Securing China's Northwest Frontier

In the first study to incorporate majority Han and minority Uyghur perspectives on ethnic relations in Xinjiang following mass violence during July 2009, David Tobin analyses how official policy shapes identity and security dynamics on China's northwest frontier. He explores how the 2009 violence unfolded and how the party-state responded to ask how official identity narratives and security policies shape practices on the ground. Combining ethnographic methodology with discourse analysis and participant-observation with in-depth interviews, Tobin examines how Han and Uyghurs interpret and reinterpret Chinese nation-building. He concludes that by treating Chinese identity as a security matter, the party-state exacerbates cycles of violence between Han and Uyghurs who increasingly understand each other as threats.

DR DAVID TOBIN is Hallsworth Research Fellow at the University of Manchester.

Securing China's Northwest Frontier

Identity and Insecurity in Xinjiang

David Tobin
University of Manchester

CAMBRIDGE
UNIVERSITY PRESS

University Printing House, Cambridge CB2 8BS, United Kingdom

One Liberty Plaza, 20th Floor, New York, NY 10006, USA

477 Williamstown Road, Port Melbourne, VIC 3207, Australia

314–321, 3rd Floor, Plot 3, Splendor Forum, Jasola District Centre, New Delhi – 110025, India

79 Anson Road, #06–04/06, Singapore 079906

Cambridge University Press is part of the University of Cambridge.

It furthers the University's mission by disseminating knowledge in the pursuit of education, learning, and research at the highest international levels of excellence.

www.cambridge.org
Information on this title: www.cambridge.org/9781108488402
DOI: 10.1017/9781108770408

© David Tobin 2020

This publication is in copyright. Subject to statutory exception and to the provisions of relevant collective licensing agreements, no reproduction of any part may take place without the written permission of Cambridge University Press.

First published 2020

A catalogue record for this publication is available from the British Library.

Library of Congress Cataloging-in-Publication Data
Names: Tobin, David, 1979– author.
Title: Securing China's northwest frontier : identity and insecurity in Xinjiang / David Tobin, University of Manchester.
Other titles: Identity and insecurity in Xinjiang
Description: Cambridge, United Kingdom ; New York, NY : Cambridge University Press, 2020. | Includes bibliographical references and index.
Identifiers: LCCN 2020009135 (print) | LCCN 2020009136 (ebook) | ISBN 9781108488402 (hardback) | ISBN 9781108726313 (paperback) | ISBN 9781108770408 (epub)
Subjects: LCSH: Internal security–China–Xinjiang Uygur Zizhiqu. | Xinjiang Uygur Zizhiqu (China)–Ethnic relations. | Uighur (Turkic people)–Ethnic identity. | Uighur (Turkic people)–Cultural assimilation–China–Xinjiang Uygur Zizhiqu. | Uighur (Turkic people)–Government policy–China–Xinjiang Uygur Zizhiqu. | Uighur (Turkic people)–Violence against–China–Xinjiang Uygur Zizhiqu. | Ethnic conflict–China–Xinjiang Uygur Zizhiqu. | Nationalism–China. | Nation-building–China.
Classification: LCC DS793.S62 T58 2020 (print) | LCC DS793.S62 (ebook) | DDC 951/.60611–dc23
LC record available at https://lccn.loc.gov/2020009135
LC ebook record available at https://lccn.loc.gov/2020009136

ISBN 978-1-108-48840-2 Hardback

Cambridge University Press has no responsibility for the persistence or accuracy of URLs for external or third-party internet websites referred to in this publication and does not guarantee that any content on such websites is, or will remain, accurate or appropriate.

This book is for my friends of all ethnicities in Xinjiang whose lives can help us understand China.

Contents

List of Figures		*page* viii
List of Abbreviations		x
Introduction		1
1	Securing China on the Multi-Ethnic Frontier	27
2	Mass Education as an Identity-Security Practice	59
3	'East Turkestan' in China's Identity and Security Narratives	87
4	Identity and Insecurity after '7-5'	114
5	Performing Inclusion of the Uyghur Other	139
6	Han and Uyghur Narratives on Ethnic and National Identity	166
7	Han and Uyghur Narratives on Identity and Insecurity	192
Conclusion: Identity and Insecurity in Xinjiang		222
Appendix 1 Cast of Characters		244
Appendix 2 Lyrics to 'One Family' (Yi Jiaren) Song – Original Mandarin and English Translation		246
Bibliography		248
Index		278

Figures

2.1 Photograph of image, (a) 'Bilingual Education Hastens Buds (*Shuangyu Cuibeilei*)', from exhibition celebrating 60th anniversary of the People's Republic of China (PRC), organised by XUAR government. Photograph of image, (b) 'Rain and dew moisten seedlings', from XUAR government's 60th anniversary exhibition. *page* 81
4.1 Photograph of unofficial slogan pasted around residential areas: 'Xinjiang has been an indivisible part of the motherland since ancient times', taken in Ürümchi. 130
4.2 Photograph of vandalised People's Armed Police public display on '7-5' outside Children's Park in Ürümchi: 'Regional Party Secretary Wang Lequan makes his important speech regarding the "7-5" incident'. 135
5.1 Photograph of MG car dealership advertisement with government slogan ('The Han can never leave ethnic minorities, ethnic minorities can never leave the Han, and all ethnic minorities can never leave each other'), taken in gent's urinal of an Ürümchi coffee shop. 144
5.2 Photograph of image, 'Alika Kedehan, "Loving Mother"', from official exhibition celebrating 60th anniversary of the People's Republic of China. 145
5.3 Photograph of public political slogan and art: 'I look to the party as I look to my mother'. 147
5.4 Photograph of exhibit from PRC 60th anniversary exhibition celebration: 'The mighty army – the troops of Xinjiang's People's Armed Police'. 150
5.5 Photograph of image from PRC 60th anniversary exhibition celebration: 'Ürümchi People's Square'. 150
5.6 Photograph of public political slogan: 'Strengthen *Minzu Tuanjie*, Strike Hard against "The Three Evils"'. 151

5.7 Photograph of public political slogan: 'Ethnic Unity is prosperity, ethnic separatism is disaster'. 151
5.8 Photograph of two public banners. Top slogan: 'Joyfully celebrate National Day, happily welcome Mid-Autumn Festival'. Bottom slogan: 'Strengthen ethnic unity, protect social stability'. 155
5.9 Photograph of patriotic stickers distributed across Ürümchi: 'Love China (*Zhonghua*), Love Xinjiang'. All photographs taken by the author. 155

Abbreviations

CCP	Communist Party of China
ETIC	East Turkestan Information Center
ETIM	East Turkestan Islamic Movement
IR	International Relations theory
PAP	People's Armed Police
PLA	People's Liberation Army
PRC	People's Republic of China
SCO	Shanghai Co-operation Organisation
WDP	Western Development Project
WUC	World Uyghur Congress
XUAR	Xinjiang Uyghur Autonomous Region

Introduction

Since the 2008 global financial crisis and US military interventions in the Middle East, China's leaders consider themselves in an unparalleled strategic 'window of opportunity' under 'new conditions' of Western decline that could enable transformation of world order for centuries.[1] China's Leading public intellectuals draw attention to Western failures combined with China's double-digit growth figures to argue the world has entered a 'post-American century'.[2] These politically influential thinkers believe China will be a 'new type of superpower' that rules by consent and attraction instead of 'Western' coercion and assimilation (Hu & Hu, 2012).* This optimism amongst Chinese elites and scholars has driven public debate in popular books and online commentary, culminating in Xi Jinping's signature slogan of the 'China Dream' of the Great Revival (*weida fuxing* 伟大复兴) to become a 'strong and prosperous nation' (*fuqiang daguo* 富强大国) again. However, this optimism conceals deep pessimism at the heart of these debates that identity and insecurity on China's ethnic peripheries could derail the Great Revival. While the 2008 Beijing Olympics slogan, 'one-world-one-dream', circulated across official media, riots and inter-ethnic violence exploded in Lhasa, Tibet. The 60th anniversary of the founding of the People's Republic of China (PRC) was subsequently overshadowed by ethnically targeted violence between Turkic-speaking Muslim Uyghurs and the Han ethnic majority. The events of July 2009 claimed at least 197 lives in Ürümchi, the capital city of the Xinjiang Uyghur Autonomous Region (XUAR) (Xinhua, 2009a). The violence sparked broad debates amongst China's ethnic policy thinkers about the relationship between identity and national security.[3] Wang Yang, Guangdong Party Committee Secretary, now head of the Central Committee's Xinjiang Work Group, suggested that

---

* Note: Chinese naming practices list surnames first and this book follows this practice in text and in the references section, e.g. Ma Rong is listed as Ma, Rong (2007) in the references.
[1] For example, see: Xi MFA (2014); NDRC (2013; 2017).
[2] For example, see: Hu & Hu (2012); Wang, Yiwei (2014); Yan, Xuetong (2013); Zhang, Weiwei (2012).
[3] A self-described '2nd generation' of *minzu* policy scholars challenged the '1st generation' historical materialist focus on economic development, arguing for a policy shift towards 'fusion'

1

China must re-adjust its ethnic minority policies 'or there will be further difficulties' (Smith Finley, 2011, p.78). This book analyses the social and political dynamics in Xinjiang that led to the turning point of 2009, culminating in a rethink of identity and security in China and ethnic policy shifts towards 'fusion' (*jiaorong* 交融).

On July 5, 2009, Uyghur rioters violently targeted ordinary Han Chinese residents in Ürümchi. On July 7, hundreds of Han residents organised into vigilante groups targeting random Uyghurs. Uyghurs, Han, and the security services were all perpetrators and victims (Roberts, 2012, pp.15–16). The 2009 violence was disarming for officials and for analysts of China. Unlike outbreaks of political violence in Xinjiang during the 1990s,[4] it was committed by ordinary, unarmed people against other ordinary, unarmed people. Ethnic relations have since become understood as a significant challenge to the party-state's capacity to provide political stability and economic development. Since 2009, a shared national identity built on 'ethnic unity' (*minzu tuanjie* 民族团结) has been officially described in existential terms as a prerequisite to China's rise and a 'zero-sum political struggle of life or death' (XEP, 2009, p.15). China's leading thinkers and policymakers conjure nightmarish, mirror-images to dreams of prosperity and power that foretell national collapse if ethnic minorities and Han do not identify as the same timeless nation. To secure dreams of unity and revival, the Chinese Communist Party (CCP) has operated mass extra-legal internment camps as 'Education and Transformation Centres' (*jiaoyu peixun zhongxin* 教育培训中心) in Xinjiang since 2017. Internment camps are part of increasing controls over the Uyghur population since the 'de-extremification' (*qujiduanhua* 去极端化) campaign's intensification in 2015, under new regional party-chief Chen Quanguo (Roberts, 2018, pp.246–250). Scholarly estimates from official sources suggest approximately 1 million people, 10 per cent of the adult Uyghur population, have been interned, though figures are constantly rising (Zenz, 2018, p.1).[5] These exceptional policies towards 'fusion' are logical conclusions of the ethnocentric insecurity cycles analysed in this book. The party-state has long targeted Uyghur identities as causes of violence and obstacles to China's revival. The party-state frames China's survival hinging on identification with its narrative of Chinese identity (*Zhonghua Minzu* 中华民族)[6] and minority identities as

---

into a race-state (*guozu* 国族). For an example of the public debate, see: Zhongguo Minzu Zongjiao Wang (2012).

[4] For example, see Bovingdon (2004a; 2010).

[5] US Defense Department estimates go as far as 3 million, nearly a third of the Uyghur population in China, referring to them as 'concentration camps'. See Stewart (2019).

[6] *Zhonghua Minzu* can be simply translated as 'China'. However, as Chapter 1 briefly discusses, the term's history of racial connotations predates the adoption of nationalism and China (*zhongguo* 中国) as the name for the PRC. The term has historically been used in different

Introduction

security problems to be solved. This ethnocentric blindspot overlooks the role of the state and the majority in ethnicised violence, enabling inconsistent policy that exacerbates insecurity in Xinjiang. This book then interrogates the triadic relations between majority, minorities, and the state in the production of identities and insecurities in Xinjiang. It examines the relationship between identity and security in contemporary China by analysing Han and Uyghur responses to the party-state's grand identity narratives and its securitised approach to everyday ethnic relations in Xinjiang. How do official nation-building narratives and unofficial self-identifications of Uyghurs and Han in Xinjiang shape each other? To what extent does official promotion of identity in Xinjiang as a national security matter make the region secure? The book argues that China's nation-building project in Xinjiang exacerbates insecurity and hardens ethnic boundaries.

The book speaks to traditions of scholarly works at the intersection between detailed micro-empirics of Chinese studies, and broader conceptual approaches of International Relations (IR). It analyses how the party-state's nation-building project to build a shared multi-ethnic, national identity in Xinjiang is practiced as a security matter, shaping Han and Uyghur identities and insecurities on the ground. The book assesses the outcomes of nation-building through its popular reception amongst Han and Uyghurs, whose identities are articulated through narratives of China as a 'unified and pluralistic' (*duoyuan yiti* 多元一体) nation constituted by 56 *minzu* (民族)[7] with Han as the 'nucleus' or 'centripetal force' (*ningjuli* 凝聚力).[8] Since the mid-1950s, the consensus in China's political and intellectual establishment has been that China is a multi-ethnic state (*duo minzu guojia* 多民族国家) and 'one-nation, one-state' is a Western concept unsuited to its 'national conditions' (Pan, 2008a). However, in the era of China's rise, this exceptionalism is being reconfigured to frame China's ethnic diversity as built on Chinese civilisational continuity 'since ancient times' (State Council, 2009a). There are 56 officially recognised *minzu* groups in China, re-categorised from 'barbarians' to Chinese 'ethnic minorities' (*shaoshu minzu* 少数民族) after 1949. These groups span diverse geographical and linguistic regions, ranging from East Asian majority Han and minority Koreans (*Chaoxianzu* 朝鲜族), to

---

ways, but today tends to imply racial origins. It is used over the more civic-minded *Zhongguo* and is supplanting references to 56 different ethnic groups in conceptualising the Chinese nation (see next footnote and Conclusion to the book).

[7] Official translation of *minzu* changed from 'nationality' to 'ethnicity' during the 1990s to avoid associations with self-determination (Barabantseva, 2009). Following Harrell (1990), *minzu* is left untranslated because it does not entail self-identification as is often assumed in Euro-American anthropology.

[8] These are official concepts primarily drawn from the seminal work of Fei Xiaotong (1980; 1988).

South East Asian Thai (*Daizu* 傣族), to South Asian Tibetans (*Zangzu* 藏族), to Inner Asian Mongolians (*Mengguzu* 蒙古族), and Central Asian Uyghurs (*Weiwuerzu* 维吾尔族). The CCP categorises diverse ethnic groups and contains their identities within Chinese civilisational history *and* the sovereign boundaries of the modern territorialised state. Since Zhou Enlai declared 'Five Principles of Peaceful Co-existence' after the 1954 Pancsheel peace treaty negotiations with India, territorial conceptualisations of statehood (sovereignty and non-interference) have been the core of China's foreign policy. However, the era of China's rise has seen intellectuals and officials re-conceptualise China through narratives of an exceptional, non-Western, and unbroken 5,000-year-old civilisation. *Zhonghua Minzu*, therefore, is built through competing logics of imperial civilisation *and* the modern nation-state, producing policy tensions between equal inclusion of minorities in the nation and exclusion as non-Chinese barbarians.

Many scholars, dazzled by 5,000 years of civilisation and complex relations between socialism, capitalism, and nationalism in contemporary China, assert that China is exceptional and beyond comprehension of social sciences. Lucian Pye, the American political scientist, built on Sinological approaches standardised by John King Fairbank (1968), famously conceptualising China as 'a civilisation pretending to be a state' and a '*miracle*' of 'astonishing unity' (Pye, 1990, p.58). The late, great expert on nationalism, Eric Hobsbawm (1990), considered China a unique 'historic nation', historically avoiding European problems of secession due to ethnic homogeneity. More recent critical approaches, which analyse diverse political narratives in contemporary China, such as Callahan's (2013) *China Dreams*, show how exceptionalist narratives are just one popular interpretation of China that drives scholars and officials to construct policy by distinguishing China's unique path from Western civilisation. The re-emergence of *cultural* nationalism tells a story of unbroken, civilisational continuity through '5,000 years' of *Zhonghua Minzu*, rather than the modernising, transformative impulses of socialism.[9] Former diplomat Zhang Weiwei echoed the orientalist undertones of Western Sinology infusing this trend when he wrote that 'China is a unique civilisation-state' with an unbroken, unified history (Zhang, 2011; 2012). Former President Hu Jintao repeated the socialist narratives of Mao Zedong, Deng Xiaoping, and Jiang Zemin, that the 'new China' was established after a century of revolutionary struggle against Western imperialism and reactionary domestic separatists. However, Hu and leading thinkers also reassert that China is held together by its unique civilisational identity of 'teaching without discrimination' (*jiaohua*), allowing non-Han barbarians to *become* Chinese through

---

[9] On the rise of cultural nationalism and the harmony concept, see Callahan (2012; 2013) and Nordin (2012).

acculturation, as opposed to the ethnic exclusion of Western nation-states (Ma, 2007, p.7). Narratives of China as a modernising state that transforms tradition *and* China as unbroken civilisation circulate in the same official and intellectual conceptualisations of China. China is thus produced somewhere between the 'extremes of modern/traditional, barbarian/civilised, margin/core, and inside/outside' (Barabantseva, 2011, p.276). China paradoxically includes ethnic minorities as timelessly Chinese and excludes them as less Chinese than Han, constituting ambivalent boundaries that externally demarcate and internally structure *Zhonghua Minzu*. Minorities must identify through logically incompatible visions of identity: socialist transformation of tradition *and* continuity as marginalised barbarians in Chinese civilisation. China's inclusion of minorities is as ambivalent as the identity within which they are being included.

Most studies of nationalism in contemporary China focus on construction of Japan and the West as threats in the post-1989 'patriotic education' campaign (*aiguozhuyi jiaoyu* 爱国主义教育).[10] The CCP positions itself as guarantor of security against existential threats of Japanese and Western imperialist designs to split China or contain its economic development, because 'without the CCP, there would be no new China'. However, the position of 'domestic strangers', what Sun Yat-Sen called 'internal foreigners', is crucial to understanding the origins and boundary production practices in contemporary nationalisms we label *Chinese* (Callahan, 2010, p.128). The CCP has always described itself as the guarantor of Chinese identity and security against intertwined existential threats of Western imperialism and barbarian separatists within. The external boundaries of China and internal boundaries between different ethnic groups are inseparable in constituting what it means to be a non-Western Chinese civilisation. This book focuses on the 2009 violence in Xinjiang as a turning point in official approaches to identity and security, marked by the party-state's announcement that domestic 'ethnic unity' is necessary to secure China at domestic and global levels. The book will show how competing nationalisms in Xinjiang from above and below (official, Han, and Uyghur) challenge and complement mainstream understandings of Chinese nationalisms because they redirect external boundaries inwards to identify Chinese friends and non-Chinese enemies within. Nationalism in China is state-driven but also a grammar of resistance against the party for failing to protect the nation against the West and Japan (Gries, 2004, p.181). However, in Xinjiang, dynamics of legitimation and resistance are turned inwards. People speak to the state to secure their identity against internal others at a neighbourhood level.

---

[10] For example, see: Callahan (2006); Gries (2004); Hughes (2006); Zhao (1998; 2004).

The Chinese state has faced historical recurrences of Uyghur resistance, following incorporation of the 'Western Regions' (*xiyu* 西域) into the Manchu Empire in 1759 and after the region was renamed 'new frontier' (*Xinjiang* 新疆) in 1884.[11] Naming the region as a frontier perpetuates Xinjiang's position as a newly discovered periphery ruled by and defined in contrast to the *old* centre of China. Xinjiang has been integrated into China through inscriptions of difference and inferiority that maintain its frontier status and constant cultural conversion to make 'domestic strangers' identify themselves and their history as Chinese. Popular exceptionalism in Sinology and Chinese scholarship, which frames contemporary China as an unbroken civilisation, invisibilises how different peoples in Xinjiang have been incorporated into China through imperial state expansion and only later through nationalist discourses. Critical Asian Studies scholars who look to China's cultural frontiers and analyse the diverse ethnic groupings concealed by *national* history have deeply challenged the way Sinological knowledge can support this political project.[12] Historians and social scientists writing about Xinjiang focus on 'multiple centres' and 'in-between-ness' of the region between China, Central Asia, and Russia.[13] The languages and religions of many groups within the PRC's contemporary borders, including Uyghurs, are the result of thousands of years of trans-border, inter-civilisational exchange, blurring the lines between Chinese, Islamic, Turkic, Mongolian, Tibetan, and Indian civilisations. These complexities are obscured by China's rise and the party-state's growing power to represent multiple peoples within its territory as historically Chinese. As James Leibold tells us, 'it would seem that with each passing day, China is becoming more "Chinese", and the mythomoteur of the frontier is fading into the red sun of the centre' (Leibold, 2007, p.183). China's most politically influential scholars have now pushed ethnic policy towards promotion of 'fusion' to become a nation-state (*minzu guojia* 民族国家) or race-state (*guozu* 国族), to compete with other states and resist attempts of 'western enemies' to prevent China's rise (Hu & Hu, 2012; Zhu, 2012). Conceptualising China through 'fusion' of many peoples into a singular identity represented by the state is a shift towards what Chinese scholars and official discourse have traditionally termed a European 'one-nation, one-state' model. This transformation is conceived as the means to maintain Chinese civilisation in a Western global order, but its identity is deeply shaped by that order. Furthermore, 'fusion' cannot succeed without mass state-violence because the

---

[11] For example, see: Clarke (2007a; 2007b; 2010).
[12] See: Elliot (2001); Jacobs (2008; 2016); Leibold (2007); Millward (1994; 1996; 2007); Newby (1999; 2005; 2007); Perdue (2005).
[13] For example, see: Brophy (2016); Millward (2007); Perdue (2005); Starr (2004).

more the CCP demands assimilation in Xinjiang, the more resistance it engenders.

Looking to the northwest frontier (Xinjiang) to understand the centre of China addresses pressing gaps in mainstream Chinese Studies literature that overlooks how official policy and national identity narratives in Xinjiang sometimes complement but often contradict mainstream understandings of China. Contemporary classics on the formation of modern China in the early twentieth century pay limited attention to the region and some avoid mentioning it altogether.[14] During this period, loyalties to Pan-Turkism, Islam, and the Soviet Union were fiercely debated in Xinjiang, contesting different conceptualisations of nationhood and provide fertile analytical ground for scholars of Xinjiang's history and identities.[15] By overlooking Xinjiang, Chinese Studies can neglect how the conceptualisation and governance of peripheralised regions constitute the centre's boundaries. Confucian historians, including Tu Wei-ming, explain that conceptualising and governing the periphery is central to defining Chinese-ness, that is always a 'geopolitical concept' and a cultural 'living reality' (Tu, 2005, p.145). Chinese Studies' Sinocentric blindspot inadvertently subsumes Xinjiang into its conceptualisations of China or leaves it untouched as an exotic anomaly beyond analytical comprehension. The omission of Xinjiang from detailed analysis in Chinese Studies reflects and reinforces the official ambivalent position of the region where its territorial inalienability *and* incomprehensible cultural otherness are taken for granted. Xinjiang covers one sixth of the PRC's territory. Linking analysis of the region to national-level identity and security discourses enables more complex and intriguing understandings of contemporary Chinese politics and society. For example, repressive political controls and ongoing state dominance of Xinjiang's economy challenge standard understandings of the 'opening and reform era' (1978 onwards)[16] as a distinct break from communist 'authoritarianism' towards political pluralism and economic liberalisation.

More than 30 years ago, Vivienne Shue (1988) argued that economic reform and increased political controls could co-exist. However, unproblematised liberal assumptions that consider markets and authoritarianism mutually exclusive persist despite the empirical evidence. A partial story of China has been constructed by overlooking regions and issues that show evidence of decreasing openness and pluralism, while failing to address links between economic development and state-violence. Scholars of contemporary Xinjiang note too

---

[14] For example, see: Duara (1988); Fairbank & Goldman (2006); Harrison (2000); Mitter (2004); Spence (1990).
[15] For example, see: Schluessel (2009) on Turkish flags in Uyghur classrooms, Millward (2007) on the Jaddids, and Brophy (2016) on the role of the Soviet Union.
[16] For example, see: Becquelin (2000; 2004a); Bovingdon (2010).

many similarities between classic European colonial forms and metropolitan dominance in Xinjiang to dismiss claims that its governance represents a 'colonial endeavour' (Cliff, 2016, pp.7–9). Narratives of 'backward' and dangerous Uyghur identity justify Xinjiang's state of exception, enabling conflation of vernacular alternatives to CCP historical narratives with armed resistance to China's rise (Bovingdon, 2010, pp.7–9; Cliff, 2016, p.216). The XUAR government's work, overseen by the State Council, runs counter to assumptions of increasing local autonomy nationwide, which draw from studies excluding the region from their conclusions.[17] National-level discourse drives Xinjiang policy, even if the state is not entirely in command. Local conditions mediate concrete effects of policy on the ground. Analysing identity and insecurity in Xinjiang show how the centre articulates and securitises China as 56 *minzu* united by *Hua* civilisation. However, Han and Uyghur identities in Xinjiang constrain the state's ability to achieve its intertwined nation-building goals of a shared *Zhonghua Minzu* identity and global power.

This book contributes to understanding how the broader context of China's identity and security shaped the 2009 violence in Xinjiang and the subsequent security response. It asks, *Who* is the China narrated by the party-state's nation-building project in Xinjiang? How do its identity narratives and related policy practices shape identities and insecurities on the ground? The book argues that the party-state's framing of Uyghur Turkic and Islamic identities as ever-present security threats demarcates ethnic boundaries and constructs an ethno-hierarchy, producing different insecurities for different groups in Xinjiang. This is the first book to use detailed ethnographic fieldwork in Xinjiang since the violence of July 2009. It is also the first to use interviews and participant-observations on Han perspectives in Ürümchi, erroneously assumed to be indistinguishable from the party-state. Its analysis of nation-building is inspired by literature on Xinjiang that focuses on interaction between CCP strategy and Uyghur counterstrategies (Bovingdon, 2010, p.6). However, the book analyses nation-building narratives and their effects through triadic relations between the state, majority (Han), and minorities (Uyghurs), and how each category is under constant reconstruction through this process.

The book's core argument is that the party-state's deeply ethnocentric approach to nation-building hardens ethnic boundaries and produces widespread insecurity in multi-ethnic Xinjiang. Chinese nation-building valorises the Han ethnic majority as China's active nucleus, objectivising their identity as Chinese, whilst violently including Uyghurs on terms that entail rejection and transformation of their own identities. The party-state seeks to secure the

---

[17] For example, see Zheng Yongnian's (2007) classic on China, the de facto federal state.

perceived culture of the Han majority as the standard for all 56 *minzu* against the threat of Uyghur Turkic and Islamic identities. However, framing this identity narrative as a security matter increases insecurity amongst Uyghurs because their identity, articulated through Turkic language and Islam, are treated as problems to be converted, contained, or eliminated. Official identity narratives also exacerbate insecurity amongst Han in Xinjiang because they represent Uyghurs' visible attachments to Islam and Turkic language as ever-present sources of violence and threats to China's prosperity and identity. The party-state's approach to nation-building thus perpetuates cycles of mistrust and violence between Han and Uyghurs, who often view each other as existential threats. Widespread identity insecurity on the ground subsequently exacerbates state insecurity because protest and violence by Uyghurs are interpreted as existential threats to China. The state conflates non-violent resistance, including Turkic or Islamic identity practices, with violence, demanding assimilative 'fusion' that makes Uyghurs more insecure. The more the state securitises homogenous identity, the more insecurity and heterogeneous resistance it produces amongst peoples it seeks to include. This book analyses these multiple identities and insecurities to show how tensions in ethnic inclusion mean China is both a multi-ethnic civilisation pretending to be a state *and* a homogenising nation-state pretending to be a civilisation. This multiplicity of meaning includes groups who identify as Chinese in different ways but is a perplexing source of insecurity for those who do not.

Theoretical Framework

As the so-called Asian century unfolds, eastwards power shifts in global politics[18] have precipitated cultural anxieties about China's rise in policy and media circles across Europe and the United States. When interviewed by the BBC during the 2012 Chinese leadership transition, I set aside my pages of prepared notes on the impact of policy shifts on Chinese people, the biggest winners and losers of political change in China. I was repeatedly asked by BBC Manchester, Coventry, and Cardiff, 'Should *we* be worried?', as if the 'China threat' loomed large on the streets of Britain. Although these anxieties explicitly address shifts in material power, the underlying nationalist ontological referent of security was identity and cultural power. 'We' referred to *us* in the West and not *them*, the Chinese, outside. Some of the abundant IR literature on potential threats to the current international order posed by China's rise is empirically rigorous and sensitive to history.[19] However, mainstream IR tends to build knowledge through this domestic/international

---

[18] For example, see Buzan & Lawson (2014); Kerr (2011).
[19] For example: Fravel (2005; 2007); Goldstein (2001); Johnston (1995; 2003).

dichotomy, reflected in debates about China's rise. Structural realists frame China's rise as an inevitable threat because all rising states are drawn into military conflict as their interests expand and clash with existing great powers (Mearsheimer, 2010). Neoliberals consider China an opportunity for Western gains if it continues 'co-operation' with prevailing norms of international relations (Ikenberry, 2014; Shambaugh, 1996; 2013). However, these approaches are not diametrically opposed but intimately related complementary opposites (Callahan, 2005, p.712). Mainstream 'problem-solving' IR rationalises the rules of global politics as legitimate by asking how *they* (China) affect an unproblematised *us* (the West), ethnocentrically constructing China at the infant stages of inevitably becoming like us. Instead, this book speaks to these debates through critical IR theory to construct research questions that ask how taken-for-granted categories are constituted through relations between disciplinary knowledge (identity, security, etc) and social practices (China, nation, *minzu*, etc).[20]

This book analyses the mutual interplay between China's domestic and international discourses of identity and security as ethnographic questions, broadly located in the critical paradigm that considers power as productive of identities, rather than simply repressive. Mainstream IR considers China's rise a question of material power in relations with other states. This book's approach offers a fresh perspective on how China's rise shapes and is shaped by domestic identity and ethnic politics. The analytical framework draws from works in the intersection between post-structuralist IR and postcolonial theory that historicise knowledge and bring non-European voices into mainstream analysis. The postcolonial historicisation and deconstruction of binaries in knowledge production overlap with post-structuralist and feminist critiques of IR to reveal its Eurocentric discursive power in constitution of the international.[21] These critical hermeneutic accounts retell the discipline's foundational narratives, moving away from 'teleological accounts of progressive journeys towards a secular liberal modernity', in Chakrabarty's (2000) words, to 'provincialise Europe' (Tickner, 2011a, pp.5–6). Postcolonial theory invokes the Foucauldian power/knowledge nexus, locating power in the construction of discourse to create dominant 'regimes of truth' that favour the West through binarism (Darby & Paolini, 1994, pp.385–387). The illusion of rational, cultural neutrality in world order marginalises non-Western perspectives that reveal the historical constitution of IR's foundational concepts and contradict realist orthodoxies, according to Morgenthau (1948) and Waltz (1979), that international life has changed little over 'millennia' (Acharya,

---

[20] For example, see: Ashley (1984); Brown (2013); Cox (1981).
[21] For example, see: Butler & Spivak (2007); Campbell (1998); Doty (1996); Enloe (1990; 2000); Franks (2003); Masters (2009); Tickner (2011a; 2011b); Weber (1998); Zehfuss (2002).

2014, p.648; Agathangelou & Ling, 2004, p.21).[22] 'Europe' was long thought of as the sovereign, universal subject of all histories, including 'Indian' and 'Chinese', while histories of non-Western Others have been subordinated to master narratives of West and East (Chakrabarty, 2000, pp.1 & 27). However, postcoloniality in China is complex and puzzling because China is postcolonial with reference to itself as much as with the West and Japan (Fiskesjö, 2017, p.6). The analysis here, therefore, is a theoretically oriented study of how ethnic minority others in China are discursively constituted by master narratives of a self-identified Eastern state navigating integration into a Western-built global order.

The book's identity-security framework, understands identity and security as mutually constitutive practices, and broadly enquires why people categorise other people and how these categorisations make people feel either secure or threatened. This framework is used to analyse intimate relations between identity and security in the interplay between top-down ascriptive official discourse and bottom-up daily social practices. Its ontological assumptions follow post-positivist turns in social anthropology and Xinjiang studies that moved from analysing social practices as reflections of identity to explore how identities are constituted and reconstituted through these practices (Bellér-Hann, 2008; Roberts, 2004). The framework links nation-building attempts to produce a shared securitised identity and different ethnic groups' everyday experiences of identity and security. This approach problematises the internal power relations and state-centric assumptions in everyday thinking of who we are, concealed by invoking security as an existential matter. Identity and security are analysed as boundary instantiating practices and mutually performative referents of each other. Regulated and repetitive performances enforce rules of identity, often by identifying and excluding undesirable elements, through what Judith Butler termed performative 'negative elaboration' (Butler, 2007, p.132). The concept of re-performance is used to frame how Han and Uyghurs both adopt official framings of identity-security but use them to resist and reconfigure its narratives without necessarily offering alternative ontologies of identity. Re-performances adopt underlying assumptions in official discourse, such as *minzu*, frontier, backwardness, and modernity, to contest it and articulate alternative self-identifications. 'Reading between the lines', to borrow Homi Bhabha's (2009) phrase, shows how Han and Uyghurs use inter-textual inversions of hegemonic discourses to narrate the meaning of daily practices and resist their official social positions.

---

[22] Also, see: Barkawi & Laffey (2006), pp.343–344; Bhambra (2011), pp.667–669; Darby (1998), pp.10–11; (2004), pp.6–7; Darby & Paolini (1994), pp.371–373; De Carvalho et al. (2011), pp.741–742; Grovogui (2001) pp.445; Hobson (2007), pp.93–97; Prakash (1992), pp.10–13; Sankara (2001), pp.404–408; Seth (2011), pp.169–170; Tickner (2011b), pp.610–611.

This identity-security framework enables analysis of the identity and security contestations produced by Chinese security discourses, which perform a multi-ethnic, Han-centric China under threat from ethnic minority identities in Xinjiang.

The post–Cold War flurry of security studies literature widened the meaning and analytical referents of security beyond traditional state-centric conceptualisations in the theory and practice of international relations.[23] State-centric security analyses failed to adequately theorise or tackle global and local dimensions of contemporary threats to human lives, including ethnic conflict and poverty (Walker, 1990, p.3). Security is not an objective thing, and it measures neither the quantity nor quality of physical safety or human well-being. Rather, people frame their *desire* to secure things, by violence or threat of violence, as existential *needs* using the available socially meaningful narratives. The Copenhagen school, led by Barry Buzan (1991) and Ole Wæver (1995), showed how various social realms, including identity, can be *securitised* by elevating them to levels of existential importance seemingly beyond the political. Identity is securitised when represented as an existential matter and universally desired state, which must be secured to eliminate threats to the nation's sense of 'we-ness' (Buzan et al., 1998, pp.4 & 119–121; Wæver, 1995, p.60). However, state-centric security involves spatial inclusion and exclusion that define identity and security inside the state, while relations with the 'outside', between states and their peoples, are defined through difference and anarchy (Walker, 1990, pp.11–12). State-centric approaches to securitisation obscure internal hierarchies and power relations that shape who we think we are and who should be secured. What Brent Steele (2007) termed 'ontological security' produces state-centrism rather than simply reflecting pre-existing identities.

Security discourses perform 'who we must be' by distinguishing the domestic, civilised self to be secured against the threat of the international, barbaric other (Callahan, 2004, p.27; Walker, 1997, pp.71–72). These performances produce nation-ness by making territorial and cultural boundaries congruent and representing alternatives as security threats (Campbell, 1998, pp.61–70; Shapiro, 2004). States draw boundaries between safe insiders as referents of security and dangerous outsiders as existential threats through 'discourses of danger' (Campbell, 1998, pp.1–3). Securitisation can exert state power beyond military and economic coercive measures through 'productive cultural governance that institutionalises borders between self and other, and between patriotic citizens and foreign enemies' (Callahan, 2007, p.7). Securitisation is

---

[23] For example, see: Booth (2005); Bubandt (2005); Buzan (1991); Buzan et al. (1998); Campbell (1998); Jarvis and Lister (2013); Kaldor (2006); Steele (2007); Stevens and Vaughan-Williams (2014; 2016); Walker (1997); Wæver (1995); Weber (1998).

conceptualised here as a performative enactment that articulates internal and external boundaries, producing them as taken-for-granted referent objects of security. Identity is reproduced through regulated and repetitive performances to enforce its rules, but these are in constant process and contestation (Campbell, 1998, p.9; Butler, 2007, p.185). The inside and outside of identity and security are mutually constitutive binaries that are stable only through reference to each other and open to constant contestation. Official security discourses inscribe coherence and threats to national identity, but struggles over identity are equally located in unofficial sites such as art, film, and literature, which are never fully controlled by the state (Campbell, 2003, p.57). As Foucault (1991) taught, power, like identity, is omnipresent, but its decentred and fractured constitution produces resistance to itself. Identity and security are never complete, and they are always unstable.

State-centric approaches overlook how securitising national identity hierarchically orders domestic identities and can exacerbate insecurity by positioning groups as cultural insiders or outsiders. Securitising national identity performs particular national narratives as incontestable and normatively orders identities by positioning the majority as the taken-for-granted national standard. For example, Cold War–era 'Soviet Threat' discourse represented communist 'sympathisers' in cultural and geopolitical terms as infections of the nation's cultural coherence, blurring internal and external security threats to constitute what it means to be American (Campbell, 1998, pp.25–27). Thongchai Winichakul's *Siam Mapped* similarly showed how national inclusion and exclusionary boundary demarcation were inseparable in Thai narratives of national security, producing internal enemies to justify social control over ideological rivals (Winichakul, 1994, p.167). Official designations of security/danger and self/other *within* state boundaries link groups and alternative cultural characteristics to external threats. This strategy produces national identity as homogenous and enables internal differences to appear external (Winichakul, 1994, pp.169–170). This book will show how official identity discourses in Xinjiang construct Uyghurs as 'constitutive outsides' to eliminate alternative national narratives and secure *Zhonghua Minzu* identity.

'Security often produces insecurity' (Weber and Lacy, 2011, p.1021). Attempts to fix and impose singular narratives of national identity-security provoke security for some and insecurity for others. It is the micropolitics of producing the nation which can lead to its unravelling (Krishna, 1999, pp.xvii & xxxvii). The power of the state may be everywhere but its essentialisations have very different implications for differentially essentialised groups (Chowdhry and Nair, 2004, p.18; Krishna, 1999, p.xxix). Discourses of essentialised identity produce feelings of security for groups whose identified characteristics represent the nation at the expense of insecurity and exclusion for others. Security discourses, therefore, tend to produce domestic ethnic hierarchies, provoking insecurity and resistance amongst groups who feel their identity is threatened. For example, Chapter 4 will show how the Chinese party-state frames violence as ordinary incidents of crime *or* as exceptional security threats, contingent upon *who* is threatened by them. Including the majority as the core of the nation to be secured at the expense of minorities provokes resistance through alternative configurations of identity and insecurity. Security is not simply produced from above and should be treated as a socially situated and discursively defined practice (Bubandt, 2005, p.275). Analysing the voices of real people avoids the depoliticised abstraction of state-centric logics and reveals the politically contested character of security (Jarvis and Lister, 2013, p.173). 'Who are we?' and 'How are we to be secure?' are intimately linked questions in mutual interplay between state and society, best analysed and problematised together.

Official Chinese texts frame inclusion and exclusion of ethnic minorities as national security matters. The story of China as a unified nation with Han at the centre (*Zhonghua Minzu*) will be analysed as a repetitive performance of securitised boundaries between China and the West and between Han and minorities. The party-state describes China as locked in a 'zero-sum political struggle of life or death' (*nisiwohuo de zhengzhi douzheng* 你死我活的政治斗争) *for* a shared identity *against* the 'inside/outside Three Evils' ('terrorism, separatism, and extremism') (XEP, 2009, p.15).[24] The party-state narrates a story of Turkic ethnic enemies inside China supported from outside by violent 'Islamic terrorists' and Western 'enemies of China' (*fanhua shili* 反华势力) (State Council, 2009a; 2009b; XEP, 2009). The attributive phrase 'inside/outside' (*jingneiwai* 境内外) links disaffected Uyghurs inside China with external threats, particularly those who frame their identity as Turkic or Central Asian. Although Uyghurs identify through Turkic language and Islam,[25] official Chinese texts assert that only 'mistaken understandings' of 'The Three Evils' (*sangu shili* 三股势力) could possibly understand Uyghur identity as Turkic, Islamic, or Central Asian (XEP, 2009, pp.47, 61, & 94). From the CCP's declaration of its own 'war on terror' following 9/11 until July 2009, Xinjiang had the lowest rates of incidents of violence and unrest than any region of China, but violence committed by Uyghurs is always represented as an existential threat (Bovingdon, 2010, p.112). The referent object of security in official texts is the party-state's narrative of China as a unified multi-*minzu* nation with Han at the centre.

---

[24] '*Sangu Shili*' can be literally translated as 'three forces'. However, the party-state's official translation used in English-language white papers is 'The Three Evils'. For example, see State Council (2009a; 2009b).

[25] For example, see: Bovingdon (2010); Smith Finley (2011).

The global 'war on terror' enabled intensification of the party-state's pre-existing 'Strike Hard' campaigns. Nevertheless, Islam is neither the source of Uyghur discontent nor the party-state's insecurity. Chapter 1 shows how China's insecurity stems from Xinjiang's history of problematic integration and anxieties that Uyghurs are not Chinese. Prior to 9/11, policy announcements described violence in Xinjiang as 'separatism' (*fenlie zhuyi* 分裂主义) without mentioning religion, extremism (*jiduan zhuyi* 极端主义), or terrorism (*kongbu zhuyi* 恐怖主义) (Dwyer, 2005, p.52). Every Uyghur interviewed in this book identified as Muslim. However, most described Xinjiang's problems as stemming from what they understood to be Chinese colonialism. The repression of Islamic practices was understood as one component of a long-term colonial project to exploit and convert the region that would not change course if Uyghurs renounced religion. Following the July 2009 violence, Alim Seytoff, spokesperson for the World Uyghur Congress (WUC) repeated one widespread Uyghur perspective that tensions were rising 'because of the Chinese government's political propaganda, indoctrination of the Chinese people ... and portraying Uyghurs ... as terrorists, separatists, and Islamic radicals' (PBS, 2009). Uyghurs feel insecure in China *because* of the state's security policies, including facilitation of mass Han in-migration, rapid and unequal development, and monolingual education.[26] Promoting Chinese nationalism in Xinjiang is a double-edged sword because it includes Han but its violent inclusion of Uyghurs makes them feel excluded. This book will show how the party-state's model of national inclusion excludes cultural characteristics such as Uyghur language and Islam as threats to Chinese identity. These exclusions exacerbate both Uyghur fears of assimilation and Han fears of Uyghurs as internal enemies. The party-state's securitisation of its *Zhonghua Minzu* narrative contributes to uncontrollable cycles of identity and security contestations between the state and different ethnic groups, the medium of which ranges from subversive poetry to mass violence.

Methodology

This book combines discourse analysis and ethnographic methods to examine identity and security in contemporary China through analysis of relations between Han, Uyghurs, and the state in Xinjiang. It analyses official narratives on Chinese, Han, and Uyghur identities, before examining the effects of these performances through their reception and in micro-level social practices amongst Han and Uyghurs. The analysis draws on ethnographic fieldwork in Ürümchi (2009–2010), including discourse analysis of official texts, participant-observations of security practices, and in-depth interviews with Han and Uyghurs.

---

[26] See: Becquelin (2000; 2004a); Bovingdon (2002; 2004a; 2010); Clarke (2007a; 2007b); Dwyer (2005); Smith (2002).

The book builds on sparse available research on the July 2009 violence.[27] It is the first detailed study to use interviews and participant-observations on Han perspectives in Ürümchi, erroneously assumed to be indistinguishable from the party-state. It will analyse how Han and Uyghurs in Xinjiang both deploy official nation-building discourse against itself to articulate alternative configurations of identity and insecurity that make the state feel insecure. Chapters 1–3 use discourse analysis of official government documents and education texts on ethnic identity and national security to understand official Chinese nation-building narratives. Chapters 4 and 5 move from the classroom to the street, using participant-observation and discourse analysis of everyday security practices, political slogans, and public festivals to analyse dissemination of official identity-security narratives on the ground. Chapters 6 and 7 turn more distinctly to unofficial politics and the effects of nation-building, using detailed, semi-structured interviews with Han and Uyghurs on their own identity-security narratives. The costs of overt resistance in most authoritarian states are so high that political alternatives are not officially recorded. Scholars must look below the surface to what James Scott (1985) famously termed 'infrapolitics'.

Before conducting fieldwork, several Chinese Studies scholars repeated widespread assumptions that Han are naturally aligned with party-state identity narratives, saying that 'Han will just tell you what the party says they should say'. However, because Han identities are never officially framed as threats in Xinjiang, Han were eager to privately discuss ethnic relations and anger towards Uyghurs and the party-state with foreign outsiders.[28] Nationalist grammars of official legitimation are deployed by Chinese public intellectuals to argue the CCP allows the West to dominate global politics to overtly resist the party-state's claims to guarantee national glory (Shue, 2004, p.28). Han in Xinjiang often overtly and covertly use the party-state's grammar of legitimation to articulate insecurity and ethno-nationalist identities, excluding Uyghurs and resisting the party-state's model of a multi-ethnic China. Analysing covert resistance in social realms thought of as non-political is pivotal to understanding the sensitive politics of ethnic identity in Xinjiang.[29]

---

[27] See: Cliff (2016), chapter 7; Millward (2009b).

[28] During a follow-up field trip in 2015, this atmosphere had changed, with several friends explaining that people were given more strict 'education' on 'how to talk to foreigners'.

[29] Due to the region's sensitive politics, the first research priority is preserving participants' anonymity (Bovingdon, 2002; Smith, 2006). Balancing 'thick description' against political realities that identity is a security matter is intellectually unfortunate but ethically essential. Therefore, relatively limited details are revealed, namely, ethnicity, gender, age, occupation, and approximate interview locations. All names and key concepts were coded in recording of data. All notes were stored in files with passwords on disks in locked, hidden storage. There were many revealing stories that must remain untold, despite express consent of interviewees. These could reveal people who identify themselves on terms officially framed as security threats to China.

In Xinjiang, the costs of Uyghur resistance to official identity and security narratives are considerably higher than for Han, which makes analysing what they say and do outside the public record all the more important. Anthropologists have shown that because Uyghurs feel stateless in China and across Central Asia, they are less susceptible to state-inspired hegemony than ethnic majorities, and their multiple modes of political reflexivity emerge in jokes, 'personal' stories, and asides outside the official record (Roberts, 2007, p.204). When writing this book, a leading international scholar on ethnicity in China advised that 'Uyghurs can't tell you anything about nation-building' because they have no active input into official politics. Every leader of the PRC and every Xinjiang party chief has been a member of the Han ethnic majority. However, listening to peripheralised perspectives of Uyghurs, and working-class Han in Ürümchi, is essential to understanding both the social dynamics engendered by China's nation-building project and the obstacles it faces. To analyse the identity and security dynamics produced by official nation-building, the book explores how Han and Uyghurs respond and relate to official texts in their daily practices.

The production of official texts on identity and security is understood here as 'a practice through which things take on meaning and value' (Shapiro, 1988, p.11). In official security texts, the powerful speak *for* the powerless in processes of 'epistemic violence' to establish a singular, normative narrative of reality (Spivak, 1988, p.76). Representations of marginalised groups derive from other texts and are written to relationally define the self in a superior position by categorising and dominating the other (Said, 2003, pp.36 & 92). In Xinjiang, epistemically violent texts include policy documents, official news reports, textbooks, museum exhibitions, political slogans, and SMS texts sent by the party-state's security organs. They are found on the street, in the classroom, and in public bathrooms. They are *everywhere*. Power is omnipresent and exercised from 'innumerable points' (Foucault, 1991, pp.93–94). Although this omnipresence exerts state power, identity is one area where it meets limits. Official texts on identity and security establish a singular national reality, but different ethnic groups mediate this reality and use these texts to reproduce their own identities. As Chapters 6 and 7 will show, the public repetition of these texts is widely dismissed as propaganda. The party-state's omnipresence inadvertently reveals limits to its power because it reminds people it cannot engineer their identities; otherwise, these texts would be unnecessary.

Understanding the identity and security dynamics produced by official nation-building, therefore, requires asking *who* reads its texts and *how*. A textual approach by itself would leave 'discourse's address unaddressed' (Prakash, 1995, p.211). Neither the power of the party-state above nor resistance from below takes ontological precedence; rather, they shape, challenge, and reinforce each other. It is, therefore, best to analyse power relations between state and society in terms of the 'mutually conditioning interplay between unlike elements' (Shue, 1988, p.27). There is no absolute outside of power because multiple modes of resistance take place within the strategic field of power relations, each relying on the other to play the role of adversary and reinforce themselves (Foucault, 1991, pp.94–96). However, alternative identities threaten the state's 'power to identify' and the producer of the text becomes the inverted, projected object of the argument turned against itself (Bhabha, 2009, p.35). Understanding intertextual processes of political antagonism, including negotiation and resistance to identities offered by states, involves 'reading between the lines' (Bhabha, 2009, p.35). This approach enables analysis of how Han and Uyghurs read between the lines of official identity-security narratives, and then how these readings shape *and* are shaped by official texts. Analysing official party-state discourse reveals *what* Han and Uyghurs read before asking *how* they do so through interviews and participant-observations.

Political education (*zhengzhi jiaoyu* 政治教育) in Xinjiang is extensive., Even prior to the turning point of 2009, every official body, from police stations to universities, came to a standstill every Wednesday afternoon for political education of all employees of the state, cadres, teachers, and students. Most public buildings were closed with signs posted on locked doors, including the Public Security Bureau (PSB) announcing, 'Closed this afternoon for political education'. The texts analysed throughout the book and key primary sources for Chapters 2 to 5 were selected as the most widely read political education texts published by the party-state, written by officials at the Ministry of Information, the State Ethnic Affairs Commission, and Xinjiang People's Publishing Press. These texts represent the party-state's official attempts to convince people of its identity-security narratives and the effectiveness of its governance in achieving goals of economic development and political stability. These texts are written primarily for state-employees and students, emphasising history and student behaviour, but almost everyone in Ürümchi had to mediate their narratives through reading, memorising, and reciting their content at school, the workplace, or residential unit. These texts are divided into those publicly available, focusing on broad historical-cultural narratives, and 'internal circulation' (*neibu faxing* 内部发行) texts offering more focused, detailed explanations of the violence. Xinjiang's internet access and international communications were blocked for approximately 10 months following the July 2009 violence 'to prevent unrest' (Xinhua, 2009a). People were largely quarantined from outside information, from international media, and the Uyghur diaspora during the book's primary fieldwork period.

Methodology

The book's analysis, therefore, focuses on how Han and Uyghurs responded to identity and security narratives in publicly available sources, local media, and education.

Publicly available texts that emerged after the July 2009 violence have not been systematically analysed by scholars and they are easy to dismiss as 'propaganda'. However, they are an invaluable window into the intent of the party-state's nation-building project, particularly region-wide, universal 'ethnic unity education' (*minzu tuanjie jiaoyu* 民族团结教育). These texts were the primary component of compulsory classes for all schools, universities, public bodies, work-units (*danwei* 单位), and cadre and state-employee training. Classes were composed of lectures by officials and teachers, mass recitation of sections of the texts, and written examinations determining whether people could continue their employment or studies. The exams required writing essays on their content in response to leading questions (e.g. 'Why say that Xinjiang has always been an indivisible component of the motherland?' and 'Why say "7-5" was not a *minzu* problem, not a religious problem but a political problem of defending the unity of the nation and the fundamental interests of the masses?').[30] Almost all Xinjiang residents were very familiar with the narratives throughout this book and most recognised the specific texts analysed. The core texts from these courses were identified and selected through interviews and discussions with teachers and students of political education. One text utilised here is *The Xinjiang Cultural Knowledge Study Guide* (Hereafter: *Xinjiang Cultural Knowledge*), used for training local cadres on the history and cultures of Xinjiang. It was also used in other 'ethnic unity' classes and publicly available for a meagre 12 renminbi in the 'hot topics' section of Ürümchi's *Xinhua* bookstores.

The book's analysis also uses two important texts unavailable for public purchase and marked for 'internal circulation'. The first is *The 50 Whys: Protecting National Unification, Opposing Ethnic Separatism, Strengthening Ethnic Unity Study Book* (hereafter: *The 50 Whys*). During fieldwork (September 2009–August 2010), this text was published by the Xinjiang Education Press[31] and studied by all teachers and students at every higher educational institute in Xinjiang. *The 50 Whys* originally came into my possession by chance after asking a university lecturer if I could borrow the copy on their desk. They were eager to express how 'interesting' it was and how I would learn about China by reading it. However, when leaving with the book, I was

---

[30] '7-5' refers to the incident of mass violence in Ürümchi on July 5, 2009.
[31] There was considerable online official promotion of this text at the time, particularly by the Ministry of Information, that suggests the content came directly from higher levels of authority. However, most online discussion of the text has since been deleted.

subsequently chased across campus by a Communist Party University supervisor, demanding I return it and questioned on what I knew about the book. The following day, another teacher laughed off the incident and told me it wasn't 'secret' but was 'only for Chinese people because foreigners wouldn't understand it'. Later, another staff member gave me a copy because they wanted 'the world to know the truth about 7-5' and 'what the Uyghurs have done to us'. The second text, *Common Knowledge of Ethnic Theory* (hereafter: *Common Knowledge*), was used for all middle school children aged 12 to 15 in Ürümchi as part of ethnic unity education. This text was less focused on violence than *The Fifty Whys* but contained the same historical explanation of Xinjiang as an indivisible component of China, describing Uyghurs as 'not a Turkic *minzu*' and 'not an Islamic *minzu*'. Like *The Fifty Whys*, the text was taught through lectures, memorisation, and group recitation. Passing the related assessment was a requirement to complete one's education.

To assess the effects of nation-building, Chapters 4–7 use participant-observations and interviews to analyse the public performance and popular reception of its narratives. Chapters 4 and 5 use discourse analysis of official texts but move from classroom to the street, analysing how China's nation-building narratives are performed through everyday security practices and political slogans. Chapters 6 and 7 directly analyse how the party-state's nation-building project is received on the ground through detailed, semi-structured interviews with Han and Uyghurs in Ürümchi. Living in Ürümchi for a year in 2007 enabled development of networks of relationships based on trust, as well as knowledge of the city and local social practices. I conducted over 100 semi-structured interviews with Han and Uyghurs in Ürümchi between September 2009 and August 2010. Initial conversations took place in public and any political or social topics were initially raised by the interviewee. Any further, detailed discussion of sensitive topics took place in private, mainly in people's homes. However, most Uyghur interviewees preferred to go for long walks in quiet areas while talking as 'even the walls have ears'. Informal, semi-structured interviews using Mandarin were conducted over several meetings in private, enclosed apartments or quiet public places in the south of the city with approximately 50 Uyghurs and in the north with approximately 50 Han. Long, semi-structured interviews with three key Uyghur and three key Han interviewees were conducted after building long-term relationships based on trust. These were each about 8 hours long and conducted in private over several sessions with Uyghur interviewees named Aynür, Mahigül, and Mukhtar, and Han interviewees named Mrs Du, Miss Lan, and Mr Qiang.[32] These were focused interviews, but follow-up questions

---

[32] See Appendix 1 for details on key interviewees.

responded to how interviewees led the conversation, allowing them to highlight the specific issues they understood as central to identity and security.

Interviews used directed conversations in ordinary settings after building enough trust to stimulate discussion that is impossible in formal social contexts and can lead to standardised, formalised answers. Methodologies employing such 'conversations' appear to be formless to participants, but through thorough preparation and background knowledge, the researcher establishes frameworks within which the 'conversation' takes place, so that it is flexible and controlled (Burgess, 2015, p.107). Following established methods in studies of ethnic relations in Xinjiang, the researcher proceeds with set questions and concepts in a 'progressively structured' manner (Smith, 2006, pp.136–137). Interactions began with informal conversations to establish the social groupings of participants (occupation, hometown, age, gender, and political views) before selecting key representatives of these groupings. Non-directive questions allowed participants to guide more detailed discussions and highlight issues they deemed important. Finally, as relationships developed, my emerging hypotheses were checked using more directive questions.[33] Interviewing techniques departed from Burgess' (2015) methods by allowing participants more involvement to raise topics they deemed important and ask questions before, during, and after interviews. This flexibility maintained the conceptual focus on narrative patterns in identity and security throughout the research. However, it enabled interviewees to redirect conversations to empirical areas they felt were the crux of identity and security in their own lives. As a scholar trained in political science and IR theory, I did not expect to analyse narratives of language and hospitality in Uyghur pop music lyrics nor the cultural significance of Uyghur fashion. However, flexibility opened fruitful areas to understand identity narratives beyond official discourse that they were specifically highlighted by Uyghurs in their own narratives on identity and insecurity. The interviewees are loosely organised following Joanne Smith's (2000) adoption of Weberian 'ideal types', not as straitjackets but to provide context of participants' social position and idiosyncratic personalities. Through attention to detail, participants' individual idiosyncrasies are actively explored to gain deeper understanding of personal narratives within grander discourses of identity and security.

My position as a 30-year-old white male during fieldwork inevitably shaped research access. This position is reflected in the age range of interviewees, all aged between 20 and 60, as well as gender imbalance in the shorter interviews

---

[33] For example, broad questions, such as 'Do you feel safe in the city?' and 'Where are you from?', stimulated discussions, which led to openings for more directive questions about specific instances where people felt insecure or when their ethnic, hometown, and national identities came into conflict.

of both groups (about 60 per cent male, 40 per cent female). Given the region's politics, this is a relatively successful balance, though I had no access to people working in religious institutions and most people interviewed worked in public spaces (e.g. *getihu* entrepreneurs,[34] administrators, and service staff) or education (teachers and students). Every Uyghur interviewed identified as Muslim, and religious repression, which prevents state-employees and young people from even entering mosques, means that Uyghurs who appear 'secular' are often most representative of balancing acts between private religious devotion and public identity. Those interviewed were all at the forefront of China's nation-building project, either through direct involvement in teaching and studying ethnic unity or working in public with direct experience of the July 2009 violence. Interviews with Han were less problematic and time-consuming, as most were eager to share their stories and did not face political repercussions for their identity. Interviews with Uyghurs were split approximately 50-50 between those working in state-employment (teachers and administrators) and private or self-employment (small-business owners, entrepreneurs, students, and service staff). Interviews with Han leaned towards private or self-employment (70 per cent), though this reflects how most Han migrate to Xinjiang for short-term employment or business.

Ürümchi is a hub for education and employment, so approximately 25 per cent of Han and Uyghurs interviewed were born in Ürümchi and 75 per cent moved to Ürümchi for opportunities in employment or education. According to official statistics, the Han proportion of Xinjiang's population grew from less than 5 per cent in 1949 to an absolute majority in the twenty-first century, if military and *Bingtuan* paramilitary farms are included (Rudelson, 1997; XUAR Statistics Bureau, 2007; 2018). Ürümchi's population is approximately 80 per cent Han and its gross domestic product per capita (GDPpc) is about average in a region ranked at 76 per cent of national GDPpc and 21/31 administrative units at RMB 45,000 (XUAR Statistics Bureau, 2007; 2018). Ürümchi is a large, modern city where government-built apartments mean Uyghur traditions of 'open-doors' is practically impossible. Ürümchi is spatially and ethnically divided, broadly between Han-populated north and Uyghur-populated south (Taynen, 2006; Smith, 2002). All interviews with Han were therefore conducted in the north of the city and those with Uyghurs in the south. Almost all Uyghurs in Ürümchi were able and willing to converse in Mandarin Chinese after gaining trust using basic Uyghur, though Mahigül and Mukhtar preferred to use English. Conducting research primarily using Mandarin Chinese in Ürümchi focuses the book on urban Uyghurs who are the

---

[34] *Getihu* (个体户) is a social class of self-employed, small-scale entrepreneurs, emerging after 1978 with the dismantling of some industrial state-owned enterprises and loosening of state controls on markets.

most deeply engaged with nation-building narratives and interact with Han on a near-daily basis. As the most exposed to Chinese nation-building, they are models of how Uyghurs respond to the project. This approach parallels Thomas Cliff's study in Korla to observe nation-building and the 'colonial endeavor' in Xinjiang (Cliff, 2016, p.4). However, focusing on densely populated, urban Ürümchi, where employment is less concentrated in ethnically stratified natural resource sectors, enables closer analysis of nation-building's impact on ethnic relations between Han and Uyghurs.

Chapter Outline

The book argues that the CCP exacerbates insecurity and hardens ethnic boundaries in Xinjiang by treating identity as a security matter. The book analyses the party-state's production and securitisation of its *Zhonghua Minzu* narrative: the China the party-state seeks to build (Chapters 1–3). It then analyses public dissemination and circulation of these narratives in everyday security practices, political slogans, and traditional festivals (Chapters 4 and 5). Finally, it analyses the effects of nation-building in Xinjiang by asking Han and Uyghurs how they receive these official identity and security discourses (Chapters 6 and 7). The book examines the puzzle of Xinjiang's ambivalent position in China, included as timelessly Chinese *and* excluded through perpetual need for cultural conversion. It will show how Xinjiang's ambivalent position, as inalienable component of a modern territorial state *and* frontier on the periphery of timeless Chinese civilisation, illustrates that China is a hierarchical, multi-cultural civilisation and homogenising nation-state at the same time. China violently excludes ethnic minorities who narrate alternative identities, while also including them as barbarians to be civilised by a boundless empire *and* as ethnic minorities in a unified, territorialised state. These tensions between inclusion and exclusion open perpetual possibilities of cultural resistance to *Zhonghua Minzu* using its own terms. The securitisation of identity that excludes how people identify themselves guarantees it. Han and Uyghurs in Xinjiang respond to nation-building by articulating identity and insecurity in ways that destabilise the party-state's narrative of China as a unified multi-ethnic nation with the Han at the centre.

The first three chapters focus on the identity, which the party-state's nation-building project seeks to produce and securitise. These chapters analyse how official texts, particularly the 2009 ethnic unity education drive, demarcate the internal and external boundaries of Chinese identity-security. The first chapter focuses on the history of China's politically contingent narratives on Xinjiang's integration. Chapters 2 and 3 analyse how contemporary narratives include and exclude Uyghurs, respectively. Chapter 1 examines how the historical context of empire, nationalism, and ethnic relations in Xinjiang shape identity and security narratives in contemporary nation-building practices. This explores how China has historically understood Xinjiang through an imperial geopolitical prism, gradually shifting towards contemporary cultural nationalism to include its historical identity as a security matter. Xinjiang's status as a timelessly inalienable component of Chinese territory is now a non-negotiable security matter. However, its peoples are never unambiguously framed as Chinese, either by the state or by themselves. Xinjiang is a site of exotic difference on the frontier of imperial civilisation *and* an indivisible component of a modern territorial state. Chapter 2 examines how mass education as an identity-security practice includes Uyghurs in official *Zhonghua Minzu* narratives. It offers a critical reading of Xinjiang's integration into China in ethnocentric national history. The chapter will analyse how the party-state's historical narratives on Xinjiang demarcate hierarchical boundaries between majority Han (*Hanzu* 汉族) and ethnic minorities (*shaoshu minzu* 少数民族) in publicly available political education texts, particularly ethnic unity education. These texts narrate China by unifying histories of all peoples within the PRC's contemporary borders as timelessly Chinese. However, they order *Zhonghua Minzu* into an ethno-hierarchy by demarcating stark boundaries between modernising, active Han nation-builders and backward, passive minorities. Official narratives of Chinese national history securitise this hierarchical, ethnocentric mode of Chinese-ness by framing Uyghur ethnic identity as a backward threat to China's unity and security.

Chapter 3 will examine the exclusion of Uyghur identities in official *Zhonghua Minzu* narratives. It will analyse the production and circulation of the party-state's 'East Turkestan' (*dongtu* 东突) narrative, which articulates Uyghur-ness as an external Turkic threat. Official 'East Turkestan' narratives articulate Uyghur Turkic identities as Western 'imperialist' fabrications and culturally external threats to *Zhonghua Minzu*. These narratives transgress popular Uyghur understandings of their own identity, exacerbating insecurity and enabling Uyghurs to highlight this exclusion. Official policy documents and ethnic unity education texts link 'East Turkestan' to the 'inside/outside Three Evils' of 'terrorism, separatism, and extremism', explaining Uyghur protest and violence as security threats to China caused by Turkic identities. Exclusion and inclusion are two sides of the same nation-building process that tells Uyghurs they must not be Turkic Muslims and they must become Chinese ethnic minorities. This transgression of ethnic boundaries threatens Uyghur identities while offering a vocabulary to resist nation-building from within its own logics by identifying as an alternative, parallel Turkic civilisation to China.

Chapters 4 and 5 move from the classroom to the street, analysing how official identity and security discourses are publicly performed using participant-observations and discourse analysis of everyday security practices, political slogans, and traditional festivals. These chapters focus on the dissemination of exclusionary and inclusionary dimensions of nation-building narratives, respectively. Chapter 4 will explore how hierarchical ethnic boundaries between Han and Uyghurs were performed and re-performed in everyday politics following the July 2009 violence. Official media and education narratives framed violence as dangerous, outsider terrorism if committed by Uyghurs or as rational attempts to improve security if committed by insider Han. The party-state exacerbated insecurity by securitising ethnocentric narratives of a Han-led nation under threat, excluding Uyghurs as sources of insecurity and activating pre-existing ethnic stereotypes amongst Han. Hierarchical identity-security narratives produced insecurity for Han, as many felt they must enact violence to secure themselves and China from Uyghur terrorists. Uyghurs felt insecure because they were ethnically targeted both by the state's security practices and by Han nationalist violence. Chapter 5 moves from exclusion to the inclusion of Uyghurs in public performances of 'ethnic unity' (*minzu tuanjie*) and celebrations of traditional festivals of the Han (*Zhongqiu jie* 中秋节) and Uyghurs (*Roza Heyti* روزاھېيت). Minority festivals are officially framed as private and ethnic, while majority Han festivals are celebrated as nationally significant events for all *minzu*. 'Ethnic unity' is ethnocentric and hierarchical because it normatively orders identities into binaries between the trans-ethnic, national standard of the Han against anomalous ethnic minorities. Unity (*tuanjie*) offers inclusion contingent upon identification with narratives of Han superiority and Uyghur marginality.

The final chapters analyse the effects of nation-building in Xinjiang using detailed, semi-structured interviews and participant-observations. Chapters 6 and 7 directly ask how Han and Uyghurs understand official narratives and their own identity-insecurities. These two chapters explore the intersections between official and unofficial politics by analysing how identity categories, China, Han, and Uyghur are interpreted and reinterpreted on the ground to articulate multiple identities and insecurities. Chapter 6 will explore how Han and Uyghurs interpret and reinterpret official 'ethnic unity' narratives of national inclusion. It will show how Han and Uyghurs in Ürümchi dismiss 'unity' as propaganda but re-perform its content to articulate alternative ethno-national boundaries. Han in Ürümchi, particularly *getihu* and working classes, employ pre-communist discourses of lineage and language that still circulate in official discourse, to define identity and position Uyghurs outside China. Identity narratives amongst Han intellectuals tend to draw on official culturalist conceptualisations of China, including Uyghurs but replicating Xinjiang's ethnocentric inclusion as a frontier to be converted. Uyghurs tend to define their identity through cultural practices, particularly Turkic language and Islam, highlighting how official exclusion of these practices and in everyday ethnic relations show they are not Chinese. Chinese nation-building in

Xinjiang is failing because its model of inclusion makes little sense in daily experiences of ethnic boundaries amongst Uyghurs and Han. Han and Uyghurs contrast self-constructed visceral ethnic identities against the multi-*minzu* conceptual imagination of *Zhonghua Minzu*. They both use tensions between inclusion of Xinjiang as Chinese territory and its cultural exclusion as a frontier to identify themselves as distinct nations built on lineage and language.

The final chapter will explore how Han and Uyghurs respond to security narratives in official nation-building discourse. Han and Uyghurs in Ürümchi both tend to resist official nation-building through ethnicised conceptualisations of security, positioning each other as threats and securitising their own identities. *Getihu* Han in Ürümchi use the party-state's discourses of danger to articulate China as an ethnic Han nation under threat from Turkic and Islamic Uyghurs. Han intellectuals emphasise that their willingness to include Uyghurs in Chinese civilisation represents the real essence of *Zhonghua Minzu* that should be secured but without addressing its Han-centric mode of inclusion. Uyghurs in Ürümchi re-perform official discourses and unofficial Han framings of Uyghur-ness by articulating China as a threat to their Turkic and Islamic identities. They invert the party-state's discourses of danger and articulate the Han population as part of the party-state's project to culturally assimilate Uyghurs through demographic and linguistic transformation. The Han-Uyghur ethnic boundary is then redirected inwards, securitising boundaries between 'real' Uyghurs who are educated in Uyghur (*minkaomin* 民考民) and those Sinicised by being educated in Mandarin (*minkaohan* 民考汉). Uyghur narratives on the *minkaohan-minkaomin* boundary reflect and reproduce identity anxieties amongst Uyghurs that they are a dying Turkic nation in a Han nation-state, *Zhonghua Minzu*.

The book's core argument is that the party-state's nation-building project in Xinjiang hardens ethnic boundaries and produces widespread insecurity. Nation-building produces insecurity amongst Uyghurs by including them on terms that entail extinction of their Turkic and Islamic identities. It emboldens Han ethno-nationalists to securitise their identity through ethnocentric narratives, which frame Uyghurs as culturally inferior threats. The party-state's ethnocentric conceptualisation of *Zhonghua Minzu* perpetuates cycles of mistrust and violence between Han and Uyghurs in Xinjiang by making both groups feel threatened by each other's identities. The party-state has securitised a narrative of China that makes Han and Uyghurs feel identity-insecurity and they respond by securitising alternative identities. Han and Uyghurs in Xinjiang build alternative Chinas by making sense of ethnicised daily practices using the narratives available to them. This book tells the story of how these many Chinas are built every day.

1 Securing China on the Multi-Ethnic Frontier

Introduction

Although China's twentieth century territorial borders have remained relatively stable, the problematic inclusion of its frontiers illustrates the historically contingent identity of one of the world's oldest, most stable civilisations. During the Manchu's eighteenth century expansion into Central Asia, Xinjiang ('the new frontier'), previously referred to in Chinese sources as the Western Regions, became a military colony and geopolitical 'buffer zone'. The region only became Xinjiang province in the late nineteenth century and by the 1950s, was still described by Zhou Enlai and Mao Zedong as a piece of a geopolitical 'chess game' in anti-imperialist struggles with the West and Russia (Zhou, 1950b, p.63; 1951, p.66). Following the 1949 revolution, a region that had been integrated into the Chinese state for geopolitical purposes gradually became understood as an inalienable component of modern Chinese socialist identity. The second half of the twentieth century saw state-led economic development and demographic transformation of Xinjiang with mass Han migration. Xinjiang's inclusion as part of China's national territory helped redefine China as a modern, multi-ethnic state, rather than the Han race. Xinjiang found itself in an ambivalent position of peripheralisation *and* centrality to Chinese identity in the twentieth century struggle to build a modern nation within the territorial boundaries established by Manchu empire-building. Xinjiang has been integrated into the Chinese nation as a non-Chinese frontier. However, the twenty-first century shift towards cultural nationalism in Chinese politics, which defines *Zhonghua Minzu* as 5,000 years of unbroken civilisation, invisibilises these historical shifts while inadvertently drawing attention to them. Despite 5,000 years of shared civilisation, the region remains a 'new frontier' in need of transformation, and ambivalently positioned between inclusion as Chinese territory and exclusion as culturally un-Chinese.

This chapter explores how this historical context of empire, nationalism, and ethnic relations shapes contemporary Chinese nation-building practices in Xinjiang, specifically, the tensions between ethnic inclusion and exclusion. Primordialist or 'ethno-symbolic' approaches that define nations as territorial communities of shared history and culture, 'founded on antecedent ethnic ties' (Smith, 1991; 1995) offer limited understanding of how identity is reproduced in modern, multi-ethnic states such as China. Antecedent ethnic ties cannot explain how the Han, an East Asian, largely atheist, Sino-Tibetan-speaking ethnic group, have come to consider a region populated by Central Asian, Turkic-speaking Muslims as an inalienable component of their national identity. The modern, multi-ethnic sovereign Chinese state re-imagines China as a 5,000-year-old, unbroken, singular civilisation. If nationalism is about 'stretching the short, tight skin of the nation over the gigantic body of empire' (Anderson, 1991, p.86), then Chinese national identity emerges from social processes that imbue groups with convictions that they are naturally and eternally linked. These processes can be understood through Ernest Gellner's classic conceptualisation of nationalism as the principle 'that holds that the political and the national unit should be congruent' (Gellner, 2006, p.1). Nationalist literature, public media, monuments, and museums *imagine* the nation by linking people who have never met into 'finite and sovereign' communities based on shared identification (Anderson, 1991, pp.7, 25, & 36). However, nationalism does not simply arise from the state-seeking demands of pre-existing, bounded social entities (Brubaker, 1998, p.278). Nation-building is a process of cultural governance where states exert power through 'historical practices of representation', which institutionalise boundaries between self and other (Campbell, 2003, p.57; Callahan, 2007, p.7). Many nations, including China, already have their own states and many, like Uyghurs, do not. The territorial and cultural boundaries of nations represent contested political claims, which seek to define the boundaries of political identity (Brubaker, 1998, p.278). Ethnic majorities often deploy the state's resources in attempts to culturally transform minorities within existing national borders and make them congruent with majority culture. Despite 5,000 years of unbroken civilisation, majority Han Chinese elites today construct policy and devote considerable resources to eliminate contestation of identities in ethnic minority regions and to establish Han culture as the national standard.

The party-state frames territorial integrity as an existential matter for China and uses Deng Xiaoping's phrase that 'stability is above all else' (*wending yadao yiqie* 稳定压倒一切) in most policy and education documents on Xinjiang. While the CCP emphasises political stability, China's nation-building project in Xinjiang seeks to radically transform its cultures and make its identity congruent with the PRC's contemporary territorial borders. This invocation of national identity is a form of cultural governance, which inscribes coherence to the self by identifying alternative identities as threats in official and unofficial arenas. Nation-building is often an act of power, demarcating group boundaries between safe insiders and dangerous outsiders, within nominally timeless, modern territorial units. However, *whose* identity represents what Gellner called the nation's 'high culture' and the ramifications for minorities whose culture is deemed 'low' reveals the ethnocentric tensions within these projects. That 56 officially recognised *minzu* are distinct, unequal ethnic groups *and* equal members of a nation produces state insecurity because they respond with claims to heterogeneity based on China's own narratives of cultural difference. The paradox of the nation is that its story can only be told with continual slippage between timelessness and modernity and between preexisting homogeneity and continual marking of internal others through cultural difference (Bhabha, 1990, pp.292–293). Modernists, including Anderson and Gellner, overlook the 'profound ambivalence' and contestation that emerges when telling 'the story of the fullness of the nation's life' (Chatterjee, 2001, p.402). 'Where there is power, there is resistance' and the nation fractures itself with its own logical tensions (Foucault, 1991, p.95). The party-state's securitisation of identity is clear, nevertheless, the national narrative it securitises is ambivalent and destabilises itself. The orientalist changelessness of colonial subjects and desires to reconstitute them through progress and nationalism split all colonial projects (Prakash, 1992, p.16). The ambivalent tensions between inclusion and exclusion and between timelessness and modernity unintentionally open multiple possibilities of alternative self-identifications within the nation. The story of the nation offers homogeneity and finality, but this homogeneity invites heterogeneous frames of resistance and perpetual redefinitions of its story.

Nation-building projects are effective when the bounded self-identifications they offer are internalised and shared by its subjects. However, the ambivalence of the Chinese nation is amplified in Xinjiang because 5,000 years of continuity are overlaid on long histories of pre-existing linguistic and religious practices. When official articulations of identity and security run counter to practiced boundaries, as they do in Xinjiang, we can expect assertive responses from ethnic groups to preserve the boundaries they feel encapsulate their identity. This boundary encroachment produces existential identity conflicts as people feel they face external threats and 'if they do not speak out now, they will be silenced forever' (Cohen, 1985, p.108). Ethnic boundaries are fluid and they are not maintained through difference itself but through the social organisation of difference (Barth, 1969, p.15). Boundaries encapsulate groups, but the content that gives them meaning constantly changes (Cohen, 1985, p.91). Ethnic groups deploy pre-existing, self-ascribed cultural differences, in our case Turkic language and Islam, as organisational vessels that reproduce ethnic boundaries, to resist the conversion offered by nation-building. State-led nation-building performs and securitises a specific national narrative that people resist by articulating alternative and inverted ethnic configurations of identity and insecurity. China, therefore, is officially performed and unofficially re-performed in a mutual interplay between state discourse and social practices, mediated by pre-existing identity boundaries built from above and below. Like all nations, China is subject to constant change, and its transient existence is found in these interstices.

This chapter illustrates how contemporary nation-building practices in Xinjiang are shaped by shifting historical contexts of empire, nationalism, and ethnic relations in China. The chapter is divided into three sections, each of which introduces the historical context of Xinjiang's problematic integration into China. The first section analyses the intersection between identity and security in Chinese nation-building by examining shifting boundaries of inclusion and exclusion of non-Han. It asks, How have non-Han been included and excluded in official national narratives? *Who* is the China to be secured by nation-building narratives? The analysis builds on the nationalism literature to analyse Chinese nation-building as a politically and historically contingent process of cultural governance of its frontiers. The territorially bounded conceptualisation of China that emerged in the twentieth century represented a relatively dramatic shift to sovereignty and national identity. However, imperial framings of difference between civilisation and barbarians continued to co-exist in tension with nationhood and intermingled with Chinese nationalism. The second section asks, How has Xinjiang's position in China been officially conceptualised throughout modern history? This examines how Xinjiang's identities and its contingent position in China have been historically viewed through a geopolitical prism. It argues that twentieth century Chinese nation-builders subsequently articulated and securitised a new multi-*minzu* Chinese national identity in Xinjiang. The final section asks, How have nation and ethnicity been organised in China's inclusion of ethnic minority others? How are Xinjiang's peoples included and excluded in this majority-minority relationship? This explores how Chinese nation-building conceptualises ethnicity and organises ethnic relations by articulating hierarchical relations between Han majority and ethnic minorities. The section bridges literatures on ethnic politics in China[1] and Uyghur identities in Xinjiang,[2] analysing the mutual interplay between grand state-led goals of Chinese nation-building and everyday ethnic relations in Xinjiang. The three sections together show how Xinjiang's position in China is primarily viewed through the prism of security. Uyghurs are framed as threats to official *Zhonghua Minzu* identity because they challenge hierarchical ethnic relations that constitute its boundaries.

---

[1] For example, see: Barabantseva (2008; 2009; 2011); Baranovitch (2003); Gladney (1996; 2004); Schein (2000).
[2] For example, see: Bellér-Hann (2001; 2002; 2008); Bovingdon (2002; 2004; 2010); Brophy (2016); Clarke (2010); Dautcher (2009); Dwyer (2005); Harris (2008); Newby (2007); Roberts (2004; 2009), Smith (2000; 2002).

This chapter introduces the historical context behind the book's core argument. The party-state exacerbates insecurity in Xinjiang by producing an ambivalent narrative of Chinese identity as the referent of national security. Chinese nation-building began long after the establishment of territorial and bureaucratic control in Xinjiang in the eighteenth and nineteenth centuries. Today, narratives of imperial dominance and national integration continue to overlap uneasily, producing tensions between ethnic inclusion and exclusion within official conceptualisations of identity and security. The party-state's story of a unified *Zhonghua Minzu* with the Han at the centre is drawn from Fei Xiaotong's 'unified and pluralistic' (*duoyuan yiti*) narrative. This ethnocentric performance of timeless boundaries excludes minorities from the core of China, Central Plains (*Hua* 华) culture, including them as 'new blood' 'for the Hans' (Fei, 1988, p.188). The party-state therefore frames Xinjiang as an indivisible, equal component of a modern territorial state *and* a site of exotic difference on the frontiers of imperial civilisation. Xinjiang and its peoples are never unambiguously framed as Chinese either by the state or by themselves. China's nation-building in Xinjiang thus reproduces and securitises civilisational boundaries between Han and Uyghurs by framing the preservation of Uyghur marginality as central to the survival of the modern, multi-ethnic Chinese state. Xinjiang's status as an indivisible component of China and Uyghur identification with their marginality in an ambivalent China (56 equal *minzu and* civilisational boundaries) are non-negotiable, existential security matters in official discourse. Uyghur Turkic and Islamic identities transgress the hierarchy constituted by this internal boundary through expressions of identity-insecurity and demands for cultural equality, which are framed as existential threats to China, the civilisation, and China, the modern, territorialised state. For *Zhonghua Minzu* to be a benevolent, attractive civilisation *and* a modern state of 56 equal *minzu*, it needs Xinjiang to be Chinese *and* to be marginal. However, it is this perceived need that lies at the heart of China's security problems in Xinjiang.

Nations and Nationalisms in China

This section analyses the intersection between identity and security in Chinese nation-building by examining its historically shifting boundaries of inclusion and exclusion of non-Han. How have non-Han been included and excluded in official national narratives? *Who* is the China to be secured by nation-building narratives? Twentieth century Chinese nation-building re-conceptualised permeable internal boundaries of an imperial, pre-modern civilisation, re-classifying barbarians through relatively impermeable *minzu* categories in a territorially bounded China. The civilising project and contemporary nation-building are based on competing and logically incompatible ontologies of human community (pre-modern, inclusive culturalism versus modern, exclusive nationalism). In practice, however, these often work in creative tension as mutually reinforcing discourses (Callahan, 2010, p.131). Twentieth century nation-builders conceptually inflated *Zhonghua Minzu* to include all barbarians within the PRC's new borders as one of 55 minority *minzu*. However, using critical theory to de-centre official national narratives reveals the sociohistorical contingency and power relations behind the constitution of these taken-for-granted identity categories. Chinese nation-building is a historically contingent identity performance that seeks to secure China against existential threats of alternative identities by making their histories congruent with contemporary borders. This section analyses how contemporary official identity narratives have been politically imposed on China's entire history by exploring shifting configurations of difference emergent in China's nation-building. Twentieth century Chinese nation-building articulated a territorialised conception of nationhood (56 unified, equal *minzu*). However, this shift reconfigured rather than replaced imperial, pre-modern framings of difference between civilisation and barbarians, which continue to guide nation-building practices and ethnic relations in Xinjiang. China's uneasy integration of Xinjiang reflects the ambivalent inclusion and exclusion of cultural difference in *Zhonghua Minzu*.

The boundaries of China today are somewhat different to those of the Qing dynasty (1644–1911 CE), let alone those of the Han dynasty (206 BCE–220 CE). National history is an unavoidable reality but superimposes a timeless identity category ('China') upon thousands of years of multiple interacting and overlapping histories, concealing its contingency. Chinese Studies can reproduce these nationalist narratives on history by uncritically taking its object of analysis for granted, i.e. 'China', the nation. For example, Paul Cohen's (2010) 'China-centred perspective' takes 'Chinese perspectives' as the starting point to counter academic Orientalism with *national* history. Taking 'China' as an analytical starting point countered the Eurocentrism of 'impact-response' frameworks, which understood Chinese modernisation as passive responses to the 'advanced', 'active' 'West' (Cohen, 2010, p.12). However, simply reversing this binary reproduces Eurocentric logics, which conceptualise the world as a series of impermeable civilisations with European nations at the centre, into a Sinocentric mirror image where China replaces Europe. More critically minded Chinese Studies literature tends to understand modern Chinese nation-building as a response to both internal imperial decline and external conflict with the West.[3] The critical history literature on the 'Qing Frontier' (present-day Xinjiang, Tibet, and Mongolia) goes further to de-centre

---

[3] For example, see Duara (1988); Harrison (2000); Mitter (2004); Thornton (2007).

the China category altogether by analysing interaction between world history and the region's own historical specificities[4]. Historians such as Peter Perdue (2005), Laura Newby (2007), and James Millward (2007) have shown how Xinjiang's history sits 'in between' the Chinese, Islamic, Indian, and Mediterranean worlds, none of which predominated across the whole of Xinjiang or for extended periods (Millward, 2009a, p.55). This regional approach to social histories within and across national boundaries rejects the naturalising ontology of nations as givens. The 'Qing frontier' literature shows how the Manchu empire-state departed from Chinese rituals and the Sinocentric 'tribute' system, exemplified by John Fairbank's *The Chinese World Order* (1968), which profoundly shaped contemporary understandings of Chinese history. The Manchu invasions of Mongolia, Zhungaria, Tibet, and Tarim Basin, during the eighteenth and nineteenth centuries, seized and ruled these territories as military colonies, long before they were reimagined as part of China's national community in the twentieth century.

The construct of a Chinese premodern 'tribute system' derives from orientalist historical thought and was never an uncritically accepted 'system' by 'vassal' states that traded with or had been militarily conquered by China (Perdue 2015, p.1007). Military considerations tended to take prominence and there are common features between Qing expansion into its frontiers and the early modern European socioeconomic structures described by Tilly (1992) as state-making (Perdue, 2005, p.530). Attempts at mass conversion of frontier peoples to Chinese culture were a later, more modern project, gradually initiated long after Manchu state-making but building upon earlier configurations of social difference. Centring 'China' as an unproblematised unit of analysis ahistorically adopts the PRC's contemporary borders as natural givens, concealing how different peoples within those boundaries are constantly imagined and reimagined in fundamentally different ways. Official texts and popular usage still refer to Xinjiang today as the frontier (*bianjiang* 边疆), alongside the northern and southwestern regions of Inner Mongolia and Tibet. In the Chinese imagination these are regions historically occupied by barbarians (*yi* 夷) and they became repackaged as Chinese ethnic minorities in transition from empire to nation-state (Di Cosmo, 2002, p.2). Uyghurs, Tibetans, and Mongolians who inhabited the territories acquired and settled during the mid-eighteenth century Manchu imperial expansion were only officially re-categorised from external barbarians to internal ethnic minorities in the 1950s. The conceptual opposition between Han-populated 'inner China' (*neidi* 内地) and ethnic 'frontier' (*bianjiang* 边疆) constitute China in official and unofficial narratives of national history and nation-building today.

---

[4] See: Elliot (2001); Jacobs (2008; 2016); Leibold (2007); Millward (1994; 2007); Newby (2007); Perdue (2005).

Analysing the mutual constitution of China's centre and margins through interplay between the state and different peoples, therefore, counters the master narratives of both Eurocentric world history and Sinocentric national history.

Chinese nation-building in Xinjiang adopts both the grammar of civic nationalism (56 equal *minzu*) and positions the Han category as the cultural nucleus of its national identity narratives. Critical Han Studies[5] has shown how the origins and meaning of the Han category itself are historically contingent and unstable. The contemporary Han ethnonym emerged through intercultural translations of race and ethnicity from Europe to Japan and then to China but became contested in ideological struggles between early twentieth century Chinese revolutionaries and reformers (Chow, 2001, p.48). However, the modern Han ethnonym built on older interactions and distinctions between the sedentary dwellers of the central plains and nomads of the northern steppe (Leibold, 2010, p.10). The Han concept emerged with the intervention of marginal barbarians as Western Hu labelled sedentary dwellers of the Central Plains as Han despite being politically and culturally divided for much of their history (Elliot, 2011, pp.173–175). Older discourses that divide the civilised Central Plains (*Hua* 华) from northern barbarians (*Yi* 夷) and nomadic from sedentary peoples inform the symbols, such as the dragon, and boundaries, such as the Great Wall, that define Han China today (Leibold, 2010, p.10). The fluidity of the Han ethno-cultural marker reflects the tensions it conceals between inclusive cultural universalism and exclusive ethnocentrism. The former seeks to attract and assimilate non-Han groups into Chinese culture, where the latter excludes them from exclusivist ethnic majority identity. Chinese nation-building offers marginal Xinjiang an ambivalent space between civic and ethnic nationalism but also reveals how this ambivalence is found at the heart of China.

Unlike most European states, nationalism emerged in China *before* the nation could claim control of the state in debates about preservation of Chinese culture in the face of Western and Japanese encroachment. Drawing on the history of European nation-states, Charles Tilly (1992) distinguished state-making, the social penetration of centralised, coercive taxation and security, from nation-building, the subsequent creation of citizen identification with the centralised state (Tilly, 1992, pp.1–3). Prasenjit Duara (1988) critiqued Tilly's distinction between nation-building and state-making as inherently Eurocentric because, unlike Europe, state-making and nation-building were simultaneous and inseparable historical processes in China (Duara, 1988, p.2). During anti-imperialist and anti-Manchu rebellions of the late nineteenth and early twentieth centuries, Chinese intellectuals conceptualised state-making within a

---

[5] For example, see Chow (2001); Elliot (2011); Leibold (2010).

nationalist framework to unify national identity and ensure state strength vis-à-vis European and Japanese empires (Duara, 1988, pp.2–5). However, stark contrasts between Chinese and European nation-building are too nation-state-centric to capture their shared experiences or regional variations in how indigenous cultures and resistance shape nation-building projects during their expansion. The shifting nature of Xinjiang's integration into China offers a more complex picture that defies orientalist binaries, which construct China as an exceptional unbroken Chinese civilisation against the discontinuity and violence of Western nation-states. The Manchu had already built an imperial state in Xinjiang by the end of the eighteenth century, but it was the mid-twentieth century before Xinjiang became seen as Chinese, rather than simply belonging to the Chinese state (Jacobs, 2008; 2016; Kamalov, 2007). Tilly's separation of state-making and nation-building is problematic when applied to China's Central Plains. However, China's problematic integration of Xinjiang shows how tensions between logics of empire and nationalism in ethnic inclusion parallel tensions between orientalism and nationalism in European colonial projects.

Chinese thinkers' interaction with nineteenth century Western imperialism triggered nationalist thought as elites grappled with the internal atrophy of empire and external threat of imperialism, in Sun Yat-sen's words, to 'save China'. However, discontinuity between the Confucian moral ordering of traditional China and geopolitical ordering of sovereign China is too often overemphasised in fixed binaries (Kerr, 2011, p.159). Sinocentrism amongst Han Chinese elites was not replaced by modern nationalism when concerns of national sovereignty and cultural identity became intertwined for the first time during the late-Qing. Competing conceptualisations of community were absorbed from European colonialism, namely, identity as a fixed racial category, but intersected with Sinocentric culturalism, blending and creating new meanings through intercultural translation and semantic hybridity (Chow, 2001, pp.48–50). The institutionalisation of genealogy under the Manchu had become a primary marker of identity, and this tradition became intermingled with racialised identities when the Taiping Rebels labelled the Manchus a 'race of demons' and the Emperor a 'Tartar dog' of 'barbarian origins' (Leibold, 2007, p.29). The insertion of race and the territorially bounded state reinforced Sinocentrism, giving leading thinkers such as Sun Yat-sen vocabulary to argue that 'common blood' is the Chinese nation's greatest force and exclude the Manchu as a 'different lineage' (Dikötter, 1994, p.406; Leibold, 2007, pp.30–31). China's racial identities emerged in the late imperial period through cultural interaction between many schools of thought, led by reformers who actively responded to the decline of imperial cosmology (Dikötter, 1994, pp.410–411). China's nationalisms were neither generated by a self-contained system called 'Chinese culture' nor imposed through 'Western' hegemony, but instead, emerged through semantic hybridity and intercultural translations.

The uneasy incorporation of non-Han peoples has been a question for Chinese nation-builders at least since the early twentieth century, when they lamented the lack of a consistent name for the Sinic community. Debates between revolutionaries and reformers during the Republican era (1912–1949) blamed China's weakness and economic inferiority in the face of Western imperialism on an absence of shared modern national identity. Liang Qichao and Zhang Binglin argued that China's 'backwardness' could only be overcome by building a 'race-state' (*guozu* 国族),[6] the most advanced stage of human evolution, to unify China as a modern nation against European and Japanese empires (Duara, 1988, pp.2–5; Leibold, 2007, pp.9–11). Nationalism and racism reconfigured and reinforced Sinocentrism at the same time. Revolutionaries, such as Yan Fu and Zhang Binglin, framed China's anti-imperial resistance as a struggle between races and saw the Manchu as a foreign non-Han race. They defined the Chinese nation (*Zhonghua Minzu*) as the Han race, a lineage descending from the mythical Yellow Emperor (Chow, 2001, p.53). The reformer, Liang Qichao, built on the 'Five Constituencies' (Han, Manchu, Mongolian, Tibetan, Muslim), institutionalised under the Qing empire to govern barbarians, and recast them as races (Leibold, 2007, p.32). However, for Sun Yat-sen and Liang Qichao, these races were now Chinese subjects to be assimilated for the purpose of strengthening *Zhonghua Minzu*, the Han race (Callahan, 2010, p.134; Leibold, 2007, pp.32–33). The Xinhai revolution that ended Manchu rule played a crucial role in establishing China as a modern state and placed as much importance on hierarchical domestic ethnic relations as anti-colonial international relations. Its participants strove to 'expel the Manchu' and 'restore the Han' in order to unify the five races and save China against the threat of Western imperialism (Chow, 2001, p.53; Leibold, 2007, pp.30–31). This racialised lens shaped the Xinhai Revolution as visualised in its 'five colour' flag to represent the 'five races' and the overthrow of the Qing as non-Chinese 'Tartar dogs' (Harrison, 2000, p.101; Leibold, 2007, p.37). Although the Manchu were excluded from Chinese identity, their homeland and their imperial conquests remained part of the modern territorial unit of 'China' after Sun Yat-Sen came to power. Barbarians on the fluid frontier became ethnic minorities within the closed boundaries of the nation-state (Leibold, 2007, pp.19–28). The idea of the Han as a core, modernising group of a new 'race-state' was superimposed on to older ideas of Sinic civilisation (Leibold, 2007, pp.9–11). This uneasy transformation of barbarian outsiders to marginal minority insiders blurred distinctions between China's imperial domain and its sovereign territory.

---

[6] This conceptualisation of China, once criticised by Mao as 'Han chauvinism', has re-emerged in contemporary ethnic policy, as celebrated by Hu and Hu (2012).

The ambivalent inclusion of non-Han peoples in China, as Chinese but not *as* Chinese as the Han, persists in post-1949 official narratives that China has been developed by the cultural and economic superiority of the Han 'nucleus'. The construction of a multi-ethnic China emerged from tensions between the Han concept, Qing territorial expansion in regions populated by other ethnic groups, and conflict with Western imperialism (Leibold, 2007, p.19). Manchu strangers, like other barbarians, officially became Chinese after the founding of the 'new China' under Mao Zedong. The CCP celebrated the 1949 revolution as 'liberation' (*jiefang* 解放) of every *minzu* from a century of 'divide and rule' by Western imperialists as the 'new China' 'swept away' China's 'old system' of '*minzu* oppression' (Liu, 1954, pp.118–119). Mao Zedong and Deng Xiaoping both described 'Great Han chauvinism' (*Da Hanzu zhuyi* 大汉族主义) as a fundamental and pressing problem in Xinjiang, Tibet, and Inner Mongolia (Mao, 1949, p.21; Deng et al., 1953, p.99). However, despite this explicit rejection of discrimination against minorities, the CCP was blind to its own ethnocentrism in its claims that the Han were the most advanced and most culturally significant group in China. The 'new China' was to be built on Fei Xiaotong's (1988) idea that China is unlike Western nations because it has always exemplified 'plurality and unity' (*duoyuan yiti* 多元一体), with the Han as a unifying 'nucleus' (Liu, 1954, p.119). Fei Xiaotong remains China's most celebrated social scientist, and his deep influence on Chinese political thought is seen in references to *duoyuan yiti* in all official texts analysed throughout this book. Fei was trained at the London School of Economics under pioneering structural functionalist Bronislaw Malinowski, and his thought exemplifies tensions between culturalism and ethnic nationalism in official Chinese identity discourses. Fei's (1988) story of China is a semantic hybrid of European structuralism and traditional Chinese exceptionalism where the Han have *always* been the 'guiding force' of the Chinese nation via natural attraction of barbarians to their superior economic and cultural development. In this officially endorsed history of China, non-Han groups are described as 'new blood' 'for the Hans' (Fei, 1988, p.188). Non-Han history is narrated solely through the function of the telos of Chinese assimilation. Minorities were now Chinese but could never become part of the Han 'nucleus' whose identity forms China.

The ethnocentric Han nucleus concept fractured China's nation-building project from its outset because it tells the story of Han building China to strengthen themselves and ambivalently including domestic others. Defining *Zhonghua Minzu* through a Han nucleus produces tensions between integration of minority regions as imperial vassals populated by barbarians *and* as equal regions of a modern state built on a shared national identity. The origins and contemporary practices of Chinese nationalisms show how 'domestic strangers', or what Sun Yat-Sen called 'internal foreigners', are crucial to producing boundaries that encapsulate and construct the meaning of China (Callahan, 2010, p.128). Modern state-making and nation-building emerged simultaneously in China during the nineteenth and twentieth centuries in cataclysmic movements to unify its peoples and rejuvenate the Han to rise against threats of European imperialism and the internal Manchu other. However, because non-Han barbarians were to become Chinese, instead of establishing their own states, nation-building began later on the Manchu frontier and continues today. Modern Chinese identity, therefore, continues to be produced through conceptualisation of its own shifting and blurry internal peripheries as much as by consistent political positioning as non-Western in reference to relatively fixed external borders.

Nation-Building on China's Northwest Frontier

This section explores relations between identity and security in Chinese nation-building by analysing the inclusion and exclusion of Xinjiang in China's official national narratives. The previous section examined ambivalent tensions between Han ethnonationalism and Chinese culturalism within the *Zhonghua Minzu* narrative. This section turns to how this ambivalence plays out in Xinjiang. It asks, How have Xinjiang's peoples been included and excluded in official national narratives? *Who* is the China to be secured in nation-building narratives in Xinjiang? An exploration of the historical shifts in Xinjiang's position between inclusion and exclusion illuminates the sociohistorical contingency of China's identity boundaries. The Chinese state has historically approached Xinjiang primarily through the prism of security. The region was integrated into modern China in the eighteenth century as a geopolitical 'buffer zone' and then as a site of anti-imperialist, nationalist struggle in the nineteenth century. Under twentieth century Chinese socialism, Xinjiang became a place in need of 'peaceful liberation', before being gradually re-framed as an indivisible component of timeless, unbroken Chinese civilisation in the twenty-first. The securitisation of a new and fixed Chinese national identity in contemporary Xinjiang fractures itself further by building on but concealing Xinjiang's ambivalent inclusion in China throughout modern history.

The Qing project in Xinjiang that followed Emperor Qianlong's 1759 conquest of the 'Western regions' was less a civilising mission to convert barbarians, than a geopolitical project to extend state power and secure inner China. The Manchu exercised pragmatic political control adapted to local conditions with policy often designed to prevent potential corrupting contact of barbarians with civilisation (Perdue, 2005, p.338). The Qing state adapted its governance of different regions under the banner of 'rule by custom', permitting the development of different languages, maintaining existing local structures of governance, and institutionalising genealogical records as the primary marker of identification in Xinjiang (Leibold, 2007, pp.19–28). Under the Qianlong Emperor (1735–1796 CE), Tibetan and Mongolian religious leaders and symbols were co-opted and incorporated into imperial rituals but no attempts were made to include Islamic leaders or Turkic identities into China (Newby, 2005, p.42). The Manchu permitted the maintenance of Islamic law in southern Xinjiang and co-opted indigenous local leaders (*begs*) to maintain power (Leibold, 2007, p.28). At the same time, Muslims of Central Asia were prevented from being symbolically incorporated into the Qing system or from being socially connected to China through migration in or out of the region (Perdue, 2005, pp.339–342). This 'Emperor-Centric' system prevented regional separation by punishing disloyalty to the Emperor and the state, as opposed to earlier Sino-centric Han Chinese dynasties that sought but failed to produce group identification (Leibold, 2007, p.28). Instead of seeking to eradicate difference, the Manchu state was an 'empire of difference' (Jacobs, 2016, p.14). The Qing re-inscribed, highlighted, and institutionalised difference while Manchu elites maintained separateness from the Han masses through marriage policies, separate residences, and ethnic 'nomenklatura' in military institutions (Perdue, 2005, p.338). The eighteenth century Chinese state deeply penetrated Xinjiang society through centralised taxation and the military apparatus, but its imperial state-making proceeded without nation-building.

The Chinese state has historically faced resistance in Xinjiang when attempting to increase security through deeper integration (Clarke, 2007b, p.325). Nationalist discourses emerged in China's eastern metropoles during the Opium War (1839–1842 CE) to build a nation and a state to resist Western imperialism and the internal Manchu enemy[7]. However, by 1830 the Daoguang Emperor (1820–1850 CE) had only just permitted Han Chinese settlement in Altishahr, the southern region of today's Xinjiang, and interethnic marriage continued to be outlawed (Clarke, 2007a, p.265). The Qing had created loyalty in Xinjiang but not a shared Chinese identity (Newby, 1999, p.459). Rebellions in Xinjiang over land rights and treatment of local peasants by officials grew with settlement and integration of the region, most notably in Hami, 1831 (Forbes, 1986, p.29). Before and after 1759, Xinjiang's value was debated within the Qing court through the prism of geopolitical security, and local rebellions intensified the seriousness of these questions. Many Han officials, including influential maritime defence advocate, Li Hongzhang (1823–1901), viewed the region as a 'barren wasteland' and its political control as a drain on the Empire's resources (Millward, 2007,

---

[7] For example, see Chow (2001), Leibold (2007), and Mitter (2004).

p.126). However, following military success, Han officials became gradually convinced by frontier defence advocates, such as Zuo Zongtang (1812–1885), that Xinjiang was a source of imperial glory as a 'forward defence dividend' (Perdue, 2005, p.560). From the outset, Xinjiang's incorporation into China was a geopolitical military project viewed through the prism of security for inner China rather than shared identity or nation-building. The maritime versus frontier security debate ended with the conclusion that insecurity in Xinjiang was an existential matter, a 'sickness of the heart', rather than a mere 'disease of the limbs', as had been claimed by Li Hongzhang. This perceived need to retain political control of the region stemmed from existential fears that China would collapse if, as expected, Mongolia and Beijing would follow Xinjiang's lead and separate from China (Millward, 2007, pp.126–127). As we shall see in subsequent chapters, Xinjiang's eighteenth century integration as a geopolitical 'buffer zone' and a 'wasteland' resonates today because its marginality as a site of insecurity remains central to China's nation-building project.

In 1884, Xinjiang ('new frontier') province was established in the Western Regions and it became subject to Chinese civil law for the first time, ceasing to be ruled as a formal military colony. The very idea of Xinjiang was a geopolitical invention of a 'new frontier' and 'strategic buffer' between China and the West but laid the institutional foundation for later nation-building efforts, which made it possible to begin to think of the region as Chinese. The north and south of Xinjiang were united as a singular political unit and became seen as the same place in Chinese discourse after Emperor Qianlong's military conquest and this new naming (Millward, 2007; Newby, 2005). It was only after taking the North that the Qing armies realised conquering the south would be necessary to hold the north. People in the south saw themselves as culturally distinct from the nomadic north. Even culturally and linguistically similar groups from the Fergana Valley in present-day Uzbekistan were referred to as 'Andijanis' and outsiders (Newby, 2007, pp.24–25). Qing documents indicate that prior to unification, considerable networks of inter-oasis trade, travel, and marriage linked the oases of Southern Xinjiang (Newby, 2007, p.18). Spurred on by the reformers' drive to build a modern state to resist European and Japanese imperial aggression, the southern oases and northern steppes were politically transformed from multiple colonies into a single province at the end of the nineteenth century. The establishment of Xinjiang province produced new socio-spatialised ways of thinking of north and south as a singular region intimately tied to China's survival, deeply shaping Chinese nationalisms and Uyghur resistance ever since.

If Xinjiang is a frontier between Sinic and Turkic civilisations, then Ürümchi, the primary fieldwork site of this book, exemplifies this frontier and China's approach to nation-building. Contemporary official Chinese histories of Ürümchi still describe it as a 'frontier city' today (SEAC, 2009). Ürümchi is located between Xinjiang's nomadic north and sedentary south, and between the east, where city states such as Qumul had closer historical contact with China, and Uyghur majority cities, Kashgar and Khotan, in the far West. Until the eighteenth century, the city was only seasonally inhabited by nomadic peoples, unlike the famous Uyghur-majority oases of Kashgar, Khotan, and Qumul, which enjoyed autonomy if not independence until 1949. Most of Ürümchi was built by Manchu settlers and officials as a strategic outpost and tax base. Manchu soldiers burned down Jiujawan, the nearest indigenous settlement 5 km away, recognising Ürümchi's strategic importance in securing all the 'Western Regions' (Gaubatz, 1996, pp.45–46). This 'frontier city' was built as an 'outpost of Chinese settlement in non-Chinese territory' to secure what later became known as Xinjiang (Gaubatz, 1996, p.45). With the nineteenth century arrival of Han traders in Xinjiang, their settlements became known as 'Han cities' (*Hancheng* 汉城) and older cities became known as 'Muslim cities' (*Huicheng* 回城) (Pan, 1996b, p.86). 'Frontier cities' such as Ürümchi, Hohhot, and Xining were small, separated Chinese enclaves, based on architectural ideals of the Chinese classics, but later became multicultural cities as non-Chinese groups settled (Gaubatz, 1996, pp.2–3). A policy of Chinese-Muslim segregation was implemented after Xinjiang's unification in the 1880s. A walled boundary was built, connecting the small, walled Manchu and Han cities (*gongningcheng* 巩宁城 and *dihua* 迪华) but separating them from the Uyghur and Hui Muslim city in today's *Erdaoqiao* (二道桥) / *Döngköwrük* (دۆڭ كۆۋرۈك).

Manchu state-making, the 1830 opening for Chinese settlement, and establishment of Xinjiang province in 1884 laid foundations for twentieth century Han-led nation-building amongst Turkic peoples in Central Asia. In contrast to nation-building experiences of the central plains and east coast, Chinese nation-building, a designed project to produce shared identity, only began to emerge in Xinjiang *after* the *Guomindang* (GMD) overthrew the imperial Qing state in the 1911 Xinhai Revolution. With the collapse of Republican authority in the 1940s, China turned to historical appeals as rationale for its rule over Xinjiang, drawn more from key Nationalist (GMD) than Communist (CCP) thinkers. Anhui-born General Zhang Zhizhong (1895–1969) negotiated the disbandment of the East Turkestan Republic (1944–1949) after defecting to the CCP from the GMD in 1949. Zhang, like Mao Zedong and Zhou Enlai, acknowledged that Uyghurs were indigenous to Xinjiang but was the first Chinese official to claim Xinjiang was also the homeland of Han Chinese people (Jacobs, 2008, p.548; Kamalov, 2007, pp.34 & 40). The GMD began to present Xinjiang as a relatively safe frontier in the 1940s. In 1947, General Zhang publicly criticised Han chauvinism and commissioned the Tianshan pictorials (*Tianshan huabao* 天山画报), a series of visual representations of exoticised, non-Han others, presenting Xinjiang as an open, untapped frontier, safe for Han settlement (Jacobs, 2008, pp.551–553). Its peoples were represented unthreateningly as elderly, bearded men or young, lively, naïve girls in colourful costumes, welcoming Han Chinese settlers and the civilisation they brought with them (Jacobs, 2008, p.556). Chinese nation-building reimagined Xinjiang as an integral but peculiarly foreign part of Chinese civilisation: an internal, ethnic frontier on the periphery of the civilised self.

Upon taking power in 1949, the CCP inherited this legacy of ambivalent nation-building in Xinjiang. The changes in Chinese leaders' understanding of the relationship between China and its northwest frontier, from military to identity logics, illustrate the ambivalence and historical contingency of Xinjiang's position in post-1949 China. Chinese leaders' public speeches and private communications during the 1950s discussed the CCP's role and ethnic relations in Xinjiang, first, in terms of military strategy and then, socialist transformation, to eradicate the 'oppressive' nature of China's traditional treatment of ethnic minorities (Zhou, 1949, p.4; 1950a, p.53). From the 1950s to the 1980s, Xinjiang was still understood as a 'strategic buffer' and described as the 'frontline in China's struggle against Soviet hegemonism' (XUAR Party Committee, 1982, p.257). Like earlier eras, the region was viewed through a geopolitical prism, but for the first time, official strategy included the political project to fit national identities to state borders. The CCP's long-term strategy for political control proceeded with Western and Soviet influence at the forefront of its thinking (Liu, 1954, p.119). Unified ethnic relations were part of China's ongoing geopolitical strategy to unite Xinjiang's many peoples against the West and Japan. Zhou Enlai's repeated appeals to the Han, China's 'core *minzu*' (*zhuti minzu* 主体民族), to show minorities 'benevolence' and cease 'discrimination and humiliation' in racist banners and placards, were on the grounds that ethnic relations in Xinjiang are a 'strategic chess game' of existential importance (Zhou, 1950b, p.63; 1951, p.66). Mao Zedong and Deng Xiaoping both described Uyghurs as the 'core *minzu*' in Xinjiang and highlighted 'Han chauvinism' as the fundamental, pressing problem (Mao, 1949, p.21; Deng et al., 1953, p.99). During the 1950s, Han chauvinism was conceptualised, like 'minority nationalism', as a remnant of the old China that 'haunted' Chinese minds and hindered social progress, so much so that even loyal Han cadres were considered unconsciously chauvinist by party leaders (Zhou, 1950a, p.53; Deng, 1953, p.104). The party leadership worried that Han chauvinism could incite Uyghur unrest and destabilise CCP control because ethnic discrimination undermined its claims of religious freedom and equal participation for minorities. A disunified identity was considered a geopolitical weakness and Western empires would take advantage.

The CCP originally considered ethnic identities as remnants of class exploitation. Both minority nationalism and majority chauvinism were considered obstacles to constructing a unified, modern China to defeat imperialism. The CCP sought to eradicate Han chauvinism as a source of disunity and political instability as much as 'local nationalism' in Xinjiang's many 'patriotic education' campaigns (Deng et al., 1953, p.99; Liu, 1954, p.121). Deng Xiaoping described economic discrimination as symptomatic of the 'haunting' of China by 'bourgeois nationalist thought' and considered the economy 'the foundation of the resolution to the *minzu* problem' (Deng, 1953, p.104). Patriotic education campaigns ran from the early 1950s until the early 1980s in Xinjiang and sought to produce a shared identity by preventing violence against non-Han and enabling inclusion of Uyghurs in the CCP. The party leadership frequently reined in former GMD members who became Xinjiang's regional leaders, explicitly reminding them that these were national priorities (CCPCC, 1953, p.106). However, the Han population in Xinjiang was so minimal that the CCP was dependent on demobilised nationalist soldiers to quell unrest among Uyghurs and Kazakhs in the 1950s and early 1960s, including leading political defectors such as Wang Zhen and Tao Zhiyue, who ran the regional government and the *Bingtuan* (兵团) paramilitary farms.[8] The CCP had to compromise between anti-chauvinism and anti-imperialism, relying on Han chauvinists to put anti-imperialist principles into practice. The chaos of the Cultural Revolution saw Han factions fighting for power in Xinjiang[9] but ended with 'opening and reform' and Deng Xiaoping's celebration of China as a nation enjoying 'genuine equality' without *minzu* conflict (Deng, 1979, p.245). The party-state now began to officially present China as a timelessly unified nation and Chinese scholars debated how to promote *more* 'patriotic education' to prevent China sliding into domestic disunity and international weakness (Bai, 1981, p.46). Historical materialism was never abandoned by the party-state. However, 'opening and reform' marks the party's gradual shift towards its reconfiguration as a 'scientific Development outlook' (*kexue fazhan guan* 科学发展观) with development the solution to the *minzu* problem (*minzu wenti* 民族问题) that will secure unification of Chinese identity (Hu, 2007, pp.13–14; MOI, 2008, p.26). 'Opening and reform' marks the party-state's official gradual shift away from conceptualising identity as a function of class struggle in a socialist dialectic towards identity as a function of economic development in dialectics tinged with what Deng himself termed 'bourgeois nationalist thought'. The teleological end-state of

---

[8] The Xinjiang Production and Construction Corps is popularly referred to as the *Bingtuan* and is frequently described as a state within a state by scholars of the subject. The *Bingtuan* was the institution responsible for communist-era 'reclamation' of land in Xinjiang. The *Bingtuan*'s unusual status as a quasi-state persists today. It owns more than half the arable land in Xinjiang and administers its own courts, police, schools, and hospitals. For example, see: McMillan (1979); Becquelin (2004a).
[9] For example, see: McMillen (1979); Millward (2007).

this dialectic is 'fusion', a *Zhonghua Minzu* ethno-hierarchy, defined, led, and held together by the Han nucleus.

The CCP has explicitly embraced the idea of China as a 'unified, multi-*minzu* nation' built through '5,000 years' of 'fusion', at least since the leadership of Hu Jintao (Hu, 2006, p.632). Ethnocentrism continues to haunt socialism in China. This haunting continues not simply because Communists had to compromise with Nationalists in Xinjiang but because the 'new China' was built by people whose thinking was unavoidably shaped by the ethnocentric traditions and social attachments they sought to eradicate. During the 1950s and 1960s, Jian Bozan, the influential Inner Mongolian anthropologist, warned that new and fashionable claims of timeless 'fusion' emerging in official circles would gradually promote majority chauvinism and minority assimilation by concealing China's history of class conflict and *minzu* oppression (Jian, 1960, pp.14 & 19–21). The significance of these claims resonates in China today because official policy has explicitly shifted towards 'contact, communication, fusion' (*jiaowang, jiaoliu, jiaorong* 交往交流交融) under Hu Jintao and then Xi Jinping, whose approach is security first, development later (XUAR Government, 2018). Today, the term 'separatist history'[10] conceals China's complex histories, securitising official narratives of *Zhonghua Minzu*, and excluding authors who challenge the 5,000 years of fusion narrative as threats to China.

The project to build a 'new China' without letting go of non-*Hua* peoples and territories acquired through imperial state-building produced unresolved tensions between political stability and identity transformation and between inclusion and exclusion. These tensions emerge in contemporary official explanations of the regional autonomy system for ethnic minority regions, which emphasise both stability and transformation. The autonomy system is a highly limited and territorial-based form of cultural autonomy for regions and sub-regions with high proportions of non-Han populations, namely, Xinjiang, Tibet, Inner Mongolia, Ningxia (Hui), and Guangxi (Zhuang) (Clarke, 2007a, p.278). Before the CCP took power, Mao Zedong had promised self-determination (*zijue* 自决) for minorities and Zhou Enlai insisted 'every *minzu*' has the 'right to self-determination' (Zhou, 1949, p.4). However, after coming to power, the CCP's approach shifted from *zijue* to regional autonomy (*zizhi* 自治) to hold these territories and placate calls for independence, particularly on the former Qing Frontier (Clarke, 2007a, pp.278–284). Xinjiang was subsequently divided into smaller administrative units to counter potential calls for further Uyghur autonomy. For example, 'gerrymandering' assigned Daur and Mongols the Tacheng and Emin autonomous counties,

---

[10] For example, see: XEP (2009).

despite only having 17 per cent and 12 per cent of the populations, respectively (Bovingdon, 2004a, pp.13–14). The establishment of 'sub-autonomies' countered Uyghurs' demographic and political weight by entrenching the idea that Xinjiang belonged to 13 officially recognised ethnic groups (McMillen, 1979, pp.66–70; Clarke, 2007b, p.333). From the outset, the establishment of autonomy was driven both by the party-state's desire to maintain its own power and the transformative impulses of nation-building that disrupted the ability of Uyghurs to claim Xinjiang as their nation.

Mainstream Chinese Studies scholars, such as Zheng Yongnian (2007), frame China as a de facto federal state, pointing to increasing fiscal and economic provincial autonomy in the 'opening and reform era'. However, the autonomous regions, unlike the provinces, are directly supervised by the State Council, the highest level of central government and designed to counter claims for federalism or separation. The Deng Xiaoping slogan, 'stability overpowers everything', is used in most official texts and political slogans on Ürümchi's streets. However, it highlights the need for political stability, including the regional autonomy system, to guide the transformative identity project of Chinese nation-building. The *National Law on Regional Autonomy*[11] states the purpose of the autonomy system is to ensure that ethnic minority regions can 'never be separated' from China *and* are 'modernised' by raising their 'scientific level'. Official explanations tell the story that prior to 'liberation' (*jiefang* 解放) by China, minorities in Xinjiang were 'enslaved' and 'oppressed', and their economy was 'backward' (*luohou* 落后) (State Council, 2009a; 2009b). Since 'liberation', regional autonomy has made minorities their 'own masters' such that they enjoy equality, freedom, and development (most specifically 'tall buildings'), in a modern China (XEP, 2009, pp.72–73). A stable regional autonomy system was thus designed to secure political stability by transforming Uyghurs into Chinese *minzu*. However, official autonomy narratives reproduce ambivalent tensions between inclusion of Xinjiang as an equal unit of a modern territorial state and exclusion as an exotic, orientalised frontier.

In the 'opening and reform' era, Ürümchi exemplifies Xinjiang's ambivalent position for Uyghurs, Han, and the Chinese state. Uyghurs tend to deride it as 'Hanified' or 'a Chinese city' with no 'real' Uyghurs. Han migrants from all over China arrive in seasonal labour migrations, and, as Chapter 6 will show, few have intentions of settling while many understand Uyghurs as dangerously backward, non-Chinese others. The Manchu-era walls were demolished in the 1980s, but Ürümchi remains spatially and ethnically divided between Han-populated north and Uyghur-populated south (Taynen,

---

[11] See: Zhonghua Renmingongheguo Minzu Diquyu Zizhifa ('National Law on Regional Autonomy') (2001) Articles 9, 14, 55, and 71.

2006; Smith, 2002). This de facto segregation between Chinese (Han) and Muslims (Uyghurs) follows pre-modern civilisational boundaries built before China superimposed the logics of modern nationalism on to its empire. The walled division of the city into north and south ran across what is now *Renmin Lu* (People's Street), a key military position separating Han and Uyghur rioters during the imposition of martial law after the July 2009 violence. These are not immutable, civilisational fault lines. They are performative boundaries, maintained and reinforced by the power of official ethnocentric historical narratives, which frame the city as a frontier point between civilisation and barbarism. Ethnically organised violence emerges at this frontier point and in the discursive tension between China as a modern, multi-ethnic state and China as a civilisation with the potential to transform barbarians.

The party-state's historiography invisibilises the ambivalence of Xinjiang's inclusion in China and the dramatic significance of the shift away from condemning Han chauvinism towards adoption of its cultural nationalist logics. Official historiography in the PRC has arguably been more effective than armies at incorporating Xinjiang into China and severing linguistic, cultural, and religious links to Central Asia (Millward & Perdue, 2004, p.36). The party-state has re-imagined the 1759 Manchu conquest as Xinjiang's inevitable 're-incorporation' into China, following the decline of the Tang dynasty (618–907 CE) military outposts. Ethnic unity and history textbooks at all education levels insist that only 'separatists' and 'terrorists' who seek to 'distort history' and 'harm ethnic relations' claim this was a conquest (XEP, 2009). The CCP's nation-building project in Xinjiang is built on identity-security narratives, which reproduce, reconfigure, and securitise traditional internal boundaries between civilised Han frontier builders and willing or unwilling barbarians. Literary works and traditions that identify themselves as Turkic, locate themselves outside Chinese culture, or present negative representations of contemporary life are treated as security threats to China (Friederich, 2007, p.95). Public burning of Uyghur history books and clamp-downs on campaigns for Uyghur language education are officially explained alongside arrests of suspected terrorists through the prism of national security and territorial integrity (Becquelin, 2004b, p.45). The Chinese nation's emergence at the confluence of imperial and modern domains, therefore, requires reading China's territoriality and the self from Beijing's view and suppressing all alternatives (Sautman, 1997, p.364; Callahan, 2009). Uyghur Turkic and Islamic identities challenge their status as willing barbarians in *Zhonghua Minzu* narratives and are subsequently framed as omnipresent threats. They are no longer raw barbarians, but they are not yet civilised.

Nation-building in Xinjiang today continues nineteenth century narratives that Chinese civilisation is faced with extinction in the face of the internal barbarian threat in collaboration with external threats of Western interference.

The 'struggle' for a shared identity against the 'inside/outside Three Evils' ('terrorism, separatism, and extremism') is a 'zero-sum political struggle of life or death' for China (XEP, 2009, p.15). The party-state routinely claims that internal Turkic ethnic enemies are supported from outside by violent 'Islamic terrorists' and Western 'enemies of China' (*fanhua shili* 反华势力) seeking to split the nation (State Council, 2009a; 2009b; XEP, 2009). The attributive phrase 'inside/outside' links disaffected Uyghurs inside China, particularly those who frame their identity through Turkic language and Islam, with external threats. Official Chinese texts assert that only the 'mistaken understandings' of 'The Three Evils', which 'distort history', could frame Xinjiang history as Central Asian or Uyghur identity as Turkic and Islamic (XEP, 2009, pp.47, 61, & 94). Chinese nation-building in Xinjiang thus configures identity and security by constituting a unified, civilised self against ever-present threats of Uyghur identity within China's territory but from outside its cultural frontiers. Nation-building invisibilises the historical contingency of Xinjiang's integration into China and intensifies the perceived existential need to convert Uyghur identity and pacify its threat to Han cultural centrality in *Zhonghua Minzu*.

One example of the contemporary resonance of historical tensions between inclusion of Xinjiang as an inalienable, timeless component of China and exclusion as an exotic, often dangerous frontier is exemplified in competing meanings of the 'fragrant concubine' (*Iparhan* ئىپارخان / *Xiang fei* 香妃) (1734–1788 CE). Iparhan's story today has been re-appropriated by the state as a tale of 'ethnic unity' (*minzu tuanjie*) represented by her marriage as a Uyghur with a Chinese Emperor. The explanatory text at her tomb just outside the Uyghur city of Kashgar tells visitors that Iparhan's entrance into the 'imperial harem' expresses 'the good wish for unity and mutual love between different nationalities since ancient times'.[12] Iparhan is symbolic of ethnic unity and an integral part of the Chinese nation. However, she is still an exotic, ethnic Uyghur outsider, symbolising that 'to Han minds, Xinjiang was in the empire but not yet of it' (Millward, 1994, p.442). The continuing competition over visual representation of Iparhan as Chinese by the state and ethnically Turkic by Uyghurs reflects how the Qing expansion of China's physical boundaries has never been resolved in the realm of self-identification (Millward, 1994). Xinjiang is included as part of the Chinese nation through the party-state's discourse on ethnic unity but as an exotic frontier on the periphery of the Han nucleus.

Xinjiang is ambivalently positioned between the Chinese self and barbaric other, both timelessly Chinese and a perpetual frontier. In the words of Gong

---

[12] Quotes drawn from three research trips (2007–2008 and 2012).

Yufeng, spokesperson for the Chinese embassy in Egypt, Xinjiang is 'a fairyland, ever and forever' (Gong, 2009). Minority identities, therefore, are produced somewhere between barbarism and civilisation. Alternatives that challenge this ambivalence are treated as existential threats to China's cultural boundaries and the territorial integrity of the modern state. On the surface, nation-building in Xinjiang is a stark, binarising security discourse, but *Zhonghua Minzu*, the party-state's referent of security, is deeply ambivalent in its inclusion of non-Han others. *Zhonghua Minzu* confounds and blurs the logics of civilisation and nation and of empire and state, securitising the identity of China as a civilising nation and Xinjiang as a perpetual frontier. Civilisation and nation in Xinjiang are mutually reinforcing, hybrid configurations of identity and security. They reinforce the ethnic boundaries they seek to eliminate by consistently highlighting a peoples' identity as a problem to be eliminated. Nation-building in Xinjiang began long after establishment of the state and much later than is assumed in the Chinese Studies accounts on the emergence of nationalism. The geopolitical concerns of the Manchu and the CCP regarding Western and Russian territorial encroachment drove the incorporation of Xinjiang into China between 1759 and 1949. The analytic focus of the next section is turned to the concerted political efforts that began in the 1950s to make Xinjiang and its peoples Chinese.

Securitising Ethnic Boundaries in Xinjiang

This section shifts focus from territory to people, exploring how nation-building in China shapes and is shaped by ethnic politics. It analyses the historical relationship between nation and ethnicity, and between majority and minorities, in the CCP's approach to ethnic relations. The section then turns to the construction of Uyghur identity and the implications for nation-building, to ask how these identities are included and excluded in this majority-minority relationship. Identities in Xinjiang tend to be understood as contemporary political science questions of integration into China or through historical questions of cultural and social practices in two fairly distinct streams of literature (Bellér-Hann et al., 2007, p.2). The top-down approaches of scholars, usually trained in Chinese Studies, primarily analyse the region through state-centric framings of physical, territorial integration into China or through majority/minority configurations as understood by the party-state.[13] The bottom-up approach, adopted by scholars trained in Central Asian Studies or social anthropology, begins analysis from below using micro-fieldwork to understand social change through self-identifications and

---

[13] See: Blank (2003); Gladney (1990; 1996; 2004); Rudelson (1997).

'daily practices'.[14] These different approaches represent analytical emphases rather than fixed ontologies. This section draws from both to examine mutual interplay between the top-down official project to produce a shared *Zhonghua Minzu* identity and bottom-up articulations of identity in Xinjiang, understanding China as produced and re-produced somewhere between the two. The analysis links studies of Chinese state nationalism and ethnic relations, bridging the two literatures' core ideas by understanding identities in Xinjiang through relations between top-down ascriptions and bottom-up self-identifications.[15] The section argues that Chinese nation-building securitises hierarchical relations between Han majority and ethnic minorities, constituting *Zhonghua Minzu* in official national narratives. Transgressions of these hierarchical boundaries, either through calls for self-determination or greater cultural equality within China, are thus officially framed as existential threats to China.

The peripheralisation of China's ethnic margins is often central to what it means to be Chinese. Louisa Schein's study of China's southwestern Miao people (*Miaozu* 苗族), *Minority Rules*, showed how official and unofficial discourses of 'internal Orientalism' circulate in contemporary China, representing minorities as agricultural, feminine, and out of step with modernity but also as integral components of *Zhonghua Minzu* (Schein, 2000, p.130). In nineteenth century European colonial discourse, 'the Orient' was an inferior and backward frontier to be dominated by the West, mutually constituted as superior and advanced (Said, 2003, pp.6–7 & 54). Orientalist logics circulate within China and are directed inward to exclude minorities from the modern core of the nation, while forcibly including them in *Zhonghua Minzu* on a lower, non-modern level of the ethno-hierarchy. This peripheralisation of minority identities is central to majority identity construction. Dru Gladney's *Dislocating China* (2004) illustrated how Chinese representations of minority *minzu* as exotic, erotic, and primitive relationally constitute majority Han identity as the national standard and an economically advanced, civilising force. Minorities are represented as backward, external, and dependent, thus in need of the superior, modern, benevolent Han to be civilised and absorbed into China (Gladney, 2004, pp.13–16). The policing of minority identities in *Zhonghua Minzu* is built on Fei Xiaotong's Han nucleus concept, and its ambivalent inclusion of non-Han others exemplifies tensions between Orientalist and nationalist thought in European colonialism, highlighted in Partha

---

[14] See: Bellér-Hann (2001; 2002; 2008); Bovingdon (2002; 2010); Dautcher (2009); Roberts (2004; 2009); Smith (2000; 2002).
[15] There is a modest but growing literature that more explicitly explores the intersections between ascription and self-identification in Xinjiang. For example, see: Bovingdon (2002; 2004; 2010); Brophy (2016).

Chatterjee's classic, *Nationalist Thought and the Colonial World* (2001). In Orientalism, the Orient is eternally backward and passive. However, in universalist nationalism, all humanity is capable of progress, even if defined in ethno-centric terms (Chatterjee, 2001, p.38). Non-Han internal others are subject to these two logically contradictory, disciplining identity discourses at the same time. Ethnic inclusion in *Zhonghua Minzu* assumes the backwardness of non-Han and, thus, their postulated need to be civilised by China. 'Internal orientalism' in Xinjiang represents minorities as backward and exotic, but unlike Gladney's and Schein's analyses of southwestern minorities, Uyghurs' Turkic and Islamic identities are officially framed as security threats to China. On the surface, Chinese nation-building in Xinjiang is stark and absolute, but historicising and decentring the ethnic boundaries it articulates reveal the project's ambivalence and historical contingency. Chinese nation-building secures an identity within unresolved tensions between exclusivist Orientalism and inclusionary nationalism, opening perpetual possibilities for internal critique.

From 1955 onward, the party-state led an official ethnic classification project (*minzu shibie* 民族识别) to unify and modernise China by categorising all peoples within the PRC into 56 *minzu*. All party-state discourse, including the constitution, describes an unshakeable de facto and de jure equality enjoyed by all *minzu* in China (Constitution of the PRC, 2004). The party-state 'scientifically' determined who belongs to what ethnic group and its *minzu shibie* formulated the contemporary ethnotaxonomy of 56 *minzu* (Mullaney, 2011, pp.1–4). More than 400 groups applied to become *minzu* but only 56 were eventually accepted (Fei, 1980, p.165). Subjective identifications were bypassed in favour of 'political exigencies' and 'expert determinations', making the undifferentiated mass of 'alien peoples' within China's borders intelligible to the state in new ways (Schein, 2000, pp.82 & 95–96). This process was understood as 'scientific research work' because it used historical records to determine the genealogical lineage and historical migrations of peoples to categorise *minzu* identities (Fei, 1980, pp.170–174). Fei Xiaotong's influential review of *minzu shibie* explained that researchers had to tell the *Chuanqing* of Guizhou that they were Han and groups of self-identified Mongolians in Hulunbuir, Inner Mongolia, that they were Daur (*Dawoerzu* 达斡尔族). *Minzu* is in the first instance a politically imposed category that does not comfortably translate as *ethnicity* because it does not necessarily include self-identification.

Scholarly literature and official documents ordinarily cite Marxist-Leninism, particularly Stalin's four principles of nationhood (language, territory, economic life, and psychology), as the foundation of the party-state's ethnic policies and the solution to the *minzu* problem.[16] However, the party-state

---

[16] For example, see Hu (2009); Pan (2008).

radically departed from Stalin and Engels by rejecting the idea that nation and ethnicity only emerge under the historical conditions of a capitalist stage of development and considered these categories as timeless in China (Ya, 1965, pp.117–119). The party-state drew from nationalist discourses to frame the Han as a timeless *minzu* that transcend the materialist dialectics of history, within which minority identities emerge. Fan Wenlan, one of the most politically influential historians during this period, explained that the Han's advanced culture derives from their formation during the Qin-Han period, two millennia prior to the development of capitalism, uniting and leading all *minzu* in China (Fan, 1954, pp.12–13). In practice, the first task of *minzu shibie* was to differentiate which groups were majority Han and which groups were ethnic minorities (Fei, 1980, p.166). Its focus on distinguishing between Han Chinese and non-Han others owed as much to the persisting binary between civilisation and barbarism as the modernising impulses of Marxism. The complex identities of a broad range of ethnic groups were overlooked, ethnocentrically and negatively defined as non-Han. Ethnic minority groups in China today are still defined 'negatively', according to a lack of Han Chinese attributes, constituting a hierarchical China (Callahan, 2010, p.132). Ethnic minorities were understood as non-Han *internal* others, a construction of the Han's modern nation-building project, later re-framed as a continuation of civilisational identity. Conservative Han Chinese traditions shaped modernising socialist nation-building practices and their ethnocentrism has haunted the party-state's project to produce a post-ethnic, modern nation.

The project to re-categorise and modernise all peoples formerly known as barbarians has saturated subsequent modes of Chinese ethnographic knowledge. However, the national project of creating a multi-ethnic shared identity and the imperial project of civilising barbarians continue to co-exist uneasily. The party's binary division between majority Han and ethnic minorities structured ethnic policy narratives in all its legal documents, including the constitution and white papers.[17] The party-state's project to categorise China's many peoples depended on 'unceasing efforts' to intervene through modern techniques in education, museums, dance performances, and language policies (Mullaney, 2011, p.135). Official *minzu* identities in contemporary China are 'the outcome of government policy during the last four decades' (Schein, 2000, p.80). Although the political ascription of ethnonyms encloses the vocabulary available to people to contest their meaning, it cannot completely enclose the meaning itself. Minoritisation is a powerful political discourse in China, but *minzu* are positionalities, which take on a life of their own

---

[17] For example, see: State Council (2009a; 2009b). The dramatic disappearance of the ethnic minority concept under Xi Jinping and the more explicit policy shift towards 'fusion' is addressed in the book's conclusion.

(Schein, 2000, pp.96–99). For example, Stevan Harrell's classic study of the Yi of Yunnan showed how they self-divide into various ethnic groups unrecognised by the state. *Minzu* is an officially defined positionality, through which the group, the other, and the state negotiate the relationship between the category and the group (Harrell, 1990, p.516). Ethnicity, *minzu*, and nation are blunt instruments, concealing contestation over their meaning and the competition for power to articulate them. The party-state has relatively successfully engineered the *minzu* category. However, mutual interplay between top-down and bottom-up processes of articulation, maintenance, and resistance shape multiple meanings of the category, emerging in daily practice.

The position of Uyghur identities in this process and the social dynamics it has engendered illustrate how the meaning of the *minzu* category emerges through interplay between official politics and unofficial identities. Analysing Uyghur identities from above, Dru Gladney (1990) argued that the Uyghur category was constructed by the Chinese state. Gladney, like Rudelson (1997), built this argument on how the Uyghur ethnonym fell into disuse for five centuries after conversion to Islam due to association with the Qocho Buddhist Kingdom in ninth to fourteenth century Turpan. Gladney claimed the 'ethno-genesis' of the Uyghur[18] was a 'gradual evolution' through successive stages of integration into the Chinese state, crystallising in 1934 with the official adoption of the Uyghur ethnonym at a Xinjiang provincial government conference (Gladney, 2004, pp.205–210). The official reinvention of the Uyghur ethnonym is then considered an external imposition onto disparate peoples. As Chapter 2 will show, the absence of Uyghur agency in this narrative is a theme in official discourse, which identifies Uyghurs as less authentic and timeless than Chinese civilisation, which will inevitably absorb them. Justin Rudelson's *Oasis Identities* (1997) built on Gladney's 'ethno-genesis' to argue that Uyghurs had no *national* identity prior to *minzu shibie*. Geographical obstacles, namely, the Taklamakan desert and Tian Shan Mountains, restricted inter-oasis contacts between Uyghurs who identified themselves purely by localised place of birth. Uyghurs today do continue to speak with pride regarding birthplace, and oasis-based stereotyping *within* the Uyghur community, both positive and negative, is commonplace (e.g. see Dautcher, 2009). However, Rudelson's fieldwork was conducted before the upsurge of political violence and ethnic consciousness in the 1990s and his empirical claims have been re-assessed to emphasise the growth of ethno-national identities in the 'opening and reform' era (Smith, 2000; 2002). Furthermore, the top-down 'ethno-genesis' arguments overlooked how multiple identities (local, ethnic, national, etc) can co-exist and intermingle without necessarily

---

[18] References to 'the Uyghur' in this book denote the identity category, particularly its representation in official narratives.

precluding one another. Local (oasis) identities are real but are not formally institutionalised, so must be understood from below. Whereas ethnic and national identities are more politicised, located in the interplay between official ascription and unofficial self-identification.

Uyghur narratives of history and identity that emphasise distinctiveness from Chinese nationalisms forced a rethink of the absence of Uyghur agency in state-led ethno-genesis arguments. Ildikó Bellér-Hann's (2008) study of official native documents from Xinjiang (1880–1949) showed how they universally used the Turk ethnonym, suggesting a longer-term, shared Uyghur identity than ethnogenesis arguments allow. Laura Newby (2007) showed that inter-oasis trade and marriage flourished during the eighteenth and nineteenth centuries, despite the geographical obstacles asserted by Rudelson as impediments to group identity. Uzbeks, the most linguistically similar ethnic group to Uyghurs, were even referred to as *Andijanis*, and children from 'mixed marriages' were called *Chalgurts* ('half breeds') (Newby, 2007, p.18). These histories indicate that Uyghurs' group identity emerged prior to questions of *national* identity that arose with Uyghur integration into the Soviet and Chinese states. The Uyghur category has been shaped by political shifts as much as Han, but their group consciousness had a life of its own prior to the institutionalisation of state-sponsored, fixed ethnonyms. Uyghur nationalism, like Han nationalism, emerges through intercultural translation and semantic hybridity. Uyghur nationalism that conceptualised group identity as congruent with bounded territory was articulated in response to the emergence of the nation-state with the collapse of Russian and Chinese empires. During the 1910s and 1920s, Uyghur intellectuals in Russian Turkestan began to explicitly articulate the Uyghur nation to identify sedentary Turkic speakers in nationalist newspapers and in engagement with Soviet officials (Roberts, 2009, p.361). Debates between Uyghur nationalist intellectuals and Kashgari traders in Soviet Central Asia proceeded within the institutional bounds of the Soviet political system and ideological framings of national revolution moving towards socialism (Brophy, 2011, p.5). Debates amongst Uyghurs culminated in official Soviet adoption of the ethnonym for sedentary Turkic speakers at the 1921 Tashkent conference to identify newly acquired 'minorities' in Soviet Central Asia (Kamalov, 2007, p.32). Uyghur articulation from below spoke to Soviet power above, resulting in institutionalisation of the Uyghur category, and the ethnonym was then directly imported by the Chinese state in its 1950s *minzu* classification project. The Uyghur category emerges, similarly to the Han category, through intercultural interactions between people, states, and empires.

The post-1949 institutionalisation of the Uyghur category in Xinjiang reflects the interplay between Uyghur articulations of national identity and the party-state's nation-building project. After 1949, Turkic-speakers in China were for the first time called Chinese minorities, rather than Muslims (*hui*) or barbarians (*yi*), and were officially permitted to maintain their own language and religious customs. The system of ethnic regional autonomy in Xinjiang, established in 1955, was designed to secure Xinjiang as Chinese territory but provided a more distinct and bounded 'territorial frame' for Uyghur grievances and political aspirations (Bovingdon, 2004a, p.3). However, while the Uyghur category became territorially bounded and delinked from Uyghurs across Central Asia, Xinjiang faced rapid demographic transformation through mass state-sponsored immigration of Mandarin Chinese–speaking peoples to produce and secure the region's Chinese identity. According to official statistics, the Han Chinese proportion of Xinjiang's population grew from less than 5 per cent in 1949 to an absolute majority in the twenty-first century, when including military and *Bingtuan* paramilitary farms (Rudelson, 1997; XUAR Statistics Bureau, 2007; 2018). Chinese nation-building reconfigured Uyghur's self-selected ethnonym denoting linguistic and cultural identity as a state security matter, to be made congruent with Chinese territory. The party-state went further by transforming Xinjiang's demographics to be more congruent with China's hierarchical cultural boundaries. Demographic and linguistic transformation produced considerable identity-insecurity for Uyghurs that resonates in their identity narratives today as they rapidly became a numerical minority within Xinjiang.

In the 'opening and reform' era, the meaning and political significance of the Uyghur category has been transformed again as the party-state's conceptualisation of Chinese-ness gradually shifts from historical materialism to cultural nationalism. The identity of Turkic-speaking peoples has become redefined as a 'mistaken' identity because Uyghurs are framed as having always been culturally Chinese.[19] This shift intensified Uyghur identity-insecurities, and the political violence of the 1990s[20] suggested that ethnic boundaries in Xinjiang were hardening and that Uyghurs did not consider themselves Chinese. Politically targeted violence throughout the 1990s sparked waves of bottom-up literature as scholars grappled with how Uyghurs understood identity and ethnic boundaries. Bellér-Hann (2002) and Smith (2002) used longitudinal perspectives to show how Han-Uyghur relations deteriorated in the 'opening and reform' era due to demographic transformation and subsequent employment squeeze, coupled with growing ethnic discrimination since the party dropped public concerns about Han chauvinism. During the 1990s, Uyghurs in southern Xinjiang and Ürümchi employed strategies of everyday resistance, including the Islamic pork taboo and dress codes to reinforce and reproduce symbolic, social, and spatial boundaries vis-à-vis Han Chinese

---

[19] For example, see: XEP (2009), p.47.
[20] Chapter 3 more fully analyses the political violence of the 1990s.

(Smith, 1999; 2000; 2002; Bellér-Hann, 2002; 2007). Uyghurs challenged official discourses of time and progress as value-free representations by using 'Xinjiang time', two hours behind official 'Beijing time' used by Han Chinese in the region, thus creating parallel temporal worlds (Smith Finley, 2013, pp.139–141). With deterioration of ethnic relations in the 'opening and reform' era, Uyghur fears of being minoritised and discriminated against by state-supported Han Chinese migrants grew alongside the perception of threat to Uyghur 'we-ness' (Clarke, 2007b, p.325). The project to build the Chinese nation by telling Uyghurs who they must be was frequently resisted through both peaceful and violent challenges to the state's authority throughout the 1990s (see Bovingdon, 2002; Dillon, 2002; Millward, 2007). The policy shift towards monolingual education, analysed in Chapter 2, has exacerbated this sense of threat. Uyghurs are no longer the 'core *minzu*' of Xinjiang, as described by Mao, and the securitisation of identity encloses the discursive space to negotiate their identity without transgressing officially ascribed boundaries.

Neither party-state discourse nor everyday social practices indicates the withering away of ethnic identities with economic development as envisaged by the CCP's initial historical materialist approach to nation-building. Instead, an increasing activation of ethnic boundaries in China's 'opening and reform' era revolves around language, religion, and indigeneity. Political, economic, and discursive inequalities have persisted and contribute to the maintenance of notions of cultural separateness (Bellér-Hann, 2002; Bovingdon, 2002; Smith, 2002). The recent content-based approaches to identity, which partly emerged as responses to the boundary literature that drew from fieldwork during the 1990s, critiqued the tendency to view Uyghur identity as a binary construction of ethnic otherness vis-à-vis Han Chinese. This shift coincided with the broader ontological turn in social anthropology to studies of 'visceral' social practices over conceptual, 'imagined' communities and adds depth to studies of identity in Xinjiang (Bellér-Hann, 2008, p.11). Jay Dautcher's *Down a Narrow Road* (2009) argued that the focus on ethnic boundaries in the 1990s reified Uyghur identities as intrinsically ethnic, which overlooks how everyday, face-to-face social practices at the neighbourhood level construct a shared sense of Uyghur community. Ildikó Bellér-Hann's *Community Matters* (2008) showed how studies of Uyghur cultural boundaries are 'insufficient to understand the repertoires on which group members may potentially draw in order to assert their sense of belonging' (Bellér-Hann, 2008, p.21). Ethnic boundaries, which hardened during the 1990s in Xinjiang, are constructed by people through daily practices, but, informed by the historical content of the category. This book analyses how Han, Uyghurs, and the party-state demarcate and securitise these boundaries in their daily practices using the meaningful cultural and historical repertoires available to them.

The Chinese state has historically faced what Michael Clarke (2007b) termed an 'internal security dilemma' in Xinjiang. China's goals of increasing security through further 'integration' has always faced resistance, as it conflicts with Uyghur identities, thus decreasing security and destabilising the nation-building project (Clarke, 2007b, p.325). Uyghurs continue to identify themselves through Turkic language and Islam, despite these being officially designated as threatening, non-Chinese attributes.[21] The romantic and exotic representations of ethnic otherness that circulate in southwest China are applied to the Northwest, but Uyghurs face the additional disciplining discourse of identity-security. The 'backward' identity of Uyghurs is thus at once a romantic vision of a pre-modern, natural past and a threatening alternative to Chinese identity. Chinese identity-security discourses highlight Uyghur alternatives to *Zhonghua Minzu* as existential threats to the nation *because* of their backwardness. What Stevan Harrell (1995) called the Chinese 'civilising project' is securitised in Xinjiang by framing it as central to the survival of China's cultural identity and territorial integrity. The nation-building drive to convert Uyghurs *and* maintain their marginality securitises an ambivalent identity, opening the possibility of perpetual critique because Xinjiang is positioned as an equal component of the modern state *and* a frontier on the periphery of civilised China. The party-state's *Zhonghua Minzu* narrative requires loyalty and transformation of Uyghur identity to maintain China's self-identification as a unified, non-Western multi-*minzu* nation held together by consent rather than coercion. As will be shown throughout this book, the party-state's securitisation of *Zhonghua Minzu* as a zero-sum 'struggle of life or death' against Uyghur Turkic and Islamic identities exacerbates cycles of identity-insecurity in Xinjiang. Han and Uyghurs use official narratives to securitise their own conceptualisations of identity and frame each other as existential threats.

Conclusions

This chapter showed how China has historically understood Xinjiang through a geopolitical prism that has gradually shifted towards cultural nationalism, which includes Uyghurs but frames their identities as security threats. The historical context of empire, nationalism, and ethnic relations shape China's contemporary nation-building practices in Xinjiang, which highlight its cultural otherness *and* its timeless Chinese-ness. Chinese nation-building in contemporary Xinjiang is an identity-security discourse, which is performed from above but re-articulated from below in mutual interplay between official

---

[21] For example, see Bovingdon (2010); Smith Finley (2011).

Conclusions

and unofficial politics. The chapter's first section built on the nationalism literature to analyse Chinese nation-building as politically contingent processes of frontier cultural governance and relations between Han and non-Han peoples. It showed how Chinese nation-building began to articulate and securitise a specific narrative of nationhood (*Zhonghua Minzu*) as an existential matter in mid-twentieth century Xinjiang. This conception of nationhood represented a shift to a territorially bounded national identity but was informed by and continues to co-exist in tension with imperial, pre-modern framings of difference between civilisation and barbarians. The second section analysed shifts in the official conceptualisation of Xinjiang's position in China throughout modern history to show how Xinjiang's identities have been historically viewed through a geopolitical prism. Chinese state-making and nation-building emerged in China as simultaneous processes in nineteenth and twentieth century movements against European imperialism and Manchu domination. However, Xinjiang was governed by the Manchu as a distant, barbarian colony under imperial protection for strategic purposes. Xinjiang only began to be understood as part of the Chinese *nation* in the twentieth century struggle to build a modern national Chinese identity. Transformed from a military colony in the eighteenth century, Xinjiang's marginality is central to official *Zhonghua Minzu* narratives and is now seen as an inalienable component of China's self-definition as a modern, multi-ethnic state. Twentieth century nation-builders articulated and securitised a new multi-*minzu* Chinese national identity in Xinjiang. The chapter's final section explored how Chinese nation-building produces and securitises ethnic boundaries in Xinjiang, which people mediate and reorganise in daily ethnic relations. Chinese nation-building and its ethnic classification project conceptualise and organise ethnicities by articulating hierarchical relations between Han majority and ethnic minorities. Chinese nation-building shapes Uyghur identity, but Uyghur national identity also builds on older ideas of belonging. Through intercultural translation, the Uyghur category, like China, has adapted to modern conceptualisations of statehood that bind and fix identities to territories.

Xinjiang today occupies an ambivalent position in China as an indivisible, equal component of a modern territorial state *and* a site of exotic difference on the frontier of imperial civilisation. Xinjiang's status as an inalienable component of China is a non-negotiable security matter, even though its peoples are never unambiguously framed as Chinese. The party-state, therefore, securitises an ambivalent *Zhonghua Minzu* where Uyghurs are included as internal others. The CCP has superimposed multi-*minzu*, socialist modernity onto older boundaries between civilisation and barbarians. This ambivalent boundary has been securitised in Xinjiang. When Uyghurs identify through Turkic language or Islam, or simply express dissatisfaction with policy or inequality in *Zhonghua Minzu*, they transgress this boundary and are framed as existential threats to China's cultural constitution and its territorial integrity. The ongoing conversion of Xinjiang and its peoples, labelled 'internal foreigners' by Sun Yat-Sen, constitutes what it means to be Chinese in the twenty-first century. Contemporary narratives of *Zhonghua Minzu* reflect a confluence of ancient and modern identity politics by building on traditions of defending and defining China against internal foreigners and barbarian others. Contemporary nation-building in Xinjiang securitises this older cultural boundary and frames it as central to the preservation of the modern Chinese state's territorial integrity. Barbarism and backwardness require perpetual nation-building in Xinjiang to transform a multiplicity of ethnic self-identifications into a timeless multi-*minzu* nation with the Han as the central, centripetal force. From its outset, Chinese nation-building constituted internal and external boundaries through each other as it sought to defend China's internal civilisational boundaries from imperialism and external cultural influence. China's nation-builders sought to prevent the West from dismembering Chinese civilisation by building a modern national identity, and today they seek to avoid becoming Western by rejuvenating Chinese civilisation. China needs Uyghur self-identification to maintain its identity as a non-Western multi-*minzu* nation built on consent. The in-between-ness of Uyghur identity and Uyghur dissatisfaction with policy, therefore threaten to China defined through internal hierarchy and fixed external boundaries against the West.

The securitisation of *Zhonghua Minzu* produces cycles of identity-insecurity in the region because, as will be shown throughout the book, the state's identity narratives exacerbate tensions between different ethnic groups who perceive each other as existential threats. Chinese nation-building nominally aims to collapse ethnic boundaries, but it reinforces them by securitising an ethnocentric national narrative that emboldens Han nationalism and threatens Uyghur identities. Nation-building in Xinjiang organises ethnicity by securitising the internal and external boundaries of *Zhonghua Minzu*, inevitably producing identity-security for some and identity-insecurity for others. The next chapter analyses how official narratives on China's historical role in Xinjiang and Xinjiang's position in China are taught in universal 'ethnic unity' (*minzu tuanjie*) education to cadres and students of all ages. These texts are a crystallisation of China's nation-building project and tell a story of China as a modern, multi-*minzu* civilisation securing itself from the backward threat of Uyghur ethnic identity.

2   Mass Education as an Identity-Security Practice

Introduction

After the July 2009 violence, the party-state instituted compulsory 'ethnic unity education' (*minzu tuanjie jiaoyu* 民族团结教育) in all state institutions across Xinjiang to 'promote ethnic unity consciousness ... with patriotism as its core content' (XUAR Government, 2009, article 3). This chapter examines mass education in Xinjiang as an identity-security practice, specifically how its narrative of *Zhonghua Minzu* history ethnocentrically includes ethnic minorities. The universal coverage of ethnic unity education is a crucial component of broader drives for 'patriotic education' (*aiguo zhuyi jiaoyu* 爱国主义教育) and nation-building.[1] To complete compulsory 'ethnic unity' education, all schoolchildren, students, teachers, and employees of the state in Xinjiang are required to link their identity to official narratives of history in exams and oral repetition of official texts. Several students interviewed explained that exams focused on answering leading questions such as, 'Why say that Xinjiang has always been part of the Chinese nation (*Zhonghua Minzu*)?' and 'Why say that by 60 BCE, Xinjiang was already an inalienable part of the motherland (*zuguo* 祖国)?' Intensive political education is universalised in Xinjiang but deemed out of date for Han-majority regions of China, reinforcing Xinjiang's uneasy integration and unequal position in *Zhonghua Minzu*. For example, during the 2012 Chinese leadership accession, the 'Chongqing model' of Bo Xilai was widely de-legitimised by state-media, academics, bloggers, and even the World Bank, for reinstituting political education and 'singing red songs'.[2] The use and content of intensive ethnic unity education in Xinjiang reinforces its otherness in China as an exceptional problem, which needs perpetual Han guidance. These texts ethnicise national-level political concepts, such as 'scientific development', explaining conversion of Uyghur identity as a natural and progressive process. They also introduce concepts rarely encountered across China because of their associations either with the Mao era or Han

---

[1] For example, see: XUAR Government (2009); EUAB (2009).
[2] For example, see: Freeman and Wen (2012); World Bank (2012); Xinhua (2012).

chauvinism, such as Han-led 'fusion' and 'ethnic extinction' (*minzu xiaowang* 民族消亡) of minority identities. This chapter offers a critical reading of the writing of ethnocentric national history in mass 'ethnic unity' education and the ideological training of cadres. It examines Xinjiang's integration into China by analysing how ethnic minorities, particularly Uyghurs, are ethnocentrically included in official *Zhonghua Minzu* narratives.

The literature on patriotic education in China focuses on the party-state's post-1989 efforts to bolster its legitimacy following the Tiananmen protests by presenting Japan and the West as external cultural threats.[3] However, it overlooks how patriotic education campaigns ran from the early 1950s until the 1980s in Xinjiang. Patriotic education was originally focused on domestic identity dynamics and designed by the party leadership to eradicate Han chauvinism and rein in former GMD members who became Xinjiang's regional leaders (CCPCC, 1953, p.106). In Xinjiang's many 'patriotic education' campaigns, the CCP sought to eliminate both Han chauvinism and 'local nationalism' as sources of disunity and political instability, described by Deng Xiaoping as the 'haunting' of China by 'bourgeois nationalist thought' (Deng et al., 1953, p.99; Deng, 1953, p.104; Liu, 1954, p.121). Following the disunity of the Cultural Revolution, Chinese scholars debated how to promote *more* 'patriotic education' and prevent China from sliding into domestic disunity and international weakness (Bai, 1981, p.46). However, these campaigns' proponents were blind to the ethnocentrism of their own national narratives, for example, in Liu Shaoqi's description of the Han's 'higher levels' of 'political, economic, and cultural development', which confers a 'special responsibility' (Liu, 1954, p.120). Mao Zedong explained that this 'special responsibility' required Han to 'enthusiastically help develop ethnic minorities' economy and culture' (Mao, 1956, p.143). In the 1950s, these narratives were tempered by explicit warnings against Han chauvinism. Today, the party-state does not address ethnic discrimination, and its domestic narratives of patriotism are solely directed at minority nationalism and Uyghur identity as threats to a timelessly unified *Zhonghua Minzu*.

Most 'nation-builders' see the creation of a 'long and proud national historical consciousness' as a means to 'construct nations and national identity' (Berger, 2007, p.1). Slogans such as 'Xinjiang has been an indivisible component of the motherland since ancient times,' and 'Xinjiang has been a multi-*minzu* region since ancient times' are visible in almost all urban spaces across Xinjiang. Contemporary official histories of Xinjiang begin with assertions that Xinjiang has always been an indivisible component of China and that ethnic Han have occupied and ruled the territory since antiquity

---

[3] For example, see: Callahan (2006); Gries (2004); Hughes (2006).

(Bovingdon, 2004a, p.355). A 'regime of authenticity' in China's *national* history secures the unity of an 'unchanging core' for the contested and contingent nation, a national subject, moving and progressing through linear time (Duara, 1995, p.4; 1998, pp.288–291). Although patriotic slogans narrate the timeless history of a unified *Zhonghua Minzu*, they exemplify tensions between Xinjiang as an imperial possession of Han-led civilisation and Xinjiang as an autonomous region of an equal and modern state. China's national narratives build historical consciousness on 5,000 years of 'fusion' to secure the superiority of the timeless Han core's superiority and its domination over minority peripheries. The unification and teleological unfolding of *Zhonghua Minzu* are the start and endpoint of this narrative. Alternative historical interpretations, including Turkic identities, are explicitly excluded as 'false' and dangerous. China is thus defined both through lineage as an ancient cultural nation (*zuguo* 祖国, or 'land of our ancestors') *and* as a rational, progressive socialist nation bringing development to Xinjiang. As Prasenjit Duara (1995) argued, scholars should 'rescue history from the nation' by exploring the contested and contingent meanings of historical identities that are concealed by ascribed categories from above. The China-centred perspective in official historical accounts of Xinjiang conceal and undermine alternative histories and regional centres of identity, specifically those self-selected by Uyghurs (Bovingdon, 2004b, p.355).

This chapter asks, How do political education texts in Xinjiang produce and constitute relations between nation and ethnicity? How do they narrate China's internal boundaries between majority Han and ethnic minorities? The texts analysed were the most widely read political education texts in Xinjiang, published by the party-state and written by officials and employees at the Ministry of Information, State Ethnic Affairs Commission, and Xinjiang Education Press.[4] The chapter is divided into three interlinked sections. The first explores how the party-state unifies the histories of all peoples within China's contemporary borders by projecting 5,000 years of history and identity formation through the contemporary *minzu* category. Mass education texts narrate China's political jurisdiction over Xinjiang since ancient times by ranking the central plains and Han identity as timelessly progressive against a backward and passive ethnic Xinjiang. The second section analyses how these texts relationally articulate Han identity in China's nation-building project against ethnic minorities (*shaoshu minzu* 少数民族). This explores how official *Zhonghua Minzu* narratives in Xinjiang produce a dichotomy of self/other, what Judith Butler called the performative 'negative elaboration' of self (Butler, 2007, p.132). The undesirable identities of minority others are

---

[4] See the methodology section of the book's introduction for full explanation of their selection and significance.

negatively elaborated as an absence of the progressive majority self and problems to be overcome to produce a timeless, unbroken civilisation. This section specifically examines the party-state's construction of a normative binary between pre- and post-'liberation' Xinjiang that contrasts the 'backward' dangers of Xinjiang's ephemeral, feudal identities against the Han's modernity and timelessness. The oppositional framings of Han/minority, modern/backward, active/passive, and security/danger are mutually constitutive and mutually reinforcing dichotomies where the Uyghur is marked as a problematic absence of the Han self. The final section analyses how the party-state includes Uyghurs in *Zhonghua Minzu* by narrating their teleological identity progression, moving from backward ethnicity towards progressive, modern Chinese nationhood. This narrative assumes that minority identities will die out (*minzu xiaowang*) and progressively become Chinese through 'fusion'. The analysis then turns to how 'bilingual education' policies (*shuangyu jiaoyu* 双语教育), in practice Mandarin-medium education, were presented in the media and political education as a means to achieve this 'fusion' and for China to become Chinese.

The chapter argues that mass education in Xinjiang is an identity-security practice that teaches the meaning of *Zhonghua Minzu* as a timeless ethno-hierarchy, structured by relations between modernising, active Han nation-builders and backward, passive minorities. Timeless Han culture is positioned as China's progressive force, while minority identities are marginalised as historically ephemeral transitions to be contained before they are absorbed and disappear. Mass education represents Han-centred China as a unified, modern, multi-ethnic nation in contrast to dangerous and backward ethnic identification of Uyghurs, manipulated by Western 'one-nation, one-state thinking'.[5] Uyghurs are only included in this story as peripheral, threatening remnants of imperialism and feudalism. The referent of security is the timeless *Zhonghua Minzu* narrative. However, these texts securitise an ambivalent *Zhonghua Minzu* as a modern multi-*minzu* national identity *and* a continuation of timeless, hierarchical civilisation.

Producing China's Timelessness

This section analyses the production of the contemporary *minzu* category in mass education and its projection onto 5,000 years of unbroken Chinese history. Historiography in the PRC has incorporated Xinjiang into the Chinese

---

[5] Most of the analysis here draws from the contrast between official representations of the categories of Han majority and ethnic minorities in Xinjiang. Kazakh and Mongolian interviewees expressed disgust at these essentialisations but also explained these study courses were primarily directed at Uyghurs.

state by severing its linguistic, cultural, and religious links to Central Asia (Millward & Perdue, 2004, p.36). The party-state's *Zhonghua Minzu* national narrative unifies the histories of China's many peoples as timelessly Chinese and timelessly *minzu*, invisibilising and reconfiguring discourses of civilisation and barbarism that framed what it meant to be Chinese for centuries. As Jian Bozan (1960) warned, this 'fashionable' shift towards timeless 'fusion' conceals China's long history of class conflict and *minzu* oppression by reframing barbarians from culturally alien to backward *minzu* lagging behind the superior Han. The grammar of socialist transformation merges with ethnocentrism in Fei Xiaotong's (1988) idea that the Han's status as China's 'guiding *minzu*' is a natural outcome of superior agricultural development, which builds on Fan Wenlan's (1954) chauvinist narrative that the Han's ancient formation naturally led to contemporary demographic and economic superiority. The normative binary between Chinese civilisation and barbarian minorities persists and merges with nationalism and socialism, ordering Chinese identity and security by placing Han at the apex of cultural and economic development.

China's contemporary identity is presented as timeless and inevitable but growing in strength throughout history. The 'overall direction' of history has always moved towards 'national unification' and 'all *minzu* took the establishment of central Chinese authority as national orthodoxy ... today, *Zhonghua Minzu* has already become the common name and ascription for the universal self-identification of every *minzu*' (State Council, 2009a, pp.5 & 7). Since 1949, Xinjiang has reached the highest stage of ethnic unity, national prosperity, and common identification with *Zhonghua Minzu* under the CCP's guidance (State Council, 2009a, p.7).[6] This writing of China's *national* history secures a fixed national subject moving in a linear progression (Duara, 1995, p.4; 1998, pp.288–291). However, by demarcating timeless boundaries between modern Han and backward ethnic minorities, ambivalent Chinese nation-building produces national subjects within its tensions between ethnic inclusion and exclusion. The State Council's white paper *Development and Progress*, like all official statements on Xinjiang history,[7] opens by establishing ancient Chinese jurisdiction over Xinjiang to legitimate contemporary political and cultural policies:

Since the First Century BCE, the region of Xinjiang has been an important formative component of the Chinese nation. Furthermore, it has played an important role in the building and development of a unified, multi-ethnic nation. (State Council, 2009b, p.3)

The production of a 'long and proud national historical consciousness', which encloses Xinjiang history in a timelessly progressive China, is a central

---

[6] Also see: State Council (2003) p.54; MOI, ED (2009) p.5; MOI TD (2009b) p.150–151.
[7] For example, see: *Xinjiang Cultural Knowledge*, *Common Knowledge*, and *The Fifty Whys*.

narrative of nation-building. All peoples who have ever lived on the soil of what is today known as Xinjiang, 'from ancient times until today', are retrospectively categorised as 'self-identifying' (*rentong* 认同) members of *Zhonghua Minzu* (XEP, 2009, pp.49–51):

> From ancient times until today, many ethnic groups have lived on the territory of Xinjiang. Every ethnic group who has ever laboured, existed, and multiplied in Xinjiang has been a member of the Chinese nation (*Zhonghua Minzu*), including those *minzu* who once existed but are now extinct. (XEP, 2009, p.49)

The contemporary boundaries of Chinese-ness are naturalised by stretching *Zhonghua Minzu* back in time prior to the concept's existence, conflating imperial and modern domains to establish territorial and cultural jurisdiction over Xinjiang. Xinjiang's entrance in official *Zhonghua Minzu* narratives always begins with the arrival of Chinese military forces in Xinjiang, who progress the teleology of China's unification. Xinjiang's active centre in official historical narratives is China's central plains. Xinjiang is peripheralised as a place to be conquered and pacified (Bovingdon, 2004b, p.355). All official chronologies begin with the Han dynasty's (221–206 BCE) 'jurisdiction' over the 'frontier' (*bianjiang*), established with a military protectorate (State Council, 2009a, p.4).[8] These narratives remind readers of the pre-modern boundaries between Han civilisation on the central plains and barbarians of the frontier through each dynastic period of history, paradoxically reinforcing Xinjiang's timeless other-ness while containing it within the PRC's contemporary borders.

Official historical narratives characteristically leap more than eight centuries from the Han dynasty to the Tang (618–907 CE) when Chinese 'jurisdiction' included Xinjiang (State Council, 2009a, p.5).[9] Dynasties representing discontinuity in Chinese control are written out of these narratives to identify Xinjiang as timelessly Chinese. The eight-century period between the Han and the Tang is known for the absence of Chinese presence and rise of Uyghur city-states such as Qocho/Gaochang and Yarkhoto/Jiaohe, which continued to exist during the Tang era (Millward, 2007). Readers are instead frequently reminded that the 'overall direction' of Chinese history has *always* moved towards 'fusion'. The scant mentions of periods of disunity between the Tang and the Yuan dynasties (1206–1368 CE), such as the Liao (907–1125 CE), Song (960–1279 CE), and Jin (1115–1234 CE), explain that war on the central plains simply meant that the Chinese state was too busy to 'look after' Xinjiang and failed to 'persist' in its 'mission' (MOI TD, 2009b, pp.149–150). Readers are then immediately reminded that close but

---

[8] Also see: State Council (2003) p.52; MOI, ED (2009) pp.1–2; MOI TD (2009b) p.149.
[9] Also see: MOI, ED (2009) p.2; MOI TD (2009b) p.149.

unspecified political links mean the 'overall direction' of *Zhonghua Minzu* cannot be shaken by exceptions counter to this teleological flow (MOI TD, 2009b, pp.150–151). The narrative then leaps again to when China's territory was at its most expansive, the Mongolian Yuan dynasty (1206–1368 CE) and then to the Manchu Qing dynasty (1644–1911 CE). Nevertheless, these texts are silent about the diverse peoples within China's genuinely multicultural history, including how the Mongols and the Manchu helped establish China's contemporary borders. Instead, these sections tell readers the Yuan and Qing helped 'guarantee' China's borders and the centralised rule that was already established by the Han dynasty's military protectorate in Xinjiang (State Council, 2009a, p.5)[10]. Xinjiang is officially written into *Zhonghua Minzu* by selecting specific periods of history when Chinese military forces are present and neglecting those when absent. Xinjiang, therefore, has no history of its own and is only present when Chinese imperial conquests drag the region towards the teleological end of *Zhonghua Minzu*.

Official *Zhonghua Minzu* narratives conceal China's complex histories and historically contingent representations of non-Han. The concept of ethnic minorities (*shaoshu minzu*) only appeared in Chinese for the first time in the 1924 United Front Manifesto, which reconfigured ethnic difference from distance from the Chinese centre to a series of nominally equal, bounded ethnic units (Leibold, 2007, pp.9–11). The GMD General Zhang Zhizhong, who negotiated the dismantling of the East Turkestan Republic (1944–1949), followed the Republican-era warlord Sheng Shicai's ethnotaxonomy of Xinjiang into 14 'indigenous' ethnic groups. Although the CCP avoids the term 'indigeneity', these 14 *minzu* are still officially recognised today as 'long-term residents' of Xinjiang (SEAC, 2009, p.17; XEP, 2009, p.50). The nationalist emphasis on lineage and indigeneity shaped how ethnicity was first conceived in Xinjiang, despite running counter to Stalin's four principles of nationhood in the emerging *minzu* project (Jacobs, 2008, p.551; Millward, 2007, p.208). The 1950s ethnic classification project (*minzu shibie*) is described as a scientific Marxist project in Chinese scholarship. However, its 'scientific research work' used historical records on genealogical lineage and migration to determine people's *minzu* identity (Fei, 1980, pp.170–174). The party-state further departed from Stalin and Engels' ideas that nation and ethnicity only emerge during a capitalist stage of development because the Han are an innately 'socialist *minzu*' formed more than 2,000 years ago (Fan, 1954, p.12). The differentiation between Han and ethnic minorities, therefore, was always built on the older distinction between civilisation and barbarians (*hua/yi* 华夷) that socialist narratives claimed to eradicate.

---

[10] Also see: MOI, ED (2009) pp.2–3; MOI TD (2009b) pp.149–150.

The party-state and anthropologists consciously produced the *minzu* concept during the communist period (1949–1978) as a modernising nation-building project. However, *minzu* merged with traditional ideas about civilisation and barbarism to reinforce and weave cultural difference between majority and minorities into a timeless *Zhonghua Minzu* narrative. *Minzu* theory was considered the 'theoretical frontline' in 'resolving the *minzu* problem' (*minzu wenti* 民族问题) (Ya, 1965, p.224). In the 1960s, Ya Hanzheng, today considered a moderate *minzu* theorist, wrote that 'the essence of the *minzu* problem as a class problem does not only apply to a capitalist stage of development but also fits all historical periods prior to capitalism' (Ya, 1965, p.255). *Minzu* has been applied to every period of history but there are 'backward *minzu*' and 'civilised *minzu*' (Ya, 1962, p.116). The ethnic minorities concept, a modern and self-conscious political construction of the Chinese state, reinforced older Sinocentric world-views by normatively identifying minorities as inferior and dependent on Chinese civilisation. The party-state then had to devote considerable resources to re-writing Marx to fit Chinese history as much as re-writing Chinese history to fit Marx. In the spring of 1962, the CCP held a conference in Beijing to 'unify' translations of Marx, Engels, Lenin, and Stalin into Chinese. The conference decided to abandon all use of 'tribe' (*buluo* 部落) and 'clan' (*shizu* 氏族), thus translating all social groupings in Marxist analysis from the beginning of time and forever as *minzu* (Ya, 1962, pp.125–126). Control over the Marxist conceptual framework, so central to all political vocabulary in contemporary China, erased self-identified differences between tribes and clans throughout history. The history of China's many peoples became conceived as ephemeral, peripheral blips in the telos of *Zhonghua minzu*, led by Han nation-builders on the contemporary territory of the PRC. This official reorganisation of knowledge laid foundations for the contemporary resurgence of cultural nationalism in Marxist clothing that articulates *Zhonghua Minzu* as an ethno-hierarchy and differentiates identities according to their majority/minority or *hua/yi* status.

The ethnic minorities concept, a modern and self-conscious political construction of the Chinese state, reinforced traditional Sinocentrism. The concept's construction uses circular reasoning to ascribe minority identities as inferior and dependent *because* they are modern constructs institutionalised by the Chinese state. Uyghur lineage is framed as the binary opposite of Chinese civilisation, as broken and without connection to the past, since 'extinction' of the Turks (*Tujue* 突厥) and the Huihu/Uighurs (*Huihu* 回鹘) (SEAC, 2009, pp.8–9). *Huihu* is a transliteration of Uighur, the ethnonym for the group who migrated from the Orkhon valley in present-day Mongolia to the Turpan region in the ninth century. Despite the ancient origins of the term 'Uyghur', the party-state describes identification with Turks or Turkic-ness as 'distortions of truth' and 'distortions of history', because, since 60 BCE (Han dynasty), 'every *minzu* identified with the command of the central government' (XEP, 2009, pp.47 & 49-50). This narrative conflates the eighth century Gok-Turk kingdom and the broader Turk category, employed in many twentieth century nationalist movements in Turkey and Central Asia. However, *The 50 Whys* tells readers that Uyghurs are 'not a Turkic *minzu*' because 'after the Turk Khanate collapsed in the 8th century, they did not form a modern *minzu*' (XEP, 2009, p.57). The consensus in Chinese scholarship is that Turkic identity is a 'myth fabricated by Pan-Turkism' (Pan, 2008a, p.12). Modern nation-building stretched back in time to convert and Sinicise dead barbarians (*yi*) who identified as Turks. *Huihu* is always translated as *Uygur* or *Uighur* and never *Uyghur* in Chinese academic literature, conceptually separating ancient from modern ethnic categories when defining Uyghur identity. Conversely, the connotations of authenticity and continuity by using the same character for the Han dynasty and contemporary Han category are never problematised. The *minzu* problem is thus resolved in Xinjiang by writing the Turk out of history as an extinct *Chinese* group and articulating the Uyghur as a modern, artificial Chinese construction.

The party-state's approach to the '*minzu* problem' during the 'opening and reform' era has been that development resolves 'national contradictions' and all *minzu* will be unified into *Zhonghua Minzu* (NPC, 2001; Hu, 2007, pp.13–14; Bekri, 2008). Deng Xiaoping described economic discrimination as symptomatic of China's 'haunting' by 'bourgeois nationalist thought'. However, Deng and the party-state remained wedded to an ethnocentric historical materialism. 'The economy is the foundation of the resolution to the *minzu* problem' but *Zhonghua Minzu* is its teleological outcome (Deng, 1953, p.104). Hu Jintao's 'scientific Development outlook' is explained as a continuation of 'scientific Marxism' that secures the unification of *Zhonghua Minzu* identity (NPC, 2001; Bekri, 2008). When applied to Xinjiang, 'scientific development' (*kexue fazhan* 科学发展) denotes an evolutionary cultural framework that conceives its peoples' identities as superstructural to economic development, the basis of the party's 'ethnic minority work' (*minzu gongzuo* 民族工作) (Hu, 2007, pp.13–14; MOI, 2008, p.26). Contemporary representations of minorities in development policies as 'ethnic' and 'backward', contrasted against advanced, mobile Han, reproduce this hierarchical socio-spatial order where they must learn from the Han (Barabantseva, 2009, p.250). The normative ranking of cultures during the communist-era considered the existence of minority identities as transient leftover effects of class exploitation from earlier stages of development (Shijian Bianji Bu, 1965, p.213). *Minzu* identities are still associated with separatism and explained away as 'remnants of class exploitation' today, as 'historical leftovers of old thinking' that 'threaten national security' and 'want to destroy socialism' (XUAR Dept. of Information, 2009, p.84). Although universal stages of human development are central themes in Chinese Marxisms, but anthropologists in the 1950s and 1960s never applied this analysis to the Han category. The cultural nationalism, described by Deng as a haunting from China's past and European imperialism, is now celebrated in narratives of 5,000 years of unbroken civilisation moving towards a culturally Chinese modernity. The '*minzu* problem' discourse reveals how contradictory narratives of nation and civilisation co-exist and intermingle in mass education and the writing of China's national history. The '*minzu* problem' frames and targets Uyghur ethnic identity as a backward threat to be eliminated by Han-led economic development. The problem is resolved in the short term by teaching 'factual' national identity to minorities who will be attracted to the timelessness and superiority of ancient Chinese civilisation and the modern state.

Producing Han, Producing Minorities

This section analyses how mass education in Xinjiang relationally produces Han identity as the active, timeless centripetal force of *Zhonghua Minzu*, contrasted against passive, ephemeral ethnic minorities (*shaoshu minzu*). Nation-building texts produce the Han category through a normative binary between pre- and post-'liberation' Xinjiang, written into the timeless order of *Zhonghua Minzu* and superimposed on the boundary between Han majority and ethnic minorities. Dru Gladney (2004) and Louisa Schein (2000) showed how the peripheralisation of ethnic minorities relationally produces Han-ness as China's modern core. The party-state's binary division between Han majority and ethnic minorities defines non-Han groups 'negatively' according to a lack of Han Chinese attributes in binarising, hierarchical identity narratives (Callahan, 2010, p.132). In Xinjiang, this majority–minority relationship is securitised, which demands Uyghurs identify their cultural existence as a transient historical moment, passing with their absorption in *Zhonghua Minzu*. The oppositional framing of Han/ethnic minorities, modern/backward, active/passive, and security/danger are mutually constitutive dichotomies where the Uyghur other is marked as a dangerous absence of the Han self. The party-state's ongoing project to articulate China's internal constitutive boundaries, represents what Judith Butler (2007) called the performative 'negative elaboration' of the self. The undesirable identities of minority others are negatively elaborated as absences of the progressive majority self and as problems to be eliminated. Xinjiang's history is marked as backward, ethnic, and dangerous due to 'pre-liberation' absence of the Han self. Han-ness is relationally defined against the non-Han ethnic minority category as China's timeless, advanced essence, liberating minorities from their feudal tribal politics.

Most contemporary policy statements on Xinjiang's histories and identities quote Fei Xiaotong's ethnocentric conceptualisation of China as a 'unified and pluralistic' (*duoyuan yiti* 多元一体) nation, whose formation has been driven by the superior force of the Han 'nucleus' since ancient times (Fei, 1988, pp.214–215). The official narrative in *Xinjiang Cultural Knowledge*, a text on the region's history studied by political cadres, describes the Han nucleus as an ancient and unbroken lineage, before contrasting it against China's modern political construction of ethnic minorities. It describes Han culture (*Han wenhua* 汉文化), the ancient basis of modern Han identity, as rising during the Han dynasty and flourishing during the Tang, before being fused with a modern ethnic identity (*Hanzu* 汉族) (SEAC, 2009, pp.13–19). The formation of a 'unified and pluralistic' China was driven by Han, engaging in advanced agriculture on the central plains of the lower reaches of the Yellow and Yangtze Rivers (Fei, 1988, p.168). The Han have driven 5,000 years of 'nation-building' and the history of the Chinese soil is one of inevitable development, unification, and 'assimilation' into *Zhonghua Minzu*, while ethnic minorities provide 'new blood' 'for the Hans' (Fei, 1988, p.188). 'Plurality' refers to the plurality of groups, now referred to as *minzu*, who have been absorbed into and modernised by the Han through conversion and attraction rather than Western conquest (Fei, 1988, p.215). To be Chinese, therefore, ethnic minorities must identify with their benevolent assimilation into *Zhonghua Minzu*, structured through timeless boundaries between active Han and ethnic minority passivity.

These texts narrate Xinjiang's history from the perspective of Chinese civilisation absorbing barbarians on its frontiers. *Ethnic Minority Policy* adopts an implicitly Han-centric voice when referring to 'surrounding ethnic minorities', placing the central plains and the Han at its story's centre and *other* ethnic groups on the margins. *Ethnic Minority Policy* tells readers that prior to liberation, ethnic minorities engaged in herding, hunting, and fishing in grasslands, deserts, forests, and various other nameless natural habitats (State Council, 2009a, p.6). These regions are described as 'backward', then contrasted against the advanced agricultural economy of Han-populated regions (State Council, 2009a, p.6; 2009b, p.4; MOI TD, 2009b, pp.151–152). The text continues, telling readers that the 'central plains region' and nameless 'surrounding ethnic minorities' constitute a 'mutually complementary economy' (*jingji hubu* 经济互补) through 'common development' (*gongtong fazhan* 共同发展) forming the unified, multi-*minzu* Chinese nation since ancient times (State Council, 2009a, p.6). Ethnic minorities are excluded from the ancient and advanced cultural core of China but included as a 'complementary' component of an asymmetrical, economic whole. *Ethnic Minority Policy* explains that ethnic minorities provided the central plains with material goods in return for their very existence:

The surrounding ethnic minorities and the central plains region engaged in a 'mutual tea-horse market' ... as well as satisfying central plains agriculture, transport, and military needs for horses, it also supplied ethnic minorities with everything they need for daily living (*richang shenghuo suoxu*), advancing a complementary economy and common development. (State Council, 2006, p.6)

The Fifty Whys refers to this complementarity as holistic relations of dependence between advanced national core and backward ethnic periphery that produce a unified, multi-ethnic nation. The provision of horses by ethnic minorities to the central plains functions to develop their *own* living areas (XEP, 2009, p.66). This provision complements the Han offerings of silk, tea, and all daily necessities, that 'promote the development of ethnic minorities and ethnic minority regions' (XEP, 2009, p.66). Ethnic minorities provide Han with supplementary goods for *further* development, and in return, their very existence ('everything they needed for daily living') is provided by the Han. This dependency narrative relationally articulates Han as superior against the ambivalent inclusion of minorities as eternally backward but progressing since Xinjiang's 'peaceful liberation' (*heping jiefang* 和平解放) by the People's Liberation Army (PLA) in 1949 (State Council, 2009b, p.4).

The 'new China' continues to bind centre and frontier together in a 'mutually complementary economy' (*jingji hubu*). *Development and Progress* describes the 'post-liberation' period as one of rapid development and 'Xinjiang building' under the party-state's leadership (State Council, 2009b, p.4). 'Pre-liberation' Xinjiang is described as a 'natural economy' and a 'backward', 'stagnant', and entirely 'illiterate' region 'without technology' (State Council, 2009b, pp.4–7, 19–21). The party-state emerges in the Xinjiang-building narrative as a continuation of centralised rule and the benevolent provider of more than 50 per cent of post-'liberation' subsidies, which has led Xinjiang to its most prosperous period in history (State Council, 2009b, p.10). The party-state's paternalistic economic provider role on the 'frontier' is framed as the continuation of how China has historically enabled the existence and survival of ethnic minorities. Paralleling European colonial narratives, this story seeks to convince the natives that 'if the settlers were to leave, they would at once fall back into barbarism, degradation, and bestiality' (Fanon, 2001, p.37). Xinjiang's inferior status to Han settler culture is written into *Zhonghua Minzu* identity through this hierarchical relationship of dependency. *Zhonghua Minzu* is written as an ethno-hierarchy where ethnic minorities are included through dependency on the Han for their material and cultural survival.

Describing these narratives or any period of Xinjiang history as colonialism is considered 'separatist history', even though the party-state celebrates the Han military settlement of the region. *Xinjiang Cultural Knowledge* categorises Xinjiang's cultures into material divisions of oasis animal husbandry, grassland nomadic, and 'frontier-building culture' (*tunken wenhua* 屯垦文化), or literally, 'station troops to open up the wasteland culture' (SEAC, 2009, p.8). These multiple and asymmetrical poles have fused to form

Xinjiang's distinct culture but has always been a part of Chinese culture (SEAC, 2009, pp.23 & 134). The culture and 'modern formation' of non-Han in Xinjiang are explained as superstructural to their material 'base' and subsequently categorised as 'oasis' animal husbandry or 'nomadic' herders (SEAC, 2009, pp.24–55, 56–79). This crude historical materialist account explicitly defines ethnic minority identities through the concept of mode of production (SEAC, 2009, pp.2, 4, & 8). However, the passive emergence of minority identities in response to their natural environment is contrasted against the Han as active 'frontier builders' developing the wasteland of Xinjiang (SEAC, 2009, pp.24–55). The 'active spirit' of the 2,000-year-old 'frontier-building culture' of the Han has united China and developed Xinjiang, with 'simple, uncomplicated assistance of minority *minzu* armies' (SEAC, 2009, pp.24–55, 80–97). These colonial narratives reveal how historical materialism did not eradicate ethnocentrism in China because it is only applied to minority identities and never to the Han.

The official *Zhonghua Minzu* narrative is an evolutionary cultural framework that defines and normatively evaluates minority cultures through their mode of production. The Eurocentric pioneers of this essentialist and materialist approach, Lewis Morgan and Friedrich Engels, are top of leading regional universities' anthropology reading lists.[11] Friedrich Engels and Lewis Morgan's *Ancient Society* (2005 [originally published 1944]) remain widely celebrated in Chinese anthropology as central to the party's historical materialism (Pan, 2008a). Morgan's (2005) theory of cultural evolution justified colonisation of the Americas in similar terms as the CCP's story of Chinese settlement of Xinjiang, by explaining culture as superstructural to material development in three linear stages of evolution: savagery, barbarism, and civilisation. Engels described ethnic minorities as 'national refuse', which remains a 'fanatical representative of counter-revolution' until 'completely exterminated or de-nationalised, as its whole existence ... is a protest against a great historical revolution' (quoted in Robinson, 2000, p.61). Engels (2010 [originally published 1884]) explained gendered power relations, such as monogamy and polygamy, as embedded in the social relations of the mode of production. This text is often cited in Chinese anthropology to explain the matriarchal structure of the Mosuo of Yunnan as a 'living fossil' from a pre-slavery, primitive communist mode of production (Walsh, 2005, p.456). The historical construction of the modern Han category is never problematised in Chinese nation-building and remains the timeless core of *Zhonghua Minzu*, guiding the material development and cultural evolution of ethnic minorities.

---

[11] Drawn from interviews with students and teachers at Xinjiang University and Xinjiang Normal University.

Historical materialist discourses of cultural evolution merged with the culturalist binary between civilisation and barbarians, reconfiguring Chinese civilisation as the modernising, active Han and barbarians as backward, passive ethnic minorities. In official historiography, Mao Zedong's 'long march' through barbarian territory towards the 1949 revolution propelled the CCP to identify 'Han chauvinism' as a cause of *minzu* alienation' (*minzu gehe* 民族隔阂). However, that period of national self-reflection concluded by overlaying materialist, class-based explanations onto older ethnocentric narratives. In the 1960s, majority chauvinism and 'local nationalism' (*difang minzu zhuyi* 地方民族主义) were considered to emerge through the class exploitation of minorities by the majority (Shijian Bianji Bu, 1965; Ya, 1965). Contemporary narratives, emphasising development over class, frame Han 'frontier-building culture' in Xinjiang as the active, advanced culture, which 'raises the cultural and technological levels of Xinjiang' (SEAC, 2009, pp.13, 18–19, & 80–82). As pioneers and frontier builders, Han culture is positioned beyond cultural evolution, representing the communist spirit of man's domination over nature and *minzu* thought, driving economic development and the telos of Chinese history. The pioneering 'frontier-building culture' is the core of *Zhonghua Minzu* and an unbroken lineage beginning with Han dynasty military settlements and continuing with their contemporary presence as forces for 'modernisation' and 'development' (SEAC, 2009, pp.80–82):

Through the written record and cultural artefacts found in Xinjiang, as well as frontier relics of the Han and Tang, it is impossible not to see that Han culture has co-existed with all ethnic groups in a state of fusion and complementarity from beginning to end. In every aspect it has promoted the development of the culture of the Western Regions. (SEAC, 2009, p.81)

The 'frontier culture' of the Han actively advances the progression of Xinjiang's history through its introduction of advanced technology, the earliest form of writing in the Tarim basin, and patriotic poetry (SEAC, 2009, pp.81–83). The Han build *Zhonghua Minzu* for all *minzu*, relationally producing non-Han as an absence of Han culture, subject to nature and the progression of history. Ethnic minorities are included in *Zhonghua Minzu* by the arrival of the Han's advanced culture in their 'frontier' regions. The party-state's continuing usage of 'frontier' in these texts echo Frederick Jackson Turner's (1986) classic definition of the American frontier from 1893 as the 'meeting point between savagery and civilization'. The frontier is outside the self but on its margins where wilderness and savagery can be transformed into a liveable and civilised place (Smith, 1996, p.xv). However, in China's ambivalent relationship with its frontiers, they are narrated as having *always* been undergoing benevolent transformation.

The party-state's development policy narratives in Xinjiang begin with 'peaceful liberation' by the PLA in 1949 (State Council, 2009b, p.4). The

Fifty Whys explains that the PLA peacefully 'liberated' Xinjiang from its 'backward' history of being 'without tall buildings' (XEP, 2009, pp.40 & 79). *Ethnic Minority Policy* describes the new China's ongoing 'mission' to build from an 'extremely backward' base of traditional agriculture and 'low productive power' (State Council, 2009a, pp.24–25). In this narrative, all ethnic minorities in Xinjiang welcomed their 'liberation' from their 'backward condition' by the PLA (MOI TD, 2009b, pp.150–151). Due to China's 'persistence' of the nation, the 'struggle' for ethnic unity, and the party-state's 'preferential policies' (*youhui zhengce* 优惠政策), including 'bilingual education' analysed in the next section, minorities are entering their most prosperous period in history (State Council, 2009a, p.25). The colonial undertones of 'persistence' circulate widely in Xinjiang[12] and were popularly captured in the Hunan Dianshitai [Television] (2009) hit series *8,000 Flowers Go Up Tianshan Mountain*' (*baqian xiangnü shang tianshan* 八千湘女上天山). The popular series told the story of the transfer of 8,000 young girls from Hunan to Xinjiang after 'liberation' to provide wives for newly settled and demobilised Chinese soldiers. The show interspersed television drama and interviews with the real 'Hunan Flowers'. In the opening episode, the leading Communist General gives a rousing speech explaining that the Chinese military must once again 'liberate' Xinjiang because the corrupt Manchu-led Qing dynasty did not 'persist' and failed in their historical duty to advance the progression of *Zhonghua Minzu*. In these narratives, Xinjiang is an inalienable, timelessly dependent, and distant frontier of *Zhonghua Minzu*. The party-state represents the most advanced stage of historical development but also the bearer of an unbroken civilisational lineage.

The binary between civilised Han as sources of modernisation and national security converting the potentially threatening backwardness of non-Han drives contemporary ethnic policy making in Xinjiang. Ma Dazheng, the influential head of the Xinjiang-based Frontier Research Institute, explained, in a document for internal circulation only, the need for Xinjiang's demographic transformation because 'Hans are the main source of stability for Xinjiang' (Bovingdon, 2010, p.58). The Western Development Project (*Xibu Da Kaifa* 西部大开发) was conceived in terms of modernisation and political stability, to be achieved by attracting 'high-quality talents' (*gao suzhi rencai* 高素质人才) from 'inner China' that ethnic minorities can learn modernisation from, and 'develop' their material and spiritual 'civilisation' (Yang, 2005, pp.1–3). Li Dezhu of the State Ethnic Affairs Commission bluntly stated that ethnic minorities need to learn from the advanced culture of the Han, privileging Han Chinese identity as a 'civilising imperative' and

---

[12] The popular circulation of these narratives will be analysed through interviews in Chapters 6 and 7.

the ideological foundation of Chinese modernisation (Goodman, 2002, p.137; Goodman, 2004, pp.326–329). The party-state sends 'experts' from 'inner China' to the frontier to facilitate Xinjiang's 'study' of advanced technology and 'mindset' (*guannian*) (State Council, 2009b, p.11). Identity transformation, framed as modernisation, is considered a security matter because backward, historically leftover ethnic identities threaten Han superiority and cultural neutrality. Yang Faren (2005) of the Xinjiang Regional Party Political Research Office wrote that separatism only appears in less-developed, rural, ethnic minority regions. In 2008 Nur Bekri, then chair of the Xinjiang regional government, announced that those who challenge the party's modernisation policies are 'backward', 'crazed' terrorists because separatism only appears in less-developed, rural, ethnic minority regions (Bekri, 2008). The official narrative that modernising Han must secure a shared *Zhonghua Minzu* identity against the threat of backward, leftover remnants of Uyghur ethnicity is the referent of official identity-security.

In the party-state's nation-building narratives, people are either on the side of historical progress and modernisation or left behind. Only separatists, terrorists, and extremists, running 'against the flow of history' and 'modernisation', could oppose the 'sacred mission' of national unification and they will 'inevitably lose' (EUAB, 2009, p.60). Resistance to the party-state's nation-building narratives is framed as evil but also futile because it runs against the grand telos of Han-led Chinese history. 'Modernisation' is an ethno-centric security discourse that excludes ethnic minority identities as backward threats to China's identity-security. China's history is chronologically narrated as an unbroken lineage beginning with ancient economic relations of the horse and tea trades, running to the contemporary party-state's development policies. Modernisation is thus paradoxically understood as the contemporary continuation of 5,000 years of unbroken Han-centred nation-building and cultural evolution. Nation-building produces an ethnocentrically structured 'long and proud national historical consciousness' that relationally defines Han majority and ethnic minorities' identities. Chinese nation-building writes a historical materialist vision of rational progress through an ethnocentric cultural nationalist lens.

Minzu Xiaowang: The 'Extinction' of the Uyghur

This final section moves from the official production of majority-minority boundaries to the party-state's narrative on their natural and inevitable dissolution. The section analyses how the party-state narrates its teleology of identity in Xinjiang, progressing from backward ethnicity to modern nationhood, when minority identities will die out (*minzu xiaowang*) and become Chinese through 'fusion'. The analysis focuses on how 'bilingual education' policies

(Mandarin-medium education)[13] are presented in public media and political education as a national security matter and the means to achieve identity 'fusion'. Although *minzu* is represented as a timeless category, the party-state expected ethnic minority identities to wither away into *Zhonghua Minzu* with economic development. *The Fifty Whys* polices identity by reminding readers that wanting one's ethnic kin to economically succeed is 'reasonable' but that national identity *must* predominate in any individual's self-identification (XEP, 2009, pp.35–37). Despite these warnings, ethnic extinction (*minzu xiaowang*) is presented as a natural, culturally neutral process of development, and distinguished against Western ethnic nationalism. Nevertheless, the ethnic extinction concept was used in purely negative terms in the 1950s and 1960s to describe goals of assimilation and the violent organisation of ethnic relations under the GMD and in capitalist states. *Xiaowang* was explicitly distinguished from natural processes of ethnic assimilation (*tonghua* 同化) through migration and development (Jian, 1960, pp.20–21). With China's rise, the relationship between ethnic identity and national security has been revisited in scholarly and policy-making circles.[14] A self-described '2nd generation' of *minzu* policy scholars[15] rekindled older debates in a new age, urging policy makers to resolve tensions between plurality and unity through deliberate policy planning to promote 'fusion' into a singular national culture, for example, through Mandarin-medium education. Today, many self-styled Chinese Communists have reversed concerns about Han chauvinism and share the GMD's cultural nationalist goals of building a unified *Zhonghua Minzu* based on the superior Han as its 'guiding force'. The possibility that Han chauvinism or racism could exist in contemporary China is obfuscated in public discourse because ethnic extinction has been re-framed as a natural, neutral process of cultural evolution. So, what is China's official teleology moving towards and what does this mean for the relations between nation, majority, and minority?

Official ethnic unity education texts narrate Xinjiang's history as 'multi-ethnic' (*duo minzu* 多民族) or 'multicultural' (*duoyuan wenhua* 多元文化) in contrast to Western nation-states. This performative enactment of external boundaries against the West is projected inwards: China is *not* the West and is thus unified *not* divided by nationalism. To be Chinese, therefore, is to be non-Western and to be Chinese is to be a *minzu*. In the official narrative, only the 'separatist thought' of 'The Three Evils' 'ignores' the multi-cultural and multi-*minzu* history of Xinjiang by claiming that Xinjiang is a Uyghur region (XEP, 2009, p.50). Alternative historical narratives from non-Han perspectives

---

[13] On 'bilingual education', see: Schluessel (2007; 2009).
[14] See: Leibold (2012a; 2013); Tobin (2014); Zhongguo Minzu Zongjiao Wang (2012).
[15] For example, see: Hu and Hu (2012); Zhu (2012); Ma Rong (2010).

are thus framed as Westernised, separatist security threats to the territorial integrity and essence of Chinese civilisation. The unbroken, teleological 'path' of Xinjiang's 'historical evolution' runs from the pre-stone age to the present day. This path flows towards cultural 'fusion' and 'multiculturalism' of China's modern 'harmony' under the party-state's leadership: 'Since ancient times, Xinjiang's culture has always been based on fusion ... this is the historical development of evolutionary processes and unceasing raising of Xinjiang culture' (SEAC, 2009, pp.16–17). The multi-*minzu* history narrative strengthens the majority–minority dependency relationship because the active Han 'persistence' on the passive frontier is what makes the region multi-*minzu*. It is 'successive migrations' of Han into the cultural emptiness of Xinjiang that make it a timelessly 'multicultural place' through 'fusion' (State Council, 2009b, p.31). Xinjiang's other *minzu* are not present in these explanations of multiculturalism. These texts instead remind readers that 'the history of the Han in Xinjiang is very early – from before the time of Zhang Qian[16] there have always been Han living in Xinjiang' (XEP, 2009, p.50). This narrative of 'multiculturalism since ancient times' co-exists uneasily with the party-state's contemporary policies towards demographic and linguistic transformation of Xinjiang, described as 'fusion'.

In practice, official 'multiculturalism' in Xinjiang refers to demographic and cultural transformation where Han become the majority and ethnic minorities are gradually assimilated: the 'active spirit' of the Han's 'frontier-building culture' has been the driving force of multiculturalism and 'fusion' 'since ancient times' with the 'simple, uncomplicated' assistance of ethnic minorities (SEAC, 2009, p.87). The unbroken Han lineage, driving 'fusion' in Xinjiang, runs from the Han dynasty and Tang dynasty armies, to Qing-era land reclamation, to the entrance of the *Bingtuan*, and finally to reform-era mass Han migration (SEAC, 2009, p.13). Ethnic minority (*shaoshu minzu*) and ethnic group (*minzu*) are interchangeable in these texts and ethnic-ness becomes equated with an absence of the presence of Han-ness.[17] Han-ness is objectivised as the civilised national standard and ceases to be 'ethnic' and *The Fifty Whys* explicitly describes the Han as a 'transcendent *minzu*' (*chaoyue minzu* 超越民族) (XEP, 2009, pp.91–93). Official Han-ness is the trans-ethnic, objectivised nucleus of a nation that can, therefore, be simultaneously Han-centred and multicultural.

Chinese nation-building seeks political stability as a means towards cultural transformation. Nation-building seeks to ensure not only that ethnic minorities

---

[16] Zhang Qian, the second century BCE Chinese envoy, visited Xinjiang and helped establish Silk Road trade.
[17] The text *Ethnic Minority Policy*, if literally translated, would be *Ethnic Policy* (*minzu zhengce*) but outlines policy in regions populated by ethnic minorities.

identify as Chinese but also that they identify with their need to be transformed. The concept of 'ethnic extinction' emerges in these texts' discussions of 'fusion'. Ethnic unity education materials in Xinjiang explicitly state its goals as 'ethnic extinction' and the 'fusion' of 56 ethnic groups into the common identity of *Zhonghua Minzu*:

> Ethnic extinction is an inevitable result of ethnic self-development and self-improvement .... It is the final result of ethnic development at its highest stage ... in this big ethnic family every ethnic group has a *higher* level of identification – *Zhonghua Minzu*. (EUAB, 2009, pp.17 & 79)

Ethnic extinction is thus an inevitable and natural step in teleological progress where economic development and attraction to China propels ethnic minorities up the ladder of cultural evolution and they lose their group consciousness as 'national refuse'. The stated endpoint of this teleology is a global classless society where all nations disappear, as Karl Marx and Mao Zedong envisaged. However, 'ethnic extinction' first requires 'market socialism' and economic development (EUAB, 2009, p.17). National prosperity and withering away of ethnicity require planned and ideologically driven 'ethnic minority work' to teach Xinjiang's peoples to transcend ethnic consciousness and understand themselves as members of *Zhonghua Minzu*. Ethnic minority work, including ethnic unity education and Mandarin-medium education, to promote the 'common unity and development of every ethnic group' is officially described as essential to China's survival against 'The Three Evils' (XUAR Dept. of Information, 2009, pp.1 & 86–87). The contemporary party-state slogan 'Only if *minzu* exists can there be a *minzu* problem' is drawn from the Cultural Revolution period and indicates how the long-term teleological end of ethnic policy was always the eradication of ethnicity (EUAB, 2009, p.37; Shijian Bianji Bu, 1965, p.220). The Cultural Revolution's open hostility to all identities deemed ethnic and their relationship with traditional Chinese culture has never been openly debated in Xinjiang, which has enabled its goal of radically transforming ethnic identities to persist. Discourses of civilisation and nation overlap uneasily in the contemporary party-state's hybrid ideology of Chinese culturalism, Marxist historical materialism, and cultural evolution that frames history as a progressive flow towards *Zhonghua Minzu* and withering away of minority identities.

The party-state persistently narrates Turkic-ness as a 'mistaken' identity that existentially threatens China. Only the 'mistaken understandings' of 'The Three Evils' could understand Uyghur history as outside *Zhonghua Minzu* or define Uyghur identity through Turkic language (XEP, 2009, pp.47, 61, & 94):

> Turkic *minzu* is only a historical category; today there is no reality to this *minzu* ... lots of different countries use English, can you say these are one *minzu*? By this logic, if you take 'Turkic language' as to call Uyghurs, Kazakhs, Kyrgyz, etc one *minzu*, this is obviously mistaken. (XEP, 2009, p.58)

Officially ascribed Uyghur identity silences a key self-identified feature (language) of how Uyghurs conceptualise Uyghur-ness, identifying them as peripheral members of *Zhonghua Minzu*. These narratives highlight the constitutional right to 'maintain and develop' minority languages under 'multiculturalism'. However, readers are then reminded that the ever-decreasing number of minority languages across the world and the expansion of Mandarin Chinese use are universal and 'inevitable outcomes' of 'modernisation' (XEP, 2009, pp.94–95). Official sources widely describe the extinction of minority languages as a 'historical inevitability' due to the modernisation of 'ways of thinking' (SEAC, 2009, p.23). The concept of ethnic extinction is only discussed in positive terms in these narratives, but its notion that value-neutral modernisation sweeps away ethnic identities is never applied to Han ethnicity. A trans-ethnic race-state identity is, therefore, the inevitable outcome of 'modernisation', based on an essentialised vision of Han identity but framed as culturally neutral, rational progress.

In the era of China's rise, many of China's leading scholars have pushed for changes in *minzu* policy by deploying these ideas to argue that the security and prosperity of *Zhonghua Minzu* depends on the assimilation ethnic minority identities. Ma Rong, one of the most influential theorists of ethnicity in China today, argues that it is culture, not ethnicity, which has historically defined social distinction in China. Ma (2007) considers the *minzu* category as a sharp break with Chinese traditions of *hua/yi*, which must be rejuvenated to save *Zhonghua Minzu*. Ma Rong challenged the party-state's approach towards nation-building based on 56 institutionalised *minzu*, recommending the 'de-politicisation' and 'culturalisation' of ethnicity by abandoning the *minzu* category to promote *Zhonghua Minzu* identity (Ma, 2007, pp.2–5). The *hua/yi* distinction should guide ethnic relations, and 'less civilised' groups become 'civilised' through attraction to Chinese civilisation and development in the same way as 'barbarians' of the pre-modern era (Ma, 2007, pp.5–7). Ma explains the barbarian/civilisation distinction is not between *different* civilisations but between 'highly developed and less developed civilisations with similar roots but at different stages of advancement' (Ma, 2007, p.5). Barbarians are developed by *learning* Chinese culture and so, naturally, 'learn to be Chinese' (*jiaohua* 教化). This conversion process is understood as the opposite of European colonial violence, as an inevitable outcome of irresistible attraction to the superiority of Chinese culture. The 'tolerance of Chinese civilisation' extends to those who accept acculturation into 'Han-centred' Chinese civilisation, and 'discrimination' awaits those who do not (Ma, 2007, pp.6–7). Ma's vision of China intertwines difference at home and abroad where China's international exceptionalism as a non-Western, anti-colonial nation is maintained through the conversion of domestic ethnic difference.

The self-proclaimed '2nd Generation' of *minzu* policies scholars, including Hu Angang and Hu Lianhe (2012) and Zhu Weiqun (2012), are more explicitly chauvinist than ethnocentric in their recommendations to consciously engineer a mono-ethnic nation-state. These scholars argue that China's international rise to become a 'new type of superpower' requires the elimination of 'backwardness' and ethnic differentiation. These scholars mobilise official framings of ethnic minorities' 'backwardness' to argue that minorities hold back China's global progress before refracting backwardness home again to assert the need to construct a mono-ethnic China. Hu Angang of Tsinghua University, the politically influential IR scholar who helped write China's five-year plans under Hu Jintao, wrote that a new generation of *minzu* policies are essential to transform 'self-identification' (*rentong*) from *minzu* through 'fusion' (*jiaorong* 交融) into a 'race-state' (Hu & Hu, 2012). This follows Ma Rong's (2012) 'de-politicisation' model to argue for removal of *minzu* from identity cards, abandonment of the autonomy system, and promotion of Mandarin-medium education. In 2012, Zhu Weiqun, the party's leading spokesperson for ethnic affairs, recommended these measures and wrote in the party journal, *Xuexi Shibao*, that ethnic inter-mixing and 'fusion' are necessary for economic development and 'strengthening of the greater Chinese race' (Zhu, 2012). Ma speaks the language of reformers from the Republican period, such as Liang Qichao, and shares their hope for 'fusion' of the five races to unite into a strong China, yet defines these races as civilised Chinese or backward barbarians. The race-state (*guozu*) concept adopted by Hu Angang is also drawn from Republican-era debates when Liang Qichao described the congruence of state and race boundaries as the highest level of human evolution. For Liang, it was necessary for China to become a *Guozu* in order to prevail in a racial 'survival of the fittest' (Leibold, 2007, pp.9–11 & 32). For Hu Angang, socialism is a Chinese tradition and *guozu* enables China's rise as a non-Western, modern socialist state. Ma Rong, on the other hand, urges China to organise difference using pre-communist *hua/yi* distinctions to eradicate what he describes as the Western *minzu* category. Nevertheless, the teleological ends in their narratives are racial homogenisation and strengthening of the modern Chinese state to guarantee the survival of Chinese civilisation. These scholars draw on tensions in official discourse between China as an ancient civilisation and China as a modern territorial state to suggest new policy directions towards a mono-ethnic China, exemplified by shifts in Xinjiang's language policies.

The '2nd generation' of *minzu* policies scholars consider using Mandarin as the sole medium of education as essential for China 'to develop into a modernised nation' at the global level (Ma, 2007, pp.240–241). The Xinjiang Ministry of Education announced a shift in 2004 to what it termed 'bilingual education'.[18] Official explanations state that Mandarin Chinese transcends ethnicity and transmits 'modern information' in ways minority languages

---

[18] See Schluessel (2007; 2009) on how 'bilingual education' in Xinjiang describes the policy shift away from offering multiple language options towards Mandarin-medium education only.

cannot (XEP, 2009, pp.91–93)[19]. *Development and Progress* describes education of minorities as a 'national mission' and that 'practice proves' that 'bilingual education' promotes 'development, ethnic unity, and harmonious ethnic relations' (State Council, 2009b, pp.19–20). The plan declared that by 2012 every school in the region was to adopt Mandarin as medium of instruction in all courses, except for approximately four hours per week of minority literature studies for non-Han students. In Xinjiang, Uyghur and Kazakh languages are mutually intelligible and Uyghur language has long served as an inter-ethnic lingua franca among Turkic speakers and Mongolians (Dwyer, 2005, p.13). However, the political drive to produce identification with official *Zhonghua Minzu* narratives is prioritised over pragmatic or economic concerns. Shen Jianhua, Head of the CCP's Political Research Institute in Xinjiang, explained that promotion of education in Chinese (*Hanyu jiaoxue* 汉语教学) is not a pragmatic or technical matter, but will raise the overall 'quality' of ethnic minorities, which is essential to ethnic unity and identification with *Zhonghua Minzu* (Shen, 2009, p.14). As the *Ethnic Minority Policy* text explains, Mandarin-medium education is essential for the transmission of 'ethnic unity education' (State Council, 2009a, p.40).

While 'bilingual education' was a new official policy, it represented a quantitative rather than qualitative shift. The CCP had always designed language policy around nation-building goals of converting minorities by prioritising Mandarin. For example, the *National Language and Script Law* states that promotion of Mandarin-medium education is 'beneficial for the protection of national sovereignty and dignity, the unification of the motherland, ethnic unity, and the building of material socialist civilisation and spiritual civilisation' (NPC, 2001, article 5). Experimental bilingual classes were established in cities across Xinjiang by 1992, training minority students, capable of fluency in both Mandarin and their native language (*Han-min jiantong*). By 1996, the Xinjiang Regional Government issued an 'eradicate illiteracy' circular (*saochu wenmang tiaolie* 扫除文盲条列), stating that illiteracy in Mandarin must be eliminated for the 'needs of Socialist modernisation' and vesting authority in the regional government to inspect and fine work units (*danwei*) if their members failed to reach these standards (XUAR Government, 1996, Articles 1 & 4). Prior to 'bilingual education', the regional government had long echoed the party-state's national drive to promote Mandarin at the expense of minority languages across China. However, the RMB 76 million in funds made available by the central and regional governments for Xinjiang's new universal 'bilingual education' drive show this became a top political priority (Ma, 2009, p.213).

---

[19] Also, see XUAR Government (2007).

Minzu Xiaowang: The 'Extinction' of the Uyghur

(a)   (b)

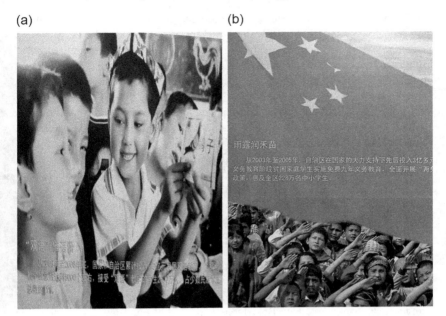

Figure 2.1 (a) 'Bilingual Education Hastens Buds'. This photograph was presented at a city-party exhibition to celebrate the 60th anniversary of the PRC's founding, in the *Xinjiang Daily*, and on *Xinhua's* national website with the caption 'I can fly'. (b) 'Rain and dew moistens seedlings: From 2003 to 2005, the regional government, under the vigorous support of the nation, has made successive investments of more than RMB 300 million, reaching a stage of comprehensive education and implementing free nine-year compulsory education for impoverished families'.

Representations of the progress of Uyghur children, whose prosperity depends on learning Mandarin, circulate widely in Xinjiang. These representations (Figure 2.1a and b) appeared in a free-of-charge, party-state-organised exhibition in Ürümchi's regional expo centre, commemorating the PRC's 60th anniversary during September 2009. The exhibition showcased examples of Xinjiang's 'ethnic unity'[20] and 'modernisation' under the party-state following the July 2009 violence. The photos in Figure 2.1 were displayed as examples of modernisation in the section on 'improving the people's livelihood' alongside photographic representations and statistics on the development of cotton field production and the oil and gas industries. The caption 'Bilingual

---

[20] These images of ethnic unity will be analysed in Chapter 5.

Education hastens buds' (Figure 2.1a) explains how Mandarin-medium education will drive young Uyghurs to blossom and prosper under the party-state's guidance. Omitting mention of the students' mother-tongue in the exhibition (Figure 2.1a: 'I can fly'), articulates Mandarin as the sole language of modernity and mobility in China, and the need for Uyghurs to be developed by this policy. Uyghurs' 'vigorous support of the nation' through salutes to the flag in return for the policy's benevolence represents identification with their position as backward ethnic minorities, attracted to China's modernisation (Figure 2.1b). Uyghur children thus become Chinese by becoming modern and they become modern by becoming Chinese. *Hanyu* ('language of the Han') and *Zhongwen* ('language of China') are conflated in these texts, which elide the category of *minzu* (Han) with the multi-*minzu* nation (China). The way policy narratives conceal tensions between ethnic and civic nationalism is central to the party-state's nation-building in Xinjiang. Han-ness is positioned as a superior and modern trans-ethnic identity into which ethnic minorities must be absorbed.

The party-state, like the 2nd generation of *minzu* policies scholars, conceptualises 'modernisation' and conversion of Uyghurs as existential identity-security matters, continually marking Xinjiang off from the rest of China as dangerously backward. Nur Bekri stated in several interviews, including for the *China Daily* in April 2009, that teaching Mandarin Chinese and 'bilingual education' policies are at the 'front-line in defeating terrorism' and developing Xinjiang (Lam, 2009). *The Fifty Whys* tells readers that only 'separatists' and 'terrorists' oppose the party's 'bilingual education' policies (XEP, 2009, pp.90–93 & 107). The framing of language use as a security matter reproduces mutually constitutive binaries of modern/backward and security/danger. Uyghurs' Turkic language use inside contemporary China is framed as a danger from 'outside' China's cultural boundaries and a historical leftover to be converted or a terrorist threat to be eliminated. Majority/minority, nation/ethnicity, backwardness/modernity, and security/danger are mutually reinforcing dichotomies, which reproduce Uyghur-ness as a backward *and* dangerous identity to be overcome by *Zhonghua Minzu*. Nevertheless, the removal of Uyghur language from the education system produced widespread identity-insecurity amongst Uyghurs.[21] In 2008, Ma Rong presented his work on 'bilingual education' at Xinjiang Normal University. According to several attendees, he was scolded by local Uyghur professors. Ma's models (2009) were based on gradual introduction of Mandarin Chinese according to different regional needs and resources, but this was dismissed as a 'fabrication'. 'Bilingual education' rapidly overhauled the education system, exacerbating social

---

[21] Chapter 7 will fully analyse how securitisation of *Zhonghua Minzu* identity produces resistance amongst those it seeks to convert.

tensions. In 2011, 20 college teachers in Ürümchi refused new lower-rank jobs imposed on them due to their limited Mandarin Chinese ability. One teacher stated, 'We are Uyghur, we should keep our language for the preservation of our culture' (RFA, 2011a). Uyghurs understood 'bilingual education' and its framing through ethnic extinction narratives as existential threats to their identity.

Conclusions

This chapter analysed mass ethnic unity education in Xinjiang as an identity-security practice and, specifically, how its narratives include minorities in a hierarchical *Zhonghua Minzu*. These nation-building texts produce the *minzu*, Han, and ethnic minorities categories, and hierarchical relations between them. Mass education in Xinjiang conceptualises *Zhonghua Minzu* as a timeless ethno-hierarchy, demarcating historically unbroken boundaries between active Han nation-builders and passive ethnic minorities. The party-state projects its contemporary *minzu* category on to the history of all peoples within the contemporary PRC's territory. However, ethnic minorities are considered historically ephemeral transitions to be contained by the state, before being absorbed by *Zhonghua Minzu*. The universal ethnic unity education texts in mass education project external boundaries between China and the West on to domestic ethnic boundaries, a key theme of the next chapter. These texts represent Han-centred China as a multi-*minzu* nation in opposition to the dangerous, backward ethnic identification of Uyghurs, manipulated by Western 'one-nation, one-state' thinking.

The chapter's first section showed how the party-state writes *Zhonghua Minzu* history by narrating and unifying the histories of all peoples within China's contemporary borders as timelessly constituted by the *minzu* category. The official historiographical narrative justifies China's timeless political and cultural jurisdiction over Xinjiang by projecting ancient boundaries between Han civilisation and non-Han barbarism on to the contemporary binary between Han majority and ethnic minorities. The second section showed how these nation-building texts relationally constitute and normatively rank the identities of the Han majority and ethnic minorities as modern and backward *minzu*, respectively. Ethnic minority identities are framed as the absence of progressive Han-ness and the frontier as the absence of the advanced central plains. These binaries structure a timeless *Zhonghua Minzu* through a boundary between the active and modernising Han 'frontier-building culture' of the central plains and the passive, backward ethnic minorities of the frontier. These texts articulate an unbroken Han lineage, occupying and developing Xinjiang since the Han dynasty through to the contemporary party-state. Chinese nation-building, thus, aims to produce self-identification with *Zhonghua Minzu* as a timeless reality for all *minzu* but minorities' inclusion entails identification with civilisational boundaries that exclude them as barbarian others.

The final section analysed how the 'bilingual education' (Mandarin-medium education) policy narrative is presented in political education texts as the means to modernise minorities and achieve 'fusion'. The analysis examined how the party-state includes Uyghurs in *Zhonghua Minzu* by narrating teleological progress in Xinjiang, moving from backward ethnicity towards progressive, modern Chinese nationhood. These texts deployed the concepts of 'fusion' and 'ethnic extinction' to write the withering away and extinction of ethnic minority identities as the teleological progression of *Zhonghua Minzu*. The official ethnic extinction narrative explains that ethnic minority policies, including 'bilingual education', will accelerate the extinction of non-Han ethnic identities and their absorption into *Zhonghua Minzu*. The party-state then securitises its *Zhonghua Minzu* narrative by framing identification through Uyghur language as an existential threat to its identity. Turkic and Islamic identities are targeted as security threats and resistance to this progress, but are ultimately futile because they run against the inevitable 'direction of history' towards *Zhonghua Minzu*'s 'sacred mission'. Han chauvinism did not wither away with the class-based revolution that promised *minzu* equality. Han chauvinism intermingled with historical materialism and is now being reconfigured in the 'opening and reform' era to frame the Han as the driving force of economic development and China's unbroken civilisation that absorbs ethnic minorities.

Chapter 1 illustrated the worries of nineteenth and twentieth century nation-builders' about defeat by the West through territorial encroachment. However, China's twenty-first-century nation-builders are equally concerned about *becoming* the West. What Gloria Davies (2009) called 'worrying about China' and Callahan (2013) termed 'patriotic worrying' is official business. China's elites devote significant resources to relationally define Chinese identity by ordering the world into civilisational camps of Western universalism and Chinese exceptionalism. Outgoing President Hu Jintao used his final speech to the 18th National Congress to reinforce China's exceptionalism by announcing, 'We will never copy a Western political system' (Xinhua, 2012b). Leading public intellectuals, such as Zhang Weiwei (2012) and Hu Angang (2012), argue that as we enter a 'post-American century', China is emerging as a 'new type of superpower', using Eastern traditions of consent over Western coercion to organise domestic politics and world order. The Chinese anthropological establishment describes China as a multi-*minzu* nation with respect for diversity in contrast to Western 'one-nation, one-state' thinking and its history of nationalist conflict.[22] Nation-building in Xinjiang is embedded in these narratives, producing and securitising *Zhonghua Minzu* as a modern

---

[22] For example, see Fei (1980; 1988); Ma (2007); Pan (2008b); Ruan (2004); Zhang (2006).

Conclusions 85

multi-ethnic nation built on consent to Chinese civilisation, in contrast to violent Western colonial conquests. Chinese nation-building produces boundaries between East and West, and civilisation and barbarians, but these depend on Uyghur consent to understand their ethnic identity as backward and to be converted to *Zhonghua Minzu*.

Chinese debates on values in global politics ordinarily contrast the 'Western' universalist human rights approach against the cultural relativism of 'Asian values' and 'Confucian values'.[23] The party-state routinely describes all commentary on human rights and appeals to 'universal values' as Western 'excuses' to 'split China' (XEP, 2009, pp.44–45). However, this binarising debate conceals how the party-state practices its own universalisms in its writing of ethnic minorities (*shaoshu minzu*) into China's history, drawn from the intermingling of Eurocentric and Sinocentric theory. Chinese historical materialism was drawn from Marx and Engels, before being transformed into China's self-avowedly 'universalist theory', and applied to all human history and potential futures (Shijian Bianji Bu, 1965, p.213). The opening of *Ethnic Minority Policy* tells readers that 'the world we live in is a world of *minzu*' and that China is a 'multi-*minzu* nation commonly created by all (Chinese) *minzu*' (State Council, 2009a, p.1).[24] *Minzu* separatism is thus not a Chinese problem but a universal human problem, which emerges at 'specific stages of socio-economic development' (EUAB, 2009, pp.26–27). *Minzu* is performed as a universal, objective truth, and boundaries between *minzu* identities are inevitable, universal human realities. Cultural relativism and Chinese exceptionalism only emerge in narratives to distinguish China's universalisms from Western universalisms and, in practice, constitute the Han as the unchanging national nucleus that drives historical progress. The party-state and Chinese anthropologists fuse historical materialist teleology and the Chinese civilisation/barbarian boundary. Ethnic unity, the national bonds that tie different Chinese *minzu* together, flow from the dawn of human beings in Xinjiang all the way to contemporary life in the PRC. China's universalist narratives describe absorption of minorities into majority-led states as a universal reality because inferior groups naturally wither away. Xinjiang's marginality, therefore, is central to the constitution of a superior and attractive *Zhonghua Minzu*. It is not enough that Xinjiang is an indisputable territorial component of the Chinese state. Xinjiang's peoples must *desire Zhonghu Minzu* and understand their own history as driven by the superior Han towards

---

[23] See contrasting human rights reports by the State Council (Xinhua, 2012c) and US Department of State (2012).
[24] As with most of this chapter's themes, this position is reiterated in most texts analysed, including *Development and Progress*, *Xinjiang Cultural Knowledge*, *Common Knowledge*, and *The Fifty Whys*.

the withering away of their own inferior identities. The party-state continues the timeless lineage of Chinese civilisation's conversion of 'barbarians' but through purportedly natural and culturally neutral processes of economic development that privilege the majority over minorities.

There are no civic nations in the world, and juxtaposition of 'good' civic nationalism against 'bad' ethnic nationalism is a 'Manichean myth' (Brubaker, 1999, p.62). Ethnic nationalism consciously foregrounds cultural components. Civic nationalism conceals them in ethnocentric celebrations of itself as a value-free outcome of rational modernity. Inclusion based on multi-ethnic formulations involve 'cultural components' as much as ethnic nationalism (Brubaker, 1999, p.61). The production of a 'long and proud national historical consciousness' in Xinjiang, like the construction of European nations, projects modern spatial domains on to ancient history. China's history is written as a cultural and ethnic hierarchy with the active Han at the centre and passive minorities on the cultural frontiers, familiar themes in the establishment of the United States and Australia by European settlers. The history of nation-building in Xinjiang is told from the Han 'nucleus' perspective. Nevertheless, Han is a contested and contingent identity category (Chow, 2001, pp.47–48). The essentialisations in official *Zhonghua Minzu* narratives speak *for* Han and non-Han alike but in different ways. Mutually constitutive and mutually reinforcing dichotomies of civilisation/barbarism, modernity/backwardness, and security/danger are narrated as timeless national realities, relationally articulating what it means to be Chinese, Han, and ethnic minority. The essentialising narratives of China's official nation-building close down all alternative social imaginations on the past, present, and future. Nevertheless, nation-building reproduces tensions between unbroken civilisational continuity and the identity transformation of Uyghurs. The official *Zhonghua Minzu* narrative includes all 55 minority *minzu* but excludes their ethnic identities as outside the 'good' nationalism of ethnic unity. The party-state's grammar of civilisation and development conceal the ethnocentrism in its universalist narratives of cultural evolution. As the next chapter shows, alternative ethnic identities are treated as irrational security threats to be defeated, eventually by historical progress but with violence in the short term. The next chapter turns from inclusion of Uyghurs in the *Zhonghua Minzu* ethno-hierarchy to this direct exclusion of their identities. Nation-building in Xinjiang relationally produces China as a progressive force by securitising *Zhonghua Minzu* and excluding Turkic identities as causes of political instability and ethnic violence.

3 'East Turkestan' in China's Identity and Security Narratives

Introduction

The narrative that China's existence is threatened by domestic traitors in collaboration with foreign imperialists has been a central theme throughout modern Chinese political history. Sun Yat-Sen urged the Han to save China from the threat of the corrupt Manchu working with the imperialist West (Chow, 2001, p.53; Leibold, 2007, pp.30–31). For Mao Zedong, the corrupt 'foreign ministries' of the GMD acted as the 'counting houses of our foreign masters' as an alliance between the domestic bourgeoisie and external imperialists, threatening China's survival (Mao, 1923; 1926). After Mao, Deng Xiaoping proclaimed that China's new 'market socialism' demanded the two tasks of 'opposing hegemonism and reunifying the country' (Hughes, 2006, p.13). Resisting global hegemonism and unifying domestic identities are always mutually reinforcing goals to make China a strong and prosperous nation again. The CCP under Hu Jintao and Xi Jinping continue to narrate the founding of the "new China" through a century of revolutionary struggle against Western imperialism and reactionary separatists. However, in the era of China's rise, cultural nationalism has re-emerged, narrating an exceptional *Zhonghua Minzu* through the continuity of '5,000 years' of unbroken, non-Western civilisation. These narratives frame minority identities as existential threats to *Zhonghua Minzu* because they identify through ethnicity, a manipulation by Western nationalist thought and remnant of China's feudal past. This intertwined struggle against external imperialist enemies and minority ethnic identities is at the heart of China's nation-building project to be a timeless, non-Western, non-ethnic nation. This chapter analyses how the securitisation of *Zhonghua Minzu* conceptualises China through the exclusion of Uyghur enemies within. The previous chapter analysed how Han and Uyghurs are included in the telos of *Zhonghua Minzu*. This chapter focuses on the exclusion of Uyghur identities in official narratives of China's history as security threats. How does exclusion constitute the boundaries of inclusion in *Zhonghua Minzu*? And how do these exclusions shape Uyghur resistance to nation-building?

Repetitions of exclusionary collocations assign characteristics to specific groups to represent peoples as a 'source of threat' (Said, 1997, p.xxi). Uyghur identification with Turkic-ness and Islam are officially framed through what David Campbell (1998) called 'discourses of danger' that demarcate boundaries between safe insiders as the referents of security and dangerous outsiders as threats. The securitisation of *Zhonghua Minzu* is a performative enactment, producing and securing a particular national narrative against alternative identities, framed as existential threats. Official CCP narratives of history exclude Turkic-ness in China today as a backward cultural threat and a distortion of history by imperialist enemies who seek to split China. The party-state explains that the 'Xinjiang problem' must never be 'internationalised' because it is an internal, sovereign matter (XEP, 2009, p.8). However, this narrative frequently emphasises its international dimensions, describing Uyghur identities as a global terrorist threat linked to both Islamism and Western human rights campaigns. It reinforces the ethnic boundaries it seeks to dissolve by drawing people's attention to these boundaries.

Nation-building includes minorities but excludes their identity characteristics deemed unbefitting of the nation as a security matter. Identity implies feelings of inclusion, based on shared practices amongst members, but these feelings require exclusion to distinguish this identity from others (Cohen, 1985, p.14). The identification and inclusion of insiders who represent the nation, contrasted against outsiders to be excluded as un-Chinese, are mutually constitutive processes of boundary production. The transformation of the internal and disagreeable into the external in nation-building narratives produces a singular and homogenous identity, promoting agendas of social control (Winichakul, 1994, pp.169–170). Linking identities within state borders that challenge official conceptualisations of nationhood to external threats is a key tactic in China's securitised nation-building project. However, communities tend to resist transgression of the boundaries that encapsulate their identification because they feel their existence is under threat (Cohen, 1985, p.91). Xinjiang is officially positioned between inclusion as an inalienable component of China and exclusion as a cultural security threat linked to a Turkic and Western outside. This in-between-ness collapses and fuses distinctions between the internal and external and between the domestic and international. Framing Uyghurs as internal *and* external enables a vocabulary of resistance that disrupts nation-building narratives using the tensions it produces between inclusion and exclusion. Power and resistance are not exterior to each other and 'where there is power, there is resistance' (Foucault, 1991, p.95). Nation-building frames Uyghur identity as the constitutive outside to *Zhonghua Minzu*. Uyghurs use this vocabulary to resist Chinese nation-building on its own terms as a colonial project to assimilate minorities and eradicate parallel civilisations.

Introduction

This chapter analyses official policy documents and ethnic unity education texts to examine how the Turk category is used to explain contemporary violence in Xinjiang and to constitute the boundaries that encapsulate *Zhonghua Minzu*. The first section will analyse the production and circulation of the party-state's 'East Turkestan' (*dongtu* 东突) narrative that articulates Uyghurness as an external Turkic threat. The official East Turkestan narrative projects external territorial borders and internal ethnic boundaries through each other by marking Uyghur language and religion as security problems *in* China from outside its cultural boundaries. The projection of external and dangerous otherness on to Uyghurs relationally produces the Han as the secure inside of *Zhonghua Minzu*, whose identity will eliminate this threat. The second section analyses the party-state's explanation of incidents of violence and protest in contemporary Xinjiang through narratives of East Turkestan and inside/outside enemies. Xinjiang was officially represented as entirely peaceful throughout the 1980s, but by the late 1990s, this shifted to narratives of a long-term ethnic *separatism* problem. After 9/11, these representations shifted again, framing Xinjiang under constant threat of infiltration by *terrorism* and religious *extremism*. The party-state today deploys the 'inside/outside Three Evils' narrative ('terrorism, separatism, and extremism') to explain all violence, historical and contemporary, as well as non-violent resistance to *Zhonghua Minzu*, articulating Uyghur identity as an inside/outside security threat to China's identity-security. This section will analyse how the party-state turns external boundaries with Islam and the West inward, demarcating ethno-spatial boundaries *within* Xinjiang between specific sub-regions that are more and less secure, more and less modern, and more and less Chinese.

The final section introduces Uyghur responses to official discourse and analyses the productive social effects of Chinese nation-building. This will examine how Uyghurs re-perform official discourses of East Turkestan and Uyghur-ness to articulate alternative configurations of identity and security. This section analyses popular deployment of the Turk category. It uses detailed, semi-structured interviews with Uyghurs in Xinjiang and discourse analysis of Nurmehemmet Yasin's short story 'Wild Pigeon' ('Yawa Kepter') as an indicative example of the category's circulation in Uyghur popular culture. Uyghurs resist nation-building from within its own narrative using its grammar of civilisational boundaries. However, Uyghurs re-perform these boundaries by reasserting cultural difference on their own terms, positioning themselves as outside but not inferior to *Zhonghua Minzu*. The chapter argues that China's East Turkestan narrative is a central component of its nation-building project to tell people whom they must not be (Turkic Muslims) and whom they must become (*Zhonghua Minzu*). The exclusion of Uyghur identity and the demarcation of boundaries, which encapsulate inclusion in *Zhonghua Minzu*, are mutually constitutive. The party-state's identity-security discourse inadvertently gives Uyghurs a vocabulary of resistance within its own logics that Uyghurs use to reconfigure their own identity-security.

Producing 'East Turkestan', Producing China

This section examines the production and circulation of the party-state's 'East Turkestan' (*dongtu* 东突) narrative that articulates Uyghur-ness as a culturally external threat inside China's territorial borders. The official East Turkestan narrative is central to Chinese nation-building processes, which demarcate the boundaries of *Zhonghua Minzu* by excluding specific identities as dangerous and external. Official East Turkestan narratives project external danger inward by framing Uyghur language and religion as security problems inside China but culturally outside *Zhonghua Minzu*. The constitution of Uyghurs as cultural threats relationally produces Han identity as the secure inside of *Zhonghua Minzu* that annuls this threat. The nation-building project to convert the history and future of Turkestan into *Zhonghua Minzu* depends on codifying and policing public language on identity and security through collocations that frame identities as safe or dangerous. Collocation is an inter-textual representational practice that produces meaning by publicly associating concepts with other concepts through ubiquitous and uncritical repetition of their connections. Repetitions of exclusionary collocations assign characteristics of danger to groups, representing cultures and peoples as 'sources of threat' (Said, 1997, p.xxi). East Turkestan has been codified through constant repetition of exclusionary key words and phrases, namely, separatism and terrorism (Dwyer, 2005, p.50). Exclusionary discourses in global politics that represent Islamic peoples as culturally inferior and backward need not be supported with evidence because these pervasive stereotypes are so often uncritically taken as truth (Said, 1997, p.xviii). Unlike European conceptions of the Orient, China includes Uyghurs in *Zhonghua Minzu* as nominal equals while simultaneously representing them as dangerous and culturally inferior. Being nominally included as Chinese citizens means the party-state can exercise what Janice Mattern called 'representational force', by threatening Uyghur identity narratives and narrating away their 'truth', pointing out inconsistencies, and dismissing alternative interpretations as false (Mattern, 2005, p.603). Chinese nation-building narrates Uyghurs' Turkic and Islamic identities out of history because they transgress the boundaries of *Zhonghua Minzu* by challenging the idea that Uyghurs have always been an inalienable but inferior component of Chinese civilisation.

The party-state describes Turkestan as an old 'undefined', 'geographical' term and a political concept forwarded by colonialists to 'dismember China' (State Council, 2002; 2003).[1] Nevertheless, the term had a life prior to any

---

[1] The term 'Turkestan' is still routinely used by mainstream historians and geographers who work on history outside China. For example, see: N. Davies (1997) *Europe: A History*.

influence from European colonialism or Chinese nation-building in Xinjiang. The earliest known use of the term 'Turkestan' comes from ninth century Persian sources, denoting the lands of Transoxiana and contemporary Xinjiang (Millward, 2007, pp.55–56). The suffix '-stan' means 'land of' in Persian and 'Turkestan' translates as 'land of the Turks' (Dwyer, 2005, p.52). Ildikó Bellér-Hann's analysis of indigenous sources written using East Turki dialects in Xinjiang from 1880 to 1949, including local historical accounts and essays collected by missionaries, used the Turk ethnonym almost universally (Bellér-Hann, 2008, pp.27–29 & 51). The Turk category included speakers of different Turkic dialects and framed community belonging through language (Bellér-Hann, 2008, p.51). The terms 'East Turkestan' and 'West Turkestan' as fixed national boundaries emerged amongst Russian scholars in 1829, dividing Turkestan along the boundary of former Russian control at the Pamir Mountains, which separates Xinjiang from Tajikistan and Kyrgyzstan today (Kamalov, 2007, p.34). During the nineteenth century, the meaning of 'Turkestan' was adapted and reconfigured to emerging national borders and came to prominence amongst Turkic nationalists across Central Asia. Turkic nationalists sought to build and disseminate the nation using pre-existing cultural markers of language and religion. They established educational institutions, including the Turkistani Youth Turk Union founded in Istanbul in 1927, to promote Turkic languages (Dwyer, 2005, pp.51–52; Schluessel, 2009, p.388). The meaning of 'Turk', like *Zhonghua Minzu*, was reconfigured through interaction between peoples who used it to define themselves and states that sought to define them in nineteenth and twentieth century nation-building processes.

East Turkestan's unique meaning in contemporary Chinese politics is embedded in narratives of China's cultural evolution when its civilisation was directly threatened by imperialism, a stage in development that the 'new China' has transcended. In official Chinese narratives, the term 'East Turkestan' is associated with the establishment of two independent Eastern Turkestan Republics in Kashgar (1932–1933) and Ghulja/Yining (1944–1949), now officially attributed to Western imperialists and Uyghur 'terrorists' (Millward, 2007, p.ix).[2] The East Turkestan Information Center (ETIC) and the World Uyghur Congress (WUC) were designated as international 'terrorist' organisations by the party-state, partly for their use of the name 'East Turkestan' (XEP, 2009, pp.17–19). It has long been de facto illegal for Uyghurs to even utter the term in the PRC (Dwyer, 2005, p.52). The generic term for East Turkestan (*dongtu* 东突) appears frequently in China, particularly in Xinjiang newspapers and party documents. However, East Turkestan is always carefully

---

[2] For example, see State Council (2002; 2003; 2009b).

enclosed in quarantined quotation marks to constitute it as a source of external danger through collocation with 'The Three Evils' (Dwyer, 2005, pp.51–52; Millward, 2007, p.x). The quotation marks that enclose East Turkestan narrate it out of history by collocating and quarantining it within a quote, as a non-existent category that only terrorists could use.

The party-state describes any claims of Xinjiang's historical separateness from *Zhonghua Minzu* as by-products of nineteenth century imperialist's 'concoction' of Turkestan to divide Chinese territory and 'split the motherland' (State Council, 2002; State Council, 2003). The party-state's historiography explains that during the 'Great Game', British and Russian empires established consulates in Kashgar, using their foothold to foment discontent amongst minorities and create the 'illusion' of Xinjiang's separate-ness (Li, 2007; State Council, 2002). East Turkestan is described as a group of 'separatists' whose outdated identity, based on language and religion, is politicised to 'unite all ethnic groups speaking Turkic languages' against China (State Council, 2002). *The Fifty Whys* tells readers 'Turkestan is a reactionary concept' and 'only used by an extremely small minority of separatists influenced by religious extremism and ethnic chauvinism on the international stage' (XEP, 2009, p.53). Its contemporary use follows 'methods of old imperialism' in 'fabricating a system of thought of so-called East Turkestan independence since ancient times' (XEP, 2009, pp.53–54). These texts dismiss 'East Turkestan' and 'The Three Evils' within the logics of cultural evolution as 'remnants of class exploitation' and 'historical leftovers of old thinking' (XUAR Dept of Information, 2009, p.84). The opposition of 'The Three Evils' to the 'sacred mission' of *Zhonghua Minzu* runs 'against the flow of history' and 'modernisation'; thus it will 'inevitably lose' (EUAB, 2009, p.60). Uyghurs are given the choice of being part of Chinese historical progress as an ethnic minority or to be left behind as 'national refuse' and extinct Turks. 'Backward' identities are exoticised as 'living fossils' that 'threaten national security' (XUAR Dept of Information, 2009, p.85). The Turk category threatens the securitised *Zhonghua Minzu* ethno-hierarchy because it constitutes Uyghurs as members of a parallel civilisation rather than less culturally evolved members of China.

Shortly after the events of September 11 focused global attention on Islam and terrorism, the State Council (2002) publicly catalogued incidents of unrest in Xinjiang in an English-language document, *East Turkestan Forces Cannot Get Away with Impunity*, the first time for a global audience. It claimed, 'There is plenty of evidence to show that most of the terrorist and other violent incidents which have occurred in Xinjiang were directly plotted and engineered by the 'East Turkistan organisation' (*dongtu*) beyond China's borders, with the collusion of a handful of people within the borders' (State Council, 2002). The State Council narrated East Turkestan out of history by explaining that only 'imperialists' and 'separatists' could possibly use the term outside quotation marks. Since 9/11, 'East Turkestan', Uyghur unrest, and religious extremism have been collocated through one another whereby '*Dongtu*' refers interchangeably to the East Turkestan Independence Movement (ETIM), the purported terrorist organisation, and East Turkestan, the geographical category. *Dongtu* is employed in all official texts and policy documents analysed throughout this book, including all media reports in subsequent chapters. The practice of shortening long transliterated names in Mandarin means that Han in Xinjiang use *dongtu* to mean ETIM *and* East Turkestan. When I used the full name for East Turkestan (*dongtu juesitan* 东突厥斯坦) during interviews, Han invariably responded using *dongtu*, thus making it impossible to discuss the category of identity or its history without securitising *Zhonghua Minzu*. Language policing has securitised boundaries and discussing 'East Turkestan' (*dongtu*) in Mandarin Chinese automatically contains reference to the terrorist organisation, ETIM (*dongtu*). This collocation renders ETIM and East Turkestan synonymous, framing any identification with East Turkestan or the Turk category as existential and organised violent security threats.

The securitisation of *Zhonghua Minzu* as a non-Western civilisation, therefore anti-colonial and inclusive of diversity, prevents any discussion of Chinese cultural hegemony over ethnic minorities by eliminating the *possibility* of racism or colonialism in Chinese history. Official narratives frame colonialism and imperialism as purely Western practices of racial superiority and the nation-state, relationally constituting *Zhonghua Minzu* as a tolerant, multicultural civilisation. Mainstream Chinese public intellectuals, Zhang Weiwei (2012) and Hu Angang (2012), both assert that imperialism and 'hegemonism' are 'Western' approaches to international relations that are incompatible with Chinese culture. The identity-security threat of the contemporary Turkic Uyghur to *Zhonghua Minzu*, therefore, is linked to the cultural outside of Islam and the West, reproducing the intertwined historical threats of domestic traitors and external imperialism in contemporary Xinjiang. 'East Turkestan' is supported by 'anti-Chinese' 'Western enemy forces' (*xifang duidi shili* 西方对敌实力), including the media, governments, and scholars who continue imperialist strategies to 'contain' China by using the violence of July 2009 'to damage China's image':

For a long time, Western enemy forces have not ceased to use the plot of 'peaceful evolution' against us. Particularly since reform, our economy has transitioned towards the market. This has made the West look upon us with so-called hope. They believe China can only lean towards a market economy to develop and will certainly move towards capitalism ... but over the last thirty years of reform, China has not moved towards capitalism; on the contrary, socialism with Chinese characteristics has enjoyed unparalleled success, achieving extreme development and China's rise and improvement in international prestige are unceasing. (XEP, 2009, p.18)

The party-state links a Western geopolitical threat to the invention of a 'fake' Uyghur identity outside *Zhonghua Minzu* in ideas targeted as 'separatist history'. The party-state's specific narratives of Chinese history and identity are the referents of security, as revealed in its explicit targeting of ideas and identity narratives:

> The Three Evils believe that under the rule of the Qing, Xinjiang became a Chinese colony. This ignores facts and distorts history. After the establishment of the Western Regions during the Han dynasty, every ethnic group identified with the rule of the central government. (XEP, 2009, pp.47–50)

Excluding alternative understandings of history as evil produces the boundaries, which encapsulate inclusion in *Zhonghua Minzu*. Popular Uyghur beliefs that the 1759 Qing military incursion into Xinjiang was a violent invasion akin to European colonial practices are framed as existential threats to China. Excluding mainstream Uyghur interpretations of history and scholarly literature on the subject as existential threats secures *Zhonghua Minzu* against Turkic self-identifications from below. This delinks the official Uyghur category, understood through the concept of *minzu*, from the broader and older Turk category that is not contained within China's borders. The *Dictionary of History and Culture of Every Xinjiang Minzu* explains that users of Turkic languages are distributed across Xinjiang, Gansu, and Qinghai (A, 1996, p.316). The text conspicuously omits mentions of millions of Turkic speakers across Central Asia, enclosing the Uyghur within *Zhonghua Minzu*. This policing of China's boundaries identifies its 'constitutive outside' to constitute its inside.

Policing the relationship between Islam and Uyghur-ness, like policing the Turk category, illustrates how the demarcation of external and internal boundaries is indivisible in China's nation-building. Political education texts such as *The Fifty Whys* repeatedly assert that Uyghurs today are 'not a Turkic *minzu*' and this 'mistaken' identity only exists due to dangerous influences of the 'inside-outside Three Evils' (XEP, 2009, pp.55–59). *The Fifty Whys* then tells readers that *only* 'separatists' and 'terrorists' could possibly understand themselves through reference to the categories of 'Turk' or 'Muslim' (XEP, 2009, pp.47–52 & 99). Interpellations of Uyghurs as Chinese and 'not a Turkic *minzu*' are ordinarily followed, in texts such as *The Fifty Whys*, with the declaration that Uyghurs are 'not an Islamic *minzu*' because religion is not one of Stalin's four defining principles of nationality (XEP, 2009, p.55). The Xinjiang military division, which governed the region between 'peaceful liberation' in 1949 and establishment of the autonomous region in 1955, originally recommended that Uyghurs must give up religion before entering the party. However, as part of the CCP Central Committee's geopolitical 'chess game', it made the tactical decision to encourage Muslims to join the party *before* insisting they 'give up religion' (CCPCC, 1950, pp.41–42). The CCP has always publicly downplayed the significance of Islam to Uyghur identity, and since 1949 Uyghurs had to choose between religion and public life.[3] *The 50 Whys* text explains that a religion cannot be the real basis of *minzu* identity because it includes followers of many different *minzu* and Uyghur history includes influence from many religions, including Shamanism of several thousand years ago (XEP, 2009, pp.55–58):

> In reality, many Uyghurs are not followers of Islam ... members of the Communist Party, members of the Communist Youth League, officials working in Government organs, students, etc are not religious. They are not devout Muslim followers of Islam, yet we cannot deny their Uyghur identity (*shenfen*[4]). (XEP, 2009, p.56)

This narrative de-emphasises Xinjiang's more recent Islamic history and Uyghur self-identification, narrating the Turk and living religion out of history and the Uyghur into Chinese telos. Uyghurs are only included through discontinuity and multiplicity, relationally producing the continuity and homogeneity of a Han-led *Zhonghua Minzu*. The party-state cites examples of Uyghurs in state employment, who are not permitted to practice Islam, defining politically acceptable Uyghur-ness as non-Islamic for its nation-building purposes. The party-state has built institutions to represent minorities and limit cultural diversity in the name of national tradition (Balzer, 2004, p.237). The China Islamic Association, which registered Imams and pilgrimages to Mecca, is one institution that articulates national traditions and limits diversity in China through 'authentic' declarations on Islam. The China Islamic Association's (2006) *Patriotic Muslim Coursebook* explains the CCP should be 'worshipped' at an 'equal level to Allah'. Such texts securitise *Zhonghua Minzu* as a modernist, atheist nation by placing this identity beyond the realm of politics and contestability. Although there are many Uyghurs who practice other religions or do not consider themselves religious, there are no studies that find any rejection of Islam as a long-term cultural influence. However, *The Fifty Whys* paradoxically reminded readers that to maintain 'religious freedom', students and state-employees are not permitted to visit mosques or practice Islam because these 'religious activities' interfere with 'freedom of choice' and 'modern education' (XEP, 2009, pp.103–104). Many interviewees explained to me that they and their colleagues would pray and fast in private to maintain their employment status or continue their studies. The logics defining Uyghur origins as multiple

---

[3] See Harris (2008) on how the official codification of lyrics in Uyghur classical music (*muqam*) omitted religious references despite Uyghur musicians explaining their meaning through Islam. Also, see Bellér-Hann (2001) on how religious practices thrived in private.

[4] *Shenfen* derives from 'identity card' (*shenfen zheng*) and usually implies 'status' more than self-identification. It is avoided in Chinese anthropological debates on identity because it does not always imply 'identification' (*rentong*).

and broken, and inferior to a timeless, unbroken *Zhonghua Minzu*, exclude Islamic social practices as threats to Chinese identity and modernity, so that to be Chinese is to be a modernist atheist.

Official narratives of *Zhonghua Minzu* as a timeless civilisation facing the backward threat of East Turkestan circulates in Chinese scholarship. Pan Zhiping, leading Chinese scholar on history and governance of Xinjiang, states without qualification or corroboration that 'Mosques are not simply places of worship; they are also fortresses for Muslims to instigate combat' (Pan, 2008, p.149). Islamic practices offer alternative cultural presence that cannot be dismissed as the absence of Han identity. The presence of Uyghur social practices, such as visiting the mosque, is therefore a security threat to the party-state's ethno-hierarchy. Ma Dazheng, a leading historian on Xinjiang who helped write many patriotic education texts, explicitly states that scholarly writing of Xinjiang's history must serve contemporary political needs of fighting East Turkestan terrorism (Ma, 2004; 2006). Ma was commissioned to write the political education text *National Interests Overpower Everything*, titled according to Deng Xiaoping slogans, which argued for rapid Han migration to secure the region's stability and identity. After the July 2009 violence, Pan Zhiping's (2008) *The History and Present Situation of 'East Turkestan'* conspicuously appeared in the 'hot topics' section of Xinhua bookstores all over Xinjiang and Beijing. Pan was awarded for contributions to social stability as part of the 'theoretical frontline' to resolve the '*minzu* problem', discussed in Chapter 2. Pan asserts that 'fake' 'Turkic history' is based on 'myths, legends, and folk-tales' that instigate 'crazed *minzu* separatist activities' (Pan, 2008, p.89). He argues that prior to the 'rise of capitalism in the West' and penetration of China by 'imperialists', Xinjiang had always been 'united' under *Zhonghua Minzu* (Pan, 2008, p.24). The Pan-Islamism and Pan-Turkism of 'East Turkestan' are dismissed as passive 'responses to 'Western politics' (Pan, 2008, pp.24–28). 'East Turkestan' is considered a 'by-product of 19th century geo-politics', first introduced to Xinjiang by traders from Russian 'Tartarstan' and Turkish political influence on students (Pan, 2008, pp.72–74). Pan frames East Turkestan through pre-modern boundaries as culturally behind the advanced evolution of *Zhonghua Minzu* because 'East Turkestan' and '*minzu* separatism' are 'completely defeated histories' and 'reactionary' leftovers that threaten 'national security, stability, and survival' (Pan, 2008, pp.73 & 146). The intertwined official and scholarly production of an 'East Turkestan' threat, that crosses national borders into Islamic, Turkic-speaking Central Asia and the imperialist, capitalist 'West', relationally produces *Zhonghua Minzu* as a multi-ethnic and inclusive mirror-image of the exclusionary and warlike West.

Official East Turkestan narratives reconfigure earlier CCP discourse that identified enemies of the revolution as external imperialism and internal feudalism. Nation-building today negatively elaborates *Zhonghua Minzu* against a threatening constitutive outside of the West, Islamism, and Turkic culture. This cultural outside is physically inside China's borders and converges through the Uyghur internal other who threatens China's indivisible internal and external boundaries by interpreting the arrival of Qing armies as invasion, identifying themselves as Turkic Muslims, or arguing for Uyghur language education. These security narratives demarcate the boundaries of Chinese-ness by framing alternatives to the party-state's identity narratives as separatism, terrorism, and extremism. The party-state has, in the words of Mao Zedong, 'turned reality upside down'. Despite the rapid growth of inequality since the end of the fully planned economy[5], the party-state employs socialism to produce China as a unique, enclosed civilisation, defined against the capitalist West. To paraphrase Voltaire, if the West did not exist, it would be necessary for China to invent it. East Turkestan exemplifies the Uyghur's threatening in-between-ness because it emerges at the intersection of internal and external boundaries that identify China's enemies as Westernisation and 'Islamic' terrorism in collusion with domestic Turks. Nevertheless, the party-state's codification of East Turkestan helps perpetuate the category's ongoing relevance by using it to mark Uyghur cultural difference as an ever-present threat.

After 9/11: China's War on the 'Inside/Outside Three Evils'

This section analyses how the party-state explains violence and protest in contemporary Xinjiang through the 'East Turkestan' narrative that articulates Uyghur identity as a threat. It examines how external boundaries constituted by the party-state's East Turkestan narrative are redirected inward, demarcating ethno-spatial boundaries within Xinjiang between sub-regions that are more and less secure, more and less modern, and more and less Chinese. The nature of Xinjiang's threat, as constituted in China's identity-security discourse, has dramatically shifted with official representations of the region as peaceful in the 1980s, beset by ethnic separatism in the late 1990s, and infiltrated by terrorism and religious extremism since September 11. From 9/11 until July 2009, Xinjiang experienced less violence and less incidents of unrest than any other region of China (Bovingdon, 2010, p.112). Despite relative political stability, compared to Han regions that experienced industrial strikes and rural protests against land seizures, Xinjiang is represented through discourses of danger. All incidents of Uyghur violence and protest are conflated and explained through the existential threat of the 'inside/outside Three

---

[5] For example, see: Wiemer (2004).

Evils', disrupting the 'overall direction' of history because they challenge narratives of equality in *Zhonghua Minzu*. These shifting security discourses articulate China's boundaries by highlighting different identities to be excluded, but these shifts are concealed by contemporary narratives of timelessness. Historicising these shifts reveals the contingency of China's identity and security, which shapes Uyghur resistance to nation-building because the inclusion it offers is ambivalent and frequently changes. Johnston (2003) and Callahan (2012) have shown how the CCP's foreign policy is organised around and shaped by China's confrontation with its domestic frontiers. In Xinjiang, the reverse is also true. As discussed in Chapter 1, the CCP always understood Xinjiang through a geopolitical prism and originally conceived its peoples' identities through their role in China's 'strategic chess game'. How Uyghur identity fits into *Zhonghua Minzu* was a much later concern and accelerated with the growth of cultural nationalism under Hu Jintao. The current official *Zhonghua Minzu* narrative requires squeezing many historical shifts in representation into a securitised framework of 5,000 years of unbroken civilisation, culminating in China's domestic unity and global 'responsible power' status.

Official explanations of Uyghur unrest have dramatically shifted over time to perform different Chinas and different threats to its identity-security. Contrary to claims of unity and social contentment following the Cultural Revolution and constant denials of the early 1990s, it was 1996 before the Party declared it had a long-term problem with 'domestic splittists' (Dwyer, 2005, p.52). Following this denial, the 'smiling, patriotic Uyghurs and Tibetans of the 1980s' gave way to the disgruntled, 'backward' separatists of the late 1990s (Gladney, 2004, p.364). The peaceful, multicultural China of the 1980s became a socialist state struggling against ethnic 'splittists' in the 1990s, and now, a 5,000-year-old civilisation battling Islamic and Western influences in the twenty-first century. The case presented by official documents and media reporting in Xinjiang is generally characterised by scholars as inconsistent and lacking evidence or independent corroboration.[6] No Uyghur group has publicly supported violence (Millward, 2004, p.30). The consensus among Xinjiang specialists is that many incidents of violence challenge the authority of the CCP but there is little if any evidence of transnational terrorism: 'few if any of these incidents resemble the premeditated, targeted, and substantial acts of violence one usually associates with international terrorist groups' (Roberts, 2012, pp.3–4). The political violence recorded during the 1990s included numerous incidents of unrest – riots, protests, assaults on individual security forces and border posts, and most notably the Baren 1990 and Ghulja 1997

---

[6] For example, see: Bovingdon (2004a; 2010); Millward (2004); Roberts (2012).

incidents. These events drew scholarly attention to changing patterns of discontent in the region and have been effectively catalogued.[7] This literature emphasises how official explanations of violence in Xinjiang are less concerned with facts than political goals. However, it overlooks how official representation of violence constitutes 'facts' that shape policy construction and resistance to its goals.

Inter-ethnic violence should always be analysed from different perspectives and no official political documents should be taken at face value. However, the power of official discourse shapes the recording of history and which 'facts' become taken for granted as the background framing of events. Massive impromptu protests in 1985 against discriminatory graffiti at Xinjiang University eventually attracted thousands of Uyghurs onto Ürümchi's streets, shouting slogans against Han in-migration, birth control policies, and nuclear testing (Millward, 2004, p.8). Ismayil Ähmäd, then Regional Government Chair, was subsequently removed from his post and 'kicked upstairs' for suggesting Uyghurs should be given employment before more Han were allowed to migrate to Xinjiang (Bovingdon, 2004a, p.7). Slogans and placards waved at incidents during the 1990s suggest ethnicised resistance against government policy rather than calls for establishment of an Islamic Caliphate, as official Chinese sources assert. For example, slogans such as 'independence, freedom, and sovereignty for Xinjiang' and 'Hans out of Xinjiang' were the most vocal and typical of these incidents (Bovingdon, 2004a, p.7). During the Baren 'uprising' of 1990, a group of Uyghurs in southwest Xinjiang attacked a border police station and stole firearms after protests in a mosque against family planning spiralled into a riot (Bovingdon, 2004a, p.8; 2010, pp.123–125; Dillon, 2002, pp.62–65). The occurrence of the Baren incident was publicly denied at the time but since 9/11, the party-state's narrative describes the 'uprising' as a 'turning point' and a 'wake-up call' for the CCP in its handling of the 'Xinjiang problem' (State Council, 2002; Bekri, 2008, sec. 3). At the time, General Secretary Jiang Zemin referred to Deng Xiaoping's speech on unity following the cultural revolution, saying the 'biggest mistake of these last few years was relaxing education' (Jiang, 1990b, pp.318–319). The Baren uprising sparked reversals of the brief post–Cultural Revolution liberalisation of speech in Xinjiang as mosque closures and arrests of Imams increased (Bovingdon, 2010, pp.87–88). Security services conducted mass seizures of Uyghur music tapes, and all lyrics then had to be vetted by a CCP censorship committee before being recorded or performed (Bovingdon, 2010, p.94). The struggle against separatism shifted focus from armed organisation to ideology and everyday identity.

---

[7] For example, see: Bovingdon (2004a; 2010); Dillon (2002); Millward (2004); Roberts (2012); Smith (1999).

The party-state narrates progressive turning points in its security approach from the 'wake-up call' of Baren in 1990 to victory against 'splittists' in Ghulja/Yining in 1997 (State Council, 2002). The 1997 Ghulja/Yining incident is described by scholars on Xinjiang and is commemorated by Uyghur diaspora groups as a massacre of Uyghurs protesting for the right to promote education against alcoholism at traditional Uyghur gatherings (*mesrep*). Police fired on protestors two hours into a peaceful march for the release of an arbitrarily detained leader of the *Mesrep* movement (Bovingdon, 2010, pp.125–126). Uyghur testimonies explain that protestors were rounded up indiscriminately by security services, forced into the local football stadium, and hosed down in sub-zero temperatures.[8] By 1998, General Secretary Jiang Zemin announced that a militarised 'Strike Hard' (*yanda* 严打) campaign was necessary in the 'long term task to fight splittism' (Dwyer, 2005, p.52). Baren and Ghulja were turning points in official representations of identity and security, articulating different Chinas, from a unified multi-*minzu* nation to a nation under threat from ethnic separatism. Violent incidents of the 1990s, such as Baren and Ghulja, saw many small-scale fights, disputes with officials, and single-issue protests rapidly and spontaneously 'snowball', attracting large numbers of protestors with varied grievances. The mass nature of protest suggested widespread discontent in Xinjiang rather than organised, premeditated violence (Bovingdon, 2004a, p.7). Unlike protests in ethnic majority regions, most disaffection in Xinjiang, as Bovingdon (2002) argues, centres on claims of cultural inequality in the PRC. Uyghur discontent with their unequal position in China threatens the party state's current *Zhonghua Minzu* narrative that insists minorities have always been Chinese and enjoy equality in the PRC. This cultural discontent is officially reframed as 'terrorism' and functions as the assumed 'facts' upon which any policy approach or identity narrative must be built.

Zhonghua Minzu was reconfigured from a nation enjoying unity and security to one engaged in 'long-term struggle'[9] against existential threats in a few short years. Discourses of danger in Xinjiang shifted from unity in the 1980s, to domestic 'ethnic splittism' in the late 1990s, then to international, religious 'terrorism' since September 11. After 9/11, the party-state reconfigured China's boundaries, claiming it has been fighting organised terrorist groups in Xinjiang, linked to Al-Qaeda and other transnational terrorist networks, such as the Islamic Movement of Uzbekistan and even Hizb ut-Tahrir (Bekri, 2008; State Council, 2002). This shift in signification enabled a re-representation of disaffected Uyghurs to 'Islamic terrorists' (Smith, 2006,

[8] For example, see sources using Uyghur testimonies: Dillon (2002); Millward (2007).
[9] On the 'long-term' *minzu* problem, see: XEP (2009); XUAR Dept of Information (2009); Pan (2008).

p.132; Starr, 2004, p.15). Jiang Zemin's famous 1996 'strike hard' statement made no mention of religion or extremism (Dwyer, 2005, p.52). When the State Council (2002) paper on East Turkestan was published, all framings of the 1990s violence were altered and 'splittists' were repackaged as 'religious fundamentalists' and 'international terrorist forces' 'inside and outside Chinese territory'. The 'Strike Hard' campaign's objective was changed to defeat of 'The Three Evils' of 'terrorism, separatism, and extremism' as part of the global 'war on terror' (Starr, 2004, p.15; Bekri, 2008; 2009a). The Chinese Foreign Ministry announced in 2002 that 'we should be cracking down on these terrorists as part of the international struggle against terrorism' (Dwyer, 2005, p.52). The Ghulja/Yining incident, for example, was re-represented as the 'victory' of a 'long-term struggle against *terrorists*' (Bekri, 2008, sec. 3). The existential threat to China was no longer domestic disunity but global-level Islamism. The party-state represents Xinjiang and Uyghur identities not simply as a source of danger to China but to the world by linking 'the Three Evils' to Al-Qaeda, the Taliban, and now ISIS. With the events of 9/11 and entry to the World Trade Organization (WTO) in 2001, the CCP's identity narratives present China as a 'responsible power' and agent of global security in its struggle against the 'inhuman' 'inside/outside Three Evils'.

The shift in representation of Uyghur discontent from 'domestic splittism' to 'international terrorism' appeals to global anti-Muslim narratives, which re-emerged following collapse of the Soviet enemy and represent Muslims as culturally inferior, backward threats to modernity (Said, 1997, p.xviii). Anti-Muslim narratives circulated more widely after 9/11 and enabled celebrated Chinese authors, such as Pan Zhiping, to write without supporting evidence that 'China's Xinjiang and outside its borders see the forces of the scum Bin Laden with the evil "East Turkestan" terrorist forces threaten the security of the life and property of the nation and the people' (Pan, 2008, p.2). Arbitrarily collocating Uyghur identity with ETIM / East Turkestan (*dongtu*) and then with Al-Qaeda represents Uyghurs as enmeshed in transnational networks of 'Islamic terrorism', seeking to establish a threatening Islamic caliphate. Unqualified representations of the few Uyghurs imprisoned in Guantanamo Bay as Islamic terrorists exemplified this approach. The Guantanamo Uyghurs were identified by the CCP as members of ETIM inside China but linked to Al-Qaeda outside (Roberts, 2012, pp.8–9). However, interrogation by US security services of the Guantanamo Uyghurs revealed they had never heard of Osama Bin-Laden until arrival at Guantanamo, they had only fired one gun in their lives, and while they declared China as 'their enemies' they expressed genuine support for the United States, not for Pan-Islamism (Roberts, 2012, pp.9–10). The Guantanamo Uyghurs were released by the United States because they were not terrorists and had no links to Al-Qaeda. Few states were willing to risk their relations with the CCP and they were subsequently re-settled in Albania, Bermuda, and Palau (BBC, 2006; NYT, 2007). These conclusions were never reported in China, yet their cases inform official narratives of Islamic terrorism in Xinjiang. The party-state's internationalisation of domestic disputes in Xinjiang emerged again in August 2011 when the Foreign Ministry and Kashgar city officials held an international media conference to blame outbreaks of protests and violence in Khotan and Kashgar on Pakistan-trained members of ETIM (Zenn, 2011). However, the following month, a spokesperson for the XUAR government admitted attackers were loosely organised using 'homemade weapons' with no links to 'extremists' in Pakistan or elsewhere (Spegele, 2011). The Foreign Ministry refused to comment on details and continued to arbitrarily link local grievances to external terrorist threats, saying that 'in Xinjiang and Central Asia, there have been a series of violent terrorist incidents in recent years. They have *all* involved domestic and foreign collaboration' (Zenn, 2011).

The CCP's confrontation with China's domestic and foreign frontiers deeply shape one another as it embeds itself in exclusionary global narratives to resolve domestic exclusions. The timing of the State Council's (2002) document seized on the opportunity to gain international legitimacy and immunity from criticism, for its policies in Xinjiang. The United States and the UN subsequently recognised the hitherto unknown ETIM as a transnational terrorist organisation linked to Al-Qaeda and China became a global player in the 'war on terror' (Roberts, 2012, p.3). In 2009, China signed multi-billion-dollar contracts for bilateral natural resource extraction with Cambodia, Malaysia, Thailand, and Pakistan through the mechanism of the Shanghai Co-operation Organisation (SCO) in partnership with Kazakhstan. These deals were all signed after these states deported Uyghur asylum seekers who had fled China after July 2009, in breach of the 1951 UN convention's principles of non-refoulment (HRW, 2009b; 2011; RFA, 2011b; UAA, 2012). These Uyghurs have since disappeared, been executed, or been sentenced to prison in closed trials (HRW, 2009b; 2011; RFA, 2011b; UAA, 2012). The CCP devotes vast economic resources to bilateral relations in Asia that enable control of Uyghur movement outside China's borders. In many senses, the CCP's foreign policy has successfully 'harmonised the world' (Callahan, 2012). The CCP's identity-security discourses have shaped global understanding of its Xinjiang policies as a battlefield in the global 'war on terror'.

The CCP redirects China's 'responsible power' status and global struggles against terrorism inward, reproducing ethno-spatial boundaries within Xinjiang between more and less modern, more and less secure, and more and less Chinese regions. Xinjiang, south of the Tian Shan Mountains, largely consists of the extremely arid Tarim basin. Party-state documents and Han Chinese in Xinjiang refer to southern Xinjiang as the 'southern frontier'

(*Nanjiang* 南疆).[10] *Nanjiang* is generally understood to be inhabited by Uyghurs, whereas the lush grasslands north of the Tian Shan, which roll into Mongolia to the east and Kazakhstan to the west, are understood as home of Kazakh and Mongolian 'nomadic ethnic minorities'. In official policy documents, Xinjiang is spatially divided into north and south, marking *nanjiang* as a particularly 'backward' Uyghur region with problems of separatism and terrorism.[11] Most incidents of violence publicised by the party-state and attributed to 'The Three Evils' are centred in Kashgar and other Uyghur-majority areas in the south such as Khotan, Aksu, and Kucha. Former regional party chair Wang Lequan stated in a press conference at the end of April 2009, 'We must fully realise the strategic value and actual meaning of accelerating the development of *Nanjiang*' (Wang, 2009a). Wang explainedthat the Uyghur cities of 'Khotan and Kashgar are on the frontline in the struggle against the Three Evils' and that 'guaranteeing stability and the mission of defending and consolidating the frontier are heavy tasks' (Wang, 2009a). Wang (2009) then explained the 'actual meaning' of 'modernisation' was to defeat 'The Three Evils' by overcoming ethnic 'backwardness' through policies such as expansion of Mandarin-medium education and demolition of Kashgar Old Town. President Xi Jinping continued this narrative in key policy speeches, announcing that there can be 'no compromise' in the 'leapfrog development' strategy to defeat East Turkestan and create long-term security in *nanjiang* (Xi, 2012, pp.314–318). Uyghurs who live in Uyghur areas are targeted as the most dangerously backward cultural frontier of *Zhonghua Minzu* because they are inside China but not yet of it.

Local development policies in Xinjiang are mediated through grand narratives of China's 'responsible power' status and ethnic boundaries, which represent Uyghurs in perpetual need of conversion through 'modernisation' to overcome their threatening 'backwardness'. The Shule County local government, adjacent to Kashgar, announced in April 2009 that all levels of government and public media must promote a patriotic, collectivist, socialist, and ethnic unity education system based on 'scientific development' using Mandarin Chinese as the medium of instruction as part of the fight against 'The Three Evils' (Shule County Government, 2009). The 2008 speech by Regional Government Chairperson Nur Bekri used in these classes, outlined that terrorism in Xinjiang was a problem of development and cultural evolution:

In Xinjiang – a remote, relatively backward ethnic minority area with complicated regional and border circumstances – only by ceaselessly quickening the pace of

---

[10] All interviewees used this spatial division both informally and in formal situations such as public lectures, language classes, and banquets.
[11] For example, see: Bekri (2008); XEP (2009).

economic and social development and greatly improving the people's life thereby allowing each ethnic group to enjoy the rewards of economic reform ... can the centripetal force of all ethnic groups be strengthened towards the party and government from the foundation, and identification with the socialist motherland. In addition, only in the above circumstances can we reduce the breathing space for 'The Three Evils', consolidate the foundation in the masses of the party, and realise lasting peace and stability. (Bekri, 2008)

Concrete policy-making is embedded in the party-state's logics of cultural evolution, whereby development and identity are intertwined facets of progress. Uyghurs are deprived of 'breathing space' to identify themselves and the 'backward' areas where 'separatism' thrives are always named as Uyghur majority cities in south-west Xinjiang.[12] The north of Xinjiang – ironically including the Han-majority capital, Ürümchi, the site of the largest outbreak of violence in Xinjiang's modern history in 2009 – is relationally represented as prosperous and secure against the arduous southern Uyghur frontier. The party-state thus produces the safe, modernising, Han-populated, urban insideness of Ürümchi against the dangerous, backward, Uyghur-populated, rural outside-ness of Southern Xinjiang. These discourses of danger demarcate internal boundaries within internal boundaries (*Nanjiang* within *Xinjiang* within *Zhonghua Minzu*), that are intertwined with external boundary demarcation between China and the threats of the West and Islam.

The 'zero-sum political struggle of life or death' for China is a struggle *for* a shared Chinese identity *against* the Turkic and Islamic 'inside/outside Three Evils' (XEP, 2009, p.15). 'Terrorism' automatically de-legitimises resistance and political opposition, particularly in the context of the global 'war on terror'. China's problems in Xinjiang can be traced to at least 1759, but the 'war on terror' has enabled the CCP's global legitimisation and incontestability of its securitisation of identity. East Turkestan (*Dongtu*) is impossible to discuss without connotations of security threats from 'outside' China, paradoxically highlighting the Uyghur as foreign while presenting their domestic Chinese status as a security matter. The collocation between East Turkestan and 'inside/outside Three Evils' links discontent Uyghurs inside China or those who frame their identity as Central Asian with external threats. The CCP ironically internationalises Uyghur unrest in claims that Turkic ethnic enemies inside China are supported from outside by violent 'Islamic terrorists' and Western 'enemies of China', using democracy and human rights as 'excuses' to 'split' and 'contain China's rise' (Bekri, 2008; State Council, 2009a; 2009b; XEP, 2009). The Uyghur (inside) is continuously marked through 'dangers' of non-Chinese cultural practices (Turkic language and Islam) in collaboration with 'Islamic terrorists' and the traditional enemy of

---

[12] For example, see: Bekri (2008; 2009b); State Council (2009b); XEP (2009).

'Western' imperialism (outside). The production of enemies appears to create a singular, homogenous China in a struggle against external forces but its production of contingent inside/outside enemies on the ambivalent frontier reproduces an ambivalent *Zhonghua Minzu*.

'East Turkestan' in Uyghur Identity and Insecurity

This section examines the productive effects of Chinese nation-building by examining Uyghur responses to its narratives using the Turk category as resistance to *Zhonghua Minzu* identity. It analyses popular deployment and circulation of the Turk category using detailed, semi-structured interviews with Uyghurs and discourse analysis of Nurmehemmet Yasin's short story 'Wild Pigeon' ('Yawa Kepter'). Uyghurs resist nation-building from within its logics by turning its grammar of fixed civilisational boundaries against itself. Uyghurs re-perform official civilisational boundaries to reassert cultural difference on their own terms and position themselves as outside but not inferior to *Zhonghua Minzu*. The epistemic violence required to transform Uyghur identities and tell them whom they must not be produces identity-insecurity for Uyghurs. Despite contemporary attempts to co-opt the meaning of Xinjiang's 1940s rebellions as the 'Three Districts Revolution' against the GMD to preserve Chinese civilisational continuity, the memories of the East Turkestan Republics have never been erased from public memory. The party-state's codification of East Turkestan has enabled new forms of resistance, or what Judith Butler called the 'taking up of the tools where they lie' (Butler, 2007, p.185). Public resistance takes place within the logics of official discourse and the 'orbit of the compulsion to repeat', so that political agency is then 'located within the possibility of a variation on that repetition' (Butler, 2007, p.185). Uyghurs embrace their otherness within China by adopting the nation-building language of civilisational boundaries between *Zhonghua Minzu* and the Turkic world to articulate their own identity and security narratives.

Prior to the establishment of the autonomous region in 1955, the imperial naming of Xinjiang ('new frontier') was debated within the CCP. Although the name implies the region is an imperial possession, it was agreed that changing it would raise questions from minorities and other states about Xinjiang's shifting position with the arrival of the PLA. Deng Xiaoping and Xi Jinping's father, Xi Zhongxun, wrote to Mao Zedong in the early 1950s to warn the party leadership that Han chauvinism was 'the fundamental problem' in Xinjiang and that ethnic minorities, particularly Uyghurs as the 'core group' (*zhuti minzu* 主体民族), may dislike the name (Deng et al., 1953, p.97). However, they recommended retaining the name and including the Uyghur ethnonym in the XUAR title as a compromise to avoid 'all manner of conjecture' about its status from inside and outside China (Deng et al., 1953, p.100).

Today, the colonial undertones of Xinjiang mean most Uyghurs use the name uneasily, while nationalist movements refute it altogether, and scholars of Xinjiang use it to avoid political controversy (Roberts, 2012, p.3). Diaspora-led organisations campaigning for autonomy and human rights in Xinjiang, the Uyghur Human Rights Project (UHRP), the East Turkestan Information Center (ETIC), and the World Uyghur Congress (WUC), use the name East Turkestan to emphasise, as Deng Xiaoping and Xi Zhongcun had, that the region was primarily populated by Turkic peoples until 1949. The integration of Turkic-speaking, sedentary peoples of southern Xinjiang with the nomadic peoples of the north and the subsequent establishment of the XUAR in 1955 provided Uyghurs with a more distinct and bounded 'territorial frame' for their grievances and political aspirations (Bovingdon, 2004a, p.3). Uyghurs adopt and adapt this 'territorial frame' to resist civilisational narratives of cultural inferiority and the politics of cultural exclusion in the PRC. The more the CCP narrates *Zhonghua Minzu* as 5,000 years of *Chinese* civilisation built on *Hua* culture, the more power and meaning it gives to Uyghurs' territorial framing because it excludes Xinjiang as a frontier of *Hua* civilisation. Civilisational narratives give Uyghurs an official vocabulary that legitimises their pre-existing framings of East Turkestan as a parallel, colonised historic civilisation.

The writings of Uyghur historians frequently respond to official histories of Xinjiang as an indivisible component of the 5,000-year-old Chinese nation by re-asserting the ancient Turkic origins of Uyghurs (Bovingdon, 2004b, p.355). In *Uyghurlar*, the famous Uyghur historian, Turghun Almas, asserted that Xinjiang has always been part of Central Asia and located Uyghur history in broader frameworks of Turkic history. Turghun responded to party-state narratives that Xinjiang's history begins with the Han dynasty, emphasising Uyghur indigeneity and repeating popular Uyghur perspectives that their ancestors inhabited the region prior to establishment of Han dynasty military outposts (Rudelson, 1997; pp.155–157; Millward, 2007, p.344). Uyghur identity narratives frame Xinjiang on its own terms, rather than a frontier of Chinese civilisation, emphasising cultural and political connections to Turkic-speaking Central Asia. Framing cultural difference through civilisational, rather than simply national or ethnic narratives, re-performs Chinese nation-building narratives, which position Xinjiang as an inalienable, timeless frontier of *Zhonghua Minzu*. Turghun Almas remained under house arrest from 1991 for publishing this civilisational framing of Uyghur identity in *Uyghurlar*, until his sudden and unexplained death in detention on September 11, 2001. Publication of *Uyghurlar* instigated a week-long conference to condemn the book, followed by public burnings (Bovingdon, 2010, p.97). One young businessman discussed the book with me, laughing aloud and saying, 'This *is* Central Asia. Han only came here recently.' China did not invent East

Turkestan. Nevertheless, the party-state gives the category profound meaning as a grammar of resistance, which Uyghurs deploy when reading themselves 'between the lines' of China's nation-building project, as Homi Bhabha (2009) termed it, as a parallel alternative to Chinese civilisation.

Despite the illegality of the term 'East Turkestan', Uyghur interviewees used it whenever discussing pre-1949 history and deployed the 'Turk' category in the present, to position themselves outside *Zhonghua Minzu*. During interviews and conversations with students from Ürümchi, Turpan, Kashgar, and Korla, 'we are Turks, we are not Chinese' was a standard interjection in discussions of identity, particularly if they felt I didn't understand Xinjiang's history. One typical response in private to the question 'Where are you from?', received from an Ürümchi-born, early 40s, male 'black' taxi driver,[13] was, 'I am a Turk, Uyghurs are Turks. We should have had our own independent country.' One middle-aged, female university lecturer explicitly referred to *The Fifty Whys* in the privacy of her own home, to explain that 'ethnic unity is just party nonsense. We are Turks.' Interviewees from all social classes, from *getihu* (个体户) entrepreneurs[14] to intellectuals, articulated a Turkic identity whenever discussing the history of *Zhonghua Minzu* or by interjecting with the topic themselves. Several Uyghur intellectuals explained they used Xinjiang instead of Turkestan solely to avoid 'offending the Han'. When I asked Uyghur interviewees, 'What was Xinjiang called before the Chinese arrived?', one typical response came from a young male student from Turpan, who told me, 'This is East Turkestan.' One middle-aged male Uyghur language teacher would only say the 'old name for Xinjiang', even in private, refusing to specify the name because in his own words, 'I have to work for the government.' Uyghur language is Turkic and their histories entwined with Central Asia with or without *Zhonghua Minzu*. Nevertheless, Uyghurs produce the contemporary political significance of the Turk category by interacting with and deploying the party-state's official nation-building vocabulary. Uyghurs re-perform *Zhonghua Minzu* as a colonial project. The Turk is narrated as a parallel, timeless civilisational identity built on shared history and language that should be recognised, like Chinese civilisation, through statehood.

China's 'opening and reform era' (1978–) has been framed by the CCP and Chinese Studies as heralding more social and intellectual freedom than any period of modern Chinese history. However, tolerance for diversity in some

---

[13] During fieldwork in Ürümchi, almost all legally registered taxis were owned and operated by Han. Many Uyghur drivers complained of discrimination and their response was to drive a 'black taxi' (*heiche*), an unlicensed car that discretely picks up passengers and is not taxed.

[14] *Getihu* (个体户), the social class of self-employed, small-scale entrepreneurs, emerging after 1978.

areas has coincided with securitisation and accelerated crackdowns in others. Xinjiang's Strike Hard campaigns, first initiated in 1996, criminalised literary works that represent a glorious Turkic past, now lying in ruins and giving way to a gloomy present as existential threats to China (Friederich, 2007, p.95). The 2002 party-state slogan 'wipe out pornography and strike at political publications' (*saohuang jizheng*) exemplified the tactical conflation of ordinary criminals, political activists, and writers as 'separatists', who were later re-packaged as 'terrorists'. The slogan's pronouncement coincided with public burning of pornographic materials alongside Uyghur history books, clampdowns on campaigns for Uyghur language education, and arrests of suspected terrorists, which were all explained together through the prism of national security (Becquelin, 2004b, p.45). The arrests of poet Tursunjan Amat and historian Tohti Tunyaz on immediate return from completing doctoral research on Uyghur history at the University of Tokyo show that how Uyghur writers *think* about Uyghur-ness has been treated as an existential security matter throughout 'opening and reform'.[15] There was a de facto policy shift from censoring Uyghur writers in the 1990s to imprisoning them in the twenty-first century, initially under the auspices of Jiang Zemin's idea of 'terrorism in the spiritual form' (Bovingdon, 2010, pp.99–100). The conflation of peaceful and violent dissent uses the 'spectre of terrorism' to silence opposition to monolingual language policies and restrictions on religious practices, which 'criminalises' Uyghur ethnicity (Becquelin, 2004, p.45). The party-state's representation of popular Uyghur identity narratives as the 'East Turkestan' threat enabled arbitrary detainment, disappearances, and prison sentences for writing poetry as terrorism.

If we turn from Xinjiang to the urban public spaces of Eastern China as a contrast, novels such as Chan Kuanchong's *The Fat Years* (2009) exemplify how artistic resistance to the party-state has often been more tolerated in the 'opening and reform era'. *The Fat Years* was banned in China but copies gradually flowed in from Hong Kong, and it became openly discussed amongst mainland journalists (Callahan, 2013, p.92). In *The Fat Years*, Chinese citizens are drugged by the party-state to make them happy and content akin to the role of soma in Aldous Huxley's seminal dystopian novel, *Brave New World*. The story opens with one character questioning the matter to be told by his friend, 'Just forget it ... look after yourself' and 'There's no country in the world as good as China' (Chan, 2009, pp.27 & 33). Chan's politics are ambiguous, but he openly acknowledges that China's golden age depends on state violence to achieve its goals (Callahan, 2013, p.97). Ai Weiwei, the dissident artist, went further, calling this Beijing's 'pretend smile' where people's external

---

[15] See Bovingdon (2010), chapter 4.

happiness is enforced to hide corrupt political structures and a lack of social responsibility (CNN, 2007). The red line of censorship is deliberately vague in contemporary China, but dissent is more tolerated when local or private than when movements, such as Falun Gong, have national appeal and they are equated with sabotage of China (Shue, 2004, p.41). Nevertheless, novels such as *The Fat Years* openly critique the Chinese political system and are treated with suspicion but are not subject to security discourses or warnings about the 'enemies of China'. Literary critiques of official politics do face bans, coercion, and even disappearances as seen in the mass arrests of Hong Kong publishers in 2016. However, critiques by Uyghurs are not treated as criminal or dissident activities that threaten public order. Their writings are elevated beyond politics and targeted as terrorist threats to China's existence because their dissatisfaction is a threat to the party-state's *Zhonghua Minzu* ethno-hierarchy. The threat of the Uyghur is countered by the securitisation of *Zhonghua Minzu*, which only perpetuates cycles of racialisation and violence, because it justifies ethnically targeted coercive measures against Uyghur identity.

'Wild Pigeon' ('Yawa Kepter'), an allegorical short story by freelance writer Nurmuhemmet Yasin, illustrates the coercive exclusion of Uyghur identity narratives as existential threats and the relations between Chinese state power and popular Uyghur resistance. 'Yawa Kepter' tells the tale of a wild pigeon who chooses to commit suicide rather than sacrifice his freedom and live under the yolk of humankind and their hordes of 'tamed pigeons' (Yasin, 2005; Laogai Research Foundation, 2008; PEN, 2013). Following the story's publication in the autumn 2004 issue of the *Kashgar Literature Journal*, Nurmuhemmet Yasin was arrested in November 2004 and all copies of the journal were recalled by the authorities (CECC, 2005). Nurmuhemmet was subsequently charged with 'inciting splittism' at a closed trial in February 2005 and convicted to 10 years' imprisonment in Xinjiang No. 1 Jail, a re-education through labour camp (*laogai*) (CECC, 2005; Laogai Research Foundation, 2008; PEN, 2013). Kuras Sayin, the journal editor, was jailed for 3 years for allowing the story to be published (Bovingdon, 2010, p.99). The wild pigeon is told by tamed pigeons not to disrupt the existing social order, echoing key themes of *The Fat Years* ('forget it ... just look after yourself'), but the pigeon's fictional unhappiness is officially conceptualised as a real-life act of separatist violence. The charge of 'inciting splittism' securitises *Zhonghua Minzu* against the threat of Uyghur identity, in the guise of a pigeon who wants to fly freely. Amnesty International and PEN campaigns for Nurmuhemmet's release simply describe him as a 'writer of children's stories' (AI, 2015; CECC, 2005; PEN, 2013). The story is clearly allegorical but if the reader is unaware that Uyghurs understand life in China through these themes, 'Yawa Kepter' would be read as a whimsical fable about the ups and downs of life in the animal kingdom.

'Wild Pigeon' illustrates how the securitisation of *Zhonghua Minzu* shapes popular resistance in Xinjiang. The Uyghur historian Dolkun Kamberi translated 'Wild Pigeon' into English, explaining that it met 'widespread acclaim among the Uyghur people' because of its 'strong portrayal of a people deeply unhappy with life under Beijing's rule' (Yasin, 2005). 'Wild Pigeon' is widely perceived as an allegorical echo of Uyghur concerns about the loss of language and identity under the party-state. A group of elders tell a youthful wild pigeon that 'the soul of the entire pigeon community has already disappeared', but they have forgotten how this occurred. The disappearance of the soul of the pigeon community articulates widespread Uyghur perspectives that Chinese nation-building is an assimilative project to eliminate Uyghur identity and history. One interpretation is that the wild pigeons represent Uyghurs in the Central Asian states outside China's acculturating influence (Bovingdon, 2010, p.100). However, the story is also a commentary on how the Uyghur-China boundary has created newer boundaries within Xinjiang between Uyghurs educated in their own language (*minkaomin*) and those educated in Mandarin (*minkaohan*). The wild pigeon is unable to understand those pigeons that have been tamed by humans because they speak a different 'mother-tongue'. This cultural confusion between the pigeons reflects and echoes Uyghur concerns about loss of mother-tongue under Mandarin-medium education where all Uyghurs essentially become *minkaohan*.

The tamed pigeons explain to the wild pigeon that humans keep them in a 'cage to feed us'. They insist that this is the right order of things but that 'no pigeon among us is permitted to object to this arrangement'. The tamed elders admonish the wild pigeon, asserting that all pigeons should be 'satisfied with what they have'. However, the wild pigeon, dissatisfied with his position in this order, describes the cage as 'supremely clever in its cruelty' because it allows 'ample view of the freedoms denied to him – with no hope of regaining them'. The visible inequality between pigeon and humans, and gifts of material survival in exchange for freedom, comments on Han-Uyghur inequality in contemporary Xinjiang, justified through ethnocentric historical narratives on their 'mutually complementary economy'. When the wild pigeon says, 'By caging my body, they hope to enslave my soul', the material force of inequality is intimately related to identity-security. The cage attempts to forcibly eliminate Uyghur culture through the hierarchical structure of *Zhonghua Minzu* where pigeons can eat as animals thanks to their human masters but can only gaze upon the freedom enjoyed by humans outside. The wild pigeon's mother represents what Jay Dautcher (2009) called Uyghur chthonic identity, by telling the young pigeon 'they want to chase us from the land we have occupied for thousands of years ... they want to change the character of our heritage ... strip us of our memory and identity'. The pigeon's mother resists the nation-building narrative that Han have always occupied Xinjiang. She frames humans as outsiders because they seek to transform pigeons and re-write history, thus re-performing Uyghur identity as excluded by Chinese nation-building.

'For the sake of our motherland', the young pigeon is released by his mother but is later captured by humans. The articulation of threats to Uyghur identity is most obvious when the wild pigeon is finally given the choice of 'freedom' or death by his mother, who offers him a poisoned strawberry. The pigeon chooses to 'die freely' to 'restore the honour of our flock'. This choice performs Uyghur identity as existing in an irresolvable state of existential crisis facing the threat of assimilation into *Zhonghua Minzu*. The pigeons wait to die while living in cruel captivity that offers hierarchical inclusion and unequal economic development ('in a cage to feed us') in exchange for giving up their ancient civilisation. 'Wild Pigeon' is a banal, everyday form of resistance to Chinese nation-building. It offers no direct political commentary but allegorically represents Uyghur identity under threat from the party-state's ethnocentric writing of history and assimilative language policies. The story resists the power of nation-building, not by rejecting but by speaking through its logics of timeless civilisation with a counter-securitising performance of Uyghur chthonic identity. Xinjiang is framed as the homeland of Turkic civilisation because Turkic peoples occupied Xinjiang before the arrival of Chinese civilisation during the Han dynasty. The direct political effect of this 'everyday resistance' is unquantifiable but illustrates how the idea of Uyghurs as a nation outside *Zhonghua Minzu* circulates despite the personal security risks (Bovingdon, 2010, p.205). If we gauge popular sentiment towards Chinese nation-building in Xinjiang through these examples of popular culture and unofficial discourse, then it is failing. Uyghurs understand the tensions within the logics of *Zhonghua Minzu* and use them against themselves to reinforce the cultural difference reproduced in official framings of China as a Han-led civilisation.

Conclusions

State-centric security discourses in global politics dominate our thinking of who we are by drawing the boundaries of *who* and *what* are to be secured: us inside versus them out there (Walker, 1990, pp.6 & 13). However, inside and outside do not always easily map on to contemporary territorial borders. The securitisation of *Zhonghua Minzu* in the CCP's 'East Turkestan' narrative reflects, to an extent, the state's 'internal security dilemma', as theorised by Paul Roe (1999) and applied by Michael Clarke (2007b) to Xinjiang. The party-state struggles to integrate two ethnic groups engaged in conflict, who both see further integration of the other as a threat to their identity. However, China's securitisation practices do not simply reflect pre-existing, objective boundaries but are central to a conscious nation-building strategy to produce identities that fit contemporary borders. The CCP's nation-building project in Xinjiang demarcates the boundaries of *Zhonghua Minzu* by articulating *who* and *what* constitute a threat to its existence, thus external to these boundaries. The identity articulated through securitisation does not objectively reflect pre-existing borders or Han-Uyghur boundaries but produces the hierarchical boundaries of *Zhonghua Minzu*. The party-state devotes vast resources to narrating identity and insecurity through education and the media that produce ethnic boundaries between the active, nation-building Han nucleus and 'simple, uncomplicated' ethnic minorities but contained within Chinese civilisation. The party-state then frames Uyghur expressions of identity as security threats because they transgress these boundaries by contradicting the inferior identity assigned to them.

On China's 'new frontier', the state's security discourses produce self-other boundaries through an interweaving of civilisational and nationalist narratives because the identified threats to China exist in the past (barbarians), present (dissatisfied ethnic minorities), and future (separatism and terrorism) in an ambiguous position inside and outside *Zhonghua Minzu*. The first section of this chapter showed how the party-state's East Turkestan narrative articulates Uyghur-ness as a threat inside China's territorial borders but outside its cultural boundaries. The identification of internal Turkic ethnic enemies, supported by Islamic terrorists and Western enemies from outside, projects external territorial borders on to internal ethnic boundaries, making the internal and external indivisible. The party-state's security discourse excludes Uyghur identity by arbitrarily linking unbefitting internal characteristics (language and religion) to external categories of danger (Islam and the West). The East Turkestan narrative is central to Chinese nation-building in Xinjiang because it tells Uyghurs who they must not be (Turks) and who they must become (*Zhonghua Minzu*).

The second section showed how the party-state's explanation of incidents of violence and unrest in Xinjiang ethnicises violence and frames Turkic-Islamic identities as the cause of physical threats to *Zhonghua Minzu*. The party-state's ambivalent inclusion of Xinjiang as a frontier between nation and civilisation and between China and Central Asia ethno-spatially orders the region into sub-regions that are more and less secure, more and less modern, and more and less Chinese. The CCP's securitisation of *Zhonghua Minzu* blurs internal and external boundaries and the domestic and international until rendered indivisible. The CCP's 'domestic' security dilemma in Xinjiang shapes and is shaped by foreign policy goals of becoming a 'strong and prosperous' nation again. Securitisation performances in 'domestic' nation-building narratives link Uyghur non-identification with *Zhonghua Minzu* to ever-present external threats of 'Islamic terrorism', which China, the 'responsible power', must

Conclusions

eliminate. The CCP constructs local development policies around ethno-spatial internal/external boundaries that demarcate between safe Han and dangerous Uyghur regions that promote or threaten China's goals of international power. The party-state's approach to its frontiers is directed outward in foreign policy seeking recognition as a 'responsible power' engaged in its own 'war on terror'.

The party-state has produced the Uyghur as an internal/external security dilemma for China's identity-security. However, the production of China's enemies inside and outside its boundaries on the ambivalent northwestern frontier produces an ambivalent *Zhonghua Minzu*. *Zhonghua Minzu* is at times a rational, technocratic socialist state and at others a mono-ethnic nation built by Han civilisation. The final section of the chapter showed how Uyghurs redeploy tensions between the ongoing attribution of danger, backwardness, and outside-ness to the Turk category and official attempts to include Uyghurs in *Zhonghua Minzu*. Tensions between progressive modernity and timeless culture circulate in most national narratives, but the party-state securitises this ambivalence, which gives Uyghurs a vocabulary of resistance to critique the conceptual inconsistencies of their inferiority in an equal, multi-ethnic *Zhonghua Minzu*. The securitisation of *Zhonghua Minzu* as a timeless civilisation produces civilisational resistance to Chinese nation-building as Uyghurs read "between the lines" of its narratives and identify with a parallel, glorious Turkic past. Uyghur popular culture re-performs the Turk as a civilisational category of identity and reasserts the centrality of those Uyghur cultural practices, which are excluded as threats to *Zhonghua Minzu* (Turkic language and Islam). The next chapter will analyse how these identity-security discourses are publicly disseminated, contributing to insecurity on the ground in the street-level, everyday politics of Ürümchi, following the violence of July 2009.

4   Identity and Insecurity after '7-5'

Introduction

The official China Dream (*Zhongguo meng* 中国梦) of the 'Great Revival' (*weida fuxing* 伟大复兴) narrates a profoundly optimistic story of the Chinese people rising to reverse subjugation by Western powers in a 'century of humiliation' and *return* to their pre-modern, rightful place at the centre of world affairs (Callahan, 2012, p.255). Since the US invasion of Iraq and the 2008 global financial crisis, China's official and public intellectual discourse has been dominated by arguments that global politics has entered a 'post-American century' and China will be a 'new type of superpower', ordering the world through Eastern consent as opposed to Western coercion (Hu, 2012; Zhang, 2012). This optimism conceals the deep pessimism and insecurity at the heart of debates about China's rise and its 'core interests' of maintaining security and producing a shared Chinese identity on its frontiers. While the 2008 Beijing Olympics' slogan ('one-world, one-dream') circulated across official media, riots and inter-ethnic violence exploded in Lhasa, Tibet. The 60th anniversary of the PRC's founding in 2009 was subsequently overshadowed by ethnically targeted violence between Turkic-speaking Muslim Uyghurs and the Han majority in Ürümchi. Since 2009, a shared national identity based on ethnic unity has been officially described as a 'zero-sum political struggle of life or death' and prerequisite to China's rise (XEP, 2009, p.15). In official policy thinking, nightmarish mirror images to the prosperity and power of the Great Revival foretell China's collapse if minorities and Han fail to share this national identity. China wants to be a 'new type of superpower' in order to secure its internal cultural frontiers and it wants to secure these frontiers because it wants to be a new superpower. This chapter moves from the classroom nation-building texts of Chapters 2 and 3 to analyse the productive effects of the boundaries they produce in Ürümchi's street-level politics of the everyday. It analyses the interplay between official Chinese

---

Chapter 4 is a refined version of D. Tobin (n.d.). 'A "Struggle of Life or Death": Han and Uyghur Insecurities on China's North-West Frontier', *The China Quarterly*, 241: 1–23.

identity-security discourses and everyday micro-level security practices before, during, and after the July 2009 violence. The chapter analyses how violence by different ethnic groups was narrated in China's identity and security discourses, and how ethnic relations deteriorated into mass violence amongst ordinary people. It considers 'Who are we?' and 'How can we be secure?' as mutually reinforcing questions that emerge in official representations of violence.

The mutually reinforcing nature of the CCP's goals of global power and securing the identity of its internal frontiers is overlooked in Eurocentric IR, which builds knowledge through domestic/international dichotomies.[1] China specialists have shown how the CCP's approach to domestic and international security is organised around sharp distinctions between a domestic, civilised self and the international, barbaric other (Callahan, 2004, p.27). Official designations of security/danger and self/other *within* the boundaries of China constitute a unified *Zhonghua Minzu* that must secure itself against the threat of Uyghur identity, linked to external security threats. The CCP explains violence in Xinjiang as a 'zero-sum political struggle of life or death' *for* a shared, civilised identity *against* the barbaric 'inside/outside Three Evils' (XEP, 2009, p.15). The referent of security is the party-state's identity narrative that frames alternative identity narratives as existential threats to *Zhonghua Minzu*. The identified threats are Turkic identities inside China supported by 'Islamic terrorists' and Western 'enemy' discourses of democracy and human rights, which are always 'excuses' to 'contain China's rise' (XEP, 2009, State Council, 2009b). Uyghurs are included as Chinese, but their identity is excluded as a source of insecurity. All violence and discontent in the region is attributed to the absence of *Zhonghua Minzu* identity. China's Great Revival and domestic identity narrative of 56 unified *minzu* are mutually constitutive referents of security in which a rising, unified China must be secured against alternative, backward Uyghur identities. What Thomas Mullaney (2011) termed the strange calculus of Chinese nationhood ('55+1') conflates Han and *Zhonghua Minzu* by separating and prioritising the Han over 55 minorities, whose identities are to be contained and transformed as a security matter. Nevertheless, as Bovingdon (2010) has shown, the *minzu* concept enables resistance from below through double use as nation and ethnicity.

Securitisation is a process of cultural governance where states exert power not only though military and economic coercion but also through 'historical practices of representation', which institutionalise self–other boundaries but are never fully controlled by the state (Campbell, 2003, p.57; Callahan, 2007, p.7). The securitisation of *Zhonghua Minzu* essentialises boundaries between

---

[1] For example, see: Mearsheimer (2010); Ikenberry (2014).

self and other by presenting them as natural and as things which must be preserved; otherwise, anarchy ensues. The constitution of danger is dependent on those to whom it is a threat, and state security practices are performative of those identity-boundaries (Campbell, 1998, p.1; Weber, 1998, p.78). However, security often produces insecurity, and securitised identity has different implications for differentially essentialised groups (Chowdhry & Nair, 2004, p.18; Krishna, 1999, p.xxix; Weber & Lacy, 2011, p.1021). Essentialising discourses of identity-security produce security for those who feel included at the cost of insecurity for those whose identities are excluded. Understanding these asymmetrical dynamics, which exacerbate cycles of violence, requires deeper consideration of popular 'vernacular' insecurities.[2] As shown in Chapter 3, in Xinjiang, vernacular resistance and even discontentment are conflated with armed organisation. Elite and popular representational politics, therefore, constitute the identity-security contention itself (Bovingdon 2010, pp.7–9, 160). Han and Uyghur responses to official security discourses in Xinjiang are, therefore, central to understanding the effects of nation-building and state-security.

This chapter analyses how the party-state performed *Zhonghua Minzu* through identity-security narratives to explain the violence of July 2009. It then turns to the productive effects of these performances, analysing how Han and Uyghurs re-performed these narratives to articulate alternative identity-securities. How was violence by different ethnic groups narrated into a story of China's identity and insecurity? How did this narrative shape official and unofficial security practices? And how did these practices produce insecurity for the state? The chapter will show how these narratives' explanations of violence produce hierarchical ethnic relations and different insecurities for different ethnic groups. It shows how material sources of insecurity are translated into identity threats and how these articulations of threats constitute the ethno-hierarchy of *Zhonghua Minzu*. The chapter links discourse analysis of official texts to ethnographic analysis of street-level security practices and protests in Ürümchi. It will show how official performances of identity-insecurities are reinterpreted by Han and Uyghurs to frame each other as threats and articulate alternative identity-insecurities. The chapter builds on sparse available research on the July 2009 violence.[3] It is the first detailed study to use interviews and participant-observations on Han perspectives in Ürümchi, erroneously assumed to be indistinguishable from the party-state. Communications technology has 'opened up new spaces ... for the articulation of alternative national imaginaries', thus loosening the party-state's monopoly on meanings associated with being 'Chinese' (Leibold, 2010, p.24).

---

[2] On vernacular security, see: Jarvis and Lister (2013); Stevens and Vaughan-Williams (2016).
[3] For example, see: Millward (2009b); Cliff (2016), chapter 7.

Introduction

However, following the July 2009 violence, internet access and international communications were blocked for approximately 10 months 'to prevent unrest' (Xinhua, 2009a). Communications technology enabled public discussions of the *Shaoguan* incident, Uyghur protests on July 5, and the subsequent violence. However, once all non-official communications with the outside world were blocked, people's alternative national and international imaginaries were only communicated in private and on the street. To analyse daily reproduction of identity-security discourses on the ground, therefore, this chapter uses local newspapers, universal ethnic unity education texts, and participant-observation of official and unofficial security practices.

The first section analyses official discourse on the events sparking the July 2009 violence at the Xuri Toy Factory in Guangdong, when Han co-workers killed two Uyghur labourers and injured hundreds.[4] This section will show how boundaries between Han as embodiments of China and Uyghurs as ethnic outsiders were securitised by downplaying organised Han violence against Uyghurs. The absence of security response produced widespread Uyghur insecurity and sparked popular protests before the July violence. The second section explores how the July violence was conversely narrated as an existential identity-security threat in the classroom and in ethnicised security practices. The analysis asks, *Who* is the referent of official identity-security practices? Uyghur violence against Han on July 5 was framed as an existential threat, while violence against Uyghurs on July 7 was considered a rational defence of personal and national security. The final section analyses these asymmetrical security dynamics following a spate of syringe assaults in the aftermath that culminated in mass Han protests for increased security and violence against Uyghurs. This section shows how Han and Uyghurs responded to official articulations of an insecure China under perpetual threat from Uyghur violence. Many Han felt *their* China was under threat, while Uyghurs felt they faced the threat *of* China. However, both Han and Uyghurs articulated identity-securitisations that were explicitly ethno-national, countering the state's multi-*minzu* narrative.

The chapter advances the book's central argument that the party-state produces insecurity for itself in Xinjiang, by showing how its security practices exacerbate ethnic tensions between Han and Uyghurs on the ground in Ürümchi. The CCP securitises an ethnocentric national narrative that values Han lives more than those of minorities. Official security practices then target Uyghur neighbourhoods and identity narratives as sources of insecurity, activating pre-existing stereotypes of Uyghurs as external cultural threats. Official discourse frames violence as ordinary incidents *or* exceptional terrorist threats

---

[4] For example, see: Hess (2009); Millward (2009b); Roberts (2012); Smith Finley (2011).

depending upon the ethnicity of *who* is threatened. This framing reproduces hierarchical boundaries in *Zhonghua Minzu* because the Han majority are the embodiment of the nation, which must be secured, while Uyghurs are framed as a security problem. This bifurcated narration of violence constitutes majority-minority identities as oppositional, making Uyghurs and Han feel under perpetual threat from each other. Han and Uyghurs then re-perform official boundaries and articulate alternative ethno-national identity-securities, which increases the party-state's insecurity regarding popular reception of its identity narratives. Many Han in Ürümchi felt they must enact violence themselves to secure China from Uyghur terrorists. Uyghurs felt insecure because they are excluded from national narratives and ethnically targeted by the state and its ethnic insiders. China's leaders now understand resolution of the insecurity produced through this dynamic in existential terms and the means to, and ends of, its global rise.

De-Securitising Uyghurs

On June 25, 2009, Han workers entered their Uyghur co-workers' dormitory at the Xuri Toy Factory, attacking them with knives and metal pipes in large skirmishes, which left two Uyghurs dead and hundreds injured (Hess, 2009, p.404). The violence occurred after a local website posted that 'six Xinjiang boys raped two innocent girls'. *The China Daily* reported the incident as 'triggered by a sex assault by a Uyghur worker toward a Han female worker' (Smith Finley, 2011, p.90). These allegations turned out to be fabrications by Zhu Gangyuan, a factory worker who failed to be re-employed after quitting his job (Xinhua, 2009b). A Han Chinese woman had accidentally entered the Uyghur men's dormitory, and when the men shouted, 'Boo', her surprised scream activated ethnic stereotypes, which framed the official story that she had been raped (Millward, 2009b; Sheehan, 2009). This section asks how the party-state conceptualised identity and security in explanations of violence by Han against Uyghurs in the lead-up to the July 2009 violence. Violence by Han was officially deemed not to be a security matter. Uyghurs who understood it as such were framed as the real threat, constituting and securitising unequal ethnicised subject positions in the nation. However, multiple perspectives on the violence circulated, articulating alternative identity-securities and challenging the party-state's narrative of *Zhonghua Minzu*.

China's 'internal orientalist' discourse represents southwestern ethnic minorities as agricultural, feminine, and backward but as integral components of China, relationally narrating majority Han identity as civilised, modern, and superior (Gladney, 2004, pp.13–16; Schein, 2000, p.130). However, internal orientalism in Xinjiang is interweaved into security discourses and reproduces popular stereotypes that Uyghur cultural inferiority and backwardness are security threats. Sexualised ethnic stereotypes, through which Han widely represent Uyghur men as primal 'sexual predators', emerged in explanations of the Shaoguan incident (Smith Finley, 2011, p.82). Xinjiang is 'dangerous' *because* it is 'backward' and Uyghurs become framed as masculine threats and too uncivilised to contain their burgeoning and primordial sexual instincts. These sexualised security discourses circulate in the post-2012 'de-extremification' struggles against 'Islamic terrorism'. Following unrest in Yecheng, 2012, then-Xinjiang party chief, Zhang Chunxian, stated, 'Show no mercy to these terrorists ... we shall not let them wave knives at our women, our children, and our innocent people' (Xinhua, 2012a). Official representations of primal Uyghur masculinity constitute threats to civilised Chinese identity, and activated popular justifications of ethnic hatred following the Shaoguan incident. *The Guardian* interviewed 20 local residents, including police, who immediately believed allegations of sexualised violence by Uyghurs and claimed published casualty figures were kept artificially low to protect them. One young man said, 'I just wanted to beat them. I hate Xinjiang people ... we used iron bars to beat them to death' (Watts, 2009). One local shop-owner told me, 'Xinjiang people have a low level of civilisation ... they chase and harass girls all the time.' The alleged rape was understood as an attack on China ('*our* women') because its violence against a Han person refuted the passive and feminine social position of ethnic minorities.

The political-economic context behind Shaoguan further illustrates the material impact of narratives that position Han as sources of identity-security, while Uyghurs are expected to imitate their culture to promote security. Reform-era policy in Xinjiang has engineered Han migration into minority areas through economic incentives, particularly labour opportunities in cotton and extractive industries, under the rubric of increased security (Becquelin, 2004b, p.358). Uyghurs, conversely, have been sent to inner China to learn 'modernisation' and transform 'traditionally compact ethnic communities', producing 'identification with the entire nation' (Feng & Aney, 2009). To reduce the Uyghur threat, they are transferred to regions with 'safe' majority Han populations, breaking up 'compact ethnic communities', 'modernising' and converting them through learning from the Han. 'Ethnic dispersion' (*minzu fensan* 民族分散) to break up concentrated non-Han populations is measured by the number of minorities living in 'scattered areas', and officially described as 'progress', and 'unity', exemplified by Xinjiang's majority-Han oil-producing cities, particularly Shihezi (State Council, 2009a, p.3). The Xuri factory was staffed through labour surplus export programmes from Xinjiang, and 96,000 workers were transferred from southern Xinjiang in the first half of 2009 (Hess, 2009, p.405). The regional government invested RMB 300–400 million to transfer labour from Xinjiang, a region with the third-lowest population density in China and a net labour importer, to regions with the highest population density. The purpose of relocation was for Uyghurs to 'become more open-minded' and 'access modernisation' through contact with majority Han (Global Times, 2009). Modernisation and economic development are thus driven by the non-economic, security logics of nation-building.

These ethnicised development strategies have produced considerable insecurity amongst Uyghurs and labour transfers raised particularly heightened concerns of ethnically targeted 'forcible relocation' (Hess, 2009, pp.405–407). On July 7, China Labor Watch (2009) tacitly acknowledged forcible relocations, stating that '*most* workers go willingly', recommending Uyghurs be allowed to 'leave the factory at their discretion'. Officials targeted vulnerable groups for relocation, specifically young women aged between 16 and 25 (Hess, 2009; UHRP, 2011). One elderly Uyghur confided that his daughter was relocated following pressure from a party cadre. A young intellectual from the same village in southern Xinjiang expressed anger that many families had done the same. While labour transfer policies aimed to transform Uyghur identity, its ethnocentrism unintentionally produced cycles of insecurity between Uyghurs and the state. Since 2017, these policies have intensified and expanded. Widespread 'forced labour' in Xinjiang's manufacturing sector is embedded in its extra-legal internment camp system for Uyghurs and other Turkic groups, enhancing China's global 'competitiveness'.[5]

Official explanations of violence by Han against Uyghurs at Shaoguan reproduced hierarchical ethnic relations, and alternative Uyghur explanations were treated as security threats. Ethnic unity textbooks and Shaoguan government spokesman, Wang Qinxin, played down the factory killings as a 'very ordinary public order incident', exaggerated to foment unrest (XEP, 2009, p.106; Watts 2009). By contrast, Uyghur rioters in Ürümchi were labelled as the 'scum of the nation' in the same passages (XEP, 2009, p.106). Violence against Uyghurs was framed as a non-existential criminal matter to be dealt with by standard legal procedures ('ordinary public order incident'). Xinjiang Regional Chairman, Nur Bekri (2009a), and Party chief, Wang Lequan (2009b; 2009c), used televised speeches on July 6 and 7 to condemn the 'distortion of facts' by 'The Three Evils' regarding the Shaoguan incident. Ethnic unity textbooks explained that 'East Turkestan' has 'distorted facts' and collaborated to use representations of the Shaoguan incident to 'harm ethnic unity' and 'split the nation' (XEP, 2009, pp.8 & 16). This narrative's internal logic was that participants were criminals who 'cannot represent every member of their *minzu*' and, unlike Uyghur complaints, this did not cause '*minzu* hatred', therefore, it was not a '*minzu* problem' (XEP, 2009, p.14). This de-securitisation invisibilised the Uyghur insecurity caused by ethnically

---

[5] For example, see: Xu et al. (2020).

targeted Han violence in the party-state's struggle for power to essentialise *minzu* identity. Furthermore, it framed alternative representations of violence as existential threats to Chinese identity. Uyghur representations of the violence as a security threat were treated as acts of terrorism committed by 'The Three Evils'. Official explanations securitised the party-state's narrative of Chinese identity as a fixed essence, which can only be represented by the state.

Downplaying Han violence and the lack of state response produced Uyghur insecurity. There was no media coverage of the incident until Uyghurs publicised their stories across the blogosphere, and it was October 10 before two Han men were sentenced (Smith Finley, 2011, pp.75–78). Guilty parties received no punishment at the time and the absence of action sparked protests in Ürümchi. The Public Security Bureau (PSB) sent SMS texts to every mobile phone in Xinjiang using the vocabulary of 'public order', rather than national security, and without specifying punishments, a sharp contrast to those addressing violence by Uyghurs. The absence of state response to the Shaoguan violence contrasted with rapid online activity of Uyghurs who posted videos of the incident on YouTube (2009), Youku, and Tudou, which went viral across Xinjiang. A protest for action against the murders of the Uyghurs in Guangdong was organised online in the early days of July. It began with a march in Ürümchi city centre at 5 a.m. on July 5 from the South Gate (*Nanmen* 南门) to People's Square (*Renmin Guangchang* 人民广场). Almost 1,000 Uyghurs protested, and those heading the march waved large Chinese flags, chanting for 'justice' and 'equality' (Millward, 2009b, pp.351–352).[6] Like Judith Butler's celebration of the American national anthem sung in Spanish, these protests were 'articulations of plurality' which *ought* to exist (Butler & Spivak, 2007, pp.60–61). The peaceful protest performatively enacted aspirations of justice and equality for Uyghurs in a multi-*minzu* China, which threatened the party-state's narratives.

Official Chinese accounts only briefly mention the protest to dismiss its representation of events as threatening 'lies' from 'The Three Evils' to stir up separatism (XEP, 2009, p.17). Unlike other protests across China, it was elevated as an existential threat to China's identity, instead of labelled as illegal interference with public order. The protest challenged the party-state's narratives on Shaoguan and *Zhonghua Minzu* where minorities are happy with their social position. This silencing of Uyghur articulations of identity and security reproduced ethnic boundaries between safe Han and dangerous Uyghurs. The narrative of equality at the protest was framed as an external cultural threat, located in 'Western discourses' of 'democracy and human rights' to 'split China' (XEP, 2009, p.16). Even claiming that Uyghurs waved

---

[6] Videos of these events were posted on YouTube (2011) but have since been removed.

Chinese flags on July 5 was designated a terrorist act and aligned with accusations of inequality from Western 'enemies of China'. The protest for genuine equality made the state insecure because it challenged *Zhonghua Minzu* identity as unified, non-Western, and built on boundaries between active, benevolent Han and passive, appreciative minorities. Framing non-violent Uyghur dissatisfaction as an existential threat demarcates the boundaries of *Zhonghua Minzu* by telling Uyghurs who they must *not* be.

Securitising Han-Centrism: '7-5' and '7-7'

This section examines how identity-security narratives framed violence by Uyghurs on July 5 as a threat to China but invisibilised Han violence against minorities on July 7. Official explanations of the July 2009 events securitised the hierarchical boundaries of *Zhonghua Minzu* by framing acts of violence as ordinary incidents or as exceptional threats to the nation, contingent upon *who* was threatened by them. Sean Roberts expressed surprise that tensions 'had not boiled over into such violence until now', particularly given the recurrences of Uyghur resistance to the Chinese state since 1759 and the explosion of political violence in the 1990s (Roberts, 2009). Just days before the incident, Uyghur journalist Heyrat Niyaz warned the regional government that monolingual education policies and labour transfers had angered nationalists and professionals whose jobs were under threat (Asia Weekly, 2009). Nevertheless, no violence in Xinjiang between 1997 and 2008 can be accurately attributed to terrorism, and it represented a 'departure from, not a culmination of, past patterns' (Millward, 2009b, pp.348–349).

During July 2009, widespread violence was committed by ordinary people against other ordinary people on a scale unseen in contemporary China. This distinguished it from paradigmatic incidents in Baren and Ghulja in the 1990s, which targeted police stations and official security institutions. According to official Chinese government figures, the violence resulted in 197 deaths, over 1,721 injuries, 'looting and burning' of 131 shops, 633 'damaged houses', and 1,206 destroyed vehicles (XEP, 2009, pp.3–4; Xinhua, 2009c). Many targets of the July 5 violence were symbols of luxury and ethnic inequality, including car dealerships, which tend to be owned by Han (Smith Finley, 2011, pp.79–80). Official narratives that dehumanise Han as instruments of 'modernisation' and security elevate them above Uyghurs in China's ethno-hierarchy, but ordinary Han people became victims of violence, trapped between the party-state and Uyghurs, whose identities it threatens. On July 7, hundreds of Han residents organised into vigilante groups, targeting and killing random Uyghurs. Uyghurs, Han, and security services were all perpetrators and victims of violence throughout July 2009 (RFA, 2009; Roberts, 2012, pp.15–16). The spiralling of events bore the hallmarks of Bovingdon's

(2004a) 'snowballing', where mass discontent during the 1990s led Uyghurs to protest when numbers grew and it became safer to participate. However, unlike the 1990s, this was inter-ethnic snowballing, illustrating how violent dynamics of identity and insecurity in Xinjiang emerge in triadic relations between Han, Uyghurs, and the state.

Videos of men, women, and children being killed on July 5 and 7 circulated on mobile phones across the city. These were initially posted on Chinese video-hosting sites but were removed shortly thereafter. Multiple eyewitnesses[7] of many ethnicities explained how the violence was ethnically targeted and they had to placate different rioting groups by declaring or lying about their ethnicity.[8] Uyghur, Han, Hui, and foreign eyewitnesses told stories of people being thrown to the ground and stamped to death by crowds. The mixed Uyghur-Han area of Zhongwan Street, southeast of Yan'an Street (*Yan'an Lu* 延安路), saw Uyghur rioters torch Han shops, dragging people from cars and beating them (Millward, 2009b, p.52). Uyghurs built impromptu roadblocks across Saimachang, Xinjiang University, parts of Yan'an Street, and the Uyghur district (*Erdaoqiao/Döngköwrük*) shopping area. According to official reports,[9] violence initially exploded at the People's Hospital on Victory Street (*Shengli Lu* 胜利路) adjacent to Xinjiang University. However, official ethnic unity education and media narratives later conflated protest and violence by asserting that the 'incident' at People's Square and violence at the University were enacted by the same 'terrorists', despite being half an hour bus ride apart.

The Chinese state understood the July violence as a pivotal security matter superseding international commitments. President Hu Jintao cut short attendance at G8 meetings and returned to Beijing (Xinhua, 2009f). By July 9, Hu publicly declared that '7-5' was a 'grave, violent incident with a deep political background' and a plot by 'the inside/outside Three Evils' to 'destroy ethnic unity, harm prosperity, and split the motherland' (Hu, 2009, pp.1–2). The '7-5' incident was unconvincingly described as an internationally funded, synchronised terrorist attack because Uyghurs involved drove buses and trucks stacked with rocks (XEP, 2009, pp.3–5). Images of dead Han bodies circulated on state television, but related violence against Uyghurs on July 7 was never explicitly acknowledged and no arrests were made. All July casualties of all ethnicities were included under the '7-5 incident' as synonymous with the 'struggle of life or death' between China and the 'inside/outside Three Evils'.

---

[7] For examples of international media coverage and other eyewitness accounts, see: RFA (2009); Millward (2009b); Smith Finley (2011).
[8] Anonymous interviews: 58 Han residents and 55 Uyghur residents, Ürümchi, September 2009 through April 2010.
[9] For example, see: XEP (2009).

The contrasting absence of media coverage or official reference to the violence of '7-7' normatively ordered meanings of materially similar acts of violence. City party secretary, Li Zhi, met Han rioters on the streets of Ürümchi on July 7 and chanted 'down with terrorists', asking rioters to 'unite and build a better Ürümchi' but without condemning their violence (Xinhua, 2009e). Then regional party chief, Wang Lequan's televised speech on the 7th solely discussed violence against Han as a 'strategy' of the 'inside/outside Three Evils' to 'destroy ethnic unity' (Wang, 2009b, p.8). In stark contrast to descriptions of rioting Uyghurs as the 'scum of the nation', Wang then addressed Han rioters as 'comrades', explaining that Han 'operations' were 'not needed' because the security apparatus was now in control (Wang, 2009b, pp.8–9). Official calls for 'clear heads' represented an increasingly insecure state's attempt to calm violence by Han but failed to address Uyghur insecurity and normatively ordered violence by ethnicity. Official descriptions of Han violence against Uyghurs as rational security 'operations' by 'comrades' ethnicised and normatively ordered violence through identity narratives. Uyghur violence was an irrational identity-security threat to China because it threatened the ethnic majority. Han violence was a non-security matter because they were rational insider 'comrades' struggling *for* China. The referent of Chinese security discourses in Xinjiang, therefore, is a Han-centric narrative of China under threat from 'The Three Evils'.

The production of '7-5' as a reified and singular event concealed the mass, decentred violence that engulfed Ürümchi and enabled its representation as a life or death struggle between good (Chinese) and evil (Uyghurs). Official conflations of peaceful protest and mass violence generally deny that protest expresses popular sentiment bearing any relation to how ordinary Uyghurs (or Han) identify themselves (Bovingdon, 2010, p.121). The meaning of '7-5' was officially narrated through constant repetition of slogans that it was 'not a *minzu* problem, not a religious problem but a political problem of defending the unity of the nation and fundamental interests of the masses' (XEP, 2009, pp.4 & 13–15; Bekri, 2009a; 2009b; Wang, 2009b). Casualty figures were officially listed by *minzu* and symbolically divided to correspond almost exactly with the city's ethnic demographics. This symbolic presentation emphasised that violence was against 'all *minzu*' but noted that only 10 of 51 Uyghurs killed were 'innocent civilians' in China's 'struggle' against the 'inside/outside Three Evils' (China Digital Times, 2009; XEP, 2009, p.14; Xinhua, 2009c). Uyghur violence and discontent were framed together as evil threats from outside China while Han violence was concealed in ethnocentric narratives of equality:

Why did the hatred of a minority of thugs cause so much damage to members of other *minzu*? ... their *minzu* consciousness is a narrow-minded *minzu* feeling and a narrow-minded *minzu* consciousness . . . they are unable to correctly distinguish the true from the false or who is friend and who is the enemy . . . so to overcome narrow-minded *minzu* feelings and consciousness we must establish the correct *minzu* feeling and consciousness, these are manifested in loving one's *minzu* as well as paying attention to the development of one's *minzu* as well as loving other *minzu* and paying attention to their development. . .and never wavering in the intense struggle against 'The Three Evils' and self-consciously protecting national unity and ethnic unity. (XEP, 2009, pp.67–68)

Official education texts, as quoted above, make everyday thinking about identity a security issue by framing acceptance of official binarising narratives as an existential matter for China's survival. These texts claim 'reactionary ideology has been instilled into the minds of youth' 'as pretexts by anti-Chinese international forces' to 'harm *minzu* relations' and 'attack the party and country' (XEP, 2009, p.96). Terrorists' 'infiltration' methods that use students to 'distort Xinjiang history and interfere with *minzu* relations' were broadly defined, including thinking that Uyghurs are a Turkic or Islamic *minzu*, 'everyday discussions' of '*minzu* history and the contemporary *minzu* situation', promoting ideas such as 'justice' and 'equality', activities like 'making friends, recognising each other's hometowns, and student parties', participation in protests, opposition to monolingual education policies, and performances of art, poetry, and songs (XEP, 2009, pp.96–101).

These everyday identity threats to *Zhonghua Minzu* were met with heightened surveillance of identity in education: 'All teachers, students, and staff must maintain a high level of vigilance' and 'protecting the unity of the nation is a political demand and historical mission of every student' (XEP, 2009, pp.102 & 107). The purpose of ethnic unity education was to disseminate the 'truth' about '7-5' such that everyone must 'dry their eyes and clearly distinguish enemy from self (*renqing diwo* 人情敌我)' (XEP, 2009, pp.104 & 106). *The 50 Whys*[10] divided participants of the July 2009 protests and riots into the instigators ('The Three Evils' and 'East Turkestan') and the 'ignorant students' who had their 'minds controlled' (*kongzhi sixiang* 控制思想) and were fooled by the instigators' 'distortion of facts' regarding 'national conditions' (XEP, 2009, pp.96–97 & 104–107). The idea that 'naïve and excitable students' are manipulated by a minority of separatists, who 'recede into the background', has long helped the party-state delink all Uyghur protest from the widespread discontent it reflects (Bovingdon, 2010, pp.119–120). Universities rounded up Uyghur students involved in the protest, who reported to party representatives before being confined and monitored in dormitories and sent to

---

[10] This was a theme in the televised speeches immediately after the violence. See: Bekri (2009a); Wang (2009b; 2009c).

additional ethnic unity education classes, using *The Fifty Whys* as a core text.[11] Official explanations stated that these students' 'thought had problems' and they 'had to learn a lesson' to 'establish the correct national outlook (*guojia guan* 国家观), *minzu* outlook, religious outlook, historical outlook, and cultural outlook' (XEP, 2009, pp.105–107). The staff responsible for identifying students with 'thought problems' explained that they were guilty of becoming 'too excited' and 'shouting bad things', including 'justice' and 'equality'.[12] The identity and social activities of Uyghur students were judged and punished outside the legal system and no students were officially charged. Alternative thought that responded to this ethnic targeting was framed as an ethnocentric security threat to China's identity. These security practices were embedded in identity narratives that gave Uyghurs an impossible identity binary: to be good Chinese *minzu* helping China rise or evil terrorists, collaborating with the West to split China.

The party-state's observably ethnicised street-level security response reproduced these hierarchical boundaries. Martial law came into effect at 9 p.m. on July 7 under the rubric of 'traffic controls' (Wang, 2009b, p.10). Two days later, tens of thousands of troops arrived from regional headquarters in Lanzhou, Gansu.[13] The People's Liberation Army (PLA) supplemented the police, People's Armed Police (PAP), and Special Police who already patrolled the city, blocking all major traffic junctions. Security practices designated Uyghur neighbourhoods as a threat through heavily armed military patrols, neighbourhood patrols, and newly installed closed-circuit television ('electric eyes') to the cost of RMB 1 million (Chenbao, 2009a). Areas where Uyghur violence had exploded, including Xinjiang University and *Erdaoqiao/Döngköwrük*, were heavily militarised for months with PLA patrols, armed PAP stations on most street corners, security gates, bag-checks, and constant flashing of surveillance cameras. In the lead-up to National Day, all bus stops, street corners, and mosques in the south of the city were guarded by three or four armed PLA positioned together to deal with crowd control. PLA patrols of about a dozen troops with machine guns, batons, and riot-shields marched up and down every surrounding street. On October 1, a dozen PLA trucks, containing approximately 30 troops armed with machine guns, parked about 20 feet apart in front of Xinjiang University's back gate on *Yan'an Lu*. While additional soldiers paraded, the trucks were adorned with large slogans, including 'defend the frontier' and 'protect ethnic unity'. Images of PAP officers

---

[11] Anonymous interviews with two university staff, Ürümchi, October 2009.
[12] Anonymous interviews with two university staff, December 2009.
[13] Following Xi Jinping's reform and restructuring of China's military divisions, these are now located in Xinjiang.

armed with machine guns appeared in local newspapers alongside children raising the flag, under the headline 'Ceremony Held, the People's Police Protect the National Flag' (Chenbao, 2009e). Street-level security practices designated Uyghur neighbourhoods as a threat through military patrols, neighbourhood patrols, and electronic surveillance.

By contrast, Han-populated hotspots of violence against Uyghurs on July 7, such as Xinjiang Normal University and Youth Street (*Qingnian Lu* 青年路), were only lightly patrolled by the PAP and left to neighbourhood watch patrols of Han volunteers approved by local work units. Posters advertised for volunteers who wore 'patrol' armbands but openly armed other Han residents. By September's end, I had observed dozens of neighbourhoods in the north with Han men aged from 18 to mid-60s, armed with large clubs and parading without training, in the name of security. Videos online showed the PAP distributing large wooden clubs to random Han Chinese residents during the violence of July (UHRP, 2011). On *Qingnian Lu*, potentially lethal extendable batons were displayed for sale for 20 *kuai* in windows of a discount underwear shop and sold out in one day. Ethnically targeted surveillance perpetuated the ethnicised and ever-present threat of violence, while Han children played on busy streets with their new deadly toys, attracting no attention. Ethnicised targeting by military and neighbourhood patrols reflected an activation of ethnic stereotypes and acceleration of the pre-existing 'heightened surveillance' of Uyghurs' daily lives (Anthony, 2011, pp.51–52). Ethnicised surveillance perpetuated the street-level identity-security politics of a city where the threat of violence and insecurity was ever-present and strictly ordered by official discourse into safe Han and dangerous Uyghur neighbourhoods.

Hu Jintao's speech on July 7 stated that '7-5 was over' (Hu, 2009, p.1). However, lingering Han insecurity was evident through observation and conversations with local Han residents even during September. Most Han interviewees warned me never to visit 'dangerous', 'terrorist' Uyghur areas. Several told me they had not even left their street since July. Within a single day of walking across the city I observed six instances of Han Chinese parents physically dragging their children away from random Uyghurs. Most Han interviewees were eager to tell me the 'truth about 7-5' with 12 interviewees expressing pride regarding the events of July 7, saying, 'We battered the Uyghurs!' or 'We proved we *too* are a unified *minzu*'. Like popular interpretations of the Shaoguan violence, official discourse activated rather than produced ethnic hatred, but people often framed their everyday insecurities using grand geopolitical discourse. Ordinary residents redeployed 'The Three Evils' narrative against Uyghurs and designated them as culturally external terrorist threats. Seventeen local Han interviewees explained that ethnically targeted violence against Uyghurs was necessary because the government was 'too slow' and 'too soft' in dealing with 'Uyghurs', 'terrorists', 'The Three Evils', and 'East Turkestan'; these terms were all used interchangeably by the same people. *Ethnocentric* official discourse was redeployed to articulate an explicitly *chauvinist* mono-ethnic identity where all Uyghurs are culturally external, inconvertible Turkic threats to China.

The subsequent insecurity felt by Uyghurs in fear of state violence and Han vigilantes has remained relatively undiscussed in English and Mandarin sources. One young, politicised intellectual explained the July violence by saying, 'If you have a boiling pot of water and keep the lid on too tight, it will eventually boil over'. World Uyghur Congress (WUC) spokesperson Alim Seytoff explained that tensions had been rising 'because of the Chinese government's political propaganda, indoctrination of Chinese people ... and portraying Uyghurs ... as terrorists, separatists, and Islamic radicals' (PBS, 2009). The WUC claimed that the casualty figures were too low and that over 600 people had died, many of whom were Uyghurs killed by the PAP (BBC, 2009). Official figures were constantly disputed in interviews with Han and Uyghur locals who all believed many more had died. Where Uyghurs point to China's need to conceal the targeting of Uyghurs, several Han Chinese residents explained that the casualty figures were kept low because the UN would visit Ürümchi and 'interfere with China' if they exceeded 200. State Media explained that the 'international community' (namely, Belarus, Thailand, Cambodia, and Laos) supported China's efforts and agreed it was an 'internal affair' (Xinhua, 2009g). However, Uyghur campaign groups reconceptualised the inside and outside of identity-security by viewing these events as an opportunity to invite the 'outside' in and articulate Uyghur insecurities to international news agencies. Most Uyghur interviewees and several eyewitnesses explained the outbreak of violence as a response to heavy handed policing at the peaceful protest. Several claimed a policeman struck a female Uyghur at the square. Uyghur eyewitness interviews with Radio Free Asia (2009) claimed the protestors only moved to *Nanmen*, where reports of violence eventually emerged, *after* the police moved into the square to detain people. All non-Han interviewees expressed insecurity by explaining they were too frightened to leave their homes for days because they could see Han mobs with weapons and hear constant screams. Multiple Uyghur interviewees described continuous police gunshots in the city centre, *Erdaoqiao/ Döngköwrük*, and university area on July 5. They assumed the gunshots of security forces targeted Uyghurs, staying inside and, in many cases, hiding overnight to escape. For many Uyghurs, the state was understood in tandem with ordinary Han residents as a violent threat.

Official explanations of the July 2009 violence securitised boundaries within *Zhonghua Minzu* by narrating Uyghur violence as a threat to China's unified identity and by downplaying Han violence. The party-state framed alternative interpretations to its identity-security narrative as terrorism from outside China's cultural boundaries. The struggle between China and its enemies is thus one over how to understand and think about the relationship between the 'domestic' self and 'international' other. The greatest threats to China were not invading states or armed separatist groups but alternative minority conceptualisations of identity and security, which challenge notions that they are happy with their inferior social position in *Zhonghua Minzu*. The referent of official identity-security in Xinjiang, therefore, is not living, breathing Han people but an ethnicised identity-security narrative that constitutes hierarchical majority-minority relations.

Insecuritisation and the Ethnic Threat

In the aftermath of the July violence, a spate of small-scale assaults and robberies by Uyghurs using syringes against Han broke out across Ürümchi. These continued for several months and culminated in mass Han Chinese protests for increased security measures. The syringe assaults were narrated into identity-security narratives as terrorist threats to China, reactivating and heightening existing popular Han Chinese insecurities. This section links official discourse analysis to participant-observations, exploring how securitisation produced different insecurities for Han and Uyghurs by essentialising these groups in hierarchical relations. Official explanations of the violence performed China as an insecure nation under perpetual threat from ethnic Uyghurs, securitising boundaries between majority and minorities as objectively existing facts to be preserved for China's survival. When the violence dissipated, many Han-owned shops and homes displayed flags and official slogans about Chinese history and ancient Han jurisdiction over Xinjiang (see Figure 4.1). Military trucks, stationed on the streets since imposition of martial law in July, displayed the slogan 'Deeply love the frontier' (*reai bianjiang* 热爱边疆). In Chinese political slogans, 'deep love' is reserved for aspects of the self, such as the family, motherland, or workplace during the communist era. However, this modification of the slogan 'deeply love the motherland' (*reai zuguo* 热爱祖国) ambivalently loves Xinjiang as a frontier, as part of the self but not quite of it. This narrative loves the region's frontier otherness but needs the Chinese military, under the Han's ancient jurisdiction, to secure its restive, exotic peoples. The use of 'land of our ancestors' (*zuguo* 祖国) in popular slogans (Figure 4.1) exemplifies Xinjiang's ambivalent inclusion because it conceptualises China as both a civic *and* a racial nation. *Guojia* (国家), the amalgamation of state (*guo* 国) and people as a united family (*jia* 家) attempts to define China in civic terms. However, *zuguo* explicitly racialises China by amalgamating physical lineage (*zu* 祖) with the state (*guo* 国). *Zuguo* conceptualises China through common physical origins, excluding non-Han who share different lineages. These slogans illustrate Xinjiang's ambivalent

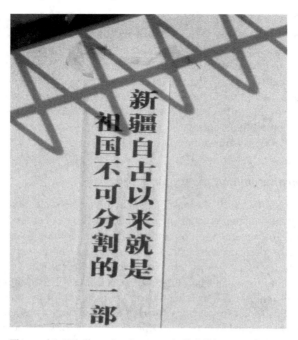

Figure 4.1 'Xinjiang has been an indivisible part of the motherland since ancient times' (*Xinjiang zigu yilai jiu shi zuguo buke fenge de yi bufen*). This standard political slogan (*kouhao* 口号) appeared across the city and in state media broadcasts. However, this home-made, improvised banner was pasted on the front of a large Han Chinese-owned apartment block in the north of the city and remained there until at least August 2010.

inclusion as a cultural frontier, *belonging* to a Han frontier-building lineage who must secure the contemporary PRC's territory by preserving *and* civilising Xinjiang's barbarian otherness.

The spate of syringe assaults in the aftermath of mass violence was officially represented as an ongoing, ever-present security threat to China's physical and cultural integrity. On September 5, *Xinhua* reported that syringes used in assaults across the city contained drugs, despite China's Academy of Military Medical Sciences' announcement that 6 months of close observation was required to make this determination (Xinhua, 2009h; 2009i). Xinjiang residents received SMS messages on September 13 from the PSB stating, 'Syringe attacks are a continuation of 7-5' committed by terrorists and all citizens have responsibilities to 'resolutely struggle' for ethnic unity. The PSB explained that 'no matter what tool is being used', these attacks 'create an atmosphere of terror and interfere with social order' and would be met with a prison sentence of between 5 and 15 years, regardless of the medical diagnosis (XUAR Gonganting, 2009). By September 16, the PSB announced 75 arrests for related incidents (Chenbao, 2009b). By contrast, a copycat spate of syringe stabbings, committed by Han perpetrators in Xi'an, was treated as an 'ordinary criminal investigation' (Chenbao, 2009g; 2009h). Xinjiang suffers from some of the highest rates of HIV and heroin use in the PRC, and AIDS and drug use are frequently stereotyped as Uyghur problems across China (CSIS, 2007, pp.3–4). These stereotypes are activated in periodic regional health scares triggered by official representations of Uyghurs. In late 2007, the Ürümchi City Health Department sent public SMS messages stating that 'Uyghurs' had strategically infected kebabs with HIV across the region.[14] In November 2011, the Ministry of Public Security and Ministry of Health in Beijing had to publicly deny rumours that 20,000 HIV-infected terrorists had again laced food with blood (People's Daily, 2011). Syringe assaults in Xinjiang were narrated through these stereotypes into framings of violence by minorities as biological threats to China's organic cultural integrity. What Sean Roberts (2018) termed the 'biopolitics of exclusion', to describe post-2017 narratives of Uyghur identities as 'ideological viruses', emerged in framings of the syringe attacks, not as dangerous assaults on people, but as infectious, medicalised threats to the health ('life or death') of the Chinese body. Uyghurs are officially represented as biological threats to the organic cultural integrity of the unchanging core of *Zhonghua Minzu*, which in the aftermath of mass violence re-activated and elevated popular stereotypes and insecurities to the level of national survival.

The party-state securitised its *Zhonghua Minzu* narrative by elevating what later transpired to be minor assaults to the level of national security threats, further exacerbating street-level insecurity. The Xinjiang News Centre texted residents on August 28 with a security warning that 'some people' had been attacked with syringes and that all residents should 'be on their guard' to 'defend national security'. Citizens were reminded by the PSB to 'raise their guard and increase self-defence' and that ordinary individuals were 'responsible for national security' (Chenbao, 2009c; 2009d). Although '7-5 was over', Xinjiang residents received SMS texts on September 13 stating that 'syringe attacks were a continuation of 7-5' committed by terrorists, against whom all citizens had a responsibility to 'resolutely struggle' for the cause of ethnic unity. The city government placed public announcement posters across the city on September 2, stating that syringe attacks were 'not normal public order incidents but attempts by the minority of enemies to destroy the city's peace and unity'. The insecurity produced by official narratives was exemplified in

---

[14] I was living in the city at the time and would receive regular security-related SMS messages.

huge gaps between genuine attacks and erroneous claims. The Regional Government originally announced that between August 20 and September 2 there had been 476 incidents at hospitals in which 531 people were injured (Chenbao, 2009c). However, by September 4, only 89 of 476 officially reported incidents were confirmed as cases of syringe attacks (Xinhua, 2009g). On September 3, a PSB SMS text told the city that only 15 people had been genuinely injured in syringe attacks. By mid-September 2009, *Xinhua* explained that bodily harm committed by the syringe assaults was minimal and no victims had contracted any diseases (Chenbao, 2009m). Jackie Sheehan (2009) reported that many such incidents even turned out to be mosquito bites.

These narratives heightened different insecurities for Han and Uyghurs as the PSB and Regional Government publicised new regulations, demanding that ordinary residents, 'the frontline' in fighting 'East Turkestan terrorism', remain 'on guard' to report neighbours and family for everyday 'abnormal behaviour' (XUAR Government, 2010, articles 2, 5, 9, & 16). Many syringe incidents were openly explained as muggings but listed as terrorist incidents and added to the casualty figures of '7-5', compounding perceived levels of identity-security threat (Xinhua, 2009i). Local newspapers reported numerous cases where victims chased and apprehended alleged attackers, but public reports ignored the security threat this posed to Uyghurs. Several non-Uyghur eyewitnesses described one incident on September 3 at *Nanhu Lu* where three Uyghurs were dragged from a public bus and battered to death by Han residents. The victims were accused of syringe attacks and the mob prevented the PLA and ambulances from entering the scene until they were dead. The state was unable to prevent groups of Han from killing Uyghurs and unwilling to prosecute them for doing so. It had heightened Han insecurities by positioning them as the 'frontline' in fighting terrorism and exacerbated cycles of violence by framing assaults by the majority as 'operations' to secure China.

The heightened and ethnicised insecurities drawn from official narratives culminated in a mass rally on September 3, which the party-state struggled to control. Tens of thousands of residents, almost entirely Han Chinese, assembled across Ürümchi at the North Gate (*Beimen*, 北门), South Gate, and People's Square.[15] State-media described the rally as 'protests against syringe attacks' and 'for security', informing readers how protestors waved Chinese flags and shouted, 'Severely punish the mob' (Xinhua, 2009d). Chinese media overlooked the vast numbers involved and subsequent violence against Uyghurs in revenge for syringe attacks. Han protests were never linked to this associated violence, sharply contrasting against official narratives that wrote

---

[15] Verified by foreign eyewitnesses, several Uyghurs, and most Han interviewees.

Uyghur protests and waving of Chinese flags out of the public record. Protests by minorities were existentially threating to Chinese identity, but Han protests were officially framed as *for* security and aligned with the party-state against the 'inside/outside Three Evils'.

Analysis of the protests, however, reveals more complex identity-security politics than suggested by binary divisions between pro-CCP Han and separatist Uyghurs. The party-state struggled to contain the Han protest and restored martial law as state insecurity grew. Chinese media failed to mention the PAP's use of tear gas to disperse the Han crowd.[16] Nor did it mention that thousands of PLA troops and PAP were posted on September 3 to block their passage on all major thoroughfares running south towards Uyghur neighbourhoods. Groups of Han protestors attempted but failed to break past military cordons to reach the Uyghur district. Liberation Street (*Jiefang Lu* 解放路), which runs from the symbolic centre of the city, *Nanmen*, all the way through the Uyghur district, was fenced off and guarded with tanks, armoured cars, and approximately 1,000 troops armed with machine guns and riot shields, facing north to block potential Han Chinese rioters. Large-scale military roadblocks stayed in full force for weeks, controlling flows of people from Han-populated areas to Uyghur areas and vice versa. The military divided the city into north and south exactly where the old Qing dynasty–era city wall ran across what is now *Renmin Lu* (People's Street), separating old Chinese and Muslim cities. The securitisation of this ancient civilisational boundary reflected and reproduced Xinjiang's historical position as an unresolved frontier in *Zhonghua Minzu*.

All Han protestors interviewed confirmed that their participation stemmed from feelings of insecurity after the syringe assaults, and most expressed disappointment at the lack of executions of 'Uyghurs' following July 5.[17] Participants interviewed were all *getihu* entrepreneurs or working class. All framed it as a Han protest, using vocabulary such as 'we Han' and 'our *minzu*' to describe participants. A late-30s, female small-business owner grinned and raised her fist as she told me there were 'big protests' against Uyghurs and the government on September 3. The *New York Times* quoted a retired Han Chinese woman, saying, 'The government hasn't done anything … they haven't kept order. We're all so angry' (Wong, 2009). *The Daily Telegraph* quoted a Han Chinese interviewee, saying, 'The government is useless' (Moore, 2009). When a mid-20s male taxi driver said, '*We* fought back', *we*

---

[16] Reporting was tightly controlled. Associated Press reporters had cameras and tapes confiscated by paramilitary forces, reporting two separate instances of serious physical violence against reporters (FCCC, 2009a; 2009b; 2009c; 2009d; 2009e; 2009f; 2009g; 2009h; 2009i).

[17] Approximately half of 58 Han interviewed confirmed participation or attendance. Most Han interviewees were open and forthcoming about these issues, though all interviews were conducted in private homes, private cars, or quiet public spots.

referred to Han who attacked Uyghurs. Protestors understood violence by Uyghurs was a threat to Han cultural superiority, which the government had failed to secure. At the street level, the ethnocentric grammar of official nationalism was ironically mobilised in Han Chinese resistance to the party-state's multi-*minzu* China, articulating alternative, ethno-nationalist identity-insecurity. Since the large-scale security sweeps that had taken place in Saimachang and *Erdaoqiao/Döngköwrük* on July 6, Uyghur exile groups claimed that more than 10,000 Uyghurs had been reported missing (RFA, 2012b; UHRP, 2011; HRW, 2009, pp.21–32).[18] Hundreds of disappearances and arbitrary detentions were insufficient to calm Han protestors, who sought to restore Han superiority through violent ethnic revenge for '7-5'.

The protests called for action against Uyghurs, but discontent was directed at the state. Protesters called for then regional party chief Wang Lequan to be sacked (Millward, 2009b; Moore, 2009). A PAP poster display of '7-5' identified Rebiya Kadeer, the Uyghur campaigner based in Washington, DC, alongside the Dalai Lama, as the 'life or death enemy'. However, more vandalism was visible on the image of Wang Lequan, now seen as an ethnic traitor, than any other as Han Chinese protestors scratched and drew over his face (see Figure 4.2). Chants at the protest to 'kill the Uyghurs' were heard alongside chants of 'kill Wang Lequan'.[19] Seven different participants raised their fist to me, shouting, 'Kill Wang Lequan, kill the Uyghurs', as if synonymous, expressing anger that they were stopped from reaching *Döngköw-rük/Erdaoqiao* to 'kill the Uyghurs'. Violent chauvinist framings did predominate, but were not expressed by all participants. One male, self-employed, middle-aged Han Chinese resident explained that people took to the streets because 'Han are angry' with the 'lack of security', particularly due to the syringe attacks, but also with 'unemployment' and 'inequality between Xinjiang and the rest of China'. One late-40s *getihu* entrepreneur, from Ürümchi, explained, 'It's a political problem. Nothing to do with ordinary people ... Wang Lequan kill kill kill [raises fist]! There was no response. They

---

[18] It is impossible to quantify with any certainty the number killed or disappeared by the security services. One emblematic case is Patigul Eli, who remains under permanent police surveillance to prevent her petitioning for information regarding her missing son, Imammemet Eli (RFA, 2012a). Imammemet, an alumnus of the South China University of Technology, was detained in July 2009. He was not accused of physical violence but was claimed to have participated in the July 5 demonstrations (RFA, 2012a). Another similar case, which starkly indicates the ethnic targeting and arbitrary nature of detentions, is that of the CCP member Abdugheni Eziz. Abdugheni, a former village Party secretary in Khotan and owner of the Yang Guangcheng real estate company, volunteered to provide food and drink for the PLA and PAP in downtown Ürümchi during July 2009. He has been missing since being taken for questioning without explanation on July 31, 2009 (RFA, 2012b).

[19] This is drawn from multiple eyewitness accounts and interviews with Han who proudly discussed the protest.

Figure 4.2 'Regional Party Secretary Wang Lequan makes important speech regarding the "7-5" incident'.

did nothing. Wang Lequan is useless. He only looks out for himself, so Xinjiang is still poor compared to the rest of China. He does nothing ... things are not finished.' Like many working-class Han, he resisted official narratives that he was the centre of China and instead expressed his exclusion from politics.[20] He understood his own identity-insecurity through internal boundaries between state and society and between prospering inner China and underdeveloped Xinjiang. Like Uyghur protests, Han protests were for identity-insecurity but snowballed due to a broad range of insecurities, blamed on both the party-state and ethnic others.

Official narratives attempted to co-opt the violence and complex identity-insecurities, which emerged in conflict between Han, Uyghurs, and an insecure security apparatus. Late on September 3, the city government and PSB displayed posters across Ürümchi stating that protests were 'illegal', and participants should allow 'unity to be maintained by party and government'. By September 5, Meng Jianzhu, Minister of Public Security, visited Ürümchi, celebrating that the protest's goals to 'severely punish criminals' had been met (Chenbao, 2009p). The state response was an insecure attempt to co-opt Han resistance to ethnic unity by claiming political leaders had met their goals. However, this attempted co-option concealed violent Han chauvinism, which resisted the party-state's model of a multi-*minzu* China and created insecurity for Uyghurs. The state response failed to acknowledge, let alone resolve, the

---

[20] This point will be analysed in detail in the final chapter.

security threat that Han nationalists present to Uyghurs who were victims of physical violence.

Popular Han insecurity was exacerbated and translated into existential threats by the party-state's identity-securitisations and narratives of syringe assaults as terrorist threats. Its ethnocentric grammar was mobilised as resources of Han chauvinist resistance against the party-state's multi-*minzu* model of China. Security forces prevented Han nationalists from attacking the Uyghur 'enemy', which exacerbated their insecurity, as they felt violence was required to secure their superiority over Uyghurs. These dynamics between the state, Han, and Uyghurs heightened state-insecurity because loyalty from Han, its source of identity-security in Xinjiang, was now under threat. The Han felt *their* China was under threat, while Uyghurs felt they faced the threat *of* China. Han and Uyghurs redeployed official discourse to articulate alternative ethno-national identities, producing state insecurity as both ethnic majority and minorities challenged its multi-ethnic narrative of *Zhonghua Minzu*.

Conclusions

The interplay between China's international security discourses and micro-level security practices in Xinjiang illustrates how China's 'domestic' and 'international' insecurities are mutually reinforcing. Uyghur violence and insecurity in Xinjiang are framed as threats to China's rise and officially explained through an absence of Chinese identity. This chapter explored how the party-state performed these intertwined hierarchical boundaries, and how they were redeployed in everyday politics following incidents of mass violence in Xinjiang during 2009. Violence spread rapidly and chaotically across a city where discontent with CCP policies is widespread and individuals with different grievances became involved. The 'snowballing' of protest and violence was inter-ethnic, unfolding through asymmetrical triadic relations between state security services, and ordinary Han and Uyghurs. The chapter's analysis showed how the 'inside/outside Three Evils' discourse performed theoretically indivisible boundaries between China and the international and between majority Han and minority Uyghurs. Discourses of danger superimposed external boundaries between China and international enemies upon domestic cultural boundaries between Han and Uyghurs. Uyghur identity is officially linked to 'outside' dangers of Turkic culture, international terrorism, and the West, framed as threats to China's territorial and cultural boundaries. Violence by Uyghurs was framed as existentially threatening to China's rise and officially explained through an absence of Chinese identity. This configuration of identity and security shaped ethnically targeted security practices on the ground, producing insecurity between unequal ethnic groups and, subsequently, for the state as they turned to violence.

Conclusions

Official hierarchical identity-security narratives produced different insecurities amongst differentially essentialised groups who both re-performed official securitisations through speech, protest, and violence to articulate alternative identity-insecurities. Protests and violence did indicate 'extensive Uyghur discontent' and some willingness to brave government reprisals in expressing it (Bovingdon, 2010, p.170). Grievances regarding identity and security were held by Han as well as Uyghurs, and these complicate binary understandings of ethnic politics in Xinjiang. The chapter's first section showed how the Shaoguan violence against Uyghurs was officially designated as an 'ordinary public order incident' and unrelated to identity-security. However, failure to punish the perpetrators produced Uyghur insecurity. Uyghurs protested for action, mobilising the Chinese national flag to perform their desired position of equality, which was written out of the public record. The second section showed how subsequent violence by Uyghurs in July 2009 was framed as an existential identity-security threat to China. Violent 'revenge' by Han was conversely framed as 'operations' by 'comrades' for national security. Ethnicised security practices that target Uyghur neighbourhoods were embedded in these complementary narratives, reflecting and producing a binary approach to identity-security. Uyghur identities in China are framed as manipulations by Western 'enemies' and targeted as culturally external existential threats that *cause* violence and insecurity. The binarised meaning attributed to violence by different groups ethnicised everyday security practices of surveillance and patrols that target Uyghurs and produce insecurity. The final section showed how small-scale syringe attacks in July's aftermath were officially represented as continuing terrorist threats to China's existence. This narrative heightened Han insecurity, sparking protests for increased security and violence against Uyghurs. Protest slogans and interviews with participants showed how Han nationalists redeployed official identity-security discourse to reject the party-state's multi-*minzu* China and violently target Uyghurs as ever-present threats to their mono-ethnic national identity. The party-state's attempt to secure China from the 'inside/outside Three Evils' created insecurity for Uyghurs and ironically, for itself. The securitisation of *Zhonghua Minzu* gave Han nationalists a discursive framework with which to articulate all Uyghurs as threats, demanding and enacting violence to annul this threat. The party-state, as arbiter between Han and Uyghurs, produces insecurity between the two groups by venerating and securitising ethnocentric narratives of Han identity, while targeting Uyghurs as existential threats. These discourses of danger exacerbate insecurity in the region as Uyghurs resist the re-organisation of their identities and frame China as the outside threat to their identity-security.

On the first anniversary of '7-5', insecurity remained across Ürümchi. Public transport and streets were largely empty of residents. By July 5, 2012, the city was observably more bustling. However, ethnically targeted patterns of armed PAP patrols, bag-checks, constant flashing of surveillance cameras, and temporary security gates had intensified in Uyghur areas. There were 18,000 arrests made under suspicion of terrorism in 2005 alone, yet since 2009, a sharp rise in smaller violent incidents saw security services in Kashgar, Khotan, and Yecheng targeted in a 'self-fulfilling prophecy' of insecurity (Roberts, 2012, pp.15–17). These spiralling cycles of insecurity show how securitised identity categories continue to be violently contested from below. Between 2009 and 2017, most outbreaks of violence, for example, in Bachu, Shanshan, and Pishan, were more focused clashes between Uyghurs and security services akin to political violence of the 1990s. In 2012, Zhang Chunxian, then Party Secretary for Xinjiang, announced that all terrorists would be defeated with an 'iron fist' (Xinhua, 2012c). However, since then, many incidents were sparked during cadre patrols of Uyghur neighbourhoods under the policy of 'maintaining-stability work' (*weiwen gongzuo* 维稳工作) and President Xi Jinping's strategy of building a 'great wall of iron' to protect national unity (RFA, 2010; 2013; 2017; Xinhua, 2017). Policies perpetuating this self-fulfilling prophecy have now culminated in extra-legal internment camps, arbitrarily targeting more than 1 million Uyghurs and other Turkic-speakers as extremists, to promote identity 'fusion'. Uyghur identity is the background of potential instability that justifies this state of exception and its special policies (Cliff, 2016, pp.15–16, 216). The *getihu* interviewee who warned that 'things are not finished' captured the insecurity and Han chauvinist narratives that circulate in Xinjiang. The party-state is now attempting to break the cycles of violence it helped perpetuate and finish its 'struggle of life or death' with more state violence. In 2015, a late-40s, male Han *getihu* pointed me to the buildings and military posts armed with machine guns across the Uyghur district, explaining, 'It's so backward, like going back to the nineteenth century, but things are safe now.' The securitisation of *Zhonghua Minzu* produces hierarchical ethnic relations that shape everyday Han and Uyghur insecurities and limit the possibility of understanding each other's identity. This chapter focused on violence and exclusion in the street-level social dynamics of China's nation-building project. The next chapter will explore how narratives of ethnic inclusion were performed and re-performed through 'ethnic unity' in everyday politics after the July 2009 violence.

5 Performing Inclusion of the Uyghur Other

Introduction

In Xinjiang, grand narratives of China's non-Western, unified identity are performed and re-performed in banal everyday politics, which people must mediate in any public expressions of identity. After the violence of July 2009 in Ürümchi, former President Hu Jintao declared ethnic unity (*minzu tuanjie* 民族团结) as the means to the 'great revival of the Chinese people', contrasted against the 'disaster' of separatism (Hu, 2009). *Tuanjie* in Xinjiang is conceived as an existential security matter and central to the survival and prosperity of *Zhonghua Minzu* in the face of internal conflict and external threats. The party-state has described *minzu tuanjie* as the 'cornerstone' of its ethnic minority policies throughout the reform era, and contrasts China's unified multi-ethnic identity against Western ethnic nationalism (State Council, 2003, p.79; 2009a, p.14). *Minzu tuanjie* is the 'fundamental principle' in dealing with the '*minzu* question' (*minzu wenti* 民族问题) and organises principles of ethnicity and nation so that ethnic identity must be superseded by *Zhonghua Minzu* (State Council, 2009a, p.14). Although the party-state emphasises the unique, non-Western practice of unity (*tuanjie*), it uses this to frame a universalist approach to identity, explaining that '*all* multicultural countries need ethnic unity' if they are to be 'unified', 'stable', and 'developed' (State Council, 2009a, p.1). *Tuanjie* culturally distinguishes China from the West but it is also taken-for-granted as a culturally neutral mode of ethnic inclusion on the ground in Xinjiang. 'Ethnic unity' is taught to students and teachers in Xinjiang through these interweaved domestic and international narratives, as the basis of the 'great revival of the Chinese people', 'national strength', and expansion of China's international 'soft power' (EUAB, 2009; XEP, 2009). Studies of 'soft power' in Chinese foreign policy show how the concept is deployed to promote domestic national cohesion as much as making China attractive to the outside (Young & Jong, 2008, p.459). China's foreign policy and domestic ethnic politics are inter-related practices, constructed in reference to each other to make China more powerful and more Chinese. Chapters 3 and 4 examined how the East Turkestan and 'inside/outside Three

Evils' narratives exclude Turkic and Islamic self-identifications of Uyghurs as existential threats. This chapter turns to public performances of this identity-insecurity's mirror image by examining minority inclusion through 'ethnic unity' and its intimate relations with exclusion.

The idea of a civic, multi-*minzu* China conceals the taken-for-granted cultural content that constitutes ethnic boundaries in *Zhonghua Minzu*. Civic and cultural nationalisms are never mutually exclusive. Even in paradigmatic cases of 'civic nationalism', such as France and the United States, ideas about culture constitute statehood (Brubaker, 1999, pp.60–61). 'Civic nationalism' conceals ethnocentric assumptions about the normality of majority culture and anomaly of the minority. In China, taken-for-granted national cultural characteristics such as Confucianism are considered products of an imagined biological group known as the Han (Dikötter, 1994, p.404). However, Fei Xiaotong's (1988) 'Han nucleus' and Ma Rong's (2007) policy proposals to 'depoliticise' ethnicity by abandoning the ethnic minorities (*shaoshu minzu*) category rely on unproblematised ethnic ontologies where majority identities are non-ethnic and culturally neutral, and contrasted against narrow-minded ethnic minority identities. Unity (*tuanjie*), therefore, is a cultural project that includes minorities in *Zhonghua Minzu* by excluding their own self-defined identities. Ethnic unity practices reflect competing conceptualisations of *Zhonghua Minzu* identity. James Leibold conceptualised three modes of ethnic inclusion in China: state-sponsored Leninist *minzu* policies, Confucian ecumenism, and Han nationalism (Leibold, 2010, p.2). Leninist *minzu* discourses emerged in ethnic classification and cultural evolution narratives, discussed in Chapter 2, where economic development will naturally unify China through 'modernisation' of ethnic minorities. Confucian ecumenism entails cultural 'fusion' of all *minzu* through attraction to Han superiority and is promoted by China's leading scholars on ethnicity, particularly Fei Xiaotong and Ma Rong, who frame *Zhonghua Minzu* as timelessly built on the civilisation/barbarian binary. The public re-emergence of Han chauvinism in the 'opening and reform era' is most explicit in Hu Angang's (2012) argument for ethnic minorities' assimilation into a Han race-state (*guozu*) to propel China's rise. Ethnocentrism runs through and links all three approaches. The three models offer competing conceptualisations of 'who is China' but are all built on underlying assumptions of Han superiority and that ethnic minority identities are a *problem* to be solved. These overlapping and mutually reinforcing configurations of China stretch the confines of the PRC's contemporary territory back to 'ancient times', positioning the Han as China's centripetal, modernising driving force (Leninism), cultural attraction (Confucianism), or explicit racial superiority (chauvinism).

The drive to categorise *minzu* (Leninism) and civilise them (Confucianism) but retain the Han category as the national standard (chauvinism) are inseparable, semantically hybrid strands of Chinese nation-building. These complexities are concealed in China's official historical narratives. The historical relations of mutual military and political antagonisms between China's contemporary ethnic groups have been re-represented through narratives of timeless unity and territorial enclosure, where minorities *desire* their own destruction through formation of *Zhonghua Minzu* (Bulag, 2002, pp.1 & 22). Chapter 2 showed that ethnic unity is a temporary measure, as the 'overall direction' of history towards 'fusion' eventually produces 'ethnic extinction'. Unity articulates China as a peaceful power, attracting and converting ethnic minorities since ancient times, the binary opposite of the assimilative violence of Western 'one-nation, one-state thinking'. However, the ahistorical understanding of *Zhonghua Minzu* through timeless unity is a political construct that only emerged in official circles after 1949, concealing China's own history of class conflict and *minzu* oppression (Jian, 1960, p.21). The idea that *Zhonghua Minzu* could never be like the West closes down domestic and international critiques of China's own exclusions of minorities because this is considered an exclusively Western problem. Communist ideology did not supplant Confucian assumptions of Han superiority. These were both fused through semantic hybridity. After 1949, *Hua* civilisation became reconfigured as the Han 'nucleus' 'vanguard', and after 1978, it was reconfigured again as the means to China's rise and a source of economic development.

This chapter moves from the explicit exclusion of 'The Three Evils' to its mirror image of ethnic unity to ask, How are Uyghurs included as Chinese in the politics of the everyday? Daily 'ideological habits' can be as significant as grand-scale performances in the reproduction of nations (Billig, 1995, pp.1–6). The unobtrusive flags hanging unquestioned from public buildings help establish 'endemic conditions' of nationalism and community as taken for granted (Billig, 1995, p.6). In Xinjiang, banal nation-building texts are *everywhere* and serious reminders of the party-state's omnipresence. Power is not omnipresent because it consolidates everything under its unity but because it comes from everywhere and is produced from one moment to the next (Foucault, 1991, p.93). Understanding the consolidation of power presented by 'ethnic unity' requires looking beyond 'high' politics to explore the texts and images, encountered everywhere in the 'low' politics of the everyday. Like the previous chapter, the focus here links textual analysis in the classroom to participant observation on the street. It analyses how narratives of Uyghur inclusion in *Zhonghua Minzu* were performed through political slogans, art, and major public cultural events in Ürümchi following the July 2009 violence. The first section analyses Uyghur inclusion in China through public performances of ethnic unity in political slogans and state-sponsored songs across Ürümchi during 2009–2010, particularly 'One Family' (*yijiaren* 一家人). It will examine performative inclusion of Uyghurs through ethnic unity as an inter-textual, mutually constitutive mirror. image of the exclusionary dimensions of nation-building. The second section analyses personal displays of national emblems across the city and public celebrations of different traditional ethnic festivals, namely, Han Mid-Autumn Festival (*Zhongqiu jie* 中秋节) and Uyghur *Roza Heyti* (روزاھېيت). This section asks, How do public celebrations of different ethnic festivals articulate the relationship between ethnicity and nation? How do they balance narratives of ethnic equality and trans-ethnic Han cultural superiority?

Inclusion and exclusion are mutually constitutive, and inclusion can be as equally threatening to group identity as exclusion. The chapter argues that ethnic unity is threatening because it is hierarchical and normatively orders identities into a binary between the trans-ethnic, dynamic Han national standard and the anomaly of backward ethnic minorities in a modern world. Ethnic minorities are a perpetual and peripheral cultural frontier to be developed and converted by the active 'nucleus' of *Zhonghua Minzu*. Celebrations of traditional festivals include minorities in *Zhonghua Minzu* but reinforce their exclusion by framing minority festivals as exclusively ethnic, while majority Han festivals are national and required celebrations for all *minzu*. Nation-building in Xinjiang objectivises ethnic Han-ness as the national standard by offering inclusion contingent upon conversion of ethnic difference. Who is *minzu* and who is a nation reflect power relations that define the relationship between ethnicity and nation (Pan, 2008b, p.112). The exercise of power defines these categories, and, while Chinese scholarship generally avoids directly addressing CCP policy, the idea that power relations determine which ethnic groups gain recognition as nations has been well understood in China since the Opium War. Ethnic unity emerges from power relations between the state and different groups, which shape the meanings attributed to different *minzu*. Ethnic unity demarcates boundaries between majority and minorities, speaking *for* them without allowing them to speak. Unity includes minorities on terms set by and for the ethnic majority, namely, global power and ethnocentric 'fusion' at home.

The 'Struggle' for 'Ethnic Unity'

This section analyses inclusion of Uyghurs in *Zhonghua Minzu* through public performances of *tuanjie* in political slogans and state-sponsored songs. The conceptualisation of unity as a 'struggle' against China's enemies is everywhere, saturating news broadcasts, school textbooks, and political slogans. Most ethnic unity narratives in policy statements and education texts begin with Fei Xiaotong's (1988) notion of a 'unified and pluralistic' *Zhonghua Minzu*. *Zhonghua Minzu* is constituted by many cultures of 56 *minzu* (*duoyuan* 多元) but is held together as 'one body' (*yiti* 一体) by the 'guiding force' of the Han 'nucleus' (Fei, 1988). The exceptionalism of *tuanjie* articulates

China's nominal pluralism as distinct from Western nation-states and Soviet ethnic federalism because it unifies the nation through organic and timeless cultural bonds between superior Han and inferior ethnic minorities. *Minzu tuanjie* textbooks explain that one of its key precepts is 'The Three Cannot Leaves' (*sange libukai* 三个离不开): 'Han can never leave ethnic minorities, ethnic minorities can never leave the Han, and all ethnic minorities can never leave each other'. *Sange libukai* emerged prior to the Cultural Revolution but fell into disuse, like ethnic extinction, because of its association with Han chauvinism. *Sange libukai* imagines Han majority and ethnic minorities as complementary opposites in one indivisible, organic nation. It includes minorities but threatens them at the same time because they *cannot* leave this hierarchical relationship that is defined for them.

Following the 'turning point' of the 'Baren uprising', discussed in Chapter 3, Jiang Zemin re-introduced *sange libukai* during his 1990 August visit to Xinjiang. Jiang compared his visit to the arrival of the PLA in 1949 and emphasised that stability in Xinjiang depended on 'never giving up education and the struggle against bourgeois liberalism' (Jiang, 1990b, pp.315–318). Jiang celebrated *sange libukai* as the 'new model of *minzu* relations' (Jiang, 1990b, pp.320–321). However, asserting 'Marxism-Leninism, Mao Zedong thought, patriotism, collectivism, and socialism' simply re-emphasised pre-'opening and reform' policy. Jiang acknowledged the long-term historical construction of *Zhonghua Minzu* but instead emphasised that China is a 'unified multi-*minzu* nation' formed through a century of struggle, from the Opium War until 1949, against 'invasion, oppression, and exploitation' by 'outside forces' (Jiang, 1990a, p.304). The Hu Jintao era saw more explicit shifts towards cultural nationalism, and *Zhonghua Minzu* became reframed as a nation built by ancestral lineage (*zuguo*), 'formed through 5,000-year-long processes of joint construction by all *minzu*' (Hu, 2006, p.632). *Sange libukai* continues to denote socialism and territorial integrity but also embodies the timeless hierarchy of *Zhonghua Minzu*, reflecting how progressive, rationalist socialism and conservative, cultural nationalism are often mutually reinforcing in contemporary China. *Sange libukai* is omnipresent in all party documents, ethnic unity educational materials, and public discourse as the essence of China's ethnic relations. The advert pictured (Figure 5.1) for the 'cross-boundary' modernity offered by MG cars was combined with *sange libukai* slogans in an Ürümchi coffee shop urinal.

Unity blurs boundaries between official politics and the everyday (unofficial commercial advertising). The threatening inclusion of ethnic unity reflects and reproduces boundaries between the civilisation of the Han centre and the ethnic barbarism of the periphery. The articulation of Uyghur inclusion through ethnic unity and 'The Three Cannot Leaves' (*sange libukai*) is ethnocentric because they rely on Fei Xiaotong's idea of the Han as China's

Figure 5.1 Urinal in an Ürümchi coffee shop. Above: advert for MG cars ('City-cross-country-cross-boundary vehicle'). Below: *Sange libukai*: 'The Han can never leave ethnic minorities, ethnic minorities can never leave the Han, and all ethnic minorities can never leave each other'.

centripetal, nation-building 'nucleus'. Ethnic unity builds China upon boundaries between the timeless, unbroken culture of the advanced central plains and Xinjiang as a peripheral, backward frontier:

Sange libukai reflects the history of progress of ethnic unity amongst all of China's *minzu*. Over thousands of years of history the Han of the central plains and surrounding area's ethnic minorities have assembled, becoming the unified and stable Chinese nation with the central plain as the core ... the Han are superior in the areas of their economic cultural level, science and technology, and their labour resources. (XEP, 2009, pp.43–44)

Ethnic unity constitutes Xinjiang as a 'meeting point between savagery and civilisation' and between Chinese people (*Hua* 华) and barbarians (*Yi* 夷). Ethnic unity includes Uyghurs as Chinese but behind the Han, because

Figure 5.2 'Alika Kedehan, "Loving Mother"'.

Chinese-ness is defined through modernisation and cultural evolution. *Tuanjie* positions the party-state as the historical culmination of Han superiority whose mission is to 'defend the frontier' and develop its inferior peoples. By the end of 2009, all local newspapers in Ürümchi published daily 'people-centred' 'ethnic unity friendly stories' of ethnic minorities under the heading 'my *Minzu* Brothers and Sisters'. These personal stories were guided by political texts explaining that different ethnic groups are 'one family' (*yi jiaren* 一家人), inclusive and hierarchical, engaged in 'common ethnic unity struggle and prosperous development'. These included the story of the 'Uyghur Mother', a housewife without children of her own, who helped a Han neighbour by looking after his children when at work (Chenbao, 2009j). Another column told the story of a young Hui man who arranged his wedding on a date that his Uyghur friend could attend (Chenbao, 2009k). The ethnicised framings of these everyday experiences of banal neighbourly interactions were transformed into political acts of nation-building and contained within the *minzu* boundaries demarcated and securitised by the party-state.

Politicised and ethnicised representations of everyday social interaction were visually displayed as forms of nation-building in a free exhibition at the Ürümchi expo centre in September 2009. This was organised and curated by the XUAR Government to celebrate the 60th anniversary of the PRC's founding. The 'Uyghur Mother', representing the 'simple' love of all ethnic minorities, integrally bound into the organic fabric of *Zhonghua Minzu* appeared in the section 'Unity and Harmony Stories' (Figure 5.2). Like victims of violence in Chapter 4, the heroes' ethnicity was explicitly highlighted as part of the politicised unity narrative to tell the story that preserving the state-produced identities and social position of ethnic minorities is necessary to secure the organic cultural integrity of *Zhonghua Minzu*.

The mother-figure is particularly significant in Uyghur popular culture and often represents the natural, unbroken lineage of Uyghur-ness in China, what Duara (1998) called the 'soul of tradition within modernity'. Women's reproductive functions are often tied to 'myths of common origin' in the nationalist construction of identity (Yuval-Davis, 2008, p.26). The mother-figure plays a pivotal role in Uyghur conceptualisations of culture and national identity, exemplified in the famous folk song '*Mother*-tongue' (*Ana Til*) by Abdurehim Heyit, also recreated as a disco-pop-style song by Yasan Mukhpul. Abdurehim sings 'the language went into my body with the first drop of my mother's milk ... you are so precious to me like my dear mother'. In popular Uyghur identity narratives, Uyghur-ness is transmitted via the all-powerful mother-figure bestowed with responsibility to maintain an organic community. The deployment of the mother-figure in Uyghur popular culture resists the hegemonic orthodoxy of *Zhonghua Minzu*, which co-opts gender narratives and articulates ethnicity for Uyghurs as Chinese in origin. However, official news stories and public exhibitions that mobilised these images did not allow participants to tell their own stories, instead, deploying ethnicised representations of everyday behaviour to performatively enact a unified and harmonious Chinese national identity. Individual Uyghur behaviour was dehumanised and mobilised solely as evidence of national unity and officially co-opted as unofficial 'people-centred' stories. The 'Uyghur mother' deployed by the party-state ran counter to its practiced meaning as the timeless continuity of Uyghur-ness. Instead, the 'Uyghur mother' is transformed into a loving guardian of Xinjiang's multi-ethnic youth and desire for ethnic extinction (*minzu xiaowang*) of Uyghur culture that ethnic unity (*minzu tuanjie*) entails. The Xi Jinping–era slogan 'I look to the party as I look to my mother' (Figure 5.3) interweaves socialist progress and timeless continuity by positioning the socialist party-state at the heart of China's timeless organic integrity. The slogan threateningly displaces the mother-figure as the impeachable heart of Uyghur community. Its public display as a traditional Chinese papercutting displaces Turkic culture, simply replacing it with a form of ethnic Han culture.

After July 2009, ethnicised framings of ordinary people coping with violence circulated *everywhere* across the city in state-produced popular culture. A music video and pop ballad, 'One Family' (*Yi Jiaren*), was produced by the Regional Party Commission Information Department and the Bureau for Culture and mobilised ethnicised images of ordinary people after the violence (XUAR Party Commission Information Department, 2009b). Official explanations were posted on Chinese video hosting sites to explain the song's production and dissemination as part of the regional government's drive to

The 'Struggle' for 'Ethnic Unity'   147

Figure 5.3 'I look to the party as I look to my mother' (left).

use arts and culture to 'promote unity and protect stability' after the '7-5' attack by the 'inside/outside Three Evils' (Xin Kuan, 2009). 'One Family' was performed by a host of ethnic Han, Uyghur, Kazakh, Mongolian, Hui, Kyrgyz, and Tajik singers, though the writers claimed the music was based on an unspecified traditional Uyghur song. The song was performed at the Xinjiang People's Theatre and beamed back to China Central Television (CCTV) for a national audience in Beijing for Spring Festival (*Chunjie* 春节) during February 2010 (Xinjiang Dushibao, 2010, p.C03). From September 2009 until summer 2010 the video was played every evening on Xinjiang television as an officially assigned 'ethnic unity broadcast'. The song, like all ethnic unity messages, could be heard every day and everywhere in the city on television, radio, and even on loudspeakers on university campuses during break-times. Ethnic unity classes sang the song, and for examinations, students and staff wrote essays explaining how the song made them 'feel deeply about ethnic unity'.[1] The song lyrics[2] performed China not as a civic political unit but as an organic, unbreakable, and timeless familial bond based on common origins. The video visualised passionate performances of a multi-*minzu* chorus, interspersed with images of post-'7-5' unity exemplified by political slogans and military patrols. The chorus sang:

[1] Based on interviews with student participants.
[2] For full lyrics (Mandarin and English), see Appendix 2.

> Home is one home, the country is great China,
> If the family lives in harmony, all affairs will prosper,
> It has you and it has me,
> Home is one home; the country is great China.
> We are all one family, you cannot separate you and me.
> Warmth expels cold winds, true love becomes a true heart,
> We are all one family under the blue sky,
> We are all one heart, all one root,
> Prosperity accompanies peace, we are all one family.

This rousing and emotive song sought to overcome the troubled alienation of the 'inside/outside Three Evils' ('cold winds') with the 'warmth' of China and ethnic unity. The song adapted well-known Confucius quotes to perform the nation ('great China') through unified historical origins ('one root'), identity ('one heart'), and development ('affairs will prosper'). This performs China as an organic and hierarchical indivisible whole ('one family'), from which separation is impermissible and logically impossible ('cannot separate'). Images of people donating money to help China return to prosperity were interspersed with donations of blood to injured residents in hospital, forming organic bonds between residents who now shared life from 'one heart'. The unity between different *minzu* in the video then shifted to unity between people, government, and military, more reminiscent of 1950s conceptualisations of unity as the socialist 'struggle' for political unity between 'party and military' and 'the masses and the military' (State Council, 1950, p.45). The video visualised donations of food by the truckload being handed by the people to military forces. The People's Armed Police (PAP) appeared stern and armed with the same fully automatic, portable machine guns used in divisive, ethnicised security practices across the city. For ethnic unity, the PAP marched to the line 'the country is great China'. The final scene saw six ethnic minorities dressed in brightly coloured nylon 'traditional' ethnic costume walking against the shiny urban backdrop of an imaginary Ürümchi, visualising the relationship between modern Han and backward ethnic minorities. Official Chinese nationalism's narratives of modernisation and timelessness circulated together in the song's articulation of boundaries as timeless and organic ('I don't need to ask, you don't need to say'). The notion of family in China is inherently hierarchical and this very phrase, 'one family' (*yi jiaren*), was dismissed by Jian Bozan (1960) as a fashionable 'new way of thinking' about *minzu* relations inadvertently based on older hierarchies. Jian correctly predicted this ahistorical approach would conceal China's hierarchical history and demand assimilation, not participation, from minorities.

The mutually reinforcing inclusion of unity and exclusion of securitisation appeared together in the *One Family* video. The harmony and unity of the Han-minority relationship emerged as a state-enforced peace through threat of violence. The visual backdrop to the video was real-life military patrols in the aftermath of the July violence. At the time of the song's constant airplay, the city was heavily militarised and security services remained in position to 'defend the frontier' in Uyghur neighbourhoods. The same department responsible for education materials such as *The Fifty Whys* produced the song 'One Family'. The song, therefore, reflected the mutual constitution of the exclusion of the 'inside/outside Three Evils' and inclusion of non-Han into ethnic unity as part of the 'zero-sum political struggle of life or death' for China (XEP, 2009, p.15). The mutual constitution of unity's peaceful inclusion and violent exclusion of the 'inside/outside Three Evils' circulated across the city and in images of state-violence and social harmony in the 'Harmony Unity Stories' section of the 60th anniversary exhibition. A photo of 'the mighty army' grimacing with raised swords, representing the threat of violence to enforce unity (Figure 5.4), hung alongside doves of peace flying across People's Square (Figure 5.5). State-violence and societal peace made each other possible.

During July 2009, police and public workers arranged a background of publicly displayed political slogans (*kouhao*) across every section of the city.[3] These political texts (Figures 5.6 and 5.7) constituted inclusion and peace through the threat of exclusion and physical violence in the form of tanks, thousands of PAP and PLA armed with machine guns, attack dogs, and riot police, patrolling across the city. The slogan 'Strengthen *Minzu Tuanjie*, Strike Hard against "The Three Evils"' (Figure 5.6) again offered Uyghurs stark choices of inclusion as Chinese (unity) or exclusion as a Turkic, Islamic threat ('The Three Evils'). One of the most commonly observable slogans after '7-5' and then again after re-imposition of martial law on September 3 was Hu Jintao's signature *minzu* policy slogan, 'Ethnic unity is prosperity, ethnic separatism is disaster' (Figure 5.7). The slogan is a simple, binarising message that the party-state offers the only path to economic development, and reminds minorities that they have always required the Han for their survival, as analysed in Chapter 2. The slogan was repeated in ethnic unity education manuals and described as 'not a political slogan' but a 'political, cultural, and economic lifeline' (XEP, 2009, p.6). It performs *Zhonghua Minzu* as a nation of timeless unity *and* progressive modernity ('prosperity') but under threat from the 'disaster' of Uyghurs' backward identification with Turkic-ness. This binary repeats Uyghurs' stark choice between inclusion as Chinese (unity), with all the prosperity and ambivalence that entails, or violent exclusion as backward Turkic and Islamic threats ('The Three Evils').

The ambivalence of ethnic inclusion in *Zhonghua Minzu* is exemplified by the ethnocentrism of ethnic unity, and its message of peace is directly related to

---

[3] Many slogans remained in place for months afterward and were observable throughout fieldwork, but this is also based on multiple eyewitness accounts from July 5.

150 Performing Inclusion of the Uyghur Other

Figure 5.4 'The mighty army – the troops of the Xinjiang People's Armed Police'.

Figure 5.5 'Ürümchi People's Square'.

The 'Struggle' for 'Ethnic Unity'   151

Figure 5.6 One example of this slogan erected approximately every 20 yards on *Tuanjie Lu* ('Unity Street'), with a heavily militarised roadblock on every junction (see bottom right): 'Strengthen *Minzu Tuanjie*, Strike Hard against "The Three Evils"'.

Figure 5.7 A slogan erected by the city government's planning department supervision centre: 'Ethnic unity is prosperity, ethnic separatism is disaster'.

state-violence to eliminate alternative Uyghur identities. Ethnic unity continues to mark Xinjiang as a 'savage' frontier that requires exclusion through violence and conversion by modernisation. Violence against the enemy of 'The Three Evils' was a prerequisite to the peace offered to friends of ethnic unity in a single interlinked 'struggle' for transformation *and* continuity of *Zhonghua Minzu*. The peace, progress, and hierarchy of unity are to be maintained by state-violence against minority identities. These images and the constantly visible reminders of potential state-violence highlight how violence and ethnic exclusion are ordinary aspects of everyday life in Xinjiang, thus disrupting the party-state's own narrative of timeless unity and multi-*minzu* inclusion. When the song 'One Family' was played during breaks on university campuses and no teachers were nearby, groups of Uyghur students mocked the song by singing in faux high-pitched voices, followed by roars of laughter at the chorus, 'We are one family'. The song celebrates the visceral daily realities of violent practices such as martial law and surveillance of Uyghur neighbourhoods, which remind Uyghurs they are ambivalently included as a cultural frontier between Chinese civilisation and barbarism outside. Uyghurs found benevolent inclusion in *Zhonghua Minzu* difficult to take seriously when looking down the barrel of a gun. By the year 2020, all versions of the song circulating online contained none of these images that ambivalently narrated inclusion. Instead, a Han male and female duet have been recorded to the backdrop images of natural scenery, reflecting the recent, more explicit shifts towards organic civilisational politics.

Celebrating China: Marginalising Minorities, Objectivising the Han

Following the Cultural Revolution, China experienced a brief period of 'cultural liberalisation' in the early 1980s when official conceptualisations of minority cultures were 'fostered, promoted, and marketed' (Schein, 2000, p.88). Ethnic festivals became reworked spectacles 'clogged with tourists' (Schein, 2000, pp.89–90). However, the CCP and Han nationalists now cite 'opening' as the cause of Uyghur separatism in Xinjiang, quoting Jiang Zemin's explanation that 'relaxing education' encouraged China's enemies and Western bourgeois nationalism. This section analyses how celebrations of different traditional festivals were officially celebrated and policed in Ürümchi from 2009–2010, constituting hierarchical relations between ethnicity and nation and between Han and Uyghurs. A two-week period from September's end to the start of October witnessed celebrations for National Day, the Han Chinese Mid-Autumn Festival and Uyghur *Roza Heyti*. The proximity of these festival celebrations in space and time provided opportunities to analyse and observe differences in how they are framed and celebrated by the party-state, Han, and Uyghurs. Traditional Han festivals were objectivised as national and trans-ethnic through public promotion as celebrations for *all* Chinese people. However, Uyghur festivals were officially marginalised as ethnic and celebrations were largely relegated to the private sphere. The different meanings officially attributed to the festivals through methods that appeared apolitical articulate Han-ness as a trans-ethnic, conversionary category. The inequality between Han and minority cultures performed in these celebrations shows how the revitalisation of 'Chinese' traditional culture is deeply political and hierarchical.[4] While images of singing, dancing minorities circulate widely across China, in Xinjiang, traditional Uyghur festivals are removed from public visibility. This exacerbates Uyghur insecurity that they are being assimilated into a Han nation-state. Han culture is being revitalised as 'Chinese', while Uyghur cultural practices are being removed from public life or eliminated altogether.

The CCP has reconfigured its own identity from the revolutionary politics of eliminating tradition to endorsing and celebrating selected and curated versions of those traditions in the 'opening and reform' era. The CCP appeals to the cultural nationalism associated with traditional Chinese festivals and no longer formally celebrates socialist holidays, including International Worker's Day. During the 1990s, provincial governments sought to assert regional identities through the regional timing of holidays. The promotion of national-level festivals allowed the centre to contain rival administrations at the provincial and local levels of government (Callahan, 2010, p.192). The party-state's deployment of traditional festivals contains cultural resistance by reconfiguring itself and Chinese tradition as mutually dependent. However, the promotion of national-level festivals in Xinjiang goes beyond containment as they narrate and securitise the boundaries of *Zhonghua Minzu*. The CCP nominally includes Uyghur traditions deemed politically safe and excludes those deemed a threat, a process termed the 'folklorisation' of Uyghur ethnicity by Bellér-Hann (2002). Traditional Han festivals, such as Mid-Autumn Festival and Spring Festival (*Chunjie*), are widely and publicly celebrated in Xinjiang as *national* festivals, contrasting against the relative public absence of Uyghur festivals. This asymmetry includes ethnic minorities by objectivising the Han and demanding minority recognition of the cultural centrality of their traditions. For example, the regional government sent SMS texts to every Xinjiang resident, 'wishing all *minzu* a joyous celebration of Mid-Autumn Festival, a tradition of *Zhonghua Minzu*'. Mid-Autumn Festival is celebrated on the 15th day of the 8th month of the Chinese Lunar calendar. It was recognised as national-level 'intangible cultural heritage' in 2006 and then as a national holiday two years later (Xinhua, 2011). Mid-Autumn Festival is an official *national* holiday and celebrates the military victory of the Han over Mongolian minorities. Its origins are officially explained in moon worship from the Western Zhou period (1046–771 BCE). However, the first

---

[4] For example, see Carrico (2017) on the rise of *Hanfu*, ancient Han clothing, as part of the resurgence of exclusionary racial nationalism.

mooncakes were made in the fourteenth century when 'people' organised Chinese rebellion against the Mongols by exchanging pancakes stuck with secret messages from rebel leader Zhu Yuanzhang saying, 'Kill the Mongols on the 15th day of the 8th month' (Xinhua, 2011). Eating mooncakes in celebration of violent subjugation of non-Han who seek to dominate China, a Han responsibility, celebrates historical relations of Han superiority over non-Han. However, these celebrations conceal this cultural dominance in taken-for-granted, apolitical social practices of eating cake.

This Han-centred *Zhonghua Minzu* narrative was performed at Xinjiang University on September 30, 2009, when staff formally distributed 'love Xinjiang, love China' stickers.[5] These stickers were distributed to every student in every class along with a Mid-Autumn Festival mooncake. To love Xinjiang, one had to love China, and this entails loving China as a Han-centred nation that enacts organised violence against threats to *Zhonghua Minzu's* ethnic order. Heads of departments visited every classroom, even those with international students, confused by the visit's significance, to explain it was important to celebrate National Day and Mid-Autumn Festival for 'ethnic unity'. The conflation of civic and cultural nationalisms positioned Han culture as the guiding force of ethnic unity and equated the Han with *Zhonghua Minzu* for domestic and international audiences. Ceremonial speeches by heads of departments announced that Mid-Autumn Festival and Spring Festival were *China's* 'most traditional and most important festivals' with no mention of *Roza Heyti* that, with the exception of increased military patrols, passed without commemoration just nine days earlier. The silencing of non-Han festivals and performance of Han festivals as cultural exemplars of *Zhonghua Minzu* conflates Han-ness and Chinese-ness. This objectivisation appeared in slogans raised across the university such as 'Joyfully celebrate National Day, happily welcome Mid-Autumn Festival' (Figure 5.8). Promoting Han cultural centrality by celebrating National Day and Han festivals together whilst silencing *ethnic* festivals offers inclusion but demands identification with securitised boundaries between Han majority and ethnic minorities.

During this period, the Ürümchi *Evening Times* (*Wulumuqi Wanshibao*) produced 'I love China, I love Xinjiang' (*ai zhonghua, ai xinjiang* 爱中华爱新疆) stickers and car badges to commemorate the 60th anniversary of the PRC's founding (Figure 5.9). Newspaper staff distributed 50,000 stickers and car badges across the city at People's Square, *Beimen, Hongshan, Youhao Lu, Nanhu* Square, and the railway station (Wulumuqi Wanshibao, 2009). Other than the railway station, frequented by people from all over China, none of the areas targeted were in the Uyghur-populated south of the city. The badges

---

[5] This is based on personal observations and discussions with staff and students.

Celebrating China: Marginalising Minorities, Objectivising the Han   155

Figure 5.8 Top: 'Joyfully celebrate National Day, happily welcome Mid-Autumn Festival'. Bottom: 'Strengthen ethnic unity, protect social stability'.

Figure 5.9 Patriotic stickers given out across the city of Ürümchi: 'Love China (*Zhonghua*), Love Xinjiang'.

circulated across the Han-populated north of the city and large companies took advantage of patriotic sentiments by displaying the logo. The widely used television company Xinjiang Guangdian Wangluo displayed the logo on their cable television menu for several weeks. The stickers were displayed on approximately half of all businesses in the city centre and *Qingnian Lu* area. However, they were barely noticeable in the south. I only observed one Uyghur teacher at Xinjiang University wearing the badge and had to explain them to several Uyghur interviewees who lived in the south of the city and had not even seen them. Their distribution was announced as a response to 'popular demand'. However, the fact they were distributed and adorned by Han while ignoring and being ignored by Uyghurs reflected and further reinforced ethnic boundaries. It was visibly observable that different groups understand *Zhonghua Minzu* narratives in different ways. The personal adornment of these symbols was to 'wish happiness on the great motherland (*zuguo* 祖国) and a more glorious future for our beautiful Xinjiang' (Wulumuqi Wanshibao, 2009). The newspaper explained that the 60th anniversary had 'raised the Chinese family's self-confidence and exhibited the greatest opportunity of the new China's great achievements' (Wulumuqi Wanshibao, 2009). The newspaper wrote that since the violence of July, 'every member of the Chinese family' 'wanted to express warm love and blessings for their motherland' and that 'all children of every *minzu* will all feel pride and self-belief because they are Chinese' (Wulumuqi Wanshibao, 2009). The stickers equated love of Xinjiang with love of *Zhonghua Minzu* and pride in the hierarchy of 'One family', thus, reinforcing the exclusion of Uyghur identities.

The performances at the university represent much broader objectivisations of Han-ness as Chinese-ness where non-Han are considered *behind* the Han in terms of their acculturation to a singular form of civilisation and modernity (Ma, 2007, p.5). Ma Rong describes the term *Zhonghua* as the ancient term for Chinese civilisation instead of the modern state, *Zhongguo*. *Zhonghua* interpellates a Han-centred nation divided between the nucleus of Chinese civilisation (*Hua*) and barbarians (*Yi*) on the periphery who 'needed to be educated' (Ma, 2007, p.5). The choice of *Zhonghua* (中华) instead of *Zhongguo* (中国) to represent 'China' on the 'love Xinjiang' badge was significant because *Zhonghua* is understood as the ancient term for the Yellow River basin and central plains as the Han's place of origin.[6] Using *Zhonghua* over *Zhongguo* performs a timelessly hierarchical national community, running from ancient times to today. This objectivises Han-ness as Chinese-ness because the very name for the Chinese nation elides the difference between ethnic Han and multi-ethnic China. This objectivisation appears in the formal name for the PRC (*Zhonghua Renmin Gongheguo*) and the Chinese nation as a people (*Zhonghua Minzu*). Wearing these badges was, therefore, a banal act of patriotism that performs the Han of the Yellow River as the centre and Xinjiang as its mutually constitutive periphery. To love China, one must love the Han's dominion over the frontier, Xinjiang, and its peoples. 'All children of every *minzu*' wear these badges '*because* they are Chinese'. In practice, this means ordinary residents must not simply identify with Chinese civic

---

[6] For example, see: Fei (1988); Ma (2007).

nationalism but with China, the binary cultural hierarchy. This banal participation in the production of national boundaries was celebrated by Han Chinese residents and not by Uyghurs, reflecting the social and physical distance between the Han north and Uyghur south of the city. When I asked young and old Han Chinese residents wearing the badges why they wore them, they would say that they 'love China, love Xinjiang' as if this was self-explanatory. Ordinary people actively participated in a powerful and ethnically structured banal nationalism, concealing and reinforcing the hierarchical and contested meanings of unity.

Comparing celebrations of Han traditions with the public life of Uyghur festivals will illuminate how they reflect and reproduce their unequal social positions, which constitute the *Zhonghua Minzu* ethno-hierarchy in Xinjiang. When I asked a 40-year-old female Uyghur and Mandarin language teacher why Uyghurs use the word *bahyrem* for National Day and Mid-Autumn Festival but use *heyti* for Uyghur festivals, she explained that *bahyrem* was for Chinese national holidays, whereas *heyti* was used for '*our* traditional holidays...not for Han holidays'. Her re-performance of binaries of self and other, and ethnic and nation, in party-state discourse positioned Han China as an external culture rather than an attractive form of self-identification. *Heyti* is embraced by Uyghurs as their own private, ethnic sphere of celebration, outside the identity-security politics of *bahyrem* and Chinese nationalism. *Qurban Heyti* and *Roza Heyti*[7] mark the beginning and end of a month of fasting for Ramadan. Qurban celebrates Abraham's willingness to sacrifice for God while Roza commemorates the revelation of the Quran to the prophet Mohammed. In nineteenth century Xinjiang, locals regarded Roza and Qurban as the most important festivals, though precise interpretations over their meaning varied over time and place (Bellér-Hann, 2008, pp.350–355). Even in the few remaining traditional Uyghur *mähällä* residential areas of 2009, the month of Ramadan was a time of huge of cultural significance. The rhythms and routines of fasting and celebration punctuated daily life in ways that marked it off from other months (Dautcher, 2009, p.283). The rhythms of fasting by day and eating by night still shaped work and social life for Uyghurs, as many restaurants closed during the day and became crowded after dark. However, urban intellectuals, regardless of government restrictions, often veered away from religion and towards Turkic language as an identity marker and choose not to fast (Dautcher, 2009, p.285). Many of Ürümchi's Uyghur restaurants remained open throughout the period, in contrast to the quiet streets and closed restaurants during visits to Kashgar for Ramadan. Nevertheless, many students and teachers in Ürümchi complained to me that

---

[7] In the Arabic-speaking world these are referred to as *Eid al-Adha* and *Eid ul-Fitr*.

they were prohibited from fasting and that officials at the school would suddenly invite them out for lunches and banquets during this period.[8] The sharp contrast between celebrations of Han traditions and restrictions on Uyghur practices includes Uyghurs in *Zhonghua Minzu* by excluding their living traditions and demanding they celebrate the withering away of their identities.

In 2012, the party-state's long-standing practice of preventing Uyghurs in Xinjiang from fasting developed into more explicit, regularised policies. Government notices were posted reminding people to 'eat properly for study and work' and large banquets were recommended as 'gifts' for Muslim state-employees during Ramadan (Guardian, 2012). This month of fasting was already a period of stress and fear for many Uyghur interviewees, with little of the contemplation or celebration it is intended to inspire. Students at three separate universities during 2009–2010 complained to me that security guards monitored their dormitories to ensure they were not praying. Many students explained they would secretly leave their dormitories to visit the mosque whenever they could. Those Uyghurs interviewed all explained that the monitoring of their behaviour was a form of assimilation to prevent them from practicing their own culture by fasting or praying. Some teachers did fast but had to do so in secret. One female teacher in her mid-30s explained that fasting was a spiritual challenge, which was 'hard enough' without 'all the Han and party-members trying to make me eat and being nosy. I just tell them I'm sick and can't eat'. In 2008, she told me that fasting was a personal choice and felt it was incompatible with modern work patterns. By 2012, as restrictions tightened, she strictly participated in fasting and explained it was an important part of 'being a Muslim and maintaining our culture'. Most Uyghurs in Ürümchi explained fasting as a personal choice but the party-state's securitisation of identity exacerbated Uyghur insecurity. Uyghurs responded with secretive resistance against assimilation and imbued religious practice with meanings drawn from everyday personal experiences of politicisation and securitisation.

While Uyghur festivals were a private, ethnic affair, Han festivals are an important part of public and national life in Xinjiang. In contrast to nationwide seven-day holidays for Spring Festival, the Regional Government posted official *Roza* notifications that permitted Muslims one day off but other *minzu* had to work (Chenbao, 2009l). Excluding Uyghur traditions from national life

---

[8] Restrictions on religious practice in Xinjiang have only intensified since this fieldwork, even prior to the emergence of mass internment camps under the 'de-extremification' policy drive. For example, in Khotan, 12 children were injured in a raid by police on a religious school (Independent, 2012). Official notices of mandatory house searches in Uyghur neighbourhoods for 'illegal religious materials' and bans on 'religious clothing' in commercial shopping areas are regularly displayed (UHRP 2012a; 2012b; 2012c).

marginalises Uyghurs and other Muslims as ethnic, contrasted against the inclusive and public, national Han sphere. Furthermore, many Muslims in headscarves could be observed working for local government and universities cleaning streets and bathrooms on the day. Religious restrictions meant state-employees had to abstain from celebrations until their public duties were complete and they returned home. Universities did not celebrate any Uyghurs festivals or mention them in the teaching of Chinese culture to international students. Roza fell on September 21, 2009, a week before the Mid-Autumn Festival fanfare but passed without official celebration. Xinjiang Television news broadcasts and regional government SMS texts had invited 'every *minzu*' to 'celebrate' Mid-Autumn and Spring festivals. However, these same organisations simply warned '*minzu* who practice Islam' to '*harmoniously* celebrate' Roza. This harmonious reminder highlighted potential Islamic, ethnic threats against the security of national Han traditions. To mark *Roza*, the local *Chenbao* newspaper printed the full State Council white paper, *Development and Progress in Xinjiang*, outlining China's successful modernisation and anti-terrorism drives. The paper ordered traditional festivals in an ethnic-national binary, stating that '*minzu* who follow Islam warmly celebrate *Roza* and *Qurban*, Han, Mongolians, and other *minzu* celebrate Spring Festival' (State Council, 2009b, p.39). This tacit acknowledgement that Spring Festival is not celebrated by Uyghurs or other Turkic Muslims was coupled with an objectivisation of Han-ness as a trans-ethnic culture for 'other *minzu*'. These mutually constitutive identity constructions underline the ambivalent inclusion of Turkic Muslims in China's hierarchical multi-*minzu* family ('one family') built on common ancestral origins (*zuguo*). The following day, the *Chenbao* front page depicted an elderly Uyghur lady celebrating Roza by offering Uyghur hospitality to SWAT police with home-made *polo*,[9] alongside more extracts from the *Progress and Development* white paper (Chenbao, 2009m). The focus on identification with China and unity with the security apparatus politicised and silenced all cultural significance of Uyghur celebrations. Ethnic unity education texts and all news reports conspicuously avoided mentioning the religious significance of these festivals. Inclusion of Uyghurs in *Zhonghua Minzu* is perplexingly ambivalent and threatening towards their cultural traditions. The party-state acknowledges Islam yet de-Islamicises and reframes Uyghur traditions for political ends, while demanding they celebrate Han culture as the national standard.

On the afternoon of *Roza*, hundreds of Uyghurs spontaneously gathered and danced together at the square around *Erdaoqiao/Döngköwrük* tower. No Han

---

[9] *Polo* is the Uyghur take on pilav, served across Central Asia. This dish of rice, mutton, carrots, and raisins is seen as more luxurious than everyday noodles (*laghman*) and it is served at important social ceremonies.

Chinese residents were present, and no media covered the festivities, reinforcing the official narrative that this was a private, non-Chinese festival for Muslims only. The *Roza* dancing was semi-choreographed by a professional dancer in an open space in the middle of the growing crowd. Passers-by joined in and danced in different regional styles and in different directions, encouraging more people to join the dance as it flowed in circles but without fixed routine. The dance was a flowing, centre-less party without fixed meaning or official control, enabling Uyghurs to celebrate the festival in diverse ways. By late afternoon the square was closed and guarded by armed paramilitary forces. Increased patrols could be seen throughout the city. Military trucks used loudspeakers to broadcast exhortations that Uyghur district residents 'build a harmonious society', marking the day as particularly dangerous because Uyghurs were celebrating tradition and diversity. One early-20s male university student commented on the occasion that he was 'sad that Roza was disappearing' because 'it used to be such a long party where everyone could stay out all night but now we can't do anything, just walk around'. The language teacher who secretly fasted said, 'I don't know how they can celebrate at this time, in this terrible situation'. She later explained the political restrictions and disappearances after July 2009 meant life was unbearable for Uyghurs and it was inappropriate to celebrate unless it could be done freely. Uyghur traditions and identity performances must be mediated via the party-state's identity-security practices that marginalise Uyghur traditions in *Zhonghua Minzu* as problems. Inclusion through unity, therefore, reproduces a hierarchical *Zhonghua Minzu* because it includes Uyghurs on unequal terms that maintain their marginality while framing their traditions as threats.

Official conflation of Han-ness and Chinese-ness in ethnic unity is exemplified in descriptions of Han identity as 'transcendent' of origins and Mandarin as 'the *only* language of modernity in China' (XEP, 2009, p.92). Uyghurs resist this objectivisation of Han ethnicity because it excludes their cultural practices while demanding participation in Han festivals as loyalty to *Zhonghua Minzu*. Examples of such resistance were plentiful on *Uyghur Online*, an online message board and blog-hosting site for Uyghurs using Mandarin Chinese. *Uyghur Online* was closed down as part of a 'strike hard' campaign following the July 2009 violence.[10] During the 2008 Beijing Olympics, one anonymous Uyghur blogger explained feelings of Uyghur identity-insecurity when Han-ness is objectivised as Chinese-ness:

Zhonghua Minzu takes Han as the nucleus and includes 56 internal *minzu* groups. Perhaps because the Han *minzu* have a huge population, the national language is

---

[10] The site has since set up servers in Europe. See: http://www.uighurbiz.net/.

Hanyu,[11] culture takes Han culture as its nucleus, so in reality, we often don't consider the religious faith or cultural customs of other *minzu*. We conflate Han *minzu* and *Zhonghua Minzu*, so that it is like *Zhonghua Minzu* and the Han *minzu* are the same and other *minzu* are not considered to exist. (Bense Shouyiren, 2008)

This narrative exemplified Uyghur concerns that official Chinese nationalism is a double-edged sword that forcibly includes Uyghurs by concealing the existence of Uyghur culture. He predicted the party-state's model of inclusion as doomed to failure because 'Han symbols', such as the 'sons of the Yellow Emperor', 'the dragon', and the 'Great Wall' are ethnic traditions that cannot symbolise *Zhonghua Minzu* without eliminating other cultures within China. Echoing sentiments repeated by dozens of interviewees, these ethnic 'symbols and totems' 'do not consider the feelings of other *minzu*' who then feel they 'do not belong to *Zhonghua Minzu*' (Bense Shouyiren, 2008). In contemporary China, 'national humiliation' ordinarily refers to how European nations hurt 'the feelings of the Chinese people' first through imperial designs of the Opium War and today by criticising CCP policy (Callahan, 2009, p.141). However, ethnic minorities express alternative feelings of humiliation about the disappearance of their cultural practices in *Zhonghua Minzu*, which are entirely silenced in public life by security discourses that label these feelings as existential threats. Zhu Weiqun, vice director of the United Front work department, has acknowledged the Han 'splittist elements' and 'big-nationality chauvinism' in phrases such as 'descendents of the dragon' and 'Sons of the fiery emperor and the Yellow Emperor' (Zhu, 2012). Nevertheless, these ethnic Han symbols represent all peoples within the PRC at home and abroad. Da Wei (2010), scholar of American Studies at the China Institute of Contemporary International Relations, implicitly critiqued the influence of Fei Xiaotong in this regard, celebrating Mao's insistence that China's historically superficial approach to interacting with non-Han cultures was a case of 'watching flowers on horseback'. Da argues that it is not enough to be 'introduced' to cultures outside the central plains if China is to become a 'pluralistic and unified' nation (Da, 2010, p.6). Da Wei recommends Chinese people celebrate traditional festivals of all *minzu* because 'genuine' cultural revival cannot be based solely on celebration of Confucianism and traditions of the central plains (Da, 2010, pp.5–6). However, Uyghur websites that discuss these issues, including *Uyghur Online*, are labelled part of the 'inside/outside Three Evils' and closed down in repeated 'Strike Hard' campaigns. Ethnic targeting of speech marginalises Uyghurs from public articulations of identity,

---

[11] *Hanyu* refers to Mandarin Chinese (*Zhongwen*) but literally means 'language of the Han'. Its use by Uyghurs indicates its outside-ness. *Hanzu tili* is used in the same way in Uyghur language.

producing a Han-centred global and domestic public discourse on the Chinese nation, where the speaker's ethnicity determines their inclusion and exclusion.

Uyghurs, or Mongols, tend not to celebrate Mid-Autumn Festival or other Han festivals that are politically packaged as festivals of *Zhonghua Minzu*. Most Uyghurs interviewed simply laughed at the idea. Eventually, I stopped asking Uyghurs if they celebrated these festivals because it offended some who then ended the conversation, assuming I knew nothing about Xinjiang. Minority disinterest in Han festivals was observable across the city during Spring and Mid-Autumn festivals. Uyghur areas were quieter than usual, but Han areas were bustling with people setting off firecrackers. Spring Festival saw public celebrations at People's Square with gatherings of Han families and official banners to celebrate the occasion. In Uyghur areas, the only observable difference to daily life was heightened surveillance of Uyghurs as a threat with increases in paramilitary patrols and additional armed stations outside mosques with the threatening slogan 'The Police are here to celebrate Spring Festival'.[12] Tensions between shared national identity and exclusionary threats of violence produce an unconvincing and threatening mode of inclusion for Uyghurs. The objectivisation of Han-ness as Chinese-ness demands acculturation of non-Han and is resisted by Uyghurs through non-participation in these festivals. Most Uyghur interviewees said they 'hated firecrackers' or 'look forward to it being over'. One mid-20s male student directly acknowledged the inequality by rhetorically asking, 'Why do they get to celebrate, and we don't? Why do I have to listen to their firecrackers over and over, yet we aren't even allowed to gather in public?' After the 2008 Mid-Autumn Festival, the anonymous blogger, Uighur, published a story on the forum *Uighurbiz*, similar to those told by many interviewees. Uighur said a cadre approached him aggressively in his residential block asking him why he wasn't taking a mooncake provided by the local government:

'Aren't you going to celebrate Mid-Autumn Festival?' I replied that I wasn't. He very sharply looked at me. 'Are you not a Chinese person?' I said, 'I am a Chinese person!' He said: 'Who do you think celebrates Mid-Autumn Festival?' I was a little tongue-tied, but I said: 'Han'. I know that in Xinjiang discussion of these types of topics is very sensitive. They can casually say Uyghurs are like this, Uyghurs are like that. But if we are in front of them it is very hard to say Han are like this, Han are like that because it is said to be equivalent to opposing them!! Afterwards he then said, 'Chinese people must celebrate Mid-Autumn Festival' and repeated this several times. Without any resistance I said, 'This should be the tradition.' He then didn't pay attention to me but in my heart, I felt so uncomfortable. We get along harmoniously with them and we protect the unity

---

[12] These 'convenience stations' became permanent. They are now hubs for surveillance using real-time AI-driven facial recognition technology, determining people's threat levels and whether they should be extra-legally interned in camps. For example, see: Byler and Grose (2018).

of the nation. Yet why do we have to be subject to their culture, regardless of whether or not we have this kind of tradition ourselves? (Uighur, 2008)

Uighur proposed *unity* in a shared Chinese identity, but this resisted the hierarchy of 'ethnic unity' (*minzu tuanjie*), which frames Han culture as superior to other ethnic groups in *Zhonghua Minzu*. Framing Han cultural practices as the national standard provoked Uighur's resistance to nation-building that entails Hanification. Another Uyghur blogger repeated the family metaphor discussed in the previous section, arguing that celebrating defeat of the Mongols and a Great Wall to keep non-Han out of China only creates 'hostilities' between 'brothers' in our 'one family' (*yi jiaren*) (Bense Shouyi-ren, 2008). This inter-textual process of political antagonism rejects identifications offered by states, 'reading between the lines' to invert the text's producer and the projected object of their argument against themselves (Bhabha, 2009, p.35). Uyghurs invert *tuajnjie* against itself in performative enactments of imaginary unity and equality in *Zhonghua Minzu*.

Conclusions

This chapter showed how the inclusion offered to Uyghurs in China's nation-building in Xinjiang produces and reproduces their marginality and exclusion in contemporary China. The cultural conversion of Confucianism, modernising imperatives of the historical materialist *minzu* project, and re-emergence of 'great Han chauvinism' are alternative modes of inclusion based on competing views of Chinese identity. However, in practice, they are mutually reinforcing ethnocentric narratives. Their goal is 'fusion', which positions Han at the centre of *Zhonghua Minzu* and minority identities as problems on China's periphery. One of the most vexing aspects of theorising nationalism is its ongoing political power, which contrasts against its 'philosophical poverty' (Anderson, 1991, p.5). We need to 'break with common sense' that ethnic or national conflicts inherently involve conflict between ethnic groups or nations (Brubaker, 2002, p.166). In Xinjiang, the underlying logics of official nation-building narratives ethnicise fractured, multi-layered conflicts and reproduce the ethnic boundaries it desires to eradicate. The taken-for-granted celebration of Han-ness as Chinese-ness and reproduction of ethnic boundaries in Xinjiang are comparable to Michael Billig's (1995) description of the 'unconscious hanging of the flag' as the banal reproduction of national boundaries. However, the boundaries articulated through ethnic unity in Xinjiang are built on the taken-for-granted binary between majority and minorities that is as focused on external differentiation as it is on reproducing an internal ethno-hierarchy. On the surface, unity is a formalistic exercise in rote learning that fails to address real-life problems of violence and discrimination in Xinjiang.

However, *tuanjie* has a re-productive life of its own, and through circulation in public discourse, people critique, dismiss, and reorient the meaning of *Zhonghua Minzu* in attempts to understand their public lives and articulate their identities.

Ethnic unity (*minzu tuanjie*) positions Han as the national standard by objectivising social practices associated with ethnic Han as national and inclusive of non-Han. Inclusion of Uyghurs in *Zhonghua Minzu* demands identification with hierarchical boundaries between Han majority and ethnic minorities, with the Han nucleus guiding the 'overall direction' of history towards 'fusion' and withering away of Uyghur identity. The chapter's first section analysed inclusion of Uyghurs in *Zhonghua Minzu* through performances of ethnic unity in songs and political slogans that saturated public life across Ürümchi following the 2009 violence. The inclusion of 'ethnic unity' and exclusion of 'The Three Evils' are inter-textual, mutually constitutive aspects of the same nation-building 'struggle'. Unity is mutually constituted against the production of its alternatives as existential threats to China. Unity is the carrot to the stick of state-violence against 'The Three Evils' but offers Uyghurs ambivalent opportunities to be included in *Zhonghua Minzu* as a frontier. The second section analysed the hierarchical relationship between nation and ethnicity and between Han and Uyghurs in representations of traditional festivals. Symbols and traditions associated with the Han are objectivised as national symbols (e.g. Mandarin Chinese, traditional festivals, the dragon, the Great Wall) that transcend ethnicity and help convert Uyghurs. The framing of Han festivals as Chinese and Uyghur festivals as ethnic produces the Han as a conversionary, trans-ethnic category, relationally constituting Uyghur culture as inferior and outside the national nucleus. Unity thus converts ethnic minorities by demanding they recognise and identify with the superiority of the Han to guide them to cultural disappearance. The stories written by Uyghur bloggers and Uyghur celebration of 'ethnic' festivals reflect and reproduce their alienation from the way inclusion objectivises Han-ness as Chinese-ness. The party-state positions itself as neutral arbiter between majority and minorities, but its ethnocentric security discourses perform the Han as culturally superior *and* normatively neutral, a major obstacle to shared identity and security in Xinjiang.

'Ethnic unity' reflects China's ethno-hierarchy and exacerbates Uyghurs insecurity because it ranks Han as superior to Uyghurs without offering inclusion of their identities. Da Wei's proposal to 'rectify nationalism' suggested Chinese people ask themselves if the dragon and yellow emperor, symbols of the central plains, can legitimately represent a modern, multi-*minzu* nation (Da, 2010, pp.6 & 44). Da Wei urged Chinese people to celebrate all ethnic festivals if China is to be a genuinely multi-ethnic nation. However, the party-state instead produces a hierarchical and Han-centred *Zhonghua Minzu*

Conclusions

by celebrating Han festivals as Chinese and minority traditions as ethnic. The different streams of ethnocentric party-state narratives include Han in different ways but celebrate and rank symbols of Han ethnicity over those of all other ethnic groups. These narratives fail to produce a shared identity between Han and Uyghurs because they exclude Uyghur identities and give Han ethno-nationalists an official vocabulary of superiority and exclusion when they conceptualise *Zhonghua Minzu*. Uyghurs generally choose not to participate in 'national' festivals because they understand them as exclusion and subjection to Han-ness. The party-state inadvertently reminds Xinjiang's peoples that unity is not timeless by highlighting and reinforcing the boundaries it aims to erase from history. In the next chapter Han and Uyghurs in Ürümchi are asked directly how they understand and experience unity and identity in *Zhonghua Minzu* using detailed, semi-structured interviews. It will show how unity inadvertently produces a multiplicity of identities in the region as Han and Uyghurs re-perform official discourse to narrate alternative Chinas.

6　Han and Uyghur Narratives on Ethnic and National Identity

Introduction

Official *Zhonghua Minzu* narratives reveal multiple modes of ethnocentric inclusion (Confucian culturalism, socialist historical materialism, and Han chauvinism). However, the signature slogans of the party-state's national narratives began to distinctly shift from socialist transformation in a 'century of struggle' under Jiang Zemin to culturalist notions of '5,000 years of unbroken history' under Hu Jintao. Xi Jinping's 'China Dream' of the 'Great revival' continues to interweave these two narratives, but both China's ancient past and its future are distinctly civilisational. The reversal of a 'century of humiliation' by Western powers allowed China to *return* to its pre-modern central position in world affairs. The 'Great Revival' represents the continuous, unbroken unity and development of *Zhonghua Minzu*, distinguishing China from the disunited, stagnating West. Previous chapters showed how inclusion (ethnic unity) and exclusion ('inside/outside Three Evils') are mutually constitutive aspects of Chinese nation-building in Xinjiang. This chapter shifts emphasis from official politics above to identity narratives from below. It will analyse the social dynamics produced by nation-building on the ground that illustrate the CCP's successes and failures in its promotion of a shared identity. It asks Han and Uyghurs how they understand ethnic unity (*minzu tuanjie*) and their positions in *Zhonghua Minzu*. In the 'opening and reform' era, what Mao termed the friends and enemies of the revolution have been reconfigured to friends and enemies of the party-state's *Zhonghua Minzu* narrative. This securitisation of *Zhonghua Minzu* closes the space for public articulation of non-Han ethnic identities. Nevertheless, its ambivalent inclusion of non-Han peoples opens space within tensions between inclusion and exclusion that Han and Uyghurs deploy to critique the party-state's conceptualisation of Chinese identity. The chapter analyses intersections between China's grand security narratives and the micropolitics of everyday identities in the triadic relations between Han, Uyghurs, and the state. It will show how Han and Uyghurs read and reperform official narratives of inclusion and exclusion in *minzu tuanjie* to articulate their own friends and enemies, producing multiple Chinas.

Introduction

Synthesising the top-down[1] and bottom-up[2] approaches to ethnic identities in Xinjiang discussed in Chapter 1 enables analysis of relations between official and unofficial identity narratives and between competing visions of *Zhonghua Minzu*. The party-state's monopoly over nationalist representations of identity has gradually weakened in the reform era and does not speak for most people whom it defines as Chinese (Gries, 2004; Leibold, 2010). Contestation of identity takes place in scholarly and official debates, online discussion, and popular culture, challenging official boundaries from above and below, reconfiguring what it means to be Chinese. However, the asymmetry of what Homi Bhabha (2009) called the 'power to identify' in China's public debates mean Uyghurs have no public voice and 'representation has not withered away' (Spivak, 1988, p.104). Nevertheless, in everyday, unrecorded politics, people respond to official representations of identity and relate them to daily practices of interaction between Han, Uyghurs, and the state, reconfiguring the boundaries of *Zhonghua Minzu*. The inevitable differences between the represented and its representation then are the location of politics (Bleiker, 2001, p.510). Official representations of identity boundaries are only felt if they correspond with lived experiences of potential members and are realised in social relations symbolically close to them (Amit, 2002a, p.8; Cohen, 1985, pp.13 & 28). Group identity emerges at the interface between officially ascribed categories and visceral face-to-face interactions (Amit, 2002b, p.60). Identity is constructed symbolically and nationhood does not emerge simply through social behaviour but in the thinking about what this behaviour means (Cohen, 1985, p.98). Viscerality is a narrative itself that gives meaning to everyday life and often emerges as resistance when state-ascribed identities transgress the boundaries experienced in people's daily practices. Ethnic identities, nevertheless, feel more visceral to Han and Uyghurs because they are based on shared knowledge of how to *do* things, such as language use and religious practice. Official boundaries and visceral daily experiences intersect in Xinjiang because the ranking and securitisation of identity in official nation-building discourse mediate how nation and *minzu* can be practiced. *Minzu* are official positionalities, which people are born into, but ethnic group-ness exists through action and interaction (Harrell, 1990, p.516). 'Minoritisation' is a powerful process, but the meaning of *minzu* categories takes on a life of its own (Schein, 2000, pp.96–99). The meaning of *minzu* in Xinjiang is found in ongoing processes of interaction and contestation within and between ethnic groups and the state.

This chapter explores how Han and Uyghurs in Xinjiang understand and reconfigure the boundaries of inclusion and exclusion in Chinese nation-

---

[1] See: Gladney (1990; 1996; 2004); Rudelson (1997).
[2] See: Bellér-Hann (2008); Dautcher (2009); Newby (2007); Smith (2000; 2002).

building with their own identity narratives. It asks, How does the purported nation understand itself and renegotiate the boundaries demarcated in official nation-building? The concept of re-performance is used to frame how Han and Uyghurs deploy official framings of identity-security but invert and reconfigure their meaning to articulate alternative identities. Han and Uyghur practices of re-performance deploy the underlying assumptions of official categories, such as *minzu*, frontier, backwardness, and modernity, but uses these to contest official *Zhonghua Minzu* narratives and articulate their own identities. 'Reading between the lines' of Han and Uyghur identity narratives, to use Bhabha's (2009) phrase, shows they both inter-textually invert hegemonic discourse to resist their official social positions and narrate the meaning of visceral daily practices. Han and Uyghurs re-perform official relations between Chinese-ness, Han-ness, and Uyghur-ness through inter-textual inversions that conceptualise daily practices through ethnic difference. *Zhonghua Minzu* is performed from above and re-performed from below, producing many Chinas in triadic relations between Han, Uyghurs, and the state.

The methodology[3] in Chapters 6 and 7 links analysis of official discourse in previous chapters to qualitative analysis of detailed, semi-structured interviews with Han and Uyghurs on identity, security, and *minzu* relations. The region's politics precludes extensive, independent survey work, and my own social networks dictated the range of access available. Most people interviewed were working-class, small-scale *getihu* entrepreneurs, middle-class intellectuals, and students in their early to mid-20s. The first section analyses popular interpretations of ethnic unity through detailed, semi-structured interviews with Han and Uyghur residents of Ürümchi. It asks, How do Han and Uyghurs interpret and re-perform official identity boundaries demarcated through 'ethnic unity'? This will show that Han and Uyghurs alike tend to dismiss unity as propaganda and re-perform the narrative to construct boundaries that define *minzu* as distinct nations. Identity narratives circulating amongst Han intellectuals tend to reflect official ethnocentric narratives of a unified, multi-*minzu* nation, rather than the explicitly chauvinist ethno-nationalist narratives, which have considerable popularity amongst working classes and *getihu*. Intellectuals' conceptualisations of *Zhonghua Minzu* interweave culturalism and historical materialism, articulating Han and Uyghur ethno-nationalism as un-Chinese because *Hua* culture is inherently inclusionary and progressive. This narrative performs China through diversity but replicates underlying ethnocentric logics of Xinjiang's ambivalent inclusion as a frontier to be converted.

The second section analyses how Han in Ürümchi re-perform official nation-building discourses to articulate their identity through these

[3] See the book's introduction for a full explanation of the methodology.

interweaved narratives of socialist transformation *and* timeless civilisation. The Han interviewed tended to employ historical materialist ideas of Xinjiang's 'liberation' by the Han, sometimes positioning the Han as China's nucleus, but often as the constitutive identity of *Zhonghua Minzu*. This re-performance reflects Xinjiang's ambivalent official inclusion in *Zhonghua Minzu* and the transitory nature of life in Xinjiang for many Han. Han identity narratives on 'liberation' also used pre-communist discourses of lineage and language, re-performing boundaries between 'inner China' (*neidi*) and frontier (*bianjiang*) as timeless, unbreakable cultural divisions, positioning Uyghurs outside their *Zhonghua Minzu*. The final section links semi-structured interviews with Uyghurs to discourse analysis of popular culture narratives to examine how Uyghurs receive and re-perform the officially articulated boundaries of *Zhonghua Minzu*. Uyghurs embrace the difference through which they are articulated in China but position themselves as a nation deserving equal recognition outside *Zhonghua Minzu*, thus inverting nation-building narratives of Xinjiang's cultural inferiority. Uyghurs interviewed defined their identity through cultural practices excluded from *Zhonghua Minzu* identity, particularly Turkic language and Islam. Uyghurs distinguish their felt identity as Uyghurs from the political realities of being Chinese ethnic minorities through references to daily, visceral experiences, which highlight the persistence of exclusion and hierarchical ethnic boundaries. The chapter argues that Han and Uyghurs in Ürümchi re-perform hierarchical boundaries of official nation-building to conceptualise identities through language and ethnicised conceptions of daily practices. Han and Uyghurs generally contrast what they understand as timeless, visceral ethnic or cultural identity against the party-state's multi-*minzu* conceptual imagination of *Zhonghua Minzu*. Chinese nation-building is failing because it transgresses these identity boundaries without offering alternatives that make sense to people's daily lives. Han and Uyghurs both deploy tensions between inclusion of Xinjiang in China and its everyday exclusion as a frontier to identify themselves as distinct nations built on ethnicity and language.

Re-Performing 'Ethnic Unity', Re-Performing China

This section analyses how Han and Uyghurs interpreted public performances of 'ethnic unity' (*minzu tuanjie*) and re-performed the official *Zhonghua Minzu* narrative to articulate their own alternative identity boundaries. Most Uyghurs and *getihu* Han alike dismiss unity as state propaganda, re-performing *minzu* as distinct ethnic nations. Han intellectuals interviewed rejected ethno-nationalism as un-Chinese but echoed the ethnocentrism of *tuanjie*, which frames Han culture as a superior, centripetal force, while concealing the reality of ethnic discrimination. Many emphasised the historical and contemporary relevance of ethnic unity. For example, Miss Lan[4], a mid-20s female Mandarin Chinese teacher from the countryside north of Ürümchi, explained that 'ethnic unity is an ancient tradition of the Chinese people' whenever discussing violence in the city. One mid-40s male head of a university department, Mr Gu, often repeated the slogan 'Ethnic unity is good' when discussing ethnic relations or discrimination. Mrs Du, in her late 30s, was born and raised in Xinjiang but maintained connections with Shanghai.[5] After spending the 1950s and 1960s in Xinjiang 'opening the frontier', in her words, Mrs Du's parents had returned to their hometown, Shanghai, during the Cultural Revolution. Mrs Du represents the Ürümchi Han intellectual as a professional university teacher. Her marriage to a modestly wealthy businessman offered her luxuries such as travel opportunities across China not afforded to many other interviewees. Mrs Du could communicate in basic Uyghur, uncommon amongst Han in Xinjiang, and expressed great pride that this allowed her to 'understand ethnic minorities' in ways that her Han friends could not. Mrs Du was a proponent of ethnic unity and described herself as a 'unity model'. She was tired of being asked to justify her Uyghur language studies to her friends who would say it was a 'useless' or 'backward' language. Mrs Du's interest in diversity and unity was not shared amongst all social classes. For example, in a typical answer to the question 'Can you speak Uyghur?', in discussions about unity, one 45-year-old male *getihu* from Xi'an explained that 'this is China (*Zhongguo*), everyone should speak Chinese (*Hanyu*)'. By eliding the difference between China and Han to objectivise Han-ness (*Hanyu*) as Chinese-ness (*Zhongguo*), he was, like intellectuals, drawing from the ethnocentric official narrative of ethnic unity. However, like most *getihu* interviewed, he articulated his identity solely through the centrality of the Han nucleus with no reference to ethnic diversity or equality, which intellectuals tended to describe as an 'ancient Chinese tradition'.

Mrs Du, like many other Uyghur-speaking Han, articulated internal boundaries amongst Xinjiang Han through their attitudes to Han-minority boundaries. She contested the meaning of Han by lamenting divisions between those who identified as part of a multi-*minzu* community and those who defined themselves solely through ethnicity. Mrs Du positively stereotyped 'Xinjiang people' as 'warm hearted' and 'more accepting of difference', explained through their diverse origins from across China and experiences of living with different *minzu* in Xinjiang. This widespread stereotype draws from popular

---

[4] See Appendix 1 for details of interviewees. All names used have been altered and are for convenience only.
[5] In the 1950s, urban socialist radicals migrated en mass from Shanghai to Xinjiang, leading to considerable conflict with demobilised Nationalists over the pace of socialist reforms. On migration of 'Shanghai youth' to Xinjiang in the 1950s, see: Millward (2004), chapter 6.

Uyghur self-definition as 'hospitable' (*mehman dost*),[6] used by Uyghur interviewees of all classes, though they would never use the 'Xinjiang person' category. Miss Lan similarly described an 'authentic' Xinjiang person as someone who was born in Xinjiang, eats mutton, and treats people warmly. When I asked where Miss Lan was from, she also said, 'I am a Xinjiang person'. She articulated a Chinese socialist identity by explaining that the reason so few Han described themselves as Xinjiang people was 'because before 1949 there were hardly any Han here . . . this is a new period in history'. Miss Lan qualified these statements, saying artefacts on display at the regional museum show there have always been Han in Xinjiang. However, her awareness of demographic transformation as a political project indicates how intellectual Han understand Han-led multi-*minzu* nation-building in positive terms but as a relatively 'new period' of identity transformation. Culturalism and historical materialism offer different ontologies in their formative narratives of the nation, but are mutually reinforcing in practice because they share the same goal of integrating Xinjiang into China through Han-led 'fusion'.

Transposing unity, an 'ancient tradition of the Chinese people', onto the contemporary state has produced new boundaries not only between Han and Uyghurs, but also amongst Xinjiang Han who identify in different ways through reference to inclusion and exclusion of Uyghurs. Han intellectuals in Ürümchi tend to position the lower classes as vulgar ethno-nationalists while articulating Chinese identity through ethnic unity and nominal respect for ethnic diversity. In one of the few ethnographic studies of Han identities in Xinjiang, Amy Kardos (2010) found that 'Xinjiang Han' displayed tolerance of difference and celebrated ethnic diversity. However, this conclusion is drawn from fieldwork in Karamay, a rich oil town in Xinjiang's north, which enjoys a GDP per capita higher than most Western European states. Like interviews with intellectuals here, it is representative of privileged sectors of Xinjiang society that offer only one of many responses to official *Zhonghua Minzu* narratives. When I asked Mrs Du why there was so much discrimination against Uyghurs, she foregrounded internal class boundaries amongst Han, saying, 'That's just taxi drivers! This is a problem too, they just say anything, and it's always very extreme, it isn't objective.' While *getihu* would dismiss intellectuals as detached from Ürümchi's gritty street-level reality, Mrs Du and Han intellectuals dismissed lower-class Han perspectives as subjective in contrast to her self-defined superior, 'objective' position. Mrs Du used ethnic unity to assert her relative power vis-à-vis the working classes to identify the meaning of Han and China. This assertion of power in using state narratives to define all Han concealed the 'struggle of identifications' to identify the

---

[6] See: Dautcher (2009); Bellér-Hann (2008), pp.202–203.

meaning of heterogeneous identity categories (Bhabha, 2009, pp.42–43). These relations between subject positions illustrate 'multiple, relational degrees of subalternity' where some groups 'distinguish themselves from and speak for those 'below', while allying themselves with and speaking to those 'above' (Hershatter, 1993, p.111). Han in Xinjiang are not subaltern in Spivak's (1988) sense of being 'unable to speak'. However, hierarchical, intra-ethnic power relations show how different social classes have different levels of power to be listened to when they identify themselves and China. Intellectuals exclude the Han working class as vulgar ethno-nationalists but without problematising their own ethnocentric celebrations of ethnic unity that exacerbate Uyghur insecurity.

Despite intellectual celebrations of ethnic unity as a Han tradition, taking willingness to make friends with other ethnic groups as a proxy for ethnic solidarity revealed little evidence of such feelings amongst Ürümchi's Han. For example, Mr Qiang, a 36-year-old *getihu* from Sichuan, described himself as an ethnic Han when asked, '*Where* are you from?' He said he had no Uyghur friends and did not wish to have any. His face-to-face community was entirely Han and did not correspond to the party-state's narrative of a multi-*minzu* community. Another male *getihu*, aged 50, explained he was a local (*bendi ren* 本地人) but his 'hometown' (*laojia* 老家) was in Hunan. When I asked where he was from, he replied, 'I am from Xinjiang. Chinese Xinjiang Han person', articulating China and Xinjiang as merely attributive to his ethnic Han identity. He refused to have 'any contact with Uyghurs' and would only speak to ethnic minorities 'who want to learn more Chinese', which he said automatically excluded *all* Uyghurs. Mr Yi, a 45-year-old *getihu* small-shop owner blamed Xinjiang's security problems on Islam during our first meeting, eagerly explaining that he and all other Han refused to make friends with Uyghurs. Even Mrs Du, who could speak Uyghur, and Miss Lan, who thought unity was an ancient tradition, admitted to me they had Uyghur colleagues but no Uyghur friends. They could not explain why, which reflected the ethnocentrism of *tuanjie* that positions inclusion of Uyghurs as essential for China's survival but without listening to Uyghur perspectives on identity.

Han interviewees usually gave unproblematised notions of ethnic difference as reasons for minimal social contact with Uyghurs. Even three young, female Han Uyghur language students claimed it was impossible to make friends with Uyghurs due to 'cultural difference'. These interviewees displayed no knowledge of Uyghur culture through which they could make this claim or to substantively contrast themselves against. For example, it was evident that Mrs Du had thoroughly exaggerated her Uyghur language skills when I spoke to her using my basic Uyghur language abilities. She said I was the 'real unity model' but continued to erroneously claim that 'How is your lamb?' was a common greeting amongst Uyghurs. When I asked several Uyghur interviewees about this greeting, they simply laughed and asserted that Han know nothing about Uyghurs. Aynür, a Mandarin language teacher in her early 40s, despaired, saying, 'I can't believe people still have these attitudes'. Ethnic unity amongst Han intellectuals involved vocal commitments to defining China through diversity. However, this has little relevance to daily practices and interaction with other *minzu*, while reinforcing the underlying ethnocentrism that prioritises Han culture over Uyghur culture as a source of unity. The absence of social knowledge amongst the most educated Han illustrates the social distance between two ethnic communities and the gap between *Zhonghua Minzu*, as a multi-*minzu* nation-building narrative, and the daily intra-ethnic practices of Ürümchi residents. The ethnocentrism that frames Han as the nucleus of unity shaped intellectuals' limited, nominal commitment to diversity. Learning *basic* Uyghur alongside *fluency* in Mandarin, eating mutton, and intra-ethnic social interaction was enough to be a Xinjiang person for Mrs Du and Miss Lan, thus including Uyghurs as culturally and socially peripheral but conceptually essential to Chinese identity.

The idea of ethnic unity was dismissed outright by all *getihu* interviewed as state 'propaganda' and meaningless 'political slogans'. *Getihu* spend much of their daily lives working in public, and usually described unity as incompatible with the visceral ethnic boundaries of their daily practices. Almost all emphasised their social contact was purely intra-ethnic and articulated China via daily experiences as a mono-ethnic nation. For example, Mr Xin, a 40-year-old, local-born (*bendi ren*) taxi driver explained that 'unity is impossible' because of violence in Xinjiang: '*Minzu* contradictions! It's a *minzu* problem! Uyghurs and Han don't get along ... we Han drivers are not even willing to pick up Uyghurs. Too much trouble. Unity is impossible.' Mr Xin explained that I would have problems hailing taxis because people would mistake me for a Uyghur, and this occurred fairly frequently. I had to hail one driver by stepping in front of his car when he was deliberately ignoring me. He said, 'I nearly didn't stop. I thought you were a Uyghur but it's ok, you are a foreigner (*laowai* 老外)'! Hailing taxis was invariably a problem when travelling with Uyghur or minority friends, and even when travelling with a white European friend because she wore a flowery skirt, which Han claimed made her look Uyghur. As a *'laowai'* these daily experiences were intriguing frustrations, but for Uyghurs, the boundaries performed through these daily interactions reinforce how ethnic unity does not mean equality and includes daily experiences of discrimination.

Most Uyghurs in Ürümchi, like Han *getihu*, express little hope for ethnic unity, with many interviewees repeating expressions heard amongst lower-class Han that 'it's just a stupid political slogan'. One male, mid-20s, university-educated office worker said, 'The biggest obstacle is that people, different *minzu*, are not equal'. Economic inequality was usually explained in cultural terms. When discussing ethnic unity, Ahmetjan, a 45-year-old illegal taxi driver from Ürümchi, said unity was 'nonsense' because 'very few (Han) learn any Uyghur language. They are like this. They are the majority, there are so many of them, so they think they don't have to learn our language and our customs, but we just have to learn theirs'. They propagate their own thought.' Ahmetjan rejected the ethnocentric objectivisation of Han-ness in ethnic unity narratives by suggesting Han unconsciously 'propagate' their identity through social practices, including monolingual education, framed as value-neutral modernisation. He resisted nation-building by framing its practices as inherently Han-centric and assimilative. Aynür objected on similar terms. When discussing ethnic unity, she raised the concept of *minzu* spirit (*minzu jingshen* 民族精神), saying, 'Unity means just the Han spirit for every *minzu*'. Mukhtar, in his early 20s, had recently graduated from university and represents an amalgamation of Joanne Smith's ideal types (2000) of 'politicised teenager' and 'young urban male intellectual'. He listened to foreign radio to get 'real news', frequently criticised the government, and worried about Xinjiang's future. He also read academic literature on Xinjiang and hoped one day to study at the doctorate level. Mukhtar told me, 'I have heard this stupid '*ittipaq yakhshi*' ['unity is good'] shit all my life, I think every single day but it's stupid'. For Mukhtar, unity was a 'temporary' propaganda campaign because 'in 50 years or so there will be only one culture, Chinese culture'. When asked if ethnic unity was possible, Mukhtar laughed:

With Han Chinese people? With the Chinese Communist Party? I don't think so. After what they have done, it's hard. They really should make up for it. We sacrificed the way we lived for centuries. We are sacrificing our culture to live here. They should at least do *something* but of course they don't realise that. We are not losing our ignorance, we are losing our culture. A lot of Chinese people think that we are not well educated, let them be more modern. But they don't know what they are doing. They are assimilating us.

For Mukhtar, *tuanjie* and modernisation were temporary measures to maintain stability before the 'assimilation'[7] of Uyghurs could be completed. He re-performed the text of ethnic unity by inverting it against itself to define Chinese modernisation ('losing our ignorance') as destructive of Uyghur culture and unity as Hanification. Ethnic unity as defined by the party-state was impossible in Mukhtar's eyes because it presented a threat to Uyghur ethnic identity. Uyghur-ness as an ethno-linguistic community was Mukhtar's referent of security and the ethnocentrism of unity was a threat.

---

[7] This was Mukhtar's choice of words, which I did not initiate. In English, Mukhtar used 'assimilation', in Chinese, to assimilate (*tonghua* 同化), and in Uyghur, *khänzulishish* ('to be made Han').

Ethnic unity is often framed by Uyghurs, like Han *getihu*, as a political project with little concern for people's daily practices. When I expressed surprise to Aynür that no ethnic unity textbooks at any level of education offered information on different cultural practices or beliefs, she said, 'Of course, children here don't study that, just politics. They don't care about people.' Aynür challenged the CCP's description of its development and education policies as 'people-centred' by framing the party-state as far removed from the people. Aynür was fluent in Uyghur and Chinese and took self-conscious pride at being 'between cultures'. She expressed a strong sense of ethnic identity, but in our conversations, this primarily emerged when hierarchical ethnic boundaries and political discourse affected her daily life. Aynür taught ethnic unity classes but privately expressed frustration about publicly endorsing its views. She said she would formalistically 'regurgitate the book' without believing any of it:

You have to write self-evaluation essays – I love the Communist party, the future will be bright under the Communist party, blah blah blah. It's stupid. They can get in your brain but they cannot get into your heart. You know it's all wrong.

When I asked Aynür how she felt about teaching *minzu tuanjie* to students, she explained that life in Xinjiang was 'just like this' and that protecting one's job and personal safety depended on knowing how to repeat narratives, which she described as 'fascist' and 'extremist'. She said 'good students' would know these were lies anyway because 'these lies are everywhere'. Aynür discussed the party-state's 'inside/outside Three Evils' narrative, complaining that it excluded self-identification *between* two extremes of West and East or between being a friend of China or a terrorist. She drew the symbol for *yin-yang* to explain Xinjiang's problematic integration and said, 'You see, this is because Han culture understands the world and all things in terms of opposites – hard/soft, high/low, yin/yang, there is no in-between and no neutral.' As someone self-consciously 'between cultures' because of her ability to use Uyghur and Mandarin fluently, the 'life or death struggle' for ethnic unity threatened Uyghurs as a Turkic people, *between* China and the West. Aynür understood official discourse well and re-performed Uyghur-ness as neutrality and accommodation between epistemically violent binary opposites through critical reflections on her own identity and its official framing as a threat to *Zhonghua Minzu*. Aynür reframed 'Han culture' as a threat to Uyghur's in-between identity because its binary approach to identity-security excluded Uyghur 'between-ness' and tolerance of diversity. Like most Uyghurs, Aynür doubted the existence of the 'inside/outside Three Evils' altogether and saw it as a narrative tool to represent Uyghur identity as a threat to China:

How can we have unity when they think we are all terrorists? It's obvious there is no unity; otherwise you wouldn't see slogans everywhere. When we see these, we know there is no unity. We have to study it night and day, unity this and unity that. One day I was so depressed, studying this all day in classes. It was getting dark and we were all so tired. Then I left the class and my mood was lifted because I was on the verge of being made homeless but I finally found an advert for a new house. So I phoned to ask if they still had the house. He said yes but then asked me what *minzu* I am! I told him I am Uyghur. So he said he was not willing to rent me the house. I asked him why and he said, 'You are a Uyghur, there is no other reason'. So I feel ethnic unity is like pressing my warm cheek against their cold ass.

Aynür was angry that she participated in ethnic unity by studying it, teaching it, and by interacting with Han Chinese residents using Mandarin. However, she was rejected as unwelcome in her own homeland *because* she was a Uyghur. She even displayed her adaptation to Han cultural practices by expressing her anger at the exclusion of Uyghurs using a Chinese idiom, referring to a guest's lack of appreciation for a host's hospitality. The 'guest' is a commonly used allegory for the Han Chinese presence in Xinjiang in contemporary Uyghur music and literature (Bovingdon, 2010, pp.98–99). The widespread Uyghur perception that Han show no appreciation for how Uyghurs extended this hospitality to them is heard in Abdurehim Heyit's song, 'Stubborn Guest', an allegorical tale of an old man pleading for a guest to leave after over-staying his welcome. Aynür demarcated boundaries between herself as indigenous to Xinjiang, a chthonic identity, and Han as 'guests' in her homeland. Her 'warm cheek' represents her own individual willingness to welcome, share territory, and culturally intermingle with the Han. 'Their cold ass' represents the inhospitable and discriminatory behaviour of the Han despite their claims to desire genuine unity. Using this idiom was a complaint that the Han as a group with relative power affected her as an individual leading her daily life: *her* individual warm cheek against *their* cold collective ass. For Aynür, like many Uyghurs, ethnic unity was an ethnocentric conceptual apparatus, which conceals visceral, daily experiences of ethnic discrimination and marginalises Uyghurs as 'terrorists' if they complain about those experiences.

Re-Performing Han-ness

This section analyses how Han in Ürümchi re-perform the official boundaries demarcated in China's nation-building narratives between Han and Uyghurs and between inner China and the frontier. Ürümchi-based Han frequently use these boundaries to position themselves as a distinct *ethnic* nation liberating Xinjiang and Uyghurs from their own 'backwardness'. The modern Han ethnonym builds on older historical formations, which emerged through complex interaction and distinction between sedentary dwellers of the central plains and nomads of the northern steppe (Leibold, 2010, p.10). The Western

Hu people labelled sedentary dwellers of the central plains as 'Han' even though they were politically and culturally divided for much of their history (Elliot, 2011, pp.173–175). Older relational discourses dividing civilisation from barbarism and nomadic from sedentary peoples thus inform the symbols and boundaries that define the modern Han category today (Leibold, 2010, p.10). The fluidity of Han as an ethnic and cultural marker reflects tensions between defining Han as one of China's constitutive 56 *minzu* and as the trans-ethnic leaders of the other 55. Imperial civilising projects, multi-ethnic nation-building, and ethno-nationalism are logically incompatible ontologies of human community (conversionary culturalism versus inclusive multiculturalism versus exclusive nationalism). However, Chapter 5 showed how these multiple modes of inclusion overlap and co-exist in creative tension. Through semantically hybrid practices, they are mutually reinforcing narratives in the ongoing reconfiguration of otherness in China from *hua/yi* to race (*zhongzu*) to *minzu* that maintain non-Han as ethnic outsiders. Han racial superiority is impossible to disentangle from narratives of civilisation or cultural evolution because Han are always positioned as the culturally superior identity, which defines *Zhonghua Minzu*. Building a multi-ethnic China not only requires convincing minorities that they are Chinese, but would also require convincing Han that minorities can be Chinese too. Instead, the logical tensions that include minorities by marking them as inferior and threatening give Han an official grammar to resist any inclusion of Uyghurs. Majority ethnic chauvinism persists because it is invisibilised and framed as a Western problem, which the CCP defeated with the victory of socialism over imperialism that swept away the old China.

The more privileged Han in Ürümchi stressed the importance of ethnic unity and that their China was constituted by ethnic diversity. Many of those with longer-term ties to the region used the category of 'Xinjiang person' (*Xinjiang ren* 新疆人). 'Xinjiang person' articulates Han and Uyghurs belonging to the same territorial unit known as Xinjiang but intimately tied to the shared, conceptual community of *Zhonghua Minzu*. Jay Dautcher analysed official interpellations of Uyghur identity through the concept of 'Xinjiang person' in party-state slogans (Dautcher, 2009, p.40). 'Xinjiang person' invokes the party-state's claim, discussed in Chapter 2, that Xinjiang has been a multicultural, frontier transit point since ancient times. Xinjiang, thus defined, is framed through transitory migrations into an empty vessel rather than what Jay Dautcher (2009) termed the felt 'chthonic identity' of Uyghurs, identifying through birthplace and land. The 'Xinjiang person' category thus 'desettles' the 'chthonic identity' of Uyghurs where they are psychologically relocated from their local community to a multi-ethnic and transitory frontier (Dautcher, 2009, pp.50–59). The very naming of Xinjiang as a frontier desettles Uyghur identity because it silences the region's centrality to their identity. However,

'Xinjiang person' also desettles Han self-identification because it supplants parallel Han attachments to ethnic lineage and land with a multi-*minzu* nation. Fei Xiaotong's (1988) classic conceptualisation of *Zhonghua Minzu* through *hua/yi* boundaries, considered the Han cultural attachment to land and lineage as the driving factor behind their superior agricultural development over nomadic peoples and the centripetal force of Chinese modernity. This binarism between sedentary and nomadic cultures and between agriculture and animal husbandry define the exceptional Han and was repeated in all ethnic unity education books and cadre-training manuals analysed in Chapters 2–5.[8] Han and Uyghur attachment to land runs counter to the idea of Xinjiang person, which detaches identity from traditional attachments to land and lineage. Nevertheless, it is embedded in exceptionalist narratives of the Han as a 'frontier-building culture', analysed in Chapter 2, who transform Xinjiang and themselves through the military reclamation of land and modernisation of its peoples.

Han exceptionalism was a widespread narrative amongst those who identify through socialism and culturalism because timeless attachment to land was seen as the cultural essence that drives China's path to modernity. Mrs Du, Miss Lan, and Mr Gu all repeated the same narratives of exceptionalism, saying that 'for the Han, land is very important', particularly owning and working the land. Mrs Du was relatively politically engaged and advised me to read political slogans about ethnic unity because they 'tell you how society works'. This attitude was notably different from the widespread rejection of political slogans amongst *getihu* in Ürümchi. However, while Mrs Du embraced state-promoted identity categories, such as 'Xinjiang person', she enjoyed discussing and critically reflecting on them. I asked her why so few Han in Xinjiang identify as Xinjiang people, explaining that when asked, responses were usually a denial such as 'No, I am a Chinese person' or 'No, I am Han'. Mrs Du's response illuminated how intellectual Han in Xinjiang engage with and use official identity categories to reperform Han-ness in different ways:

This is a real problem. People here come from all over China, but they work for a while and then they leave. For Han people, land (*tudi* 土地) and their relationship with it is so important. So, your 'hometown' (*laojia* 老家) is very important. You don't just come from somewhere by living there for a while. Your family has to live there for generations. My family all worked here for decades to open the frontier. Then they retired and went back to Shanghai. But I define myself as a Xinjiang person. Because I was born here, I won't leave when I retire. But it is a real problem because people don't stay here and they don't *become* Xinjiang people. This is only in Xinjiang because people come from all over and they don't stay long. 'Xinjiang person' is a different type

---

[8] For example, see: EUAB (2009); SEAC (2009); XEP (2009).

of category altogether. It is different from saying you are a 'Beijing person' or a 'Shanghai person', it has a different conceptual meaning.

Mrs Du understood herself as a 'Xinjiang person' and lamented that Han left Xinjiang because they remained attached to their 'hometown' (*laojia*) and were not committed to building a multi-ethnic Xinjiang. Although *laojia* is translated into English as 'hometown', in practice its use includes lineage, which 'hometown' does not encompass. Han can *become* 'Xinjiang people' by choosing to move to Xinjiang to 'open the frontier' and to identify through *Zhonghua Minzu* as a multi-*minzu* nation. However, 'Xinjiang person', as Mrs Du explained, is unlike categories of Beijing person or Shanghai person, because these denote lineage. Mrs Du considered *laojia* a parochial identity, based on ancestral lineage rather than the transformative socialism of 'Xinjiang person'. 'Xinjiang person' is a different type of category to local 'hometown' identities, which constitutes China through ongoing transformative processes of multi-*minzu* nation-building on the new frontier.

Bendi ren (本地人) was used by many Han interviewees to define themselves as local or native people, who would then reject the 'Xinjiang person' category, identifying with their 'hometown' (*laojia*) in 'inner China' when asked where they were from. The issue of 'hometown' arose during every interview with Han. The vast majority would say they were born in Xinjiang but their 'hometown' is in 'inner China', distinguishing the Han-inhabited central plains from China's frontiers (*bianjiang*) in Xinjiang, Tibet, and Inner Mongolia. When asked, 'Where are you from?' almost all working-class and *getihu* Han interviewees stated firm identification with their 'hometown' and not Xinjiang. Even many born and bred in Xinjiang continued to identify through their 'hometown' in 'inner China'. One male *getihu* in his late 40s gave a standard explanation: 'I am from here but my hometown is in Shandong'. This distinction between where Han are born and where they are from exemplifies Xinjiang's ambivalent position as a cultural frontier and that Han see themselves as *in* Xinjiang but not *of* it. Another late-40s male getihu similarly explained where he was from through ethnicity, stating, 'I am Han'. When I asked if he was a Xinjiang person, he stated, 'Just now I am from here, but my hometown is in Henan'. He later explained, like many interviewees, that he had never visited his 'hometown' and that his grandparents came to Xinjiang to 'open up the frontier'. Han in Xinjiang tended to identify through the modern Han concept, but when asked for further detail, they defined themselves through traditional Chinese conceptualisations of lineage. Imagining 'hometown' as central to Han identity as a *minzu* re-performs the party-state's ethno-taxonomy by embracing and reconstituting the Han category through pre-1949 understandings of the centrality of lineage.

Intellectuals like Mrs Du with longer-term connections to Xinjiang were amongst the few Han who consistently defined China through inclusive culturalism or socialist multiculturalism without turning to exclusive ethno-nationalism. Mrs Du sharply distinguished Xinjiang from 'inner China' by saying, 'In inner China, you can see traditional Han customs preserved and celebrated, but it is different here'. She lamented the loss of culturalist traditions and respect for diversity, which she related to 'modernisation' and the growth of ethno-nationalism amongst newly arrived Han. While Mrs Du conceptualised Han as multi-*minzu* nation-builders, most interviewees and all *getihu* explicitly defined Han as the ethnic core of Chinese identity. Those *getihu* who identified as Xinjiang people often reconfigured its meaning to self-stereotype the region in negative terms, particularly 'backwardness' and Han-Uyghur ethnic divisions. For example, Mr Hu, a mid-20s male *getihu*, proudly explained he was a Xinjiang person by demarcating boundaries vis-à-vis 'inner China' and Han vis-à-vis Uyghurs through intersections of class and *minzu* from official cultural evolution narratives: 'It's still very backward, because of the Uyghurs, we are all Chinese but they are a disagreeable and repugnant *minzu*'. One male 42-year-old taxi driver, Mr Yan, who described himself as local-born (*bendi ren*) and whose parents came from Shandong to 'open the frontier', explained that he 'hated' Xinjiang, particularly Ürümchi because of 'Uyghurs': 'They are a backward, stupid *minzu*, they are very dangerous, you can't trust them. Ninety-nine per cent are all bad. Their ideology and their way of thinking is just totally different from Han'. Like many Han in Xinjiang, Mr Yan conceptualised China through Han as an ethnic concept. He discussed how Han from different hometowns came to Xinjiang to 'open the frontier' ('Shandong, Sichuan, Henan, they come from all over Xinjiang'). Differences between 'hometown' identities within the Han category were safe, but ethnic difference with Uyghurs presented dangers from outside his ethno-national identity. Mr Qiang, the 36-year-old *getihu* who had come to Xinjiang 10 years before to find work because making money was 'impossible' in the Sichuanese highlands, planned to return to his 'hometown' once he had enough money to retire. This transitory migration to Xinjiang is representative of the contemporary Xinjiang experience for many Han and contrasts against the chthonic attachments of Uyghurs. When asked where he was from, Mr Qiang immediately told me:

QIANG: I am Han, a Han of China. I don't like Uyghurs. They are a fighting-killing people. They are an offensive and savage people. They all want independence from China. They aren't a Chinese *minzu*. They aren't Chinese.
DT: Why aren't they Chinese?
QIANG: Because of their language, they don't speak Chinese. They are more like Indians or a Pakistani *minzu*.
DT: They are all learning Chinese now. So what happens after that, what will be the result?

QIANG: They still won't be real Chinese. They all want independence but it's simply not possible. It's like the Soviet Union. When a country breaks up it becomes poor and weak and other countries interfere and attack it – so we need unity.

Mr Qiang demarcated ethnic boundaries between Han and Uyghurs by adopting the language of chauvinist superiority to represent Uyghurs as culture-less obstacles to China's national strength and prosperity. Uyghurs are thus foreign, inconvertible 'savages' because they cannot master the only language of civilisation, and even if they do, they would not be 'real Chinese'. Ethnic unity was simply the means to Han power at home and Chinese power abroad. Han narrated different stories of *Zhonghua Minzu* by re-performing their identity through tensions within official discourse between China as a multi-*minzu* civilisation and China as an ethno-centric Han-led nation. For the culturalists and socialists, like Mrs Du, the chauvinist identity of Han migrants, like Mr Qiang, was as much of an impediment to nation-building as Uyghur nationalism. However, for ethno-nationalists, Uyghurs represented an inconvertible other from outside their nation. The tensions within the official Han category and *Zhonghua Minzu* narratives thus circulate in Han constitution of their identities through intra-ethnic relations in everyday relations with non-Han others.

Re-Performing Uyghur-ness

This final section explores how Uyghurs re-perform boundaries in official nation-building narratives to articulate their own ethno-national identities. Uyghurs generally stress that Turkic language and Islam are central to their identities but excluded from *Zhonghua Minzu* identity, positioning themselves outside its boundaries. Where the Han redeploy identity narratives positioning them at the centre of *Zhonghua Minzu*, Uyghurs re-perform their peripheralisation. The ancient etymology of Uyghur is frequently taken by Uyghur nationalists as 'tending to unite' (Brophy, 2011, p.1). The party-state endorses this etymology by translating it as unity (*tuanjie*) and claiming it reflects Uyghur desires to be integrated into *Zhonghua Minzu*. In the scholarly literature on the emergence of Uyghur national identity, Bellér-Hann (2008) and Newby (2007) have shown how Gladney's (1990) ethnogenesis and Rudelson's (1997) oasis identities arguments overlooked longer-term, shared group identity of Uyghurs. Uyghur group identity preceded and informed Republican era debates amongst Uyghur intellectuals about how to identify themselves through newly emerging identity categories in Soviet and Chinese transitions to national statehood. During this period, Uyghur nationalist newspapers emerged, and Uyghur intellectuals in Russian Turkestan began to explicitly articulate Uyghur as a national category (Roberts, 2009, p.361). These debates culminated in official Soviet adoption of the Uyghur ethnonym at the 1921 Tashkent conference, which distinguished sedentary Turkic speakers from nomadic Turkic speakers (e.g. Kazakhs and Kyrgyz). The Uyghur category was directly imported by the Chinese state in the 1950s *minzu shibie*. For the first time, Turkic-speakers in China were defined as a Chinese minority (*weiwuerzu* 维吾尔族) instead of barbarians or Muslims (*hui* 回) during late-Qing and Republican periods. As the sedentary Turkic Muslims of Xinjiang were negotiating transformation from barbarians to ethnic minorities, Uyghur-ness simultaneously became more territorially bounded with the establishment of the XUAR in 1955 and challenged by the region's rapid demographic and cultural transformation through mass state-sponsored immigration of Mandarin Chinese–speaking Han.

Ethnic boundaries are not maintained through difference but through social organisation of difference (Barth, 1969, p.15). Groupness is an event that forms and disintegrates under different social conditions (Brubaker, 1998, p.298). Uyghurs' complex, socially contingent identity narratives are analysed here through semantic hybridity where different, pre-existing conceptualisations of Uyghur identity overlap and exist in creative tension through relations with Han and the state, reflecting Uyghurs' ambivalent position as outside subjects of empire *and* inside members of the nation. The diversity in Uyghur identity narratives, regarding class, gender, and oasis-identities, can only be touched upon here when foregrounded in individuals' narratives. Most Uyghurs in China and across Central Asia see themselves as stateless and dismiss all state articulations of their identity (Roberts, 2007, p.204). In Ürümchi, Uyghurs often actively define their public identity through this dismissal of politics, understanding Chinese nation-building as a paradoxical combination of assimilative inclusion *and* violent exclusion. Uyghur interviewees chose to discuss boundaries with Han regularly, and most discussion of interaction with state institutions or narratives were framed through this boundary. Uyghur-ness in China is produced through daily practices mediated by identity contestations with Han and the state that blur and interweave the inside and outside of *Zhonghua Minzu*. The analysis here focuses on how Uyghurs in China articulate the meaning of Uyghur-ness through relations with Han and the state, which position them as culturally inferior ethnic minorities.

Uyghurs articulate feelings of political and cultural detachment from *Zhonghua Minzu* by framing China as distant and foreign, for example, when expressing concerns about visiting Beijing, the nominal centre of China. Clifford Geertz's 'doctrine of the exemplary centre' considered mass centralised rituals and symbols as the basis of legitimating centralised political orders (Geertz, 1980, p.13). However, Uyghurs tend to frame China's centre as culturally other and as an absence of visceral community. These concerns included 'the hotels don't accept Uyghurs'[9] from a 44-year-old *Qumul-lik*[10] male scholar and 'I won't be able to make friends' due to 'cultural differences' from several male and female undergraduate students from Korla, Turpan, and Ürümchi. One female master's degree student from Turpan said she could not go to Beijing because 'there will be no halal food'. A 30-year-old male teacher from Khotan insisted we couldn't even go north of Ürümchi city centre because 'I don't think there are any Uyghur restaurants in those areas'. Mahigül, a student in her early 20s, was a born-and-bred *Ürümchi-lik* from a professional family. She and her family were proud Uyghurs and modern, urban *Ürümchi-lik-ler*. Her understanding of 'inner China' exemplified the unfamiliarity and outside-ness that most Uyghurs expressed: 'Inner China, Beijing, Shanghai, any other part of China, these are all the same to me. They are all Chinese – same food, same buildings, same life.' Mahigül understood the centre of *Zhonghua Minzu*, like most Uyghurs, as a culturally unfamiliar and potentially hostile social environment, a Chinese frontier on the periphery of her centre of self-understanding. Uyghurs resist the party-state's attempts to radically re-map identity and transform their centre into a new frontier by rejecting Beijing's centrality.

While Han frame Xinjiang as a frontier, Uyghurs consider it the centre of their identity and refer to the region as *wätän* (homeland). Every Uyghur interviewed from all classes selected Kashgar and or their hometown in response to the question, 'What places are important to Uyghurs?' When this was followed up by the question, 'What about Beijing?' most assumed this was a joke, while one asked if I was picking a fight. Kashgar, home of the famous Id-Kah Mosque and a majority Uyghur population, is generally considered to be the centre of Uyghur Islam and frequently self-selected as a symbol of Uyghur-ness. Uyghur self-understandings contrast against how Kashgar is officially positioned in China as 'the frontline in the struggle against separatism', with many party leaders in Chapter 3 describing it as a 'backward' hotbed of 'separatism'. When I asked Mahigül and Mukhtar, the young politicised intellectual, if they were Junggo-lik ('person from China'), they found this amusing. Mahigül would say, 'I am a Uyghur *in* China', particularly to new foreign friends, explaining that she didn't want the outside world to think Uyghurs were Han or Chinese. The understanding of Uyghurs as in China but not of it echoes how Han tend to feel in Xinjiang but not of it and its ambivalent official position as a Chinese frontier. The stark contrast

---

[9] These discriminatory practices have become more explicit and widespread since 2012. However, Rayila (2011) showed how they were already visible in adverts and municipal government regulations posted at hotels prior to Xi Jinping's rise to power.

[10] The suffix *-lik* is added to place names to denote a person from that place in the Uyghur language. A Qumul-lik is then a person from Qumul where Qumul-lik-ler is the plural.

between the official centre and frontier of *Zhonghua Minzu* against Uyghur self-understanding shows how nation-building fails to include or convert Uyghurs.

The song 'Coming to Kashgar' by Perride Mamut, one of Xinjiang's most popular folk singers, is typical of how Kashgar is popularly mobilised as a symbolic centre of Uyghur-ness. Perride sings, 'She welcomed us so warmly, oh beautiful Kashgar'.[11] The CD and DVD markets across Xinjiang have spawned many famous independent artists, such as Sanubar Tursun, Perride Mamut, and Abdurehim Heyit, whose recordings are sung in Uyghur language and hugely popular amongst Uyghurs. These artists are almost entirely unknown amongst Han in the city. They write their own music but sing a blend of original lyrics and traditional folk poems, often in the medieval Turkic language of Chagatai. In many ways, Chinese and Uyghur spheres appear as 'parallel worlds' through music (Harris, 2005, p.381). However, the unofficial sphere of Uyghur music has to mediate official politics when publicised. Since the post-Tiananmen crackdown, idealism and overt political resistance in music across China generally has given way to negotiation and 'de-politicisation' for political reasons (Baranovitch, 2003, pp.36–38 & 44–45). Uyghurs have had to negotiate this political context in artistic expressions of identity because any lyrics deemed political are censored. However, more recently, as 'de-extremification' policies intensified and national narratives shifted towards chauvinist conceptions of *Zhonghua Minzu*, all artists listed here – including Perride, Sanubar, and Abdurehim – have been extra-legally disappeared in internment camps without clear explanation.[12]

The 'Coming to Kashgar' VCD begins with Perride delighted to leave Ürümchi by the modern means of airplane travel. Perride flies home to Kashgar and blissfully walks through the old town's back streets, returning to her family and a welcoming community, waving and celebrating. 'Coming to Kashgar' was released as the demolition of Kashgar old town accelerated, following the 2009 violence when thousands of Uyghurs were relocated to modern apartment blocks. The demolition is officially explained through the dependency narratives analysed in Chapter 2, as 'modernisation' of Xinjiang and preservation to 'rescue' Uyghur culture, which would disappear without the party-state (State Council, 2009b, pp.29–30). In Perride's song and in everyday speech, the party-state's modernisation and nation-building narratives are turned against themselves. *Old* Kashgar symbolises Uyghur-ness outside *Zhonghua Minzu* and Uyghurs' own timeless traditions that can survive and co-exist with modernity. Perride's performance of Uyghur

---

[11] The translators of these lyrics as well as those of Abdurehim Heyit requested to remain anonymous for their safety.
[12] For example, see: Freemuse (2019); SCMP (2019).

community and hospitality inverts the text of Chinese modernisation, positioning the 'real' Uyghur tradition in Kashgar, outside and superior to Ürümchi, a Chinese frontier city. This inversion reflects widespread Uyghur resistance to the party-state's modernisation narratives, which exclude Uyghur-ness from representations of Chinese urban modernity. Re-performing Kashgar as a site of Uyghur tradition persisting through modernity frames those features, which the party-state deems rural, ethnic, and dangerous, inside a Uyghur urban centre as an alternative modernity outside *Zhonghua Minzu*.

Widespread rejection of official *weiwuerzu* identity and the way it attempts to reconfigure Uyghurs' centre and periphery reflects how Uyghurs in Ürümchi often understand the constitution of identity through intra-ethnic daily practices. Every Uyghur interviewed, including Mukhtar, Mahigül, and Aynür, identified Uyghur language as the central feature that defines 'Uyghur heritage'. Most expressed serious concern regarding its elimination from the education system. When they discussed 'bilingual education', it was always accompanied by ironic air quotes as reminders it means Mandarin-medium education and Sinicisation. Abdullah, a 45-year-old self-employed businessman, explained, 'Language is about thought and those who are learning two languages like they do here are finding themselves confused, unable to express themselves or understand themselves properly because there is a contradiction between their thinking and religion and their language.' This narrative of language-loss, regularly heard amongst Uyghurs since at least 2004, challenges the position of Uyghur identity as a content Chinese ethnic minority and frames language policy as a threat. 'Language is a way of thinking', said Aynür before stressing that Uyghurs who could not read their mother tongue had 'no identity'. Mukhtar asked, 'How can you know your culture if you can't read the books of your elders? It's a national identity, it's just a shame we are losing it.' Mukhtar resisted the peripheralisation of Xinjiang and centrality of timeless Chinese-ness, highlighting how the 'new frontier' is an ancient centre for timelessly Central Asian Uyghurs. In discussions about the impact of language policy, Mukhtar, like Mahigül, Aynür, and Abdullah, frequently defined Uyghur-ness through the ability to communicate, read, and write using Uyghur language[13]: 'Uyghur people look so different, some of us look like Europeans, some of us look like Chinese, some of us look like they are from India. The only thing that keeps us together is our language .... I've heard there are even Christian Uyghurs ... if they *think* they are Uyghurs and they speak the same language, and share the same culture as me then yeah they are Uyghurs, they're my friends, they're my people.' Mukhtar rejected Chinese

---

[13] Elder generations of Uyghurs position religion more centrally in their self-identification. All Uyghur interviewees were still self-identified Muslims, and highlighting language does not preclude the importance of religion or other social practices.

nation-building narratives using the tools they use to define him. The synonymousness of language, nation, and civilisation was not resisted but re-performed to constitute Uyghur-ness through common mother tongue and Turkic civilisation outside *Zhonghua Minzu*.

When discussing the importance of the Uyghur language to identity, several interviewees cited the popular song by Abdurehim Heyit, 'Ana Til' ('Mother Tongue'). Almost every VCD shop I visited recommended him as both the best and most popular Uyghur musician. Most Uyghurs and every musician in Xinjiang know Abdurehim's deep, resonant singing style and call him a 'Uyghur Dutar[14] Master'. The seriousness in his lyrics and facial expressions on his album covers and his mournful singing resonate with how Yi artist Lolo used his album covers to express 'sternness' and reject representations of minorities as 'happy, smiling natives' (Baranovitch, 2003, pp.85–86). Abdurehim became known through his lyrics, including 'Stubborn Guest', and by operating outside official channels, giving away free cassettes of his recordings in the 1990s. These recordings pre-date the introduction of laws in 2001, which required artists in Xinjiang to submit all lyrics for official approval before performing or recording, leaving Abdurehim unable to tour or release recordings (Bovingdon, 2010, pp.96–97). The song 'Ana Til' celebrates Uyghur-ness through Uyghur language, imbuing it with viscerality against the conceptual belonging of *Zhonghua Minzu*:

> I want to respect the man, who knows his mother tongue,
> I want to give gold to the man, who knows his mother tongue,
> If this mother-tongue is in America or Africa,
> I would spend thousands to go there,
> Oh my mother tongue you were given by our ancestors,
> I want to be proud of you in this world.

The song symbolically constituted timeless Uyghur identity though language and reflects widespread, contemporary anxieties about the boundary-transgressing practices of Chinese modernisation and 'bilingual education' policies. The song imagines a long and unbroken Uyghur history through transmission of Uyghur language 'by our ancestors'. The song was particularly popular in Xinjiang and Mukhtar was keen to stress, 'You know this is not about mother tongue in general, it's about saving Uyghur'. 'Ana Til' performs the boundaries of Uyghur-ness and community through Uyghur language, reversing the relationship between modernity and tradition and between centre and periphery in *Zhonghua Minzu* narratives, which conceive Sinicisation as modernisation.

Uyghur language is understood by Uyghurs, much like Mandarin amongst Han, as an ancient cultural practice surviving through modernity. Mahigül, like

---

[14] The dutar is a two-stringed lute played in Xinjiang and across Central Asia.

all interviewees, used Uyghur language with her friends and family and Mandarin for work and shopping. She was trilingual but preferred not to make friends with people from Ürümchi who would not at least attempt to learn Uyghur. Like Mukhtar, she deployed the elision in official discourse, which equated the ethnic Han category with the national category of Chinese: 'I only speak Chinese to Chinese. I speak English to foreigners. I speak Uyghur to Uyghurs.' When we discussed identity and language policy, she defined herself and Uyghur-ness solely in ethno-linguistic terms:

We are Uyghur, we speak Uyghur. We are not Uyghur speaking Chinese. Uyghur is ours. Uyghur language also has many centuries of history, so it deserves to be kept. It's part of our culture. I mean if we don't speak Uyghur in the future, we can't call ourselves Uyghur. We'd be Chinese.

Mahigül demarcated community boundaries in ethno-linguistic terms, defining Uyghur-ness through mastery of mother tongue. The loss of mother tongue transgressed identity boundaries and would transform Uyghurs into members of the Han ethno-national community of *Zhonghua Minzu*. Mahigül used Uyghur for private communication and making social connections, but used Mandarin Chinese to participate in the necessary but anonymous economic transactions of public life. She explained the public need to speak Mandarin by saying, 'It's the basic thing to live in China ... we have to buy things, we can't always buy everything from Uyghurs.' She contrasted this rational negotiation of unavoidable, perfunctory interactions against the viscerality and cultural connection of Uyghur-ness. Mahigül was proudly urban and articulated Uyghur-ness through modernity by saying that Uyghur culture must 'forget about the *Muqam*' (Uyghur classical music) and 'create new things' to survive. Like Mukhtar, she responded to official narratives of 5,000 years of *Zhonghua Minzu* by re-performing Uyghur-ness as an alternative civilisation that can be preserved through and by modernity.

Although assimilation is a problematic concept that relies on a fixed, impermeable ontology of identity, outcomes are not equivalent to intent, and state policies deploying its inconsistent logics have enormous impacts. Nation-building in Xinjiang is so stark and security-focused that Uyghurs tend to understand it as an assimilative, colonial project. Mukhtar, Aynür, and Abdullah all used Chinese-speaking ethnic minorities such as Mongolians, Manchu, and Xibe as examples of pessimistic futures for Uyghurs. They all claimed these ethnic groups 'disappeared' with the 'disappearance' of their language. Abdullah explained that the Xibe were 'like other minorities – very assimilated, very Hanicised (*bei Hanhua de* 被汉化的). It's because they don't have their own language anymore, they disappear'. Aynür repeated similar narratives, referring to northeastern ethnic groups, particularly the Manchu, Mongolians, and Xibe: 'Many of these *minzu* have become extinct throughout history because their language died out. They are very much like Han.' In reference to a *New York Times* article, Mukhtar said he did not fear 'Xinjiang becoming another Tibet' but was concerned it 'would become another Manchuria'. Mukhtar meant that civilisational boundaries between *Hua* and Manchu had disappeared with decline of the Manchurian language and the Manchu became *Hua*. Mukhtar said that cultures disappear as part of 'nature' but that 'assimilation' in Xinjiang was politically imposed and 'not natural'. He said the 'bilingual education' system was a 'total failure' because 'we are losing our language ... they want to kill our language slowly then assimilate us'. Mukhtar resisted nation-building narratives that he understood as assimilation into *Zhonghua Minzu* with Han as its defining identity. He said that 'these things happen but just not them', before listing personal, visceral experiences of discrimination by the Han and the state, relating them to a need to preserve his group identity. Nation-building is failing because its culturally blind ethnocentrism articulates Han identity as the basis of national identity and conceals the daily realities of discrimination which Uyghurs experience.

Zhonghua Minzu holds no attraction or benevolence for Uyghurs because its multiple teleologies of culturalism, historical materialism, and chauvinism all end with disappearance of Uyghur identity and the rise of a Han nation-state. Official performances of *Zhonghua Minzu* offer no discursive or public space for Uyghur identity. Uyghur-ness, therefore, is privately performed and subtly re-performed in public using official narratives of timelessness, civilisation, and ethnicity. Popular culture, such as the music of Perride Mamut and Abdurehim Heyit, performs Uyghur-ness through alternative centres (i.e. language, Islam, and Kashgar), which challenge nation-building narratives and the meaning of *Zhonghua Minzu* in apolitical cultural terms. Uyghurs embrace official boundaries between Han majority and ethnic minorities and between Chinese and Turkic culture but re-perform their meaning. Uyghurs reject their position as backward and inferior ethnic minorities, re-performing *Zhonghua Minzu* as an assimilative Han nation-state. Uyghurs reframe the dissolution of boundaries through *jiaohua* ('teaching without discrimination') as a threat to a multi-ethnic China because its promotion of assimilation transgresses Uyghur identity boundaries. Uyghurs re-perform and invert civilisational boundaries between Turkic Uyghurs and Chinese Han to reject the centrality of *Hua* and seek rejuvenation of a parallel, ancient Turkic civilisation.

Conclusions

This chapter examined the effects of nation-building by examining how Han and Uyghurs in Ürümchi frame inclusion and exclusion in *Zhonghua Minzu* through their own identity narratives. The first section analysed how Uyghurs and Han interpreted and re-performed official ethnic unity narratives. Uyghurs and Han alike often dismiss unity as propaganda but deployed it to re-perform *minzu* as a distinct ethno-national boundary. Uyghurs and *getihu* Han tended to reject ethnic unity as contradictory to their ethno-national identities and disconnected from their daily practices mediated by ethnic boundaries. Identity narratives amongst Han intellectuals drew more on conceptualisations of China as a multi-*minzu* nation or civilisation and less on chauvinism. Han intellectuals identified Han ethno-nationalism as un-Chinese to perform China as a diverse, inclusive nation. Miss Lan, the Mandarin Chinese teacher, explained, 'Ethnic unity is an ancient tradition of the Chinese people.' However, this ethnocentric tradition only speaks to people who identify as culturally Chinese and ignored widespread marginalisation and discrimination against Uyghurs. The intellectual objectivisation of Han-ness as Chinese-ness sparks conflict over unequal social positions in China by prioritising one particular understanding of Han-ness and excluding Uyghur identities. The failure of nation-building to include Uyghur identity is captured in how Han intellectuals, the proponents of diversity, conceptualise *Zhonghua Minzu* through ethnocentric culturalism, which includes Xinjiang as a culturally inferior frontier to be developed and converted. Uyghurs tended to understand ethnic unity as a political narrative, which conceals China's ethnocentrism and enables daily practices of discrimination by privileged Han 'frontier-builders' ('like pressing my warm cheek against their cold ass'),

The second section explored how Han in Ürümchi re-perform official narratives of Xinjiang's 'liberation' to define identity through lineage and language, positioning themselves as the core identity of *Zhonghua Minzu*. Han nationalists re-perform officially articulated boundaries between 'inner China' (*neidi*) and frontier (*bianjiang*) as timeless and unbreakable, positioning Uyghurs perpetually outside *Zhonghua Minzu*. The tensions within *Zhonghua Minzu* shaped Han contestations of their own identity through relations with non-Han others. For culturalists and socialists, Han ethno-nationalism was an impediment to nation-building. Competing Han narratives share ethnocentric logics but challenge nation-building through their relations with Uyghurs, arguing for more or less inclusion to build the real China. The final section showed how Uyghurs re-perform the ethnic boundaries demarcated by Chinese nation-building to position their history and identity outside *Zhonghua Minzu*. Where Han re-performed identity narratives, which position them at the centre of *Zhonghua Minzu*, Uyghurs re-performed their peripheralisation. Uyghurs tended to articulate their identity as a Turkic group living in a Han nation-state, through references to their inferior position in official narratives and daily experiences of ethnic discrimination. Uyghurs in Ürümchi, like *getihu* Han, see the official multi-*minzu* China with Han at the centre as incompatible with the ethnic boundaries that mediate their daily practices.

Outside the workplace, both groups' social interaction was largely intra-ethnic. Ethnically targeted security practices and daily inter-ethnic interactions were understood by Uyghurs through the prism of ethnic boundaries that were reinforced by official narratives positioning them as a culturally inferior. Uyghurs invert and re-perform official performances of Uyghur-ness as a cultural frontier, locating their identity through Turkic and Islamic centres culturally outside *Zhonghua Minzu*. The music of popular artists, such as Perride and Abdurehim, which reflects mainstream Uyghur identity narratives, has caused those artists to be designated as security threats and extra-legally disappeared in Xinjiang's growing internment camp system.

After the violence of 2009, public life in Xinjiang was dominated by the party-state's project to build a nominally multi-*minzu* nation with the Han as the centre and Xinjiang as a frontier. Competing drives to incorporate Uyghurs into Chinese civilisation (culturalism), develop minority *minzu* (transformative socialism), and place Han at the centre (chauvinism) all co-exist in tension towards the same goals of absorbing or eliminating Uyghur culture to make China great again. To advance nation-building, the party-state seeks to transform Han identity in Xinjiang to be *of* Xinjiang rather than just *in* it. However, converting Han into Xinjiang people runs counter to popular Han self-understandings of ancestral heritage (*laojia*) as central sites of their identity. The party-state's anti-tradition campaigns have never supplanted pre-communist narratives of lineage, and these became interweaved with narratives of multi-*minzu* nationalism. Furthermore, the political construction of 'Xinjiang person' as something Han can become simply by being there runs counter to Uyghur identity because they understand themselves, like many Han, as intimately tied to the land and language of their ancestors. *Zhonghua Minzu* includes *and* excludes Xinjiang, and these tensions circulate in the way Han and Uyghurs define themselves and each other. The party-state's nominal multi-*minzu* China also runs counter to visceral experiences of many Han in Xinjiang who stay temporarily for employment and view Uyghurs as culturally foreign. Intellectuals with longer-term links to the region, such as Mrs Du, saw these transitory movements of Han in and out of Xinjiang as a problem because it threatened the region's multicultural history and demographics. Short-term migrants, on the other hand, tended to position Uyghurs entirely outside their *Zhonghua Minzu*, defined through Han lineage and language. Mrs Du's lament brought internal boundaries amongst Han to the fore through external boundary demarcation against minorities. The Han self is contested through its concrete daily relations with Uyghur otherness mediated by the competing conceptual imaginations of *Zhonghua Minzu*. Han and Uyghur are contextual and, often, relational categories within which contestation over the meaning of China takes place in interaction with the state. Nevertheless, the ambivalent position of Uyghurs in *Zhonghua Minzu*, as both 'backward' ethnic

Conclusions

minority barbarians to be converted and non-Chinese others, offers no scope for a shared Chinese identity without embracing their need to be absorbed by China.

This chapter showed that Chinese nation-building is failing because it paradoxically produces and transgresses existing ethnic boundaries while failing to offer inclusion of Uyghur identities or challenge widespread discrimination. The party-state's attempt to reconfigure difference and convince all peoples of Xinjiang that they are one national community reinforces difference because it hierarchically organises ethnic boundaries. Party-state performances of Chinese-ness have the opposite effect of their stated intention because Uyghurs and Han re-perform its narratives of timelessness and civilisation to articulate immutable difference. The party-state has promoted Han-centred nationalism in Xinjiang to secure loyalty of the Han, but this has emboldened Han chauvinists while making them feel their ethno-national identities are threatened by Uyghurs and the official promotion of multi-*minzu* China. The party-state provides Han and Uyghurs with a vocabulary to meaningfully exclude but not include each other. Official policy shifts towards 'fusion' since the end of the Hu era emphasise Han ethno-nationalism as the solution to the party-state's balancing act between different identities and resolve the '*minzu*' problem' forever. The final chapter turns to how Han and Uyghurs reconfigure identity-insecurity in response to the securitisation of *Zhonghua Minzu* to designate each other as threats. Xinjiang suffers from an insecurity dilemma because the party-state's narrative of perpetual identity-security threats produces triadic relations of insecurity between Han, Uyghurs, and the state in recurring cycles of violence.

7 Han and Uyghur Narratives on Identity and Insecurity

Introduction

The party-state's 'new China' narrative tells a story of a state founded in response to Western imperialism working with internal non-Han enemies. These twin security threats were reconfigured in the 'opening and reform' era as ethnic separatists supported by Western democracies. *Zhonghua Minzu* has many enemies because the CCP securitises many identities. The multiple logics of China the ancient civilisation, China the multi-ethnic socialist nation, and China the Han nation-state constitute perpetual insecurity and a multiplicity of threats *everywhere*. Turkic identities resist benevolent absorption into Chinese civilisation, 'reactionary' ethnic nationalists threaten teleological progression of China's modernisation, and claims of ethnic inequality are 'excuses to split China' because they challenge notions of Han superiority. Multiple securitisations of identity produce multiple enemies inside and outside Xinjiang, shaping social dynamics between Han and Uyghurs on the ground, that are marked by perpetual fear and distrust of each other. The triadic approach taken here analyses the constitution of identity and security through relations between the state, majority, and minorities. The party-state produces hierarchical ethnic boundaries between Han and Uyghurs in its *Zhonghua Minzu* narrative, objectivising Han culture as Chinese identity, and excluding Uyghur identification through Turkic language and Islam. These boundaries produce different insecurities for different groups. Han seek to secure the centrality or superiority of their identity against Uyghur calls for inclusion or self-determination. Both groups subsequently construct intra-ethnic boundaries through relations with the state and ethnic other, contesting who is authentically Chinese, Han, or Uyghur. The insecurity stemming from these fractures makes the party-state more insecure about identity and political stability. As it then seeks to secure Han loyalty and Uyghur conversion with more ethnocentric nation-building, the cycle continues and intensifies. The party-state under Xi seeks to end these intensifying cycles using chauvinist ethnic policy narratives and extra-legal internment camps to eliminate or transform Uyghur identities.[1] The previous

---

[1] The book's conclusion returns to this point in detail.

Introduction

chapter asked Han and Uyghurs in Ürümchi who they include as friends. This chapter asks who they exclude as enemies. The previous chapter showed that Han and Uyghurs in Ürümchi use different narratives within official discourse to explain their daily practices and reinforce ethnic boundaries. This chapter turns to how they articulate alternative identities by securitising those boundaries. How do Han and Uyghurs understand the party-state's securitisation of *Zhonghua Minzu*? How do they redeploy official security discourse to articulate alternative identities and insecurities? The party-state produces insecurity in Xinjiang by constructing multiple, perpetual identity-security threats, exacerbating Han and Uyghur insecurity about each other and their identities. Han and Uyghurs re-perform official identity-security narratives to resist nation-building, making the state feel more insecure, and the cycle continues with intensified state-violence.

Bellér-Hann et al. (2007) divided literature on Xinjiang broadly between historians and anthropologists of Central Asia, focusing on bottom-up identity, and political scientists trained in Sinology who analyse top-down security. Taking these approaches as analytical emphases rather than fixed ontologies helps examine mutual interplay between the top-down nation-building project and bottom-up identity articulations. 'China' is produced somewhere in between the two. Identity and security are mutually constitutive performative discourses, mediated and contested in people's daily practices. Security 'tells us who we must be' (Walker, 1997, pp.71–72), constituting the civilised self to be secured against the barbaric other, who threatens its cultural boundaries (Callahan, 2004, p.27; Campbell, 1998, pp.61–70). However, securitising national identity and superimposing it on people's daily practices provokes security for some and insecurity for others. Chapter 4 showed how nation-building produces insecurity on the ground for Uyghurs whose identity is excluded from officially securitised conceptualisations of national identity. This exclusion produces dynamic cycles of identity-securitisation and counter-securitisations between the state and different ethnic groups competing for power to identify themselves and others on existential terms. The micropolitics of producing the nation often lead to its own unravelling (Krishna, 1999, p.xvii). National identity narratives can be persuasive when they allow people to 'refract their personal and local experience', participating in the 'same' social practices without feeling subordinated (Cohen, 1985, pp.20–21; 1996, pp.807–810). Nation-building struggles to include Uyghurs as one of 55 ethnic minorities because it ignores their complaints about inequality and marks their identities as threats, while offering no space to feel Chinese *and* Uyghur. Nation-building in Xinjiang fails to produce a shared identity because it re-produces and reconfigures ethnocentric historical boundaries that categorise Uyghurs as non-Chinese barbarians, which has enabled the re-emergence of Han chauvinism. Nationalism is least convincing when it alienates personal or group experiences by extending its domain to 'people from whom one has always previously claimed significant difference' (Cohen, 1996, p.810). Chinese nation-building offers no new narratives of inclusion for Uyghur difference. Furthermore, it has ignored how official boundaries are celebrated by Han chauvinists to exclude minorities and are consistently highlighted in Uyghurs' explanations of everyday, individual experiences of marginalisation and discrimination. The production and securitisation of *Zhonghua Minzu* cannot produce self-identification because it builds the nation upon a hierarchical civilisational boundary *and* transgresses the practiced ethnic boundaries between Han and Uyghurs. Inclusion of the internal other must make sense to people's daily lives or it will produce, and struggle to contain, multiple identities and heightened insecurities from below.

This chapter is divided into two sections that use detailed, semi-structured interviews to analyse how Han and Uyghurs articulate their own identity-insecurities using official *Zhonghua Minzu* narratives. Han and Uyghurs frame each other as identity-threats by re-performing official discourses of danger. This process is termed re-securitisation because it resists official narratives but does so by deploying and inverting its object referent of securitisation, *Zhonghua Minzu*. The first section asks Han in Ürümchi how they conceive insecurity in Xinjiang. It analyses how Han in Ürümchi re-perform the party-state's discourses of danger to articulate their own insecurity and re-define *Zhonghua Minzu*. Han intellectuals tend to adopt ethnocentric multi-*minzu* narratives to frame Uyghur identity as an integration problem that can be solved by Han 'frontier-builders'. Chauvinist ethno-nationalists simply consider Uyghurs an alternative Turkic-Islamic nation that threatens Han superiority and must be dominated by China. The second section analyses how Uyghurs in Ürümchi re-perform official discourses and unofficial Han framings of security to re-define *Zhonghua Minzu* as a threat. Uyghurs understand the idea of barbarians 'learning to be Chinese' (*jiaohua* 教化), as promoted by Ma Rong (2007), not as China's peaceful attraction but as violent assimilation. Uyghurs re-perform this narrative by securitising their own identity against the violent threat of *Zhonghua Minzu*. They invert the party-state's discourses of danger by articulating ethnic unity and Mandarin-medium education as threats to Uyghur identity, redirecting official boundaries inward through narratives of insecurity and assimilation.

Uyghurs tend to frame Xinjiang's Han population as inadvertent foot soldiers in the party-state's project to assimilate Uyghurs through demographic and linguistic transformation. Nevertheless, Uyghurs often feminise the Han as physically non-threatening to articulate the Uyghur nation's strength, but understand this femininity as a threat to the survival of Uyghur-ness. The previous chapter showed how Han redirect external boundaries with Uyghurs inward, demarcating boundaries between culturalist and ethno-nationalist Han identities. Uyghurs also redirect the Han-Uyghur ethnic boundary inward, between Uyghurs educated in Uyghur (*minkaomin* 民考民) and those educated in Mandarin (*minkaohan* 民考汉). These internal boundaries are often securitised by Uyghurs because they are indivisible from external boundaries between China and Uyghurs, transgression of which threatens their existence. However, while Uyghur internal securitisation shapes daily practices and narratives, it has no history of violence. *Minkaohan* are often viewed by *minkaomin* as identity-less victims of Chinese nation-building.[2] *Minkaomin* securitise Uyghur-ness by using the *minkaohan-minkaomin* boundary to demarcate who is a real Uyghur and who is Sinicised, reproducing Uyghur insecurity that they are a dying Turkic nation in a Han nation-state.

This final chapter explores the insecurities that emerge with the party-state's securitisation of *Zhonghua Minzu*. The CCP imposes identity framings on people who understand themselves in alternative ways based on longer-term historical narratives, and they resist nation-building by re-securitising their own identities. The chapter uses interviews with Han and Uyghurs in Ürümchi to show that nation-building is failing because it produces insecurity and fractured identities on the ground. Re-securitising and re-performing *Zhonghua Minzu* are part of the same process of bottom-up identity articulation and resistance to the party-state's model of a Han-led *Zhonghua Minzu*. The core argument of the book that the party-state's securitisation of *Zhonghua Minzu* produces multiple identity-insecurities in Xinjiang is crystallised in this chapter. It shows how official narratives of *Zhonghua Minzu* exacerbate identity-insecurities amongst Han and Uyghurs because it threatens both groups' ethnic identities in different ways. Nation-building in Xinjiang produces insecurity because it includes Uyghurs on terms that entail gradual extinction of their identity and frames them as culturally inferior, which emboldens Han ethno-nationalism. The party-state's securitisation of *Zhonghua Minzu* perpetuates cycles of mistrust and insecurity between Han and Uyghurs, analysed in this chapter, by making them feel threatened by each other's identities. Popular resistance in everyday security narratives run counter to the officially securitised *Zhonghua Minzu*, creating further state-insecurity by challenging its power to define Chinese identity.

Re-Securitising Han-ness, Re-Performing China

When I arrived in the city in September 2009, '7-5' was a hot topic of conversation. For several months, almost every individual of Han ethnicity I met raised the issue with me without prompting. The openness of Han residents in discussing political topics with foreigners reflected the city's

---

[2] It was regrettable to only interview several *minkaohan*. The lack of access is mainly due to their lower numbers, but they were also less open to discussing these issues with foreigners.

asymmetrical power relations, which restrict the space in which Uyghurs but not Han are able to discuss political issues (Anthony, 2011, p.51). This section examines how Han re-perform party-state security narratives to articulate their own identities and insecurities. The analysis is divided into two sub-sections. The first analyses how Han in Ürümchi securitise Han identity through ethnicisations of physical space that frame Uyghur cultural practices, particularly the pork taboo, as existential threats to China. The second subsection explores how Han in Ürümchi tend to ethnicise violence and articulate Han ethnonationalism as the means to save China from the Uyghur threat. Han in Ürümchi re-perform the party-state's discourses of danger, securitising their own ethnocentric or chauvinist identities, which frame Uyghurs and their identities as security threats.

Securitising Han Space in Ürümchi

Han in Ürümchi tend to securitise identity through ethnicisations of space demarcating Chinese security and Uyghur danger. Ürümchi is spatially divided between the Han-populated north and Uyghur-populated south (Smith, 2002; Taynen, 2006). Interviews with Han in Ürümchi revealed that they tended to map the city according to intertwined discourses of ethnicity and danger. After the July 2009 violence, many Han who lived in the south moved north as they struggled with insecurity and feared for their physical safety. Local estate agents explained that house prices on *Jiefang Lu* (Liberation Street), the thoroughfare linking *Nanmen* (South Gate), a busy retail area, and *Erdaoqiao/Döngköwrük* dropped by 50 per cent almost overnight. Han students and *getihu* described the city's south to me as the 'enemy-district' (*diqu* 敌区). Residential districts were divided by house price into a, b, c, and d. D-*qu* literally meant 'district D', but in spoken Mandarin is a homonym of 'enemy-district'. This wordplay illustrates the open articulation of friends and enemies through Han in-jokes that frame Uyghurs as external cultural threats to Han identity-security. Aynür overheard this joke and interrupted a group of laughing Han to unwittingly explain that *Erdaoqiao* was part of B-*qu*, not D-*qu*. Aynür felt humiliated and explained to me that 'it's always just like this, unity is only superficial'. Popular articulations of Uyghur neighbourhoods as threats re-perform official discourses of friends and enemies but dispense with the culturalism of ethnic unity, viewing Uyghurs as an entirely inconvertible ethnic enemy in a Han China. Uyghurs then interpret these discourses of danger as evidence of their exclusion in an ethno-nationalist *Zhonghua Minzu*.

Many Han residents still personally struggled with fear of violence during this period, and it was common to hear official nation-building narratives used to frame Uyghur identity as a physical security threat. Although there were tens of thousands of PLA troops and PAP visible on Ürümchi's streets, many interviewees commended me for being 'fierce' for braving the danger they located in the Uyghur district. In an official welcome to foreign students at one university, a teacher told students that 'all Uyghurs like fighting and carry knives', so 'don't go to *Erdaoqiao* alone'.[3] One mid-20s, born-and-bred-Ürümchi office worker, like many Han, had still not left her apartment block three months after the violence of July. She warned me against visiting the 'dangerous' Uyghur district because 'they caused 7-5'. On the day of the 60th anniversary of the PRC's founding, Mrs Xi, a teacher from Hunan in her mid-30s, urged me to avoid the Uyghur district or city centre and to stay indoors to watch the TV transmissions from Beijing: 'I urge you not to go. You can't go to places with lots of people; 7-5 has made Han scared.' Mrs Xi explained the Uyghur district was safe for minorities but not for Han. Like most Han interviewees, she ethnicised and securitised space by explaining Han must stay within the 'security' of ethnically segregated living areas to avoid the Uyghur 'threat'.

The party-state's approach to identity-security explained that violence in the city was 'not a *minzu* problem' (XEP, 2009, p.4). However, its constant ethnocentric association of Uyghur cultural practices with threats mobilised Han to view violence across the city through the identity prism of a Uyghur threat to China. One male shop owner in his early 40s warned me on our first meeting that 'East Turkestan forces', just three miles south, were rising to separate *Erdaoqiao* from the 'motherland'. Mr Li, a 43-year-old local-born labourer, regaled me with tales of fictional violence from the action films he adored but recounted his fears of real violence in the city's south. He told me, 'Xinjiang is such a good place – even better than Beijing. It's because the people are so warm hearted. They want to help each other because they come from all over China. But don't got to *Erdaoqiao*, it's very dangerous. Rich Uyghurs pay poor Uyghurs from the south to come here and riot.' When I asked Mrs Xi who was to blame for 'security problems', she also said, 'Rich people.' These explanations of violence re-performed officially articulated dangers of 'The Three Evils', identifying China's social problems and inside/outside enemies as 'backward' Uyghurs, manipulated by wealthy Uyghurs, Islamists, and the West outside. Those in positions of public employment identified with ethnic unity but repeated the party-state's socio-spatialisations, discussed in Chapter 3, that associate Uyghur-populated areas with backwardness and terrorism. For example, Miss Lan ethnocentrically explained that Uyghur religion will disappear with 'scientific development', framing Uyghur's 'backward' identity as a problem for *Zhonghua Minzu*: 'In Ürümchi, it's not so severe but in southern Xinjiang because there are so many

---

[3] I was given the same talk when studying in Ürümchi in 2007, which shows how these narratives were heightened but not caused by violence between Uyghurs and Han in 2009.

minorities living together it is more so.' Miss Lan linked Uyghurs who live in areas with less Han and practice Islam to the 'extremism' of 'The Three Evils' by framing their identities as a 'severe' problem of 'backwardness'. The mass violence of July was a visceral threat to people's lives, but the party-state narrated it as an existential identity-threat to China, perpetuating the threat and producing Uyghur cultural practices as ever-present sources of Han insecurity.

Han in Ürümchi securitised their identity by mapping the majority-minority binary onto boundaries between the city's safe and dangerous districts, explained through references to daily practices, including dietary habits. Despite being a middle-income country, China regularly ranks amongst the top ten in the world for per capita pork consumption. The Islamic pork taboo amongst Uyghurs is a visceral everyday boundary, as most Uyghurs will not enter Han-owned restaurants that are not halal. Food is ordinarily a soft boundary because group members can share in other groups' food without being converted, but boundaries are hardened when practices function as cultural markers that constitute community (Duara, 2009, pp.112–113). Smith (2002) showed how the pork taboo is a self-ascribed vessel of difference employed by Uyghurs that maintains boundaries with Han. Uyghurs engage in a 'counter-hegemonic discourse' to 'Han superiority implicit in the Han 'civilising project' by asserting distinctiveness through frequent comparison of food preparation and styles to Han methods (Cesaro, 2007, p.196). However, Han in Ürümchi mutually engage in these boundary-production practices to reassert cultural superiority over Uyghurs. Han use pork consumption to securitise China by distinguishing who is and is not a 'real Chinese person'. Han often frame the pig as intimately tied to land and family through identity narratives as an agricultural and peaceful people, as opposed to dangerous nomadic others. Mao Zedong's commitment to eradicating Han chauvinism was often questioned because he declared pork a 'national treasure' and induced Muslim Hui farmers to raise pigs (Gladney, 1996, p.26). Miss Lan, the university teacher who expounded the ancient tradition of unity, gave me the standardised ethnocentric narrative that throughout history '*all* Chinese people' have defined the family and home (*jia*) through 'owning land, a house, and pigs'. In conjunction with standardised textbooks used across China[4], Mandarin language lessons at Xinjiang University in 2009 gave this explanation, describing the Chinese character for 'home' and 'family' (*jia* 家) as a 'herd of pigs under a roof'. The lesson passed without mention of the pork taboo or Muslim inhabitants of Xinjiang who were visible from the classroom window. This ethnocentric conceptualisation of family and home objectivises Han cultural

---

[4] Boya Chinese (*Boya Hanyu*).

practices as Chinese, invisibilising and excluding Muslims from the nominally multi-ethnic culture of China.

During fieldwork, I was constantly asked, 'Do you eat pork?' by Han interviewees, friends, and landlords. They would express relief and often camaraderie when I gave an affirmative answer with shaking of hands, being welcomed to stay in Xinjiang, and exchanging of phone numbers. Throughout interviews, Han in Ürümchi frequently insisted that all Chinese people are pork-eating atheists, mutually constituting China against ethnic Uyghur Islamic practices. During a year living in Ürümchi (2007), Han would regularly welcome me to 'taste the Xinjiang flavour', meaning Uyghur dishes of pilaf, laghman, nan, and kebabs. However, by 2009, many Uyghur restaurants had closed down in Han areas, and Han customers observably avoided those which were open. The violence of July 2009 and its official representation thus shaped how the pork taboo was employed and conceptualised by Han as a security problem. In one interview, a local city centre–based businessman explained that all Uyghur restaurants in the People's Park (*gongyuan beijie* 公园北街) area had been attacked on July 7 and could only open again when all Uyghur staff in contact with customers were replaced with Hui.[5] During 2009–2010, I was frequently warned against eating Uyghur food by many Han *getihu*, with one 40-year-old, local-born (*bendi ren*) male explaining that 'Han don't eat *minzu* food since 7-5, unity is impossible'. Mr Wang, in his late 30s and from Sichuan, had spent 11 years in Karamay as an oil executive for state-owned SINOPEC, the largest oil extraction company in Asia. He said, 'Even before 7-5, I really didn't like Ürümchi. I don't like Uyghurs. I really don't like them. So now we don't eat their food and won't buy their things.' Mr Wang openly admitted on our first meeting that, despite official employment quotas under the 'preferential policies' narrative, his SINOPEC office refused to employ Uyghurs, because 'none of them work, they don't study. We used to have one but now I won't employ them as they are too much trouble. Too much arguing. So many disagreements and ethnic contradictions.' When pressed, Mr Wang explained the only 'ethnic contradictions' were that Uyghurs wanted to pray and wouldn't eat pork during banquets. Han in Ürümchi imbue banal daily practices of eating pork with symbolic meaning using official ethnocentric security narratives to demarcate ethnic boundaries against the threat of Uyghur identity and constitute a chauvinist *Zhonghua Minzu*.

Islam is selected by Han ethno-nationalists as one vessel to demarcate and securitise boundaries specifically against Uyghurs but not Hui Muslims. The Islamic pork taboo and Han consumption of pork both have long histories in

---

[5] This practice was still observable in July 2012. I visited three restaurants on this street, all of which had Uyghur chefs but employed all-Hui service staff.

China that constitute soft boundaries, which Han ethno-nationalists harden and securitise in a city beset by visceral violence, officially explained through ethnocentric discourses of danger. Han use these discursive resources to 'think themselves into difference' by making contingent and harmless boundaries appear timeless and irrefutable (Cohen, 1985, p.86). Eating or not eating pork is unrelated to physical security, but Han in Ürümchi consistently use official narratives to frame this choice as directly impacting China's survival. Mr Yi, the 40-year-old male *getihu*, explained the violence of July 2009 by saying:

> It's religion, all Muslims, Islam is all about killing people ... ever since liberation – we liberated Xinjiang – we have had this problem. So now we hate them [points towards *Erdaoqiao/Döngköwrük*]. It's not possible to have unity and it's not possible to have harmony. It's just the government's words. Han and Uyghurs can never have the same perspective, never have the same heart. [Points to slogan 'Unity is prosperity, separation is disaster'] It's just a stupid government slogan. Do you eat pork?

Explaining that 'all people', not just Chinese people, should eat pork, Mr Yi welcomed me to Xinjiang and described me as a 'good person' when I said I did. Mr Yi did not take the party-state's multi-*minzu* China seriously. Han and Uyghurs were considered different nations based on incompatible identities, and Islam was a threatening source of violence, which constitutes immutable ethnic boundaries with Uyghurs. Han ethno-nationalists framed Islam as constitutive of timeless boundaries between atheist Han and Muslim Uyghurs. Mr Qi, a late-20s *getihu* from Ürümchi, blasted loud Russian disco music while he told me:

> Turban-heads is the name for Uyghurs, you know? The problem here is *minzu* division and *minzu* contradictions. Islam is just too extreme a religion. It's bad, makes people use violence. I mean they don't even eat pork, so they won't eat in our restaurants. Do you eat pork? [Happy at my response, says, 'Good' and continues ...] Pork is the best meat. Everyone should eat it. They think it's because it's dirty but we say it is because their ancestors are pigs and they worship them.

'Turban-head' (*chuantou* 穿头) was the official Chinese designation for Uyghurs until the Republican-era rise of warlord Sheng Shicai who rejected Han chauvinism (Millward, 2007, p.208). Its usage persists widely today amongst Han, particularly ethno-nationalists who explicitly exclude Uyghurs from *Zhonghua Minzu* as un-Chinese. Dehumanising notions that Uyghurs descend from a different species, let alone race, are heard across China, even amongst groups who consider themselves liberal. I had to repeatedly explain to numerous students when teaching in Shandong and to several friends in Beijing studying at the master's degree level that Uyghurs did not worship pigs as their ancestors. In contemporary Xinjiang, Han self-employ these stereotypes, through discourses of lineage and ancestry, to demarcate national and racial difference from Uyghurs. The pork taboo can create some physical distance because it forbids Uyghurs from entering Han Chinese-owned restaurants, a central location of socialising for Han. However, many Han narrate the banal act of eating pork as a security matter and marker of loyalty to Chinese civilisation. Han consumption of pork is objectivised as Chinese-ness and even *human* behaviour ('everyone should eat it'). Since 2012, 'de-extremification' education texts specifically targeted the pork taboo as 'religious extremism' and an attempt to 'use the Halal concept' to 'ruin close relations between Uyghurs and other *minzu*' (Zhang et al., 2014, p.37). The exclusion of Uyghur cultural practices as identity-security threats is not new. However, it has intensified and become more explicit in official discourse, reflecting shifts towards a mono-ethnic China, described by Hao Shiyuan (2012) as populist responses to chauvinist identity articulations from below, which exclude minorities from China.

Han Chauvinism in Ürümchi

This subsection analyses how Han ethno-nationalists in Ürümchi ethnicise violence and articulate a Han chauvinist identity as the means to save China from the threat of Uyghurs. Much of the literature on politics and ethnic relations in Xinjiang assumes that the identities of the Han and Chinese state are largely synonymous, for example, through passing references to 'Han rule' or 'Han China'. Party leaders in Xinjiang have all been Han since the XUAR's establishment, and it is correct to say that 'Xinjiang's government institutions... have been subordinated at all levels to the heavily Han party structure' (Bovingdon, 2004a, p.4). During the *minzu* policy debates discussed in Chapter 2, Zhang Haiyang (2012) lamented the reality that it is 'unthinkable' that a Uyghur could become a Chinese ambassador to Turkey or a Tibetan to India, let alone a top leader. Han have more power than Uyghurs to speak for China, and the party-state permits them more power to discuss their own identity. Han enjoy relative privilege because they are not subject to ethnic discrimination in surveillance, employment opportunities, or passport controls. However, it is the Han category, the narrative nucleus of *Zhonghua Minzu*, not Han people per se, who are the centre of China. Han in Xinjiang, particularly the working classes, are spoken for by the state but use official discourse against itself to perform alternative identities and insecurities. They articulate China as an ethnic Han nation which needs to be saved from the Uyghur threat *and* the party-state's complacent narratives of inclusion and diversity.

The direct links drawn in education texts and the media, between the international 'anti-Chinese chorus' and the domestic 'East Turkestan' problem, shape and fracture popular conceptions of identity and security. Most intellectuals and state employees emphasised the importance of Chinese culturalist traditions of ethnocentric unity; most working-class and *getihu* Han were less tolerant and more chauvinist in identifying threats from outside China's cultural boundaries to be defeated with violence. Mr Chen, a local-born 46-year-old *getihu*, blamed the July violence on Uyghurs' separatist identity, telling me, 'It's a political problem. Political. Uyghurs all want to separate from China. Life is better and better in Xinjiang but they still want to separate. The big problem is international. Rebiya (Qadir) and 'East Turkestan' are all abroad. They stir things up and organise trouble. They aren't even here yet they make people kill children and ordinary people (*laobaixing* 老百姓).' Most *getihu* interviewed adopted Han chauvinism to identify all Uyghurs as a 'constitutive outside' within China and inextricably linked to the 'terrorist' Islamic world outside. One 55-year-old, local-born *getihu* woman used the logics of the 'inside/outside Three Evils' in explaining, '7-5 was exactly like Iraq'. When news of suicide bombs in Pakistan reached China, Mr Qi, the local-born *getihu* in his early 20s, who described Uyghurs as 'turban-heads', said, 'They have so many terrorists in Pakistan. It's exactly what 7-5 was like. Their violence is terrible. It's better now but I worry it will be like Pakistan again'. Mr Yu, a soft-spoken 40-year-old taxi driver from Hubei who had escaped from rioters but saw a young child killed in his car, said, 'It was just like Iraq and Afghanistan. They wanted to turn our country into Iraq and Afghanistan, but we are not willing.' The standard explanation of '7-5' given to me every day by *getihu* was that Uyghurs' inherently violent nature ('their violence') was caused by their foreign-ness ('like Pakistan' and 'like Iraq') in contrast to peaceful China. Like many *getihu*, Mr Qiang explicitly referred to Uyghurs as 'foreign' and 'not real Chinese'. Many Han deployed the official 'inside/outside Three Evils' narrative to explain violence, but it emboldened chauvinists to entirely exclude all Uyghurs as foreign and inconvertible. Mr Yi, the 40-year-old *getihu* who said Islam was 'all about killing people', told me, 'It's just like Afghanistan and Iraq here – crazy. Uyghurs are exactly the same as Iraqis and Afghans'. Mr Hou, a *getihu* in his late 40s, born and bred in Ürümchi, explained the violence of '7-5' by telling me, 'Uyghurs are just like Turks, like Arabs – same languages, same religion'. These narratives re-performed *Zhonghua Minzu* as an ethnic Han nation, excluding all Uyghurs as foreign security threats by projecting chauvinist visions of international relations onto 'domestic' political conflicts.

The violence by Han against Uyghurs on July 7, analysed in Chapter 4, was officially invisibilised but privately discussed by Han. Some chose not to acknowledge the violence, such as Mr Chen, who said, 'They were all separatists – killing children, elderly, and ordinary people. It was very cruel. It was Uyghurs, all Uyghurs.' The intellectual Han interviewed, such as Mrs Du, avoided the topic altogether, claiming they didn't believe it had happened. Most *getihu* and working-class Han were more outspoken. One 45-year-old *getihu* male from 'inner China' laughed, whilst telling me, 'The rioting, looting, and killings of 7-5 was very cruel but on 7-7 we Han got together to kill Uyghurs.'[6] Mr Hu, the mid-20s *getihu* and proud Xinjiang person, told me that Xinjiang was still unstable due to the 'cruelty' of Uyghurs. I asked about the killings on the 7th but he laughed, saying, 'No, there was no trouble at all on the 7th. It was fine.' When I told him, 'Some of my Han friends said there was a lot of violence on the 7th as well', he responded, 'No, on the 7th us Han got together to kill Uyghurs. It was nothing, there was no problem.' He continued, 'The 5th was just like Iraq or Afghanistan, all the Muslims out of control with big sticks, causing chaos. The Uyghurs are such a disgusting *minzu* but then we fought back and it was ok.' Personal security was mediated by official nation-building narratives where violence against the Han is a culturally external, national security threat, but violence against minorities is 'no problem' because it maintains China's security and Han superiority. On July 5, Mr Yan, the local-born 42-year-old taxi driver, rescued his daughter from Uyghur rioters. Rioters attempted to kill them both, and his daughter was stabbed in the arm during their escape. Mr Yan explained, 'We had to attack back. If they attack your family, you have to kill them. So, on 7-7 we Han got together and attacked them. It was a nightmare. It was like Afghanistan and then us, the Americans, fighting the Taliban [laughs].' At the end of this conversation, Mr Yan shook my hand and thanked me with tears in his eyes, saying, 'No one has ever been willing to listen to this story, not even the CCP.' Mr Yan made sense of incomprehensible violence and enacted violence using the narratives available to him. As a working-class Han, he was caught between the party-state's nation-building project and the people whose identity it seeks to convert or eliminate, becoming a victim and perpetrator of violence who felt threatened by Uyghurs and marginalised by the state. The party-state's narratives mobilise chauvinism amongst Han who use official logics to make sense of the violence they experience when they arrive in Xinjiang to 'open the frontier', and exclude all Uyghurs as inconvertible security threats.

Han ethno-nationalists sought security through violence because they felt the party-state attempted to save a multi-*minzu* China not a Han China. When Mr Hu said, '*We* fought back' by killing Uyghurs, the 'we' did not mean the government. 'We' referred to ethnic Han who viewed violence by Uyghurs as a threat to their superiority, which the government would not secure. Mr Yi, the 40-year-old *getihu*, said, 'The government failed because they didn't order the police to kill them so the police were afraid, didn't know what to do.' Mr Xin, the 40-year-old, local-born taxi driver, told me, 'I was here during 7-5

---

[6] Interviewees would often say, 'We killed Uyghurs' but when asked if they were personally involved, most interviewees chose to ignore the question, change the topic, or explain they 'couldn't say'.

but I dare not speak the truth. The party dares not and the party won't let us. Ethnic minorities were killing everyone. In every other country they would respond immediately and eliminate them but not here. So, we had to defend ourselves and on 7-7 we responded. We gave them a beating [laughs proudly].'

Mr Xin's solution to security problems in Xinjiang, like other chauvinists, was to eliminate other inconvertible ethno-national groups. He securitised Han and sought to eliminate the twin threats of Uyghurs and ethnic unity. Mr Yu, the Hubei-born taxi driver, similarly framed the party-state as unwilling to provide security for the Han:

> The government did nothing, so 7-7 came and we showed them. We got together and we beat them [points south and grins] ... every *minzu* wants their own independent country – I understand that. They can protest against the government or a policy. I don't care. It's no problem but when they kill ordinary people, we are not willing, we will oppose them.

Mr Yu's referent of security was the Han, not the party-state's idea of *Zhonghua Minzu*. He explained that he turned to violence to protect 'his family and the Han'. Mr Yu claimed he had 'no problem' with Uyghurs protesting for an independent nation because that is what 'every *minzu* wants'. Nevertheless, he ethnicised the violence, and because the Han were under threat, he would kill other 'ordinary people' in response. The ethnic pride expressed by Han *getihu* in performances of violent dominance over Uyghurs ('we showed them') was embedded in popular stereotypes that Uyghurs are barbaric masculine threats to China's peace and harmony. Mr Yan, who seemed traumatised, presumably by the attack on his daughter and his own subsequent involvement in violence, used the same ethnicised framings of security to explain, 'You have to fight back and kill *them*' because it is 'human nature' to do so if 'they' attack your family:

> So on 7-7 we Han got together and attacked them. We had to but we were stopped by the special police. It's a disgrace we were stopped. They killed our families. My daughter's wounds are healed but our hearts will never heal, they will always hurt. Everything seems peaceful now as you can see, but in our minds the hurt and the hate will always be there. There is nothing we can do. The young people just need to continue working. But we will organise resistance. We will always be ready the next time, we will organise.

Organising meant using everyday social networks and telecommunications to save the Han by killing Uyghurs. During Uyghur holiday celebrations, analysed in Chapter 5, rows and rows of parked taxis unavailable for hire could be seen at major junctions of the Uyghur district with drivers congregating together and watching on with folded arms. The party-state was understood as an obstacle to Han identity-security, which could only be achieved by ordinary Han through self-organisation to eliminate the purported threat presented by Uyghurs. The party-state has staked its authority in Xinjiang on loyalty from the Han. However, this has historically been more tenuous than it appears, which partly explains the ethnic policy shift to 'fusion', described as Han populism by Hao Shiyuan (2012), and the 'de-extremification' policies in Xinjiang, which include mass, extra-legal internment camps to solve the '*minzu* problem' 'forever'.[7]

Mrs Wu was in her early 30s and had spent two years away from her 'hometown' in Fujian as a *getihu* in Ürümchi. Her slight frame and soft voice contrasted against her chauvinist celebrations of violence against Uyghurs in ethno-nationalist configurations of identity and security. On our first meeting, she asked me, 'Do you like *Hanguo (Hanguo* 汉国)?', deliberately conflating Han (汉) ethnicity and the Chinese nation (*Zhongguo* 中国) by merging the ethnonym Han, and *guo* (国), the word for country.[8] Mrs Wu dismissed my suggestion that this might be offensive to ethnic minorities. She said to me, as a foreign outsider, 'You can't understand' and became angry that I would not agree that 'all Uyghurs are bad'. She said, 'They are *all* bad. You can't understand. They all killed us'. I asked about '7-7', she responded:

WU: They killed us first. We must kill them. If they wanted to kill you, you would kill them?
DT: I would defend myself, but I wouldn't kill innocent people.
WU: There are no innocents, we have to kill them.
DT: Who are 'they'?
WU: Uyghurs.
DT: But some are innocent. Look at these people going to work, they are just people, Chinese people.
WU: No! They all kill. You don't understand.

The conversation continued in this vein. Mrs Wu confirmed that she believed all Uyghurs kill people including the elderly Uyghurs and policemen who walked past us, and even the Regional Government Chair, Nur Bekri. During July 2009, the media displayed bodies of dead Han and not Uyghurs, and this shaped and hardened perceptions on the ground (Smith Finley, 2011, pp.75–77). The party-state's ethnicised media coverage meant Mrs Wu had not even heard of the Shaoguan incident let alone subsequent protests at People's Square, so the '7-5' violence only confirmed the irrational violent nature of Uyghurs. Nevertheless, she securitised Han to re-perform a China,

---

[7] For example, see: XUAR (2018).
[8] Assuming I had heard incorrectly, I enquired if she meant South Korea (*hánguo* 韩国). However, she scorned my Mandarin tones, telling me that I 'know nothing about here'. She then rolled her eyes and assured me that she meant 'country of the Han' (*hànzu de guojia* 汉族的国家) in as patronising a tone as she could muster.

which ran counter to the party-state's multi-*minzu* nation-building project. Mrs Wu became most exasperated when I asked if proposing the killing of all Uyghurs could be construed as racism, deploying the East/West boundary discussed in earlier chapters, saying, 'Impossible! Racism is an American problem.' She then pointed to a fruit-seller setting up his stall, saying, 'Look at them! They are same as the turban-heads. They are all just turban-heads.' Mrs Wu's ethno-nationalist narratives of violence personified the nation and nationalised individual persons. 'You' and 'they' were mutually substitutable with entire ethnic groups. Visceral violence and her physical insecurity were conceptually translated into identity-insecurity because violence was officially narrated as solely associated with Uyghurs and their dangerous identities. Mrs Wu's exclusionary dismissal of Uyghurs as 'turban-heads' reflected official narratives of Islam as un-Chinese but re-performed China as a chauvinist Han nation under threat from *all* Uyghurs. I asked Mrs Wu if there was a contradiction between the idea that Xinjiang has always been part of a shared *Zhonghua Minzu* identity and saying that Uyghurs are not Chinese. She laughed and asserted colonial dominion, saying, 'No, there is no contradiction! This place is ours and these are bad people.' Mrs Wu and other *getihu* drew from official narratives to securitise the superior position of the Han as a dominant nation, holding the new frontier as China's possession rather than through shared identity. She spoke to power above in her desires for racial conquest and extermination, conceived as the rational restoration of peace.

Han is a contextual, relational category through which individuals contest their self-identifications and social positions. In China's urban centres, Han ethno-nationalist narratives are ordinarily more focused on the Western other, but Han in Ürümchi frequently re-perform official national narratives to re-securitise their everyday ethnic identities. The ethnocentrism of unity and the Han 'nucleus' speaks to Han nationalists, but the idea that Uyghurs can be converted by China held little appeal outside the intellectuals. Han ethno-nationalists did not formally resist the party-state as an institution, but their framings of identity and insecurity resisted attempts to identify China as a multi-ethnic nation and have helped drive policy shifts towards 'fusion' and internment camps. After the July 2009 violence, the party-state translated widespread physical insecurity into identity-insecurity, and the meaning of violence was constituted at the intersection between official discourse and daily visceral experiences. The ethno-centrism in official securitisations of *Zhonghua Minzu* was re-performed by Han ethno-nationalists to securitise the Han and violently exclude all Uyghurs from China. The party-state attempts to promote security by targeting Uyghur cultural practices as threats, but this exacerbates Han identity-insecurity and ethno-nationalist violence, which makes Uyghurs increasingly insecure.

Re-Securitising Uyghur-ness, Re-Performing China

This section analyses how Uyghurs securitise those aspects of their identity that are excluded as threats to China. The party-state's securitisation of *Zhonghua Minzu* identity exacerbates Uyghur identity-insecurity. Uyghurs re-perform official discourses of danger to securitise their own identities, framed through Turkic language, Islam, and chthonic belonging, articulating China as a threat. The analysis is divided into two sub-sections. The first explores how Uyghurs securitise Uyghur-ness through ethnicisations of space demarcating culturally safe and dangerous areas. The Han are often understood as unwitting participants in the party-state's nation-building project, but their intolerance towards Uyghur culture is framed as an existential threat. In response to the identity-threat of *Zhonghua Minzu*, Uyghurs often feminise Han as physically non-threatening, re-performing Chinese stereotypes of a masculine Uyghur threat and articulating Uyghur-ness as a dying Turkic identity in a feminine China. The second sub-section examines how securitisation hardens ethnic boundaries and leads to the securitisation of intra-ethnic boundaries. Ethnic boundaries with Han are redirected inward *between* different Uyghur groups, namely, *minkaohan* and *minkaomin*, framing the disappearance of Uyghur language as a security threat to Uyghur-ness. Uyghurs resist inclusion as ethnic minorities in the party-state's Han-centred *Zhonghua Minzu* by re-securitising Uyghur-ness and re-performing China as an ethnic nation that seeks to assimilate or eliminate Uyghur identity.

Securitising Uyghur Space in Ürümchi

This sub-section analyses how Uyghurs in Ürümchi re-perform official narratives that target their identities as a threat and securitise identity through ethnicisations of space demarcating security and danger. Jay Dautcher's (2009) *Down a Narrow Road* showed how performances of masculinity take centre stage in everyday Uyghur social practices, particularly jokes and proverbs used to explain social life. The Chinese stereotyping of young Uyghur men as violent and dangerous is often re-performed in ironic and sometimes genuine masculine bravado, distinguishing themselves from feminine Han. However, following July 2009, most people of all ethnicities expressed considerable fear of violence and explained they were afraid to even leave their homes. The Han violence of July 7 challenged these narratives of Uyghur masculinity. One young male Uyghur expressed a sentiment echoed by many interviewees, that 'for the first time, *we* were afraid of *them*'. By September, fear had subsided and the Uyghur district was again bustling at night, in contrast to noticeably quiet Han districts. Uyghurs narrated the Han-organised violence in ways that securitised their masculine identity against threats from an assimilative and feminine China.

Contradictions between equality in an imagined *Zhonghua Minzu* community and visceral daily practices of discrimination in China's ethno-hierarchy were raised by Uyghurs and related to identity-security in most interviews. Aynür was called into work on July 7 and she shook with fear for the whole bus journey because the passengers were 'all Han and all armed with sticks and clubs'. She explained this was particularly frightening because the state would not provide security for Uyghurs: 'No one would help me. The police, the government, they don't care if Uyghurs are killed.' For Uyghurs, the state is, at best, an observer and, at worst, the cause of violence and insecurity. Uyghurs, like many Han, imagined security as self-contained within the ethno-national boundaries of community. However, they felt doubly insecure because the state's exclusivist Chinese nationalism targeted their identity in its explanations of violence. After the July casualty figures were published and listed by *minzu*, Aynür was 'very angry' and asked, 'Are we not all human? What difference does it make what ethnic group we are? This does not help ethnic unity.' Aynür often suggested common humanity should supersede ethnicity but that China did not see Uyghurs as human, referring to terms such as 'Turban-heads', 'pig-worshippers', and 'terrorists'. She responded to this official and unofficial de-humanisation by demarcating ethnic boundaries, claiming Uyghurs 'all face this' and the Han 'are just like this'. Uyghurs vocally reject the denial of their 'human'-ness in discourses of danger and respond to visceral, everyday instances of discrimination by re-performing this de-humanisation to reject the idea that China is an inclusive multi-*minzu* nation.

Bag searches on public transport and all public buildings were immediately and seamlessly implemented across the city without visible challenge after July. Most conducting searches were not security officials but Han 'public volunteers'. All passengers' bags were checked but Uyghur passengers were observably targeted in more frequent and longer searches that many complained about in private[9]. Aynür was searched and questioned by Han security guards when bringing a box of fruit onto a public bus, while Han with similar luggage boarded freely. This visceral interaction made Aynür feel ethnically targeted and insecure, leading her to question whether the equality of *Zhonghua Minzu* had any substance:

> They think I have a bomb! It made me so angry, as if I am a terrorist, as if we are all terrorists. They all just think we are all terrorists. What are we to do? They all talk about terrorism but what can we do? It is impossible for us Uyghurs.

The securitisation of ethnic boundaries that constitute *Zhonghua Minzu* eclipsed Aynür's hope of being seen as human. Aynür was ethnically targeted and felt

---

[9] As a foreigner, I was often afforded the luxury of not being thoroughly searched. Joking with security staff that 'I'm not a terrorist, don't worry' even brought some laughs from the normally stern security guards.

treated as a 'terrorist' rather than as human. This led her to question her inclusion in *Zhonghua Minzu* and frame China as a threat to Uyghur-ness and her physical safety. Through this visceral experience, 'they' became a threatening alliance between party-state and ordinary Han because they both understood all Uyghurs as threats ('as if we are all terrorists'). On our first meeting, Aynür was enjoying watching the national-day military parade in Beijing on CCTV and did not understand why I didn't appreciate militaristic displays of Chinese nationalism. One of the last times we met, she described ethnic unity education as 'fascism' and told me, 'Now, I hate the country', relating her changed feelings to ethnic targeting, when she was a law-abiding, Mandarin-speaking citizen. Aynür had been proud of being Uyghur and Chinese ('between cultures'), but this identity and her life were threatened by the securitisation of *Zhonghua Minzu* and she securitised Uyghur-ness in response.

Aynür's personal experiences of ethnic targeting inside China reframed her inside and outside of identity. China's outside became seen as more secure for Uyghurs: 'So my situation and you know this is now the situation for the Uyghur people, it is all bad. I just want to leave this place, go as far away as possible. It is terrible here. I want to go far away to see the world, the *outside* world.' Aynür wanted to leave her home not because of cultural difference but because difference was socially organised in ways that treated her as a security problem. After July 2009, Aynür, Mukhtar, Mahigül, and Abdullah all said that they wanted to go abroad because the state targeted Uyghurs in its identity-security practices. However, they all said it would be impossible to leave because they were Uyghur. As Chapter 3 discussed, many Uyghurs seek political asylum abroad, but the party-state uses economic leverage to enable deportations of asylum seekers across Asia, notably from Thailand and Kazakhstan. Uyghurs who wanted to study abroad or to do business described how cross-border mobility was ethnicised by the party-state. Several interviewees had applied for passports and explained that for Uyghurs, standard additional application costs were bribes of RMB 30,000 and taking many influential people out for multiple dinners. After 2012, ethnic discrimination in the passport application process became more open, in one instance through the case of Atika, a Uyghur student whose application was rejected without explanation (RFA, 2012c; Tohti, 2012b). In 2015 and 2016, the Ili political and legal affairs committee and Shihezi municipal police department publicly announced pre-existing secretive practices that Uyghur residents had to submit passports for 'annual review' (RFA, 2016). Now, the official 'Population Data Collection Form',[10] using artificial intelligence through a facial recognition app,[11] determines whether individual Uyghurs are extremists to be

---

[10] See: Chin (2019).   [11] See: HRW (2019).

extra-legally detained in internment camps. This tick-box exercise tallies a simple score including holding a passport, having foreign friends, or having relatives in detention.

Several businessmen in Ürümchi, Kashgar, and Korla all complained to me in 2010 that the PSB kept their passports to 'stop us leaving China' and 'stop us doing business', which threatened their livelihood. Abdullah wished to travel abroad to build his export business, but after discovering additional costs and that he wouldn't be allowed to keep a passport on his person, he said:

> It is so hard for us Uyghurs to go abroad because it so hard to get a passport. It is nearly impossible for us to leave. We are fine in Xinjiang, but we can't go anywhere else. For Han, it's no problem. Our identity cards say what *minzu* we are and as soon as they see Uyghur, you can't do anything. You have to go home.

Physical enclosure in China and identity enclosure as an ethnic minority Uyghur threatened Abdullah's livelihood as an exporter. He understood official internal *minzu* boundaries between safe Han and dangerous Uyghurs as the reason why the party-state restricted Uyghurs' mobility and his livelihood. Uyghurs re-perform the party-state's security narratives to articulate insecurity within China and exclusion from global mobility. Their visceral experiences of discrimination contradict narratives of 'opening and reform' China as a multi-*minzu* community, and Uyghurs conclude they would be more secure outside China.

The discourses that stereotype Uyghurs as dangerous are also mocked and re-performed by Uyghurs to articulate their own identity-security. Mahigül, the student in her early 20s, was slim and soft-spoken but told me plainly that she was always safe in the city. 'I am not afraid of them, they are afraid of us.' She said, 'They don't know about Uyghurs because they are afraid, it's stupid, but we are not afraid of them. They are afraid of our men carrying knives, but this does not exist at all.' Uyghurs in Ürümchi tended to be proud of being less concerned about physical security than the Han. Mukhtar was concerned about Xinjiang's Sinicisation but re-asserted his masculinity and expressed no fear of violence when I asked him about July 7. He recounted a popular story that many young men told, in which hundreds of Han had marched to *Erdaoqiao/ Döngköwrük* only to be fought off by a few dozen Uyghur men, because Han 'can't fight and they are all afraid of blood'. Mukhtar was now a studious and law-abiding citizen. He was a little embarrassed but laughed when he told me how, as a youngster, he used to bully and fight Han Chinese teenagers. Like many young Uyghur men, he frequently mocked young Han Chinese men because they would 'carry their girlfriend's handbags' and 'can't take being teased'. Mukhtar thought fear was a characteristic of the Han vis-à-vis Uyghur masculinity. Young Uyghur men object to Chinese essentialisations of their identity but also find ways to enjoy them. Uyghurs re-perform the danger attributed to their identity as positive masculine attributes, inverting official narratives of ethnic minority passivity as a recipient of masculine Han 'frontier-building' culture.

The party-state articulates *Zhonghua Minzu* by positioning Xinjiang as 'feminine', receiving 'masculine' Han 'frontier-builders', while constituting Uyghur resistance as irrational, primal machismo. Uyghurs tend to read this text as colonialism and a threat to their nation's virility. For Mukhtar, the only way to reverse the threat of Sinicisation and preserve Uyghur-ness was Uyghur language education for all residents of Xinjiang: 'That would be a way to slow it down [Uyghur language education for Uyghurs] but no, we can't totally preserve it. I can't think of how to preserve it unless we get these people [Han Chinese] out of here or let these people start to learn Uyghur.' Mukhtar would regularly argue that language policies were designed to assimilate Uyghurs and that ordinary Han people promoted this transformative process by migrating and only speaking Mandarin. Mukhtar insisted that Han ought to study Uyghur as he had to study Mandarin, as a *living* language for *public* use. Mukhtar explained he was part of a 'dying nation' surrounded by 'brainwashed', feminine Han allied with the party-state's domination of the region's resources and jobs. He explained, 'I don't *hate* them. I only hate the Chinese government. But since most of them are so brainwashed, I can't imagine being with one. As humans we should have doubts about all things. I just don't understand this blind faith they have to the Communist party. That's brainwashed.' Aynür similarly echoed widespread concerns that continuity of Uyghurs' 'glorious Turkic civilisation' had been broken by Chinese migration and Sinicisation. Aynür gendered this loss of tradition and identity, explaining, 'Uyghur men no longer work in fields and no longer have big muscles. Now they have to work in Chinese offices and their muscles are very small.' Aynür and many other interviewees would whisper narratives about 'brainwashed Han' and the disappearance of Uyghur culture, often stopping to check the rooms and doorways of their own homes, saying that 'even the walls have ears'. Uyghurs were afraid of being overheard by Han neighbours because their identity narratives are targeted as threats to China and the Han are officially positioned as security agents of the state, 'the frontline' in 'fighting East Turkestan terrorism'.[12] The official articulations of Uyghur-ness as an ever-present threat to *Zhonghua Minzu* are re-performed by Uyghurs where China becomes the ever-present threat to the identity and masculinity of the Uyghur nation.

For Uyghurs, China's dominance as feminine outsider in Xinjiang parallels the CCP's and Han nationalists' humiliation narratives, which position the

---

[12] Discussed in Chapter 4.

West as threatening other in a 'century of humiliation'. Where Chinese nationalists articulate what Callahan (2007) termed a feminine 'victim state' identity in response to nineteenth century Western imperial encroachment, Uyghurs re-assert masculinity and their ability to endure violence as the identity of a 'dying nation' inside twenty-first century China. Joanne Smith (2002) showed how Uyghurs used self-selected vessels to demarcate ethnic boundaries in the 1990s, which were not directed against the government but towards Han migrants. However, Aynür's and Mukhtar's identity narratives show how physical threats and official securitisation of an individual's identity within *Zhonghua Minzu* has produced re-securitisations. Han and China, people and government are understood by many Uyghurs as working together in a colonial project to assimilate or annihilate Uyghur-ness. The party-state's narrative of 'people-centred' development aim to produce a shared *Zhonghua Minzu* identity, but on an individual level has produced 'people-centred' resistance. Uyghurs frame their daily, individual experiences of China's hierarchical organisation of ethnic difference through a narrative of 'humiliation' by external powers, telling them who they must be.

Identity-Security Boundaries amongst Uyghurs

This sub-section uses in-depth interviews with Mukhtar and Mahigül on the relationship between language and identity to analyse how the party-state's securitisation of *Zhonghua Minzu* produces securitised intra-ethnic boundaries amongst Uyghurs. Public meaning is 'mediated by idiosyncratic experience of the individual' (Cohen, 1985, p.14). These idiosyncrasies were explored in all interviews by allowing individuals to raise specific topics they deemed important to broader set questions on identity and security. Mukhtar and Mahigül both redirected ethnic boundaries inward, framing disappearance of Uyghur language as an existential threat. The boundary between different Uyghur groups, namely, *minkaohan* and *minkaomin*, was frequently highlighted in interviews with Uyghurs about identity. *Minkaohan* refers to ethnic minorities, educated in schools using Mandarin-medium instruction. *Minkaomin*, conversely, denotes ethnic minorities educated using Uyghur or other minority languages. *Minkaohan* are sometimes popularly referred to as China's 57th *minzu* and seen as distinct from Xinjiang's indigenous groups (Smith Finley, 2007, p.224).[13] *Minkaohan* are often economically advantaged by enjoying greater job opportunities but tend to feel socially isolated because they are more exposed to racism from Han due to easier communication (Taynen,

---

[13] I asked interviewees directly about descriptions of *minkaohan* as China's 57th *minzu* and most chose not to use this term. Mukhtar and Mahigül felt it was exclusionary and that *minkaohan* deserved greater sympathy because they were culturally isolated.

2006, p.45). *Minkaohan* are also often seen as occupying an 'ill-defined and uncomfortable middle ground' between Uyghurs and Han (Taynen, 2006, p.46). *Minkaohan* are 'betwixt and between', often seen as neither wholly Uyghur by Uyghurs nor wholly Chinese by Han, many of whom refer to them as 'half-castes' (Smith Finley, 2007, pp.219–220).

Mukhtar and Mahigül were both Uyghurs in their early 20s and former students of the same experimental bilingual schooling scheme,[14] the precursor to universal 'bilingual education'. Mahigül described these experiences as positioning them between linguistic communities: 'We are neither *minkaohan* nor *minkaomin*, we are in the middle'. Mahigül and Mukhtar both laughed when asked if *minkaohan* and *minkaomin* categories referred to the school system. They both stated that the categories referred to language use, not formal schooling. These categories are disappearing as formal, educational categories under monolingual education policies but continue to refer to Uyghur language abilities as a measure of assimilation. Mahigül and Mukhtar represent one potential future for how Uyghurs mediate conversion and exclusion in China's nation-building because their schooling model became universalised for all Uyghurs. Mukhtar and Mahigül both resisted ideas of being taught to be Chinese and articulate ethnic identities, reflecting competing Uyghur narratives on how to balance tradition and modernity and the public and private lives of Uyghur identity. Nevertheless, their narratives on the *minkaohan-minkaomin* boundary both reflect and reproduce identity-security narratives that they are a dying Turkic nation in a Han nation-state.

Mukhtar thought Uyghur should be Xinjiang's public language for the sake of the survival of Uyghur identity. When I asked Mukhtar why he had studied Mandarin, like most Uyghurs, he explained it was his parents' rational-economic decision because they knew it was an essential skill needed to find employment in China. He would describe Mandarin use through public/private distinctions, 'when I talk to Chinese people. You know, shopping or doing random stuff' and that 'before it wasn't like this but once I step out of my home, I use Chinese because everywhere is Han Chinese people'. When I asked whether all Uyghurs should have to study Mandarin, he responded:

No! I think all Han Chinese should study Uyghur. If they want to come here and live here, they should. We are the local people. You know if you come from some other place you should learn the language of the local people.

Mukhtar felt it was a common-sense demand that guests, to whom hospitality was extended in his 'homeland' (*wätän*), should study the Uyghur language, which for him defined the identity and heritage of Xinjiang. For Mukhtar, Uyghur language ought to be the official, inter-ethnic language of Xinjiang.

---

[14] See: Ma (2009).

The stigmatisation of Uyghur ethnicity should be reversed by re-elevating Uyghur language to a position of public importance representing Xinjiang's identity. Mukhtar argued that 'bilingual education' was simply the newest 'Sinicisation' tactic because 'it has always been their plan, to assimilate us'. Mandarin-medium-only education was understood as the gravest existential threat to Uyghur-ness, defined through ethno-linguistic practices. When I asked him to explain how Uyghurs would be assimilated, he responded:

> We would become more Chinese, we would lose our language, our culture ... of course the main thing is our language. If we lost that we would lose our identity, most of our identity. After that, we would naturally become like those Chinese people.

Mukhtar defined identity primarily through language. The securitisation of *Zhonghua Minzu*, which narrated Uyghurs as 'not a Turkic *minzu*', had led him to securitise this identity. On our first meeting I said Uyghurs told me his oasis hometown was a civilised place, and he responded by saying, 'Well we used to have *mädäniyät*, now we have *wenming* (文明).'[15] This stressed how his hometown had been transformed from a Uyghur place to a site of Chinese culture. Mukhtar articulated his fear of Uyghurs becoming converted to *Zhonghua Minzu*: 'The Chinese try to block our vision, make us satisfied with development. The most important thing is we keep our language alive.' Mukhtar felt Uyghurs were 'forgetting their culture' by speaking Mandarin and, like the tamed pigeons in Chapter 3, were swayed by promises of 'modernisation' and 'development', always explained in ironic air-quotes because these meant assimilation.

Mukhtar generally applied cultural characteristics he associated with Han onto *minkaohan*. 'Bad individual traits' of Uyghurs educated in Mandarin-medium schools are often framed by other Uyghurs in Xinjiang as evidence of cultural assimilation and the acquisition of 'Han disposition' (Smith Finley, 2007, pp.224 & 229). Mukhtar would sympathise with their between-ness in China's nation-building project, saying, 'It's not their fault' because their education was their parents' choice in the socio-economic context of 'life in China': 'They are different, miserable to be honest. They are just *scared*, disorientated.' Mukhtar expressed disgust at his younger cousin's adoption of Han traits when leaning over his parents to reach for his schoolbag. A 'real' Uyghur would never disrespect their elders by leaning into their physical space, and this was attributed to Mandarin-medium education and assimilation. Mukhtar said his cousin had 'forgotten his culture' and this was Xinjiang's assimilated future: 'They are supposed to have Confucius who tells them to

---

[15] *Mädäniyät* and *Wenming* are Uyghur and Mandarin Chinese terms for 'civilisation', respectively. They are both translated as equivalent terms and often used to mean that a place is safe, clean, and hospitable.

respect their elders but they just don't.' He redirected external boundaries with urbanised, feminised Han in asymmetrical relations with the state inward. The internal, Sinicised other were young Uyghur boys who spoke Mandarin instead of Uyghur and played 'Chinese games' such as cards, rather than physical games like sports and stealing apples from orchards. He described *minkaohan*, like Han, as full of fear because, due to Chinese influence, 'they were afraid to make Uyghur friends'. For Mukhtar, Uyghur language symbolised visceral community and masculinity, while China represented assimilation and femininity. *Minkaohan* represented the gradual assimilation of the Uyghur nation because their identity transgressed boundaries between Uyghurs and *Zhonghua Minzu*.

Mahigül defined Uyghur identity through language, saying Uyghurs were Turkic and those who could only speak Mandarin would become Chinese. She lamented language loss but offered different solutions to assimilation than those of Mukhtar, which reflected how she understood Uyghur-ness. Mukhtar stressed the need to maintain an imagined community with the dead through reading 'books of your elders'. Mahigül stressed the importance of individual Uyghurs in maintaining ethno-linguistic boundaries rather than public status to directly resist Chinese nation-building. Mahigül said she was indifferent whether non-Uyghurs learned Uyghur, including foreigners, because it was 'our language', unlike Mukhtar, who would express pride when he met foreigners who used basic Uyghur. Mahigül also thought ethnic relations were so antagonistic in Ürümchi that it would be better if Han did not learn Uyghur because then they would 'know we are cursing them', just like 'we know when they curse us'. She said that Uyghurs needed to 'create new things' and change with modernity to preserve Uyghur culture. She showed respect for traditional Uyghur heritage, such as the Muqam, but said it was a cultural practice for her elders, emphasising that culture had to 'progress' to survive, 'regardless of its centuries of history'. Mahigül did not dismiss popular Uyghur narratives, which emphasised tradition and continuity, but consistently objected to positioning Uyghur-ness as a frozen relic removed from the dynamism of modernity and inter-cultural interaction. When asked if she worried about the future of her language, like many other Uyghurs, she said:

If there are some languages that have disappeared, it's because there are no more people who speak in that language, but we are eight million Uyghurs. It's not possible. It wouldn't happen that *all* of us would speak Chinese and forget Uyghur. So still there would be say a million people who could speak Uyghur, so it wouldn't disappear.

Mahigül's upbringing in Ürümchi meant she was accustomed to relative anonymity and individualism in an urban lifestyle, centred on the nuclear family in gated apartment blocks, congregating in private behind closed doors. Speaking Uyghur at home in this urban environment gave Mahigül symbolic security from the boundary transgressing practices of the party-state and Mandarin-speaking *minkaohan* in public. For Mahigül, as long as Uyghur was spoken in the home, it 'wouldn't disappear' and would retain its symbolic power. Mukhtar, conversely, longed for a return to a community life where 'all families hang out together on the street' because he was accustomed to a different urban environment – Uyghur *Mähällä* where doors are left open and interaction between neighbours is frequent.[16] They both understood preservation of language as the means to secure Uyghur identity from Sinicisation, but for Mukhtar, the threat was the Chinese nation (public), whereas for Mahigül, it was Uyghur families who do not use their mother-tongue (private).[17]

When we discussed Uyghur heritage, Mahigül and Mukhtar defined community with reference to language as a shared symbolic practice but articulated different solutions to preserving the symbol. They both explained it would be laughable to speak any language other than Uyghur with family or friends, except for foreigners. Mahigül rejected the need for *public* education, taking a more individualistic approach, rooted in experience of her nuclear family life in the big city of Ürümchi:

> You can maybe speak Chinese at school or at work but at home you have your choice. I don't think it's a problem. It's our job to keep it. It's not about education. I think it's first the parents' job, not the school. If my kids went to Chinese class, I would teach them Uyghur at home when they are very small.

Mahigül saw the reproduction of identity boundaries and language maintenance as the moral responsibility of individual families within the community, rather than the community per se. Mahigül was less traditionally political than Mukhtar, but this individualism made her a fiercer critic of *minkaohan* because their individual choices did not take responsibility for preserving Uyghur-ness. Mahigül explicitly positioned her identity through between-ness but often referred to *minkaomin* as 'we'. According to Mahigül, the fundamental differences between *minkaohan* and *minkaomin* were the language and friends they *chose*. She would lament that *minkaohan* chose to date and socialise with Han Chinese people. When I asked why this was a problem, she would laugh and shrug her shoulders, saying, 'Because they are Chinese.' Mahigül positioned *minkaohan* outside the boundaries of her visceral community and inside the imagined community of *Zhonghua Minzu*. Mahigül did not socialise with *minkaohan* because they were 'like Han Chinese', explaining that *minkaomin* were 'more fun' to socialise with because they used Uyghur language. Mahigül inversed positive stereotypes of Chinese as hard-working to say this means

---

[16] On *Mähällä*, see: Dautcher (2009) *Down a Narrow Road*.
[17] This could be read as a gendered view of politics, but other female interviewees from Mukthar's oasis town shared his concerns for the public status of Uyghur.

'they are boring' and that *minkaohan* had absorbed this cultural characteristic. She contrasted this stereotype against Uyghur-ness to re-perform negative stereotyping of minorities' 'backwardness', explaining, 'We *are* a lazy *minzu*, not like the Chinese, we are good at having fun.' Mahigül inverted Chinese stereotypes so that working too hard represented the Sinicisation of *minkaohan*, but real Uyghurs, as a 'lazy *minzu*', preserved Uyghur culture by being more fun people. She securitised Uyghur-ness by articulating *minkaohan*'s Sinicised daily practices as transgressions of Chinese-Uyghur boundaries:

They are more open-minded but not in a good way … we speak Uyghur. Some *minkaohan* speak Chinese. Their Uyghur is not good. I don't like that. The Uyghur classes (*minkaomin*), they study in Chinese but they communicate in Uyghur and they hang out with Uyghur friends but *they* (*minkaohan*) hang out with Chinese. They will be influenced by the Chinese, you know, from primary school to university.

Mahigül demarcated the boundaries of Uyghur-ness through indivisible external and internal boundaries, between Uyghur and China and between *minkaomin* and *minkaohan*. She admitted to me that she felt she contravened Islam by drinking alcohol and wearing dresses that revealed her forearms. However, Mahigül claimed *minkaohan* were *less* Uyghur and *less* Islamic ('more open-minded but not in a good way') than *minkaomin*. She explained *minkaohan* dress sense was due to 'Chinese influence' through schooling and mixing with Han Chinese. They contravened Islam more gravely by wearing clothes that showed their upper arms. Mahigül articulated persistent but contingent boundaries between Islamic Uyghurs and Sinicised *minkaohan* by visually indicating a moving line with her finger from wrist to forearm and then from forearm ('We are Muslims') to upper arm ('Chinese people dress like that, not us'). Mahigül positioned *Minkaohan* as less Uyghur and more Sinicised than her *minkaomin* friends. She understood language as productive of Uyghur-ness so that speaking Chinese entailed becoming a Chinese ethnic minority and behaving in a Chinese way. Being Uyghur meant behaving as a Uyghur through banal daily practices, including dress sense and having fun, that preserve Uyghur-ness.

Official nation-building narratives made little direct sense to Mahigül and Mukhtar's lived experiences with family and friends. Instead, they re-performed these narratives to securitise Uyghur identity and articulate China as an assimilative threat. Official nation-building produces social anxieties amongst Uyghurs about preservation of Uyghur-ness defined through language, which emerges in daily practices and identity narratives. The social significance of Uyghur language was mediated through these two individuals' idiosyncratic experiences but retained its power to demarcate boundaries as a shared symbol threatened by Sinicisation. Mahigül and Mukhtar personalised and collectivised Uyghur-ness by defining themselves as authentically Uyghur but extrapolating their individual daily practices through performative enactments of collective boundaries. These performative enactments permitted inclusion of diverse individual experiences but positioned *Minkaohan* as partially Sinicised transgressors of cross-cutting internal and external boundaries of Chinese-ness and Uyghur-ness. However, the threat to Uyghur-ness was not China, the political unit, but Chinese-ness as a mode of assimilation. Mahigül did not seek to overtly resist assimilation but dismissed it because Uyghur language symbolised the home, the domestic, and small-scale community. She saw Uyghur language as domestic refuge, affording her family and her community privacy from Chinese outsiders in an urban environment. The responsibility to maintain Uyghur identity lay in the hands of individual nuclear families. These narratives of the domestic as Uyghur refuge from Chinese public life helps explain the significance of many small-scale, violent incidents sparked during residential cadre patrols and homestays in Uyghur neighbourhoods, conducted under the 'maintaining-stability work' policy since this fieldwork (RFA, 2010; 2013; Xinhua, 2017). Rather than learning to be Chinese, Mahigül and Mukhtar learned that the CCP's nation-building sought their conversion, which they re-performed as an existential threat in narratives on Uyghur identity and partially Sinicised *minkaohan*.

Conclusions

This chapter explored how Han and Uyghurs in Ürümchi securitise ethnic identity by re-performing official narratives of a Han-centred *Zhonghua Minzu* to position each other as existential threats. Relations between majority, minority, and the state produce a multiplicity of Chinas in Xinjiang. Han and Uyghurs use tensions between ethnic inclusion and exclusion in official security narratives to make sense of their daily experiences of ethnic boundaries and articulate competing identity and security narratives. *Zhonghua minzu* appears a monolithic and singular identity but reproduces its own internal fractures between culturalism, socialism, and chauvinism. Insecurity about the threat of internal and external others constitutes *Zhonghua Minzu*, and this insecurity is reproduced on the ground between and amongst Han and Uyghurs. China's grand security narratives and Han-Uyghur identity-insecurities on the ground are inter-related in the ongoing production of *Zhonghua Minzu*. The identity-insecurities of Han and Uyghurs challenge the party-state's *Zhonghua Minzu* narrative but are integral to its story. The insecurity felt by Han, Uyghurs, and the state regarding each other is woven into the fabric of creative tensions that define *Zhonghua Minzu* identity and perpetuate its timeless insecurity, establishing the conditions for ethnic policy and security practices. Disillusionment with 'propaganda' in Xinjiang is a widespread, shared experience of all ethnic groups. Nevertheless, people must mediate

Conclusions

official narratives and their securitisations to participate in and make sense of public life. Han and Uyghurs use official articulations of identity and security to make sense of daily practices of ethnic boundaries, articulating a multiplicity of identity-insecurities, located within but also resisting official narratives.

The chapter's first section analysed how Han in Ürümchi use the party-state's ethnocentric discourses of danger to securitise their own identities, defined through ethnicity, lineage, and language, re-performing *Zhonghua Minzu* either as a Han-led or Han-only nation. Uyghurs were generally understood as a Turkic-Islamic group, and ethno-nationalist Han used official narratives to frame Uyghurs as threats from outside *Zhonghua Minzu*. Many Han in Ürümchi justified chauvinism and violence against Uyghurs using the nominally multi-*minzu* conceptual apparatus of the party-state's nation-building narratives. Official narratives of Xinjiang's 'backwardness' and its 'liberation' by Han 'frontier-builders' were linked to discourses of danger and deployed by ethno-nationalists to designate all Uyghurs as inconvertible and foreign, Islamic terrorists who threaten the identity and security of the Han. Nation-building fractures identity, and the Han category itself becomes contested through relations with Uyghurs. Most *getihu* and working class Han defined China through their own ethnic identity, deploying chauvinist logics to frame Uyghurs as inconvertible and justify violent colonial domination of Xinjiang. However, intellectuals identified through ethnic unity, using culturalist and historical materialist logics, which consider the 'Han nucleus' as the source of Xinjiang's peaceful transformation from backwardness to modernity through benevolent attraction to *Zhonghua Minzu*. Han is a contextual and relational category in Xinjiang, contested through competing boundary demarcations that constitute itself against the Uyghur other in interaction with the state. Positioning the Han as the centre of *Zhonghua Minzu* (ethnocentrism) gives Han ethno-nationalists a vocabulary to resist multi-*minzu* nation-building and articulate the need to secure their cultural superiority over the Uyghur threat (chauvinism). The party-state's attempt to increase security by identifying China's friends and eliminating its enemies produces perpetual insecurity. Han chauvinist identity-insecurity leads to violence against Uyghurs and public performances of Uyghur inclusion as a threat to China.

The second section analysed how Uyghurs in Ürümchi securitise their own identities and articulate China as an existential threat by re-performing official party-state and unofficial Han narratives on Uyghur-ness. Uyghurs in Ürümchi resist inclusion as Chinese ethnic minorities by inverting party-state narratives, which position their identities as a threat, reconfiguring China as a threat to Uyghurs. Uyghurs tended to frame Han mass-migration and intolerance towards Uyghur culture as components of China's assimilation project and threats to Uyghur identity. Uyghurs often feminise Han as physically non-threatening, but that this femininity conceals state violence and constitutes a threat to Uyghur masculinity. Han-China is framed as an external security threat to Uyghur identity, masculinity, and prosperity, paralleling how the CCP and Han nationalists interpret Western encroachment in its national humiliation discourse. The boundaries that encapsulate Uyghur identity are constituted through blurry intersections of inside and outside. Uyghurs demarcate the 'internal' *minkaohan-minkaomin* boundary by redirecting external boundaries between Han and Uyghurs, in asymmetrical relations with the state, inward, and securitising Uyghur identity through narratives of Sinicisation. *Minkaohan* symbolised the transgression of these boundaries and were represented through narratives of assimilation by Uyghur-speaking Uyghurs. Uyghur narratives on the *minkaohan-minkaomin* boundary reflect and reproduce broader identity anxieties that Uyghurs are a dying Turkic nation in an assimilative Han nation-state. Han-centred *Zhonghua Minzu* narratives are understood as transgressions of ethnic boundaries by Han to convert or eliminate Uyghurs. The bilingual Uyghurs interviewed did not consider themselves 'learning to be Chinese' (*jiaohua* 教化), and their education gave them deeper insight into the epistemic and physical violence of nation-building. They considered themselves learning how *not* to be Chinese. These bilingual Uyghurs are nation-building models but understood the party-state and *Zhonghua Minzu* narratives as violent assimilation by China.

Uyghurs and Han in Ürümchi understood themselves and each other through securitised identity boundaries in a dangerous or ineffective state. The party-state attempts to convert difference by convincing all Xinjiang's people that they are *Zhonghua Minzu*, perpetually encircled and infiltrated by identity-security threats. However, its own Han-centrism hierarchically organises difference and reinforces the differences it aims to convert, making everyone insecure. The party-state faces identity-security dilemmas in Xinjiang because promoting a Han-centric *Zhonghua Minzu* has given Han nationalism a powerful securitising vocabulary to exclude Uyghurs from Chinese history as Turks, and from daily practices as the 'inside/outside Three Evils'. The party-state's attempts to increase security by targeting Uyghur cultural practices as threats converts Han physical insecurity into identity-insecurity. They subsequently demand violence to secure themselves and less-tolerant ethnic policies to solve the *minzu* problem. Many insecure Han responded with violent ethno-nationalist security practices, making Uyghurs feel increasingly insecure and perpetuating cycles of violence and mistrust. Multiple, overlapping identity-insecurity dilemmas have emerged. The imposition of the party-state's multiple identity-insecurities has increased insecurity amongst multiple groups and groups within groups. The party-state's military power has guaranteed its immediate physical security but at the cost of self-perpetuating identity-insecurity and social instability. Uyghurs and Han securitise their identities against perceived existential threats from each other and the state. The party-state's securitised *Zhonghua Minzu* narrative exacerbates spiralling cycles of ethnicised violence that are all enacted in the name of security. These cycles contribute to the party-state's perceived perpetual need for nation-building, which re-reproduces these cycles and the impossibility of security.

Conclusion
Identity and Insecurity in Xinjiang

Cycles of violence and insecurity in Xinjiang are reproduced on the ground through relations among Han, Uyghurs, and an ethnocentric state. This book has shown how the party-state's securitisation of *Zhonghua Minzu* identity produces multiple identities and insecurities in Xinjiang. These multiple identity-insecurities make the party-state more insecure and it responds with more securitisation, perpetuating cycles of mistrust and violence in the region. The party-state's production of *Zhonghua Minzu*, perpetually encircled and infiltrated by multiple threats to China's identity, hierarchically organises difference between superior, safe Han and inferior, dangerous minorities. Hierarchical nation-building reinforces the differences it aims to convert by targeting Uyghurs as perpetual identity-threats, exacerbating existential insecurities between and amongst Han and Uyghurs on the ground. Targeting Uyghur language and religion as existential threats to China leads Uyghurs and Han to securitise their own identities against perceived threats from each other and the state. The party-state, therefore, exacerbates spiralling cycles of ethnicised violence in Xinjiang that produce the perceived need for nation-building, further perpetuating these cycles and the impossibility of security.

Traditional securitisation theory embraces meaninglessness, because any referent can be securitised in beguiling combinations of the objectivism of positivism and relativism of constructivism (Barkawi, 2011, pp.702–703). Instead, the politics of identity and security in Xinjiang reveals the paradox of securitisation. It builds on long-term historical narratives but produces multiple identities and insecurities because identity is never singular or static. The party-state's *Zhonghua Minzu* narrative is fixed and securitised but interweaves different ethnocentric traditions within Chinese thought, Confucian culturalism, Marxist historical materialism, and ethno-nationalist chauvinism, reflecting different factions within the state and society. However, since Xi Jinping's rise to power, the party-state has responded to its own failures to include non-Han and inter-related cycles of violence with more explicit chauvinist 'fusion' ethnic policy narratives that justify mass, extra-legal internment camps to eliminate or transform Uyghur identities. The party-state understands that its ethnocentric narrative of unity with Han culture as China's guiding 'nucleus' cannot convince Uyghurs they are Chinese. It aims to resolve these narrative tensions and break these cycles by destroying 'the foundations' of the *minzu* problem 'forever' with 'intense stability work', 'fusion', and internment camps in a 'window of opportunity' of Western decline (XUAR Government, 2018). These policies intend to assimilate Uyghurs and guarantee support from Han chauvinists in Xinjiang by securitising an ethno-nationalist Han identity.

The inter-related multiple identities and insecurities articulated by Han, Uyghurs, and the state, analysed throughout this book, show that essentialising China as a unique, united civilisation is an elite orientalist project to contain external convergences with other cultures and convert internal difference. 'China' is mystified by grand narratives of East/West civilisations that conceal vast internal identity divergences within those categories and China's significant convergences with the West. Neither Eurocentrism nor Sinocentrism helps explain why an 'Eastern' state navigating integration into a 'Western'-built world order frames Islamic, Turkic-speaking peoples in *Central* Asia as timelessly Chinese. Uyghurs' in-between-ness threatens the stability of that grand binary narrative. The 'pluralistic universalism' of *Global* IR considers dichotomies between 'Western' universalism and 'Eastern' relativism as politically inspired because world order is a 'large, overarching canopy with multiple foundations' (Acharya, 2014, p.649). Understanding identity and security in China requires looking beyond politicised binaries to see how China understands universal human problems within its own cultural predicament that is neither uniquely Eastern nor simply Westernised. Bringing non-European voices into analysis of global politics, as postcolonial theorists and the party-state demand, reveal traditional IR's Eurocentrism. However, analysing *non-elite*, non-European voices reveals how Sinocentrism circulates in Chinese Studies. Chinese Studies can reinforce Han-centric narratives by silencing marginalised non-Han in its essentialising conceptualisations of China through the assimilative culturalism of the 'civilisation-state', the ethnocentric cultural evolution of development in the 'opening and reform' era, or the chauvinist ethno-nationalism of 'national humiliation'. 'The West' and 'China' both need to be provincialised to reveal the internal, competing particularities that constitute these categories and globalised to reveal relations between them.

The work of renowned Confucian scholar Tu Wei-ming (1995) compared the convergence and divergence in core values between Western and Chinese civilisations, urging the world not to abandon the Enlightenment principles of reason and science but to look beyond them. In a dialogue with Italian philosopher Gianni Vattimo, Tu concluded that 'the importance of rationality', found in liberal individualist traditions, is 'self-evident', but if humans are to survive and prosper in the twenty-first century, it must be supplemented with

Conclusion

respect for culture and spirituality through the 'sympathy, empathy, and compassion' of Confucian humanism (Tu and Vattimo, 2007, p.18). Tu argues that the empathy offered by Confucian humanism will help people see the world as others see it but offers no empathy for how in-between or state-less cultural groups see China or the world. 'Barbarians in the periphery' only enter Tu's narrative of 'one of the longest continuous civilisations in the world' through 'the classical distinction' between Chinese civilisation and the barbaric other, while being 'children of the Yellow Emperor' is understood as 'evoking feelings of ethnic pride' (Tu, 2005, pp.145–147).

Empathy can help accommodate otherness and look beyond the Eurocentric 'end of history' and ahistorical 'clash of civilisations' discourses, which have dominated global politics since the Soviet Union's collapse and attacks of 9/11. Nevertheless, respect for China's rise requires no empathy. The material impact of two decades of double-digit growth is unquestionable and repeatedly highlighted by world leaders and international media in almost any discussion of China. Admiration for the CCP's achievements comes from seeing the world, as Eurocentric thought already sees it, through material power and national boundaries. Empathy for the diverse peoples who are categorised as Chinese, on the other hand, requires scholarly detachment from Sinocentric and Eurocentric logics that circulate together, demanding empathy and cultural respect for state power and ethnic majorities while invisibilising identities and political alternatives that disrupt their binaries. Empathising with multiple, competing, and overlapping perspectives of different peoples within the categories of East and West, who speak different languages and enjoy different life opportunities, requires looking beyond the geopolitical demands of superpowers and their leading intellectuals' (e.g. Tu; Huntington, 1996) grand civilisational narratives. These grand narratives invisibilise ethnic difference within China and the West as well as shared ideas between them. Empathising with peoples who are called Chinese or Western requires radical rejection of essentialised categories of China and the West even when we study their circulation and power. These oppositional categories constitute perpetual insecurity between and within them as majorities mobilise scholarly and state power to securitise these identities while minorities attempt to evade their ascriptive power and seek recognition of their identities.

Just as postcolonial theory revealed the core of world politics' constitution through relations with its peripheries, understanding China requires bringing its margins into mainstream Chinese Studies analysis. Trying to understand China without reference to Uyghurs is like trying to understand world history without reference to China. Turkic-speaking peoples within China have been historically identified as outside Chinese civilisation by the state and by themselves. Uyghurs do not fit into a world imagined through grand civilisations of a collectivist, Confucian East and an individualist, democratic West.

Conclusion

Xinjiang's ambivalent position in China shows how empathy requires not only willingness to accommodate difference but also willingness to critique power when it seeks to eliminate that difference. Social anthropologist Yi Xiaocuo (2019) explains how the CCP's East-West 'friendship' narrative silences voices who challenge its hegemonic identity claims by telling a story of 'mutual aid' between majority and minorities in a struggle against 'national humiliation' that justifies 'internal colonialism and censorship' in Xinjiang. Who is deemed worthy of empathy in global politics is a matter of power that civilisational boundaries, speaking for East and West, reinforce by concealing the many peoples who struggle to be recognised and exist outside this binary. Grand philosophical demands for civilisational respect have helped recognise traditionally ignored Chinese narratives in Eurocentric approaches to world history and international politics. However, the persistent strength of 'national humiliation' and timeless civilisation narratives as reflections of the general-will of 1.4 billion people represents an intellectual failure to understand diversity in the constitution of China and its international relations. Furthermore, these narratives and their re-circulation by scholars enable chauvinist ethnic policies that seek to disappear whole peoples because their in-between identities don't *really* exist.

This book has argued that China's nation-building project in Xinjiang exacerbates insecurity and hardens ethnic boundaries. It examined the relationship between identity and security in contemporary China by analysing how Han and Uyghurs respond to the party-state's securitised approach to ethnic relations in Xinjiang. Han and Uyghurs articulate a multiplicity of alternative identities and insecurities by using and challenging official nation-building narratives. Understanding the China built by securitising *Zhonghua Minzu* required listening to perspectives from below as much as to elites. The securitisation of *Zhonghua Minzu* as a shared trans-ethnic identity with the Han category as its cultural 'nucleus' produces insecurity amongst the majority Han and minority Uyghurs on the ground. Han and Uyghurs tend to identify through lineage, language, and ethnicity. However, official securitisation of *Zhonghua Minzu* tells them their identities are under constant threat from each other and often from the state. Han and Uyghurs respond by securitising their own identities, making the state feel more insecure about resistance to its narrative and political stability. The party-state then responds by intensifying its securitisation of identity, reproducing the underlying dynamics of conflict in Xinjiang. The people identified by grand nation-building narratives then build their own Chinas using tensions in official narratives between inclusion and exclusion of cultural difference to explain visceral ethnic boundaries and violence in their everyday lives. A multiplicity of self-identifications on the ground turn official nation-building against itself, and its proponent, the party-state, is taken less seriously as *the* authority to identify who is China.

The finality, singularity, and violence demanded by identity-securitisation destabilise and multiply *Zhonghua Minzu* narratives.

The first three chapters used discourse analysis of official texts to analyse how the party-state's nation-building narratives demarcate and securitise the internal and external boundaries of *Zhonghua Minzu*. Official identity-security narratives were taught in educational texts to promote a shared identity amongst all cadres, teachers, and students in Xinjiang. Chapter 1 examined how the historical context of empire, nationalism, and ethnic relations in China shape contemporary practices of nation-building in Xinjiang. This explored how China has historically understood Xinjiang through an imperial geopolitical prism that has gradually shifted towards cultural nationalism to include minorities as a security matter. However, the party-state frames Xinjiang as both an indivisible, equal component of a modern territorial state *and* a site of exotic difference on the frontier of imperial civilisation. Xinjiang thus occupies a position of ambivalence within *Zhonghua Minzu* because its peoples have never been unambiguously framed as Chinese by the state or by themselves. When Mao Zedong's promises of independence (*zijue*) were scaled down to guarantees of autonomy (*zizhi*) after 1949, Xinjiang's status as an inalienable component of Chinese territory became a non-negotiable security matter in official discourse. The party-state gradually securitised a narrative of *Zhonghua Minzu* identity for all Chinese citizens as a multi-*minzu* nation led by the Han. However, securitising a Han-centric China reproduces internal boundaries between civilised majority and uncivilised minorities. The securitisation of these boundaries means that for Xinjiang to be safe and Chinese, it must be understood by its peoples as culturally inferior. Ethnic minority voices that challenge this boundary are officially framed as existential threats to China.

Chapter 2 examined mass 'ethnic unity' education as an identity-security practice following the violence of July 2009. It analysed boundaries demarcated by the party-state between Han and ethnic minorities in narratives of Xinjiang history taught to cadres, teachers, and students. The party-state's historiography unifies the histories of all peoples within the PRC's contemporary borders as timelessly and indivisibly Chinese. This reproduces exclusionary boundaries between Han and minorities based on oppositional and mutually reinforcing binaries of central plains/frontier, modernity/backwardness, and security/danger. These mutually reinforcing binaries perform a hierarchy of identities, interweaving civilisation, ethnicity, and development narratives, and producing Han-ness as China's ancient, modernising, active nucleus. Ethnic minority identities are narrated as backward and passive empty vessels, awaiting their own conversion and gradual extinction (*minzu xiaowang*). The official narrative of history securitises a particular way of being Chinese and of being Uyghur. It frames *Zhonghua Minzu* as a timeless *and* modernising national identity. Uyghur ethnic identities are positioned as backward and fractured, to be overcome by policies such as Mandarin-medium education that will civilise *and* modernise Uyghurs until they die out.

Chapter 3 analysed the production and circulation of the party-state's 'East Turkestan' narrative that articulates Uyghur-ness as an external Turkic threat. It showed that official 'East Turkestan' narratives target Uyghurs inside China who identify through Turkic or Islamic identities as security threats from outside China's cultural boundaries. Official policy documents routinely deploy 'East Turkestan' with the 'inside/outside Three Evils' narrative to link Uyghur identity inside China to external threats of Islam and the West. The party-state's explanation of all incidents of unrest or peaceful dissent in Xinjiang through the 'inside/outside Three Evils' frames Uyghur identities and critiques of exclusion in *Zhonghua Minzu* as security threats, blurring internal and external boundaries and intertwining China's domestic and international enemies. The official East Turkestan narrative does less to target specific armed groups than to exclude the *idea* of Turkic identities as threatening 'distortions of history'. Targeting East Turkestan is an exclusionary identity-security technique but a central component of nation-building's violent inclusion. It tells Uyghurs who they *must* become (ethnic minorities) by telling them who they must *not* be (Turkic Muslims). However, the cultural nationalist underpinnings framing China as a timeless civilisation give Uyghurs a vocabulary to destabilise nation-building from within its own logics by identifying through Turkic civilisation and deploying the civilisational identity-ontologies of *Zhonghua Minzu*. The allegorical Uyghur short story 'Wild Pigeon' was a popular example of how Uyghurs turn nation-building against itself to articulate themselves as a dying Turkic civilisation within an assimilative China. The author's imprisonment for 10 years for 'inciting splittism' shows that even allegorical articulations of Uyghur identity are understood as existential security threats to *Zhonghua Minzu*.

Chapters 4 and 5 moved from the classroom to the street, using participant-observation, discourse analysis, and semi-structured interviews to examine how China's nation-building project is performed in everyday politics. Chapter 4 showed how official security practices performed hierarchical ethnic boundaries following the July 2009 violence through asymmetrical responses to violence and ethnicised targeting of Uyghur neighbourhoods. These boundaries were resisted and re-performed from below in ways that challenge and reconfigure the meaning of *Zhonghua Minzu*. The party-state de-securitised violence against Uyghurs at Shaoguan as an 'ordinary public order incident' with no connection to identity or security. This de-securitisation produced Uyghur insecurity because the party-state failed to reassure them they were secure from the threat of ethnically targeted Han violence. Uyghur protests against this inaction performatively enacted insecurity and their desired position of ethnic equality by waving Chinese flags and chanting for 'justice and equality'. The subsequent violence on July 5, 2009, overshadowed these protests and was framed as an irrational, existential terrorist threat to China's identity and security. Han violence on July 7 was conversely described as 'operations' by 'comrades' against irrational Uyghur violence before being written out of the official record altogether. The cause of insecurity in Xinjiang was framed as Uyghur self-identification through language and religion, supported by Western 'enemies of China' and Islamists from outside. The party-state's security practices targeted Uyghur neighbourhoods and identities as sources of separatism, terrorism, and extremism through ethnicised everyday security practices of surveillance and military patrols. The small-scale spate of syringe attacks on Han in the aftermath of the July violence was officially represented as an ongoing terrorist threat, heightening Han insecurity and sparking protests for increased security and even violence against Uyghurs. Protest slogans and interviews with participants showed how Han nationalists used official narratives that target Uyghur identity as a threat to reject the party-state's model of a multi-*minzu* China. Han protestors targeted all Uyghurs as ever-present threats to their mono-ethnic China. Official narratives exclude Uyghur identity as sources of insecurity, activating pre-existing ethnic stereotypes drawn from binaries between Chinese civilisation and non-Chinese barbarians. Official identity-security narratives produced insecurity for Han who felt they were surrounded by an organised Uyghur threat and must enact violence to secure themselves and China. Uyghurs felt insecure because they were ethnically targeted by the state and by Han nationalists in the classroom and on the street.

Chapter 5 showed how the inclusion offered to Uyghurs ('ethnic unity') marginalises Uyghur-ness and places Han-ness at the centre of the nation. Uyghur festivals, such as *Roza Heyti*, were officially framed as ethnic and peripheral. Traditional ethnic Han festivals, such as Mid-Autumn Festival, despite its anti-Mongolian origins, were conversely celebrated as national festivals of cultural significance for all ethnic groups. Ethnic unity, therefore, is inherently hierarchical because it normatively orders identities into the trans-ethnic, national standard of the Han and the anomaly of backward ethnic minorities. The official ethnic unity narrative objectivises ethnic Han-ness as national Chinese-ness, thus offering inclusion contingent upon identification with Han culture as superior and a rejection of Uyghur language and religion as the basis of identity. 'Ethnic unity' and 'The Three Evils' are two sides of nation-building where Uyghurs *must* become Chinese by identifying with national symbols that are understood by Uyghurs and Han alike as symbols of Han ethnicity. Inclusion through ethnic unity is not simply limited but is inherently ethnocentric and exclusionary of Uyghur identity.

The categories of China, Han, and Uyghur are interpreted and reinterpreted on the ground to articulate a multiplicity of identities and insecurities, which build a multiplicity of Chinas. The final two chapters examined the effects of nation-building in Xinjiang using detailed, semi-structured interviews and participant-observation to analyse how Han and Uyghurs receive and reinterpret official identity and security discourses. Chapter 6 analysed popular re-performances of ethnic unity to show how Uyghurs and Han alike tend to dismiss unity but use its hierarchical boundaries to construct their own distinct identities. Han and Uyghurs in Xinjiang widely reject the party-state's model of a multi-*minzu* China with the Han at the centre but use it to contrast their visceral ethnic identities against the multi-*minzu* conceptual imagination of *Zhonghua Minzu*. The Han in Ürümchi, particularly working classes and *getihu*, employed the pre-communist discourses of lineage and language that still circulate in official discourse to define themselves as an ethnic nation and position Uyghurs outside China. Intellectual Han with longer-term connections to Xinjiang used unity to articulate multicultural conceptualisations of China. Intellectuals offered clear alternatives to chauvinism, but their self-identification as 'frontier-builders' reinforces the party-state's ethnocentric inclusion of Xinjiang as a problematic frontier to be converted and modernised, which makes Uyghurs feel threatened. Uyghurs highlighted how official and everyday exclusion of their Turkic and Islamic identity made them feel outside *Zhonghua Minzu*. Nation-building is failing because it positions the majority Han at the centre of China's national narratives and culturally superior while failing to include minority identities. Both Han and Uyghurs then use tensions between Xinjiang's inclusion as timelessly Chinese and exclusion as a cultural frontier to identify themselves as distinct ethnic nations built on lineage and language.

The final chapter showed how Han and Uyghurs securitise their own identities through competing performances of danger that invert identity and security in official nation-building narratives. Han and Uyghurs in Ürümchi tend to resist official multi-*minzu* nation-building through ethnicised conceptualisations of security that position each other as threats. Han often used the party-state's East Turkestan and 'inside/outside Three Evils' narratives to represent Uyghurs as an identity threat from outside China because Uyghurs *are* Turkic and Islamic. Uyghurs in Ürümchi resisted inclusion as ethnic minorities by framing Sinicisation and denial of their history as a threat to their Turkic and Islamic identities, thus securitising the dimensions of Uyghurness that are excluded in Chinese nation-building. Uyghurs invert the party-state's discourses of danger and position the Han as inadvertent foot soldiers in an official assimilation project through demographic and linguistic transformation. Uyghurs frame China as a cultural threat but often feminised the Han as physically non-threatening and passive, reversing official binaries that define active Han against passive ethnic minorities. Nevertheless, this femininity was framed as a threat to Uyghur identity and masculinity because it conceals violence and seeks assimilation through 'attraction'. Uyghurs redirected securitised ethnic boundaries inward through narratives that demarcate who is a real Uyghur and who is Sinicised through language use. Uyghur narratives on the *minkaohan-minkaomin* boundary reflected and reproduced identity anxieties that they are a dying Turkic nation in an ethno-nationalist China. Official Chinese nation-building produces Uyghur identity-securitisations because it frames Uyghur attachment to Uyghur-ness as a threat without offering a means to be Uyghur and part of *Zhonghua Minzu*.

Official nation-building and popular Han identity performances in Xinjiang reveal multiple, competing modes of ethnic inclusion and exclusion, which can contradict and reinforce each other. The party-state's traditional historical materialist approach to 'cultural evolution' has constructed development and ethnic policy under assumptions that economic development will naturally produce a unified China through inevitable 'modernisation' and disappearance of ethnic minorities. The Confucian culturalism of leading scholars, including Fei Xiaotong and Ma Rong, frames China as a timeless civilisation and assumes its constitutive *hua/yi* binary naturally erodes with barbarians' cultural attraction to the superior Han nucleus. These competing modes of inclusion overlap and mutually reinforce discourses of identity and security because they both frame the Han as China's cultural core and minority identities as peripheral obstacles to *Chinese* unity and power. Culturalism and historical materialism compete to define Chinese identity, but their answers are driven by the same questions about how to make China a powerful and prosperous state again without challenging Han ethno-nationalism. Each of China's three mainstream national narratives stretch the confines of the PRC's contemporary territory back to 'ancient times', positioning the Han as the centripetal force of national identity, driving cultural attraction (culturalism), modernisation (historical materialism), or racial unification (chauvinism). Communist ideology did not supplant Confucianism and capitalism has not supplanted communism. They have each been transplanted onto each other. Chinese civilisation became reconfigured as the 'Han nucleus' and the 'vanguard' driving the communist revolution in Xinjiang before being reconfigured as a source of 'development' and security in the 'opening and reform' era.

The success of *Zhonghua Minzu* lies in its flexibility to mean different things to different Han identities. However, Chinese nation-building is failing in Xinjiang because it means assimilation for Uyghurs and made people of all ethnicities feel increasingly insecure that their identities are under threat from each other and the state. The party-state's hierarchical organisation of difference between superior Han who represent the nation and inferior Uyghurs who represent potential ethnic threats hardened ethnic boundaries in Xinjiang and they are understood in terms of non-negotiable, existential security. The book has shown how the party-state's approach to nation-building through

Conclusion

securitisation of *Zhonghua Minzu* identity produces widespread inter-ethnic insecurity. The party-state has securitised a narrative of China that makes Han and Uyghurs feel insecure about the threat of each other's identities. Both groups subsequently believe their ethnic identities are marginalised in *Zhonghua Minzu* and use official discourse to frame the ethnic other as a security threat in their daily lives. The party-state's securitised conceptualisation of a hierarchical *Zhonghua Minzu* exacerbates and perpetuates cycles of mistrust and violence between Han and Uyghurs because they both feel threatened by each other's identities. Han and Uyghurs resist the party-state's nation-building project by using official narratives to articulate and securitise alternative identities against each other and the state, perpetuating the party-state's perceived need for nation-building that produced this cycle in the first place.

This book was the first study of Chinese politics using ethnographic methods in Xinjiang that incorporate the perspectives of Han in Ürümchi. This paralleled Cliff's (2016) analysis of the 'colonial endeavor' in Korla, but focusing on the urban centre of Ürümchi enabled analysis of relations between Han and Uyghurs most deeply engaged by and in official nation-building. Han perspectives in Ürümchi showed how Han and *Zhonghua Minzu* are contested categories that reflect the deeply ambivalent inclusion of non-Han others in their origins and contemporary practices. Han articulated different identity narratives through inclusion and exclusion of Uyghurs, which reflect tensions in the *Zhonghua Minzu* narrative that pull the party in different directions. Unity through attraction to Chinese civilisation, cultural evolution towards ethnic extinction, and Han chauvinism to eliminate Turkic and Islamic identities all intermingle and co-exist in creative tension in official and unofficial politics. The securitisation of *Zhonghua Minzu*, therefore, securitises a multiplicity of identity narratives from which Han and Uyghurs select to include and exclude each other and make sense of their daily lives. Ilham Tohti, the Uyghur associate Professor of Economics at Minzu University of China placed under house-arrest for writing about Han identity, found that 89.4 per cent of Han in Xinjiang wanted the government to maintain their 'superior position' (Tohti, 2012a). Many Han perspectives in this book displayed a Han superiority/inferiority syndrome, an important but under-analysed narrative in contemporary Chinese Studies, rather than *Chinese* 'middle-kingdom complex' as asserted by Pye (1990) and other orientalist thinkers. The ethnocentrism that structures official narratives of China through advanced Han cultural core and backward minority peripheries enables the persistence of Han chauvinism in Xinjiang. Working classes and *getihu* repeated widely circulating exclusionary language, calling all Uyghurs 'turban-heads', often as justification for murder. The party-state's narrative of a timelessly developing and unified multi-*minzu* China does not correspond with how people understand daily experiences of ethnic boundaries in Xinjiang, China's history of *hua/yi* boundaries, or the ethnocentrism of its Han nucleus concept. *Getihu* and working classes resent the party-state's supposed special treatment of minorities and this narrative is produced by official ethnocentric descriptions of policy as 'liberation', 'subsidies', and 'preferential'. Han intellectuals, who often identify through Confucian culturalism, reject chauvinism as un-Chinese, such as Miss Lan, the Mandarin Chinese teacher who stressed unity was 'an ancient tradition of the Chinese people'. Culturalism rejects Han ethno-nationalism by framing *Zhonghua Minzu* as inclusive of 'barbarians' but reproduces the ethnocentric inclusion of Xinjiang and Uyghurs as a problematic frontier to be converted and modernised by China. The convergence of these narratives, peaceful conversion of the Uyghur periphery and violence to eliminate Uyghur identities as China's enemies, makes Uyghurs understand *Zhonghua Minzu* as a violent, colonial project.

Discourses of Chinese civilisation, ethnic extinction, and Han superiority all speak *to* one another but *at* Uyghurs, reinforcing their marginalisation in *Zhonghua Minzu*. Unity only speaks to people who understand themselves as culturally Chinese, ignoring Uyghur concerns about inequality and assimilation by objectivising Han-ness as Chinese-ness. The '2nd generation' *minzu* policy debate, analysed in Chapter 2, essentially decided Xinjiang's current policy direction but offered no voices from Xinjiang. Ilham Tohti's 2012 survey found that 67 per cent of Uyghurs already believed that the Chinese government is a 'representative of Han interests' (Tohti, 2012a). Several Uyghur interviewees suggested Ilham Tohti was a spy because his diagnosis of Xinjiang's problems spoke to the party-state: 'without the development of ethnic minorities, there can be no revival of the Chinese people ... and without dealing with the poverty and backwardness of minorities, it will be hard to maintain long term stability in Xinjiang' (Tohti, 2006). Where Ilham Tohti diverged was in his prognosis that development cannot achieve these goals without addressing 'systemic discrimination' towards Uyghurs in 'entering the advanced productive forces', particularly the resource extraction industries, the basis of CCP development policy in Xinjiang (Tohti, 2006). The extraction and export of Xinjiang's natural resources by an almost exclusively Han workforce has long exacerbated Uyghur insecurity about resources being expropriated without benefit to the region (Bovingdon, 2004a, p.47). Post-2012 'de-extremification' education textbooks describe this claim as terrorism (Zhang et al., 2014). Mr Wang, the Han SINOPEC executive interviewed in Chapter 6, openly admitted this systemic discrimination was central to these industries' functioning. He refused to employ Uyghurs, contradicting constitutional commitments to *minzu* equality, because 'none of them work' and they cause 'ethnic contradictions' by praying and abstaining from eating pork.

In the 'opening and reform' era, discrimination against Uyghurs has been a constitutive component of the party-state's model of development. Reform-era policy engineered Han migration into Xinjiang through labour opportunities in cotton and extractive industries, which help drive China's growth, while excluding Xinjiang's non-Han groups from those opportunities (Becquelin, 2004a, p.358). This model has now shifted from marginalisation of Uyghurs to their forced integration in a political economy built on China's ethno-hierarchy. Since 2017, widespread 'forced labour' for Uyghurs and other Turkic groups in Xinjiang's manufacturing sector supports Han-owned businesses and enhances China's global 'competitiveness'.[1] This development model could not have been imagined by Confucius or Marx. It more closely resembles Cedric Robinson's (2000) theory of 'racial capitalism', where modernisation does not sweep away or homogenise cultural and regional diversity; rather, it builds on these pre-existing differences and exaggerates them. Just as China's communist revolution did not sweep away older notions of civilisation and barbarism, neither has the adoption of markets under 'opening and reform'.

This development model guarantees the persistence of Uyghur claims that Xinjiang is being colonised by China and the CCP's ongoing securitisation of *Zhonghua Minzu*. Prior to the establishment of extra-legal internment camps, Ilham Tohti spent years under house arrest for publishing research before being sentenced by the courts in September 2014 to life imprisonment on 'separatism' charges. His written essays highlighted in court as the basis of 'separatism' charges included 'Similar Events, Different Conclusions', analysing the ethnicised state responses to violence examined in Chapter 4, to ask why Uyghur violence was treated as terrorism while Han violence was not prosecuted (Xinhua, 2014). Ilham's imprisonment for 'separatism' indicates how Uyghur narratives of identity and insecurity have been officially treated as existential security threats to China for some time. However, under Xi Jinping, policy has expanded and intensified its scope to treat every aspect of every Uyghur's identity as a security problem. Uyghur claims of cultural and economic inequality are more threatening to the party-state than inequality itself because its primary referent of security is the *Zhonghua Minzu* narrative of a timelessly unified nation led by the Han.

This book has shown how multiple, historically significant narratives circulate and intermingle in China's identity and insecurity. That approach problematises notions of distinct historical turning points and analyses new policy as shifts in emphasis, which re-circulate and reconfigure pre-existing narratives. Nevertheless, how states reconfigure narrative emphasis in its policy making has dramatic effects on people's lives and political outcomes. Most of this book's fieldwork was conducted during a period officially described as a

---

[1] For example, see: Xu et al. (2020).

turning point in official ethnic policy. The party-state's self-defined approach to policy through a historical materialist framework of cultural evolution in a multi-ethnic state has shifted to more explicit, state-planned 'fusion' (*jiaorong* 交融) in a mono-ethnic *Zhonghua Minzu*. Official narratives now state that Xi Jinping's security-first approach has resolved long-term, 'important contradictions' in 'Xinjiang work', by considering 'stability' and 'fusion' as foundational to development (XUAR Government, 2018). The July 2009 violence led Wang Yang, then Guangdong Party Committee Secretary, to suggest China must readjust ethnic minority policies 'or there will be further difficulties' (Smith Finley, 2011, p.78). Ilham Tohti's detailed essay in 2009 similarly suggested periodic episodes of violence responding to policy changes meant these policies needed to be reconsidered and debated (Tohti, 2009). Illustrating the continuing ethnicised securitisation of identity under Xi, Wang Yang became the PRC's third-ranked Vice Premier and then head of the Central Committee's Xinjiang Working Group, while Ilham was imprisoned for life on 'separatism' charges. The reappearance of ethnic extinction (*minzu xiaowang* 民族消亡) in Xinjiang's 2009 education textbooks was just one signal of this coming shift and illustrates how historically significant narratives can effectively and rapidly justify policy. Ethnic extinction narratives were presented as the promotion of natural conversion of minority identities through value-neutral modernisation. However, given the parallels with European framings of earlier colonial and genocidal projects, and that Chinese scholars in the 1960s, such as Jian Bozan (1960), specifically identified *minzu xiaowang* as assimilation, it is important to note that these narratives are not new and their re-emergence should have received more scholarly attention.

The policy shift towards 'fusion' reflects the party-state's failure to include Uyghur identity in *Zhonghua Minzu*. 'Bilingual education' was understood by Uyghurs, including Mukhtar and Mahigül, as attempts to assimilate Uyghurs. The underlying logics of both sides of the brief, state-sponsored inter-generational ethnic policy debate were that minority identities are problems to be overcome to achieve China's Great Revival towards unity and power. The '1st generation' of ethnic minority policies scholars were primarily historical materialists such as Hao Shiyuan (2012), Bao Shengli (2011), and Wang Xi'en (2012). They argued that because China is a multi-ethnic socialist nation, development will inevitably resolve social conflict, resulting in *natural* disappearance of ethnicity and strengthening of Chinese identity. The increasingly influential '2nd generation' of *minzu* policy scholars, including Hu Angang and Ma Rong, adopted pre-communist Han chauvinist and culturalist narratives (*jiaohua*) to argue that ethnic minorities must be fused into a Han-led 'race-state' (*guozu*) through monolingual education. They urged policy makers to immediately engineer this race-state by eliminating the ethnic minorities (*shaoshu minzu* 少数民族) category and abandoning the regional autonomy

Conclusion   235

system that had structured ethnic policy since the 1950s. Both 'generations' shared dreams of the Great Revival but offered different policy recommendations to achieve them. Looking at policy in 2020, the party-state has pursued the 2nd generation's recommendations and pursues state-engineered 'fusion' towards a Han nation-state, despite accusations of 'chauvinism' and Western 'one-nation, one-state thinking' by the '1st generation'. Hu Angang openly celebrated his key role in authoring official slogans that explicitly signalled the 'fusion' shift in ethnic policy, such as 'contact, communication, *fusion*' (*jiaowang, jiaoliu, jiaorong* 交往交流交融), announced under Hu Jintao after the 2010 Xinjiang Work Conference to address the July 2009 violence.[2]

To resolve its own narrative contradictions and promote 'fusion', the party-state operates internment camps to eliminate adult Uyghur identities in tandem with state-run 'orphanages' to 'educate' Uyghur children. 'Fusion' policies in Xinjiang have expanded and intensified under Xi Jinping, and with his appointment of regional party leader Chen Quanguo, announcing to the National People's Congress that Xinjiang's peoples must be 'held together like pomegranate seeds', tightly and through homogeneity.[3] 'Fusion', an older, chauvinist narrative of China and last popular during the Cultural Revolution, has been reactivated as the CCP perceives itself in a position of international strength and domestic weakness in the era of China's rise. Xi Jinping (2017) has emphasised the 'collective consciousness' (*gongtong yishi* 共同意识) and organic unity (*yiti* 一体) of *Zhonghua minzu*. For the first time in PRC history, China's organic unity (*yiti* 一体) is explicitly emphasised over diversity (*duoyuan* 多元) in its *minzu* discourse (Ma, 2018, p.123). Xi's speeches and 19th Party Congress documents almost entirely abandon use of the ethnic minorities concept that saturated official discourse from 1949 to 2009.[4] *Minzu* now refers almost exclusively to *Zhonghua Minzu* in all official policy narratives.[5] Ma Rong (2018) celebrates this 'historic transformation' of the *minzu* concept as progression towards China's 'historical direction' of 'fusion'. Repeated use of what should now be translated as 'Chinese race' (*Zhonghua Minzu* 中华民族), alongside omission of ethnic minorities in official narratives, indicates official adoption of Ma's policy recommendations of ending 'special rights' (*teshu quanli* 特殊权利) for minorities and 'fusion' into the 'integral whole' of the Chinese race (Ma, 2018, p.121). Ma Rong's (2007) thinking on teaching minorities to be Chinese helped shape monolingual ('bilingual education') policies, which exacerbated Uyghur insecurity about

---

[2] For example, see: Hu and Hu (2012).   [3] See: China Daily (2017).
[4] For example, Xi's (2017) speech at the 19th Party Congress used the ethnic minorities concept only once to refer to the importance of recruiting minority cadres. However, Xi referred to the Chinese race (*Zhonghua Minzu*中华民族) 43 times, 27 of which were collocated with the Great Revival (*weida fuxing* 伟大复兴).
[5] See: Ma (2018).

assimilation before the 2009 violence. The '2nd generation' thinking on *Zhonghua Minzu* and the 'race-state' (*guozu* 国族) now drive the CCP's broader national narratives and its 'fusion' policy direction.

The party-state describes the Great Revival and its Xinjiang policies as entering a 'critical stability period' in a 'window of opportunity', while the Belt-and-Road Initiative (BRI) expands outward and the West declines, turning inward through trade protectionism and racial divisions (XUAR Government, 2018). This 'window of opportunity' shows how ethnic politics and foreign policy making are intertwined in official Chinese thought that considers the party-state in a 'life or death struggle' with Uyghurs and Western 'enemies of China' for a shared identity and global power. To secure 'fusion' and the Great Revival, the party-state has operated mass extra-legal internment camps in Xinjiang since 2017, as 'education and transformation training centres' (*jiaoyu zhuanhua peixun zhongxin* 教育转化培训中心). Approximately 1 million people, 10 per cent of the adult Uyghur population, have been interned, but these figures are constantly rising (Zenz, 2018, p.1). The camps are part of increasing controls over the Uyghur population since intensification of the 'de-extremification' (*qujiduanhua* 去极端化) campaign in 2015 under Chen Quanguo (Roberts, 2018, pp.246–250).[6] Since 2010, Xinjiang policy has been explained through narratives of 'dealing with dangers in advance' (*fangfan fengxian* 防范风险) (State Council, 2019; XUAR Government, 2018). What Sean Roberts (2018) termed the 'biopolitics of exclusion' that targets Uyghur identities as 'sickness of the heart' repeats the words of nineteenth century frontier-defence advocates from Chapter 1, exemplifying how Xinjiang is still primarily viewed through a geopolitical prism. However, the party-state looks through this prism not to Xinjiang as an empty, culture-less territory as it was conceived in the nineteenth century but to the hearts and minds of Uyghurs, who are now Islamic-Turkic threats to be eliminated or converted.

The State Council (2019) white paper on Xinjiang policy developments claims 'happiness is the most important human right' to explain mass extra-legal incarcerations and its securitisation of *Zhonghua Minzu*. It lists three vague categories of people targeted: terrorists, failed terrorists who show contrition, and people who have completed prison sentences but still 'pose potential threats to society'. Zhang Yun, CCP Secretary of the XUAR Justice Department, announced that at least 30 per cent of Uyghurs need to be 're-educated' because they are 'extremists', while the other 70 per cent are vulnerable to extremism.[7] An official 'Population Data Collection Form',[8]

---

[6] 'De-extremification' textbooks were used in mass education as part of this campaign, prior to Chen's appointment. For example, see: Zhang (2014).
[7] See: CHRD (2018).   [8] See: Chin (2019).

now collected using artificial intelligence and a facial recognition app,[9] determines whether individual Uyghurs are extremists to be interned in tick-box exercises totting up scores by religion, holding a passport, having foreign friends, or having relatives in detention. The form divides the population into 'safe, average, and unsafe', indicating the 'average' Uyghur is 'unsafe' and a threat to China's domestic unity and global power. The reasons given to released detainees or the few permitted to speak briefly to their families are listed on the *Xinjiang Victims Database*[10] that tracks individual Uyghur disappearances. Reasons include not watching state television, failing to appropriately greet officials, not smoking, wanting to travel abroad, using WhatsApp Messenger, and being born in the 1980s or 1990s ('untrustworthy generation'). The mass scale of extra-legal disappearances for innocuous reasons, alongside familiar explanations of 'fake' Turkic and Islamic identities, shows that Uyghurs as a people, not individual political dissidents, are targeted as the danger in advance that leads to terrorism. The *Xinjiang Victims Database* lists almost every known Uyghur intellectual and artist from Rahile Dawut[11] for well-known work on pre-Islamic shrines to Sanubar Tursun[12] and Abdurehim Heyit[13] for performing folk music abroad and even Adil Mijit,[14] a comedian who worked for government arts troupes. 'Eliticide', Jan Pakulski's (2016) description for the systematic targeting of public figures to prevent resistance to genocides in Eastern Europe, is considered complete. The party-state has shifted focus to eliminating or converting the broader Uyghur population for the security and 'happiness' of *Zhonghua Minzu*.

The XUAR's (2018) 'Xinjiang Work Report' uses the language of finality, suggesting these policies will seize the 'window of opportunity' to 'forever' defeat the 'foundation of separatism', Turkic and Islamic identities. Conditions in camps reported by former detainees through Human Rights Watch (2019) and international media describe cramped rooms with no sanitation, daily beatings, torture for crying or using Uyghur language, multiple gang rapes,[15] and daily renunciations of Islam and praise of Xi Jinping for bowls of gruel in return.[16] The camps themselves offer no likelihood of transformation though may eliminate the identities of individuals if they are not released or cannot physically describe their experiences afterward. The 'fusion' policies that target and break up families intend to disappear whole peoples forever. Policies of cash for mixed marriages, beginning in 2014 and accelerated under Chen Quanguo,[17] are highlighted by the Uyghur diaspora online as racial

---

[9] See: HRW (2019).   [10] See: XVD (2018).   [11] See: Scholars at Risk Network (2019).
[12] See: Freemuse (2019).   [13] See: SCMP (2019).   [14] See: Guardian (2019).
[15] For example, see: HRW (2018; 2019); Guardian (2018); Mahmut (2020); Telegraph (2019).
[16] See: See: HRW (2018; 2019); Mauk (2019); Telegraph (2019); Tursun (2018).
[17] See: Guardian (2014); RFA (2014).

assimilation and similar to forced marriages that the party-state associates with 'backward' and barbaric Islam. Mass 'inter-generational separation' through state-run 'centralised boarding facilities' for children under armed guard began in tandem with planning for camps in the first six months of Chen's tenure. These facilities raise and educate around 100,000 Uyghur children of detained parents and those who 'work' from the age of a few months old and who, according to official documents, are 'happily growing up under the loving care of Party and government'.[18]

The camps and 'orphanages' represent semantically hybrid intermingling of 'Western' and 'Chinese' political narratives. Internment camps are old European techniques to isolate peoples considered security threats to the goals of colonial state-building, for example, the Cherokee in North America and Aboriginal peoples in Australia. However, these techniques were designed to eliminate peoples, not convert identities. The Chinese concept of 'learning to be Chinese' (*jiaohua* 教化) in the camp's 'transformation education' (*zhuanhua jiaoyu* 转化教育) is seen in public relations videos to illustrate 'vocational training' benefits of learning Mandarin and chanting praise and praying to Xi Jinping.[19] This paradoxical combination of targeting a people as external security threats to Chinese identity *and* converting them into that identity perpetuates the tensions between inclusion and exclusion at the heart of *Zhonghua Minzu*, analysed throughout this book. Social anthropologist Bao Shengli (2011), one of the 'first generation' of ethnic policy scholars, warned that China should 'not repeat the same mistakes as the West' by using 'fusion'. However, mass state-violence now parallels the darkest periods of European history, seeking to eliminate indigenous peoples and transform their remnants in the name of Chinese tradition.

Zhonghua Minzu identity appears fixed and incontestable but conceals multiple, ambivalent, and historically contingent constitutive identities. Nineteenth century imperial encounters that fractured Chinese civilisation did not bring its end. Debates raged over how to build a nation through intertwined relations with cultural others: external Western states and internal ethnic minorities. Multiple meanings of Chinese-ness circulated in debates over how to save China from the West and non-Han internal others, forever reconfiguring difference and, today, culminating in colonial practices in the name of anti-colonialism. Nationalist attempts to build a strong and *modern* sovereign state used language of *ancient* civilisation (*hua*) to resist imperial powers and overthrow Manchu rule. To become strong and modern, China adopted European techniques of organising difference through territorial sovereignty and ethnocentric 'civic' nationalism. Non-*Hua* barbarians in eastern Turkestan are

---

[18] See: Zenz (2019).
[19] For example, see: 2019; HRW (2018; 2019); Mauk (2019); Telegraph (2019); Tursun (2018).

trapped in between civilisations through grand narratives of East-West conflict, which re-categorised them as Chinese ethnic minorities in the 1950s. Imperial domains and territorial sovereignty work in 'creative tension' today, inscribing the PRC's twenty-first century geo-body on all Chinese history (Callahan, 2009). 'China' always intertwines a 'geopolitical concept' in governance of its peripheries and Chinese culture as a living reality (Tu, 2005, p.145). During the nineteenth century, when 'civilisation' became joined to European imperialism, the 'white man's burden' and *la mission civilisatrice* emerged to civilise and or dominate 'inferior races' (Cox, 2000, p.218). Stevan Harrell (1995) compared this burden to China's organisation of ethnicity into superior Han and inferior minorities as its own 'civilising mission'. Pál Nyíri (2005) shows how today this civilising mission traverses contemporary borders into Southeast Asia, where Chinese migrants believe they can develop their former imperial domain as the 'yellow man's burden'. Even official BRI narratives that explain loans for infrastructure projects are infused with this self-constituting burden to build a global 'community of *destiny*' because China is the international system's only 'trailblazing' guarantor in a 'new age' (*xin shidai* 新时代) of Western decline.[20] China's confrontation with European imperialism reconfigured ancient Confucian civilising missions of teaching barbarians to be Chinese (*jiaohua*) to teach them they are 'backward' ethnic minorities in a modern state. In the increasingly closed 'opening and reform' era, ethnic minorities are redefined as timelessly Chinese. China is narrated as a powerful modern state *and* an unbroken civilisation, interweaving narratives of Han chauvinist superiority and Confucian culturalism. However, framing China as a 'civilisation-state' invisibilises non-Han histories and exacerbates the tensions between empire and nation that reproduce cycles of insecurity and violence in Xinjiang.

China's 'mission' to become a powerful and prosperous state (*fuqiang guo* 富强国) again means perpetual progress towards nationalist modernity *and* restoration of ancient tradition. Minorities are trapped in this paradoxical mission as objects of China's revival. Their 'backwardness' simultaneously supports its Han superiority narrative and resists its goals as obstacles to 'development'. China's leaders explicitly define colonialism as a Western phenomenon, insisting China is unlike Western nation-states as a 'multi-*minzu* nation commonly created by all *minzu*' (State Council, 2009a, p.1). Leading public intellectuals, such as Zhang Weiwei (2012) and Hu Angang (2012), have driven the 'new type of superpower' narrative where China's 'Eastern' traditions (tribute and fusion) are mutually constitutive of 'Western' imperialist coercion in the organisation of domestic and world order. Former President

---

[20] For example, see: NDRC (2015); Xi (2013; 2015; 2017).

Conclusion

Hu Jintao spoke through this narrative in his final speech at the 18th National Congress, announcing that China 'will never copy a Western political system' (Xinhua, 2014). President Xi Jinping racialised its logics at the 19th National Congress, explaining that 'in Chinese blood, there is no DNA for aggression or hegemony' (SCMP, 2014). Ironically, the construct of a Chinese premodern 'tribute system' derives from Western orientalist historical thought. Tribute was never an uncritically accepted 'system' by 'vassal' states that traded with or were militarily conquered by China (Perdue, 2015, p.1007). Looking to contemporary Xinjiang, there are too many similarities between classic European colonial forms and metropolitan dominance in Xinjiang to dismiss claims that its governance represents a 'colonial endeavour' (Cliff, 2016, pp.7–9). Uyghur identity has long justified a state of exception in Xinjiang, enabling conflation of vernacular alternatives to CCP historical narratives with armed resistance to China's rise (Bovingdon, 2010, pp.7–9; Cliff, 2016, p.216). A 'new type of superpower' has been narrated through tensions between orientalist understandings of China's diverse histories and modern, chauvinist ethno-nationalism. Its proponents now lead Chinese politics, seeking to secure China's internal cultural frontiers through homogenising 'fusion' and to secure those frontiers to become a new superpower.

Postcoloniality in China is always complex because China is postcolonial with reference to itself as much as with the West and Japan (Fiskesjö, 2017, p.6). Modernisation is a means to defeat Western hegemony and unite China's peoples, returning China to the world's centre *and* the Han to the centre of China. Chinese nation-building constitutes itself against Western racism and has had to appeal to multiple perspectives on identity, to satisfy Confucian culturalist desires to attract barbarians with 'benevolent' 'preferential policies', the historical-materialist drive to 'open the frontier' with economic development, and Han chauvinist violence to eliminate non-Chinese enemies. The CCP has relatively effectively navigated multiple Han demands, but at the cost that Uyghurs see China as a colonising power built on false history, violence, and social control. The Chinese Studies literature on nationalism has shown how patriotic education campaigns constituted Chinese identity by framing the West and Japan as external colonial threats. However, these campaigns also constitute Chinese identity by physically subjecting ethnic minorities inside China's territorial boundaries to coercive techniques policing and constituting their everyday identities as timelessly Chinese. Ethnic unity education sought to discipline minority identities into historical narratives of timeless *Zhonghua Minzu* that positions them as *behind* the Han's level of modernisation and civilisation. The CCP perplexingly demands non-Han identify with imperial logics as culturally empty barbarian vessels to strengthen China's expanding civilisation, with narratives of cultural evolution as 'backward' *minzu* to be modernised, and with ethno-nationalist discourses of danger that identify them as cultural threats.

Conclusion

The standard periodisation of China's history into static civilisation (until 1949), communist statehood (1949–1978), and market-driven 'opening and reform' (1978–) draws from official historiography and implicitly assumes China is on a teleological path of progress and opening. This Eurocentric vision of progress is adopted by the party-state, and often uncritically recirculated in Chinese Studies, overlooking how markets and state control co-exist in contemporary China, as they have done throughout world history. State control of the economy and centralised political power have driven Xinjiang's governance throughout 'opening and reform', indicating the deep relationship between development and security in official thought. Hu Jintao's strengthening of State-Owned Enterprises (SOEs) in 2008 and Xi Jinping's re-centralisation of political power after 2012 were techniques familiar to scholars of Xinjiang where reform and centralised power are intertwined in development and security policies. In 2020, mass, extra-legal internment camps, which racially target specific peoples and produce manufacturing goods for global markets, are central to the constitution of official Chinese identity, its securitisation, and its globally celebrated model of development. China was never a 5,000-year-old, unbroken multi-ethnic civilisation pretending to be a state, as famously claimed in the orientalist thought of Lucian Pye (1990) and Zhang Weiwei (2012). China embraced sovereignty and demarcated fixed territorial boundaries to secure itself against external state intervention *and* former barbarians within these boundaries who resist the state's nation-building narratives. Ethnic inclusion and exclusion in contemporary China are as ambivalent as *Zhonghua Minzu*. *Zhonghua Minzu* does not resolve, but perpetuates, the tensions faced by all societies between tradition and modernity and their inside and outside, most dramatically emerging in China through intertwined confrontations with barbarian frontiers, the West, and modernity. *Zhonghua Minzu* paradoxically maintains the imagined unity of Chinese civilisation that excluded Uyghurs as barbarians but un-ambivalently securitises identity to eliminate narratives that reject minorities' inferiority by demanding inclusion. China, like all nations, is a story told by different people using the available, meaningful narratives to appeal to different groups with different ideas about themselves. Neither civilisation nor the nation-state tells China's complete story, nor do they include Uyghur identity, except as objects of cultural power and conversion.

China is a nation-state that seeks to civilise its imperial frontiers using development and cultural conversion to match imperial and modern spatial domains. Xinjiang, the new frontier, must be constantly converted to Chinese civilisation to secure its congruence with the contemporary nation-state's territorial borders and ambivalent cultural boundaries. However, the daily reality of *Zhonghua Minzu* in Xinjiang refers to a multiplicity of identity contestations within its own narrative tensions, which produce direct and indirect resistance to those narratives as a colonial project. Listening to Uyghurs, one will regularly hear their descriptions of China through 'assimilation', 'colonialism', and 'fascism'. Their experiences of being forced to be Chinese echo indigenous narratives of peoples colonised by European settlers, claiming that, even when non-violent, European civilisation excluded or assimilated them through ethnocentric blindness to its culturally mediated ideas of 'modernisation', narrated as value neutral 'progress'. Uyghurs and the ethnic exclusion they experience are one important part of the 'real China'. Ethnic exclusion and assimilation policies are direct consequences of unity and modernisation. The Chinese nation is a perpetual process of building from above and re-building from below. The party-state sees itself in a historic 'window of opportunity' to resolve the '*minzu* problem' *forever* and complete this process. However, China's history shows that the more it enforces homogeneity through security on its frontiers, the more it produces insecurity and heterogeneous resistance.

Understanding China requires deeper understanding of its relations with its own self-defined frontiers, that is precluded by nonreflexive, methodological nationalist adoptions of 'China' as a unit of analysis. Additionally, understanding those frontiers, including Xinjiang, on their own terms is necessary to offer solutions that could reduce violence, but the prospects are as bleak now as they were in 2009. Mr Yan, the taxi driver who rescued his daughter during the July 2009 violence, said, 'There is nothing we can do, that's it for a generation, my generation hated *them* and my children's generation will because of what they've done.' When violence is so immediately understood through hatred and essentialised ethnic boundaries, narratives that empathise with others' identity and reject violence need to be told from above. Leading intellectual narratives demanding respect for Chinese civilisation must include empathy for those outside China's elites: those economically marginalised Han who struggle for material survival in China's competitive economic metropoles and migrate to Xinjiang to 'open the frontier' but become victims of violence in the anonymous, unfolding geopolitical telos of China's Great Revival. Mr Yan's story is not extraneous to the CCP's model of rapid development to propel China's rise but a direct consequence of it. Demands for empathy for China must also include empathy for Xinjiang's peoples whose identities are officially excluded by discourses of danger and who fear becoming victims of violence by the state and by Han nationalists. Aynür, the Uyghur Mandarin teacher, told us that 'ethnic unity is like rubbing my warm cheek against their cold ass'. Her desire for empathy, as an individual 'between cultures', as Turkic *and* Chinese, is not existentially threatening to Han people but it challenges official narratives that only 'terrorists' could identify as Turkic or Islamic. Official epistemic violence enabled Aynür's physical treatment, 'like a terrorist', when ethnically targeted and searched by unofficial security and when denied a housing lease because she was Uyghur. The young businessman, Mukhtar, explained the July 2009 violence as a 'pot of boiling water', with the lid of security screwed tightly on the pot of identity. Mukhtar believed security would immediately improve if Chinese policy permitted Uyghur language education and Han empathised with Uyghurs enough to make small efforts to speak Xinjiang's traditional inter-ethnic lingua franca. Uyghurs ask for security from assimilation through language and religion, and a small portion of the respect that China receives globally would provide that. However, the party-state targets Uyghur calls to preserve language and religious practices as *causes* of recurring violence in Xinjiang, exacerbating Han and Uyghur insecurities that have now culminated in mass 'transformation' camps.

Chinese Studies and IR must address these asymmetrical experiences of modernisation and state violence to understand the implications of China's rise and how peoples in China see China. In Xinjiang, official narratives of value-neutral 'modernisation' and timeless 'civilisation', often uncritically adopted in mainstream literature, are understood by Turkic-speaking Muslims as culturally mediated political projects that enable state-violence to eliminate their identities. Seeing China through a more multifaceted lens helps in thinking beyond friend-enemy binaries that too often frame Chinese and Western policy options as 'business-as-usual' *or* militarised conflict, neither of which are realistic, rational, or ethical. State violence against Turkic and Islamic identities as 'backward' and as 'separatism, terrorism, and extremism' has exacerbated cycles of insecurity and violence between Han and Uyghurs in Xinjiang. The adoption of mass internment camps in Xinjiang attempts to break this cycle by eliminating Uyghur identities. However, these 'fusion' policies produce more Uyghur insecurity, the material outcome of which is unpredictable and potentially volatile. What is certain is that adopting colonial techniques of targeting particular ethnic groups and isolating them as threats in camps have viscerally collapsed narrative binaries between violent, colonial West and peaceful, anti-colonial China, which will reconfigure China's identity and security.

Appendix 1 Cast of Characters

Aynür: a female Uyghur in her early 40s and Mandarin language teacher. Aynür was from a smaller oasis town but spent most of her adult life in Ürümchi with several years studying across China. She was highly qualified in formal educational attainment and language skills but was underpaid and overworked, struggling to help pay for her children's education. Fluent in Uyghur and Chinese, Aynür was proud of being 'between cultures' and her ability to make friends with Han, while also expressing a strong sense of ethnic identity.

Mahigül: a Uyghur student in her early 20s, born and bred in Ürümchi into a professional family living in a modern apartment block. Mahigül was fluent in Uyghur and Mandarin, which she said meant she understood Xinjiang and China. She was proud to be Uyghur but considered herself urban and modern, often joking about rural habits. She had Han colleagues and acquaintances but no close friends.

Miss Lan: a single, female Han in her mid-20s and early career Mandarin Chinese teacher. Miss Lan and her parents were born and raised in the countryside north of Ürümchi. She was rightly proud of her hard work to become a teacher from a rural background. She described herself as an authentic 'Xinjiang person' due to her long-term roots but did not speak any other languages or have any minority friends.

Mr Qiang: a male, 36-year-old *getihu*, small-scale entrepreneur from Sichuan. He had come to Xinjiang ten years earlier to find work because making money was 'impossible' and 'too competitive' in the Sichuanese highlands. His intended temporary migration to Xinjiang for economic reasons represents the contemporary waves of Han arrivals in the region. He said he was a proud Han and did not wish to have any Uyghur friends.

Mrs Du: a female Han in her late 30s and a long-term professional university teacher. She was born and raised in Xinjiang but her parents arrived from Shanghai in the 1950s to 'open the frontier'. Married to a modestly wealthy businessman, Mrs Du enjoyed luxuries such as travel opportunities across China not afforded by most other interviewees. She could communicate in basic Uyghur and expressed pride that this allowed her to 'understand ethnic minorities' more than her Han friends.

Mukhtar: a male Uyghur in his early 20s from a smaller oasis town, who moved to Ürümchi for his studies. He was fluent in Uyghur, Mandarin, and English, which he said meant he understood Xinjiang from different perspectives. Mukhtar had recently graduated and considered turning his hand to business. He read academic literature on Xinjiang from abroad and hoped one day to study at the doctorate level. He had Han friends but wished they were more willing to discuss the realities of life for Uyghurs.

Appendix 2   Lyrics to 'One Family' (*Yi Jiaren*) Song

Original Mandarin Chinese Version

'一家人'

花红你是哪一朵，柳绿你是哪一棵，
不用我来问，不用你来说，
花红柳绿都是春色
山青你是哪一座，水秀你是哪条河，
不用我来问，不用你来说，
山清水秀都是欢歌
家是一个家，国是大中国，
家和万事兴，有你也有我，
家是一个家，国是大中国，
都是一家人，部分你和我
温暖驱寒冷，真爱换真心，
同在蓝天下，都是一家人，
同是一颗心，同是一条根，
幸福伴样和，都是一家人
花红你是哪一朵，柳绿你是哪一棵，
不用我来问，不用你来说，
花红柳绿都是春色
山青你是哪一座，水秀你是哪条河，
不用我来问，不用你来说，
山青水秀都是欢歌
相扶风雨中，危难见真情，
病风知劲草，烈火炼真金，
你我一家人，爱才那样深，
你我一家人，请才那样真
温暖驱寒冷，真爱换真心，
同在蓝天下，都是一家人，
同是一颗心，同是一条根，
幸福伴样和，都是一家人

Appendix 2 Lyrics to 'One Family' (*Yi Jiaren*) Song

English Translation

Of all the red flowers[1] which one are you, of all the willow green which one are you,
I don't need to ask, you don't need to say,
Red flowers and green willows are the colours of Spring.
Green mountain, which one are you, Water blossom, which one are you,
I don't need to ask, you don't need to say,
The picturesque scenes are joyous songs.
Home is one home, the country is great China,
If the family lives in harmony, all affairs will prosper[2], it has you and it has me,
Home is one home, the country is great China,
We are all one family, you cannot separate you and me.
Warmth expels the cold winds, true love becomes a true heart,
We are all one family under the blue sky (*tianxia*),
We are all one heart, all one root,
Prosperity accompanies peace, we are all one family.
Of all the red flowers which one are you, of all the willow green which one are you,
I don't need to ask, you don't need to say,
Red flowers and green willows are the colours of Spring.
Green mountain, which one are you, Water blossom, which one are you,
I don't need to ask, you don't need to say,
The picturesque scenes are joyous songs.
Help each other through trials and hardships, through danger we can see the truth,
Through sickness and wind, we become indomitable, raging fire forges true gold,
You and I are one family, only love is this deep,
You and I are one family, our feelings are this genuine.
Warmth expels the cold winds, true love becomes a true heart,
We are all one family under the blue sky (*tianxia*),
We are all one heart, all one root,
Prosperity accompanies peace, we are all one family.

---

[1] This has multiple meanings, including a gift for a wedding, a bonus, or a tip, all of which imply prosperity.
[2] 家和万事兴 is from Confucius' Analects. It means if the family lives in harmony, all affairs will prosper (家庭和睦就能兴旺).

Bibliography

A, Xingliang (1996) 'Tujue Yuzu' ('Turkic Language Family') in Yu, Taishan et al. (eds) *Xinjiang Gezu Lishi Wenhua Cidian (Dictionary of History and Culture of Every Xinjiang Minzu)*. Beijing: Zhonghua Shuju Chubanshe ('Zhonghua Book Publishers'), p.316.

Acharya, Amitav (2014) 'Global International Relations (IR) and Regional Worlds', *International Studies Quarterly*, 58: 647–659.

Agathangelou, Anna M. and Ling, L. H. M. (2004) 'The House of IR: From Family Power Politics to the Poises of Worldism', *International Studies Review*, 6(4): 21–49.

Amit, Vered (2002a) 'Reconceptualizing Community' in Amit, Verid (ed) *Realizing Community: Concepts, Social Relationships, and Sentiments*. Routledge: London, pp.1–21.

——— (2002b) 'An Anthropology without Community?' in Amit, Vered and Rapport, Nigel (eds) *The Trouble with Community: Anthropological Reflections on Movement, Identity, and Collectivity*. London: Pluto Press.

Amnesty International (AI) (2015) 'China: Open Letter Re: The Current Situation of Nurmemet (Aka Nurmuhemmet) Yasin' (Available at: https://www.amnesty.org/en/documents/asa17/0004/2015/en/) [Last accessed: 26/07/19].

Anderson, Benedict (1991) *Imagined Communities: Reflections on the Origin and Spread of Nationalism*. London: Verso Press.

Anthony, Ross (2011) 'Exceptionally Equal: Emergency States and the Production of Enemies in Xinjiang', *Inner Asia*, 13(1): 51–72.

Ashley, Richard (1984) 'The Poverty of Neorealism', *International Organization*, 38(2): 225–286.

Asia Weekly (Yazhou Zhoukan) (2009) 'Caifang: Weizu NGO Gongzuozhe qian Xinjiang Fazhibao Zongbianbao Zhuren Hailaiteta zai Qiwu Shijian jiu Yujing' ('Interview: Heyrat, Uyghur NGO Worker and Former Editor-in-Chief of the Xinjiang Legal News, Gave Early Warnings before 7-5') (Available at: www.yzzk.com/cfm/Content_Archive.cfm?Channel=ag&Path=2311577102/30ag3a.cfm), 02/08/2009 [Last accessed: 11/06/18].

Bai, Shouyi (1981) 'Guanyu Zhongguo Minzu Guanxi shishang de Jige Wenti' ('A few questions regarding the history of China's minzu relations') in Peng, Wulin et al. (eds) (2013) *Zhongguo Jindai Minzushi Yanjiu Wenxian (Research Documents on Modern China's Ethnic History)*. Beijing: Shehui Kexue Wenxian Chubanshe ('Social Science Academic Press'), pp.32–47.

Bibliography

Balzer, Harley (2004) 'State and Society in Transitions from Communism' in Gries, Peter Hays and Rosen, Stanley (eds) *State and Society in Twenty-first-Century China*. New York: Routledge Curzon, pp.235–256.

Bao, Shengli (2011) 'Ye tan zhongguo ke jinyibu wanshan minzu zhengce' ('Discussion on Progressing the Perfection of *Minzu* Policy'). *Zhongguo Gongchandang Xinwen Wang (Chinese Communist Party News Online)*, 28 October (Available at: http://theory.people.com.cn/GB/16057587.html) [Last accessed: 09/04/19].

Barabantseva, Elena (2008) 'From the Language of Class to the Rhetoric of Development: Discourse of "Nationality" and "Ethnicity" in China', *The Journal of Contemporary China*, 17(56): 565–589.

—— (2009) 'Development as Localization: Ethnic Minorities in China's Official Discourse on the Western Development Project', *Critical Asian Studies*, 41(2): 225–254.

—— (2011) *Overseas Chinese, Ethnic Minorities, and Nationalism: De-Centring China*. Oxon: Routledge.

Baranovitch, Nimrod (2003) *China's New Voices: Popular Music, Ethnicity, Gender, and Politics, 1978–1997*. Berkeley: University of California Press.

Barkawi, Tarak (2011) From War to Security: The Wider Agenda and the Fate of the Study of War, *Millennium*, 39(3): 701–716.

Barkawi, Tarak and Laffey, Mark (2006) 'The Postcolonial Moment in Security Studies', *Review of International Studies*, 32: 329–352.

Barth, Frederick (1969) *Ethnic Groups and Boundaries: The Social Organisation of Difference*. Long Grove, IL: Waveland Press.

BBC (2006) 'Albania Takes Guantanamo Uyghurs' (Available at: http://news.bbc.co.uk/1/hi/world/americas/4979466.stm), 6 May [Last accessed: 01/09/18].

—— (2009) 'Scores Killed in China Protests' (Available at: http://news.bbc.co.uk/1/hi/world/asia-pacific/8135203.stm), 6 July [Last accessed: 11/06/18].

Becquelin, Nicholas (2000) 'Xinjiang in the Nineties', *The China Journal*, 44: 65–90.

—— (2004a) 'Staged Development in Xinjiang', *The China Quarterly*, 178: 358–378.

—— (2004b) 'Criminalising Ethnicity: Political Repression in Xinjiang', China Rights Forum, No. 1 (Available at: www.hrichina.org/sites/default/files/oldsite/PDFs/CRF.1.2004/b1_Criminalizing1.2004.pdf).

Bekri, Nur (2008) 'Nuer Baikeli zai Zizhiqu Ganbu Dahui shang de Jianghua' ('Nuer Baikeli's Speech at the Autonomous Regional Government Congress') (Available at: www.xj.xinhuanet.com/2008-09/11/content_14376020.htm) [Last accessed: 31/05/19].

—— (2009a) 'Nuer Baikeli Guanyu Wulumuqi "7-5" Shijian de Qingkuang Tongbao' ('Nur Bekri: Public Notification Regarding the Ürümchi 7-5 Incident') in Xinjiang Uyghur Autonomous Region Party Commission Ministry of Information (eds) *Jiaqiang Minzu Tuanjie, Weihu Xinjiang Wending: Xuanchuan Jiaoyu Cailiao (Yi)* (*Strengthening Ethnic Unity, Protecting Xinjiang Stability: Information Education Materials No. 1*). Wulumuqi: Xinjiang Renmin Chubanshe ('Xinjiang People's Publishing Press).

—— (2009b) 'Nuer Baikeli zai Zizhiqu Tingju Ganbu Dahui Shang de Jianghua' ('Nur Bekri's Speech at the Autonomous Regional Government's Cadre Conference') in Xinjiang Uyghur Autonomous Region Party Commission Ministry of Information (eds) *Jiaqiang Minzu Tuanjie, Weihu Xinjiang Wending: Xuanchuan Jiaoyu Cailiao Yi* (*Strengthening Ethnic Unity, Protecting Xinjiang Stability: Information Education Materials No. 1*). Wulumuqi: Xinjiang Renmin Chubanshe (Xinjiang People's Publishing Press).

Bellér-Hann, Ildikó (2001) '"Making the Oil Fragrant": Dealings with the Supernatural among the Uyghurs in Xinjiang', *Asian Ethnicity*, 2(1): 9–23.

— (2002) 'Temperamental Neighbours: Uighur-Han Relations in Xinjiang, Northwest China' in Schlee, G. (ed) *Imagined Differences: Hatred and the Construction of Identity*. New York: Palgrave.

— (2008) *Community Matters in Xinjiang 1880–1949: Towards a Historical Anthropology of the Uyghur*. Leiden: Brill.

Bellér-Hann, Ildikó, Cesàro, M Christina, Harris, Rachel, Smith Finley, and Joanne (2007) 'Introduction' in Bellér-Hann, I. et al. (eds) *Situating the Uyghurs between China and Central Asia*. Aldershot: Ashgate, pp.1–14.

Bense Shouyiren (2008) 'Xianhua Han Minzu yu Zhonghua Minzu' ('A Complaint on the Han Ethnic Group and the Chinese Nation') (Available at: www.uighurbiz.cn/society/2008/1008/article_7277.html), *UighurBiz*, 8 October [Access no longer available].

Benson, Linda and Svanberg, Ingvar (1998) *China's Last Nomads: The History and Culture of China's Kazakhs*. New York: M. E. Sharpe.

Berger, Mark T. (2006) 'From Nation-Building to State-Building: The Geopolitics of Development, the Nation-State System, and the Changing Global Order', *Third World Quarterly*, 27(1): 5–25.

Berger, Stefan (ed) (2007) *Writing the Nation: A Global Perspective*. Basingstoke: Palgrave Macmillan.

Bhabha, Homi (1990) 'DissemiNation: Time, Narrative, and the Margins of the Modern Nation', in Bhabha, Homi (ed) *Nation and Narration*. London: Routledge, pp.291–322.

Bhabha, Homi K. (2009) *The Location of Culture*. London: Routledge.

Bhambra, Gurminder (2011) 'Talking among Themselves? Weberian and Marxist Sociologies as Dialogues without "Others"', *Millennium*, 39(3): 667–681.

Blank, Stephen (2003) 'Xinjiang and China's Security', *Global Economic Review*, 32(4): 121–148.

Bleiker, Roland (2001) 'The Aesthetic Turn in International Political Theory', *Millennium*, 30(3): 509–533.

Billig, Michael (1995) *Banal Nationalism*. London: Sage.

Booth, Ken (ed) (2005) *Critical Security Studies and World Politics*. London: Lynne Rienner.

Bovingdon, Gardner (2002) 'The Not-So-Silent Majority: Uyghur Resistance to Han Rule in Xinjiang', *Modern China*, 28(1): 39–78.

— (2004a) 'Autonomy in Xinjiang: Han Nationalist Imperatives and Uyghur Discontent', *East-West Center Policy Studies*, 11.

— (2004b) 'Contested Histories' in Starr, S. F. (ed) *Xinjiang: China's Muslim Borderland*. New York: M. E. Sharpe, pp.353–374.

— (2010) *The Uyghurs: Strangers in their Own Land*. New York: Columbia University Press.

Brophy, David (2011) 'Tending to Unite: The Origins of Uyghur Nationalism'. Unpublished PhD diss., Harvard University.

(2016) *Uyghur Nation: Reform and Revolution on the Russia-China Frontier.* Cambridge, MA: Harvard University Press.

Brown, Chris (2013) 'The Poverty of Grand Theory', *European Journal of International Relations*, 19(3): 483–497.

Brubaker, Rogers (1998) 'Myths and Misconceptions in the Study of Nationalism', in Hall, John (ed) *The State of the Nation.* Cambridge: Cambridge University Press, pp.272–306.

(1999) 'The Manichean Myth: Rethinking the Distinction between "Civic" and "Ethnic" Nationalism', in Kriesi, Hanspeter et al. (eds) *Nation and National Identity: The European Experience in Perspective.* Zurich: Ruegger, pp.55–71.

(2002) "Ethnicity without Groups', *Archives Européenes de Sociologie*, XLIII(2): 163–189.

Bubandt, Nils (2005) 'Vernacular Security: The Politics of Feeling Safe in Global, National, and Local Worlds', *Security Dialogue*, 36(3): 275–296.

Bulag, Uradyn E. (2002) *The Mongols at China's Edge: History and the Politics of National Unity.* Lanham, MD: Rowman & Littlefield.

Burgess, Robert G. (2015) 'The Unstructured Interview as Conversation' in Burgess, Robert G. (ed) *Field Research: A Sourcebook and Field Manual.* London: Routledge, pp.107–110.

Butler, Judith. 2007. *Gender Trouble.* New York: Routledge.

Butler, Judith and Spivak, Gayatri Chakravorty (2007) *Who Sings the Nation-State? Language, Politics, Belonging.* New York: Seagull Books.

Buzan, Barry (1991) *People, States, and Fear: An Agenda for International Security Studies in the Post-Cold War Era.* London: Harvester Wheatsheaf.

et al. (1998) *Security: A New Framework for Analysis.* London: Lynne Reinner.

Buzan, Barry and Lawson, George (2014) 'Capitalism and the Emergent World Order', *International Affairs*, 90(1): 71–91.

Byler, Darren and Grose, Timothy (2018) 'China's Surveillance Laboratory', *Dissent* (Available at: https://www.dissentmagazine.org/online_articles/chinas-surveillance-laboratory), 31 October [Last accessed: 04/04/2020].

Callahan, William A. (2004) *Contingent States: Greater China and Transnational Relations.* Minneapolis: University of Minnesota Press.

(2005) 'How to Understand China: The Dangers and Opportunities of Being a Rising Power', *Review of International Studies*, 31(4): 701–714.

(2006) 'History, Identity, and Security: Producing and Consuming Nationalism in China', *Critical Asian Studies*, 38(2): 179–208.

(2007) 'Trauma and Community: The Visual Politics of Chinese Nationalism and Sino-Japanese Relations', *Theory and Event*, 10(4).

(2009) 'The Cartography of National Humiliation and the Emergence of China's Geobody', *Public Culture*, 21(1): 141–173.

(2010) *China: The Pessoptimist Nation*, Oxford: Oxford University Press.

(2012) 'Harmony, Unity, and Diversity in China's World', *The Newsletter*, 60: 22–23.

(2012b) 'Who Is Xi Jinping and Where Will He Lead China' (Available at: www.opendemocracy.net/william-callahan/who-is-xi-jinping-and-where-will-he-lead-china), *Open Democracy*, 27 November [Last accessed: 23/01/19].

(2013) *China Dreams: Twenty Visions of the Future.* Oxford: Oxford University Press.

Campbell, David (1998) *Writing Security: United States Foreign Policy and the Politics of Identity*. Manchester: Manchester University Press.
— (2003) 'Cultural Governance and Pictorial Resistance: Reflections on the Imaging of War', *Review of International Studies*, 29: 57–73.
Carrico, Kevin (2017) *The Great Han: Race, Nationalism, and Tradition in China Today*. Berkeley: University of California Press.
CCP Central Committee (CCPCC) (1950) 'Zhonggong Zhongyang Guanyu Tongyi Xinjiang Jiandang jige Wenti de Guiding de Pifa' ('Reply from the CCPCC on Several Issues Regarding Establishment of the Party in Xinjiang') in Zhonggong Zhongyang Wenxian Yanjiushi ('CCP Central Committee Document Research Office') (ed) (2010) *Xinjiang Gonzuo Wenxian Xuanbian (Xinjiang Work – Selected Documents)*. Beijing: Zhongyang Wenxian Chubanshe ('CCP Central Committee Party Literature Publishing House'), pp.??
— (1953) 'Zhonggong Zhongyang Guanyu Xinjiang Minzu Quyu Zizhi Shishi Banfa Cao'an de Piyu' ('Remarks from the CCPCC regarding the drafts on implementing *minzu* regional autonomy in Xinjiang') in Zhonggong Zhongyang Wenxian Yanjiushi ('CCP Central Committee Document Research Office') (ed) (2010) *Xinjiang Gonzuo Wenxian Xuanbian (Xinjiang Work – Selected Documents)*. Beijing: Zhongyang Wenxian Chubanshe ('CCP Central Committee Party Literature Publishing House'), pp.106–113.
Center for Strategic and International Studies (CSIS) (2007) *Demography of HIV/AIDS in China*. Washington, DC: Center for Strategic and International Studies.
CCTV (2009) 'Xinjiang Artists Preserve Traditional Performances', 01/06/09.
— (2009b) 'Xinjiang Is a Good Place', 02/10/09 (Available at: http://english.cctv.com/program/worldwidewatch/20091002/101214.shtml) [Last accessed: 23/03/19].
Cesàro, M Christina (2007) 'Polo, Laghman, So Say: Situating Uyghur Food between Central Asia and China' in Bellér-Hann, I. et al. (eds) *Situating the Uyghurs between China and Central Asia*. Aldershot: Ashgate.
Chakrabarty, Dipesh (2000) *Provincializing Europe: Postcolonial Thought and Historical Difference*. Princeton, NJ: Princeton University Press.
Chatterjee, Partha (2001) *Nationalist Thought and the Colonial World*. London: Zed Books.
Chenbao ('Morning News') (2009a) 'Dixia Tongdao dou zhuang "Dianzi Yan"' ('Electric Eyes Installed in All Underpasses'), 22 September, p.A5.
— ('Morning News') (2009b) '825 ming Xianfan bei Xingju' ('825 Criminal Suspects Detained'), 3 September, p.A3.
— ('Morning News') (2009c) 'Zizhiqu Tongbao Wushi Zhenci Shanghai Anjian Qingkuang' ('Regional Government Announces the Situation Regarding the Cases of Syringe Assault Incidents'), 3 September, p.A3.
— ('Morning News') (2009d) 'Quanjiang Zhuahuo 75 ming 'Zhenci' Zuifan' ('Seizing 75 Syringe Criminals across Xinjiang'), 16 September, p.A1.
— ('Morning News') (2009e) 'Dianli Xidezuo, Minjian Hu Guoqi' ('Ceremony Held, the People's Police Protect the National Flag'), 5 September.
— ('Morning News') (2009f) 'Zui Ming Xiangtong Weihe Zhongxing bu Tong' ('How Accusations Are Not Equivalent to Charges'), 18 September, p.A5.
— ('Morning News') (2009g) 'Xi'an Fasheng Yisi Zhenci Shanghaian' ('Outbreak of Syringe Assaults in Xi'an'), 17 September.

('Morning News') (2009h) 'Xi'an Po Liang qi Zhenza'an' ('2 Cases of Syring Assaults in Xi'an'), 22 September, p.A10.
('Morning News') (2009i) 'Meng Jianzhu lai Wu Jiancha Zhidao Weiwen Gongzuo' ('Meng Jianzhu Inspects Urumqi to Lead Stability Work'), 5 September, p.A1.
('Morning News') (2009j) 'Haizemen Youge Weiwuerzu Ma' ('Children Have a Uyghur Mother'), 15 December, p.A4.
('Morning News') (2009k) 'Tongxu weile Wo Hunli Gai Riqi' ('My Classmate Changed His Wedding Date for Me'), 15 December, p.A4.
('Morning News') (2009l) 'Rouzi jie Fangjia Tonghi' ('Roza Holiday Notification'), 15 September, p.A2.
('Morning News') (2009m) 'Huandu Rouzi Jie' ('Warmly Celebrate Roza'), 22 September, Cover.
Chan, Koonchung [Chen Guanzhong] (2009) *Shengshi: Zhongguo 2013* (*The Fat Years: China 2013*). Hong Kong: Oxford University Press.
Chen, Yangbin (2008) *Muslim Uyghur Students in a Chinese Boarding School: Social Recapitalisation as a Response to Ethnic Integration*. Plymouth: Lexington.
Child, Ben (2009) 'Old Suspicions Magnified Mistrust into Ethnic Riots in Urumqi' (Available at: www.guardian.co.uk/film/2009/sep/22/chinese-protesters-hack-website), *The Guardian*, 22 September [Last accessed: 14/09/18].
Chin, Josh (2019) 'Twelve Days in Xinjiang: How China's Surveillance State Overwhelms Daily Life' (Available at: https://www.wsj.com/articles/twelve-days-in-xinjiang-how-chinas-surveillance-state-overwhelms-daily-life-1513700355) *Wall Street Journal*, 19 December [Last accessed: 23/07/19].
China Daily (2009) 'Xinjiang Emerging from Riot Shadow', 2 September.
 (2017) 'Cherish Ethnic Unity, President Tells Xinjiang' (Available at: www.chinadaily.com.cn/china/2017twosession/2017-03/11/content_28515253.htm) 11 March [Last accessed: 23/07/19].
China Digital Times (2009) 'Death Toll in Xinjiang Rises to 184 (Updated)' (Available at: http://chinadigitaltimes.net/2009/07/death-toll-in-xinjiang-violence-rises-to-184/), 10 July [Last accessed: 11/06/19].
China Islamic Association (2006) *Musilin Aiguozhuyi Jiaocheng* ('Patriotic Muslim Coursebook'). Beijing: Zongjiao Wenhua Chubanshe.
China Labor Watch (2009) 'Labor Violations Exacerbate Ethnic Tensions in South China' (Available at: www.chinalaborwatch.org/20090706uyghur.htm#), 7 July [Last accessed: 11/06/19].
Chinese Human Rights Defenders (CHRD) (2018) 'China: Massive Numbers of Uighurs and Other Ethnic Minorities Forced into Re-Education Programs', 3 August (Available at: https://www.nchrd.org/2018/08/china-massive-numbers-of-uyghurs-other-ethnic-minorities-forced-into-re-education-programs/) [Last accessed: 23/07/18].
Chow, Kai-Wing (2001) 'Narrating the Nation, Race, and National Culture: Imagining the Hanzu Identity in Modern China' in Chow, Kai-Wing et al. (eds) *Constructing Nationhood in Modern East Asia*. Ann Arbor: University of Michigan Press, pp.47–85.
Chowdry, Geeta (2007) 'Edward Said and Contrapuntal Reading: Implications for Critical Interventions in International Relations', *Millennium*, 36(1): 101–116.
Chowdhry, Geeta and Nair, Sheila (2004) 'Introduction: Power in a Postcolonial World: Race, Gender, and Class in International Relations' in Chowdhry, Geeta and Nair,

Sheila (eds) *Power, Postcolonialism, and International Relations: Reading Race, Gender, and Class*. Routledge: London, pp.1–32.

Clarke, Michael E. (2007a) 'The Problematic Progress of "Integration" in the Chinese State's Approach to Xinjiang, 1759–2005', *Asian Ethnicity*, 8(3): 261–289.

(2007b) 'China's Internal Security Dilemma and the "Great Western Development": The Dynamics of Integration, Ethnic Nationalism, and Terrorism in Xinjiang', *Asian Studies Review*, 31: 323–342.

(2010) *Xinjiang and China's Rise in Central Asia*. London: Routledge.

Cliff, Tom 2016. *Oil and Water: Being Han in Xinjiang*. Chicago: University of Chicago Press.

CNN (2007) 'Chinese Architect Slams Olympics Pretend Smile' (Available at: http://edition.cnn.com/2007/WORLD/asiapcf/08/13/china.olympics.reut/), 13 August [Last accessed: 01/09/18].

Cohen, Anthony P. (1985) *The Symbolic Construction of Community*. Routledge: London.

Cohen, Anthony (1996) 'Personal Nationalism: A Scottish View of Some Rites, Rights, and Wrongs', *American Ethnologist*, 23(4): 802–815.

Cohen, Paul (2010) *Discovering History in China: American Historical Writing on the Recent Chinese Past*. New York: Columbia University Press.

Congressional Executive Commission on China (CECC) (2005) 'Uighur Author Sentenced to Prison for "Inciting Splittism"' (Available at: www.cecc.gov/pages/virtualAcad/index.phpd?showsingle=6759), 10 February [Last accessed: 01/09/18].

Constitution of the People's Republic of China (2004). Beijing: Foreign Languages Press.

Cox, Robert (1981) 'Social Forces, States, and World Orders: Beyond International Relations Theory', *Millennium*, 10(2): 126–155.

(2000) 'Thinking about Civilizations', *Review of International Studies*, 26: 217–234.

Da, Wei (2010) *Shei shi Zhongguo Ren?* ('Who Is Chinese?'). Changsha: Hunan Renmin Chubanshe ('Hunan People's Publishing Press').

Darby, Phillip (1998) *The Fiction of Imperialism: Reading between International Relations and Postcolonialism*. London: Cassell.

(2004) 'Pursuing the Political: A Postcolonial Rethinking of Relations International', *Millennium*, 33(1): 1–32.

Darby, Phillip and Paolini, A. J. (1994) 'Bridging International Relations and Postcolonialism', *Alternatives*, 19: 371–397.

Dautcher, Jay (2009) *Down a Narrow Road: Identity and Masculinity in a Uyghur Community in Xinjiang China*. Cambridge, MA: Harvard University Press.

Davies, Gloria (2009) *Worrying about China – The Language of Chinese Critical Enquiry*. Cambridge, MA: Harvard University Press.

Davies, Norman (1997) *Europe: A History*. London: Pimlico.

Dawut, Rahila (2007) 'Shrine Pilgrimage and Sustainable Tourism among the Uyghurs: Central Asian Ritual Traditions in the Context of China's Development Policies' in Bellér-Hann, I. et al. (eds) *Situating the Uyghurs between China and Central Asia*. Aldershot: Ashgate.

De Carvalho, Benjamin, Leira, Halvard, and Hobson, John (2011) 'The Big Bangs of IR: The Myths That Your Teachers Still Tell You about 1648 and 1919', *Millennium*, 39(3): 735–758.

Deng, Xiaoping (1953) 'Jiejue Minzu Wenti de Jichu shi Jingji' ('The Economy Is Foundation of Resolving the *Minzu* Problem') in Zhonggong Zhongyang Wenxian Yanjiushi ('CCP Central Committee Document Research Office') (ed) (2010) *Xinjiang Gonzuo Wenxian Xuanbian (Xinjiang Work – Selected Documents)*. Beijing: Zhongyang Wenxian Chubanshe ('CCP Central Committee Party Literature Publishing House'), pp.104–105.

et al. (1953) 'Guanyu Shenpi Xinjiang Minzu Quyu Zizhi Shishi Jihua Cao'an de Liang fen Baogao' ('2 Reports Regarding the Implementation of the Plans for Xinjiang Regional Autonomy') in Zhonggong Zhongyang Wenxian Yanjiushi ('CCP Central Committee Document Research Office') (ed) (2010) *Xinjiang Gonzuo Wenxian Xuanbian (Xinjiang Work – Selected Documents)*. Beijing: Zhongyang Wenxian Chubanshe ('CCP Central Committee Party Literature Publishing House'), pp.97–101.

(1979) 'Cujin ge Minzu Gongtong Fanrong' ('Promoting Common Prosperity for All *Minzu*') in Zhonggong Zhongyang Wenxian Yanjiushi ('CCP Central Committee Document Research Office') (ed) (2010) *Xinjiang Gonzuo Wenxian Xuanbian (Xinjiang Work – Selected Documents)*. Beijing: Zhongyang Wenxian Chubanshe ('CCP Central Committee Party Literature Publishing House'), pp.244–245.

Di Cosmo, Nicola (2002) *Ancient China and Its Enemies: The Rise of Nomadic Power in East Asian History*. Cambridge: Cambridge University Press.

Dillon, Michael (2002) *Xinjiang: China's Muslim Far North West*. London: Routledge Curzon.

Dikötter, Frank (1994) 'Racial Identities in China: Context and Meaning', *The China Quarterly*, 138: 404–412.

Doty, Roxanne (2000) 'Desire All the Way Down', *Review of International Studies*, 26: 137–139.

Doty, Roaxanne Lynn (1996) *Imperial Encounters: The Politics of North-South Relations*. Minneapolis: University of Minnesota Press.

Duara, Prasenjit (1988) *Culture, Power, and the State*. Stanford: Stanford University Press.

(1995) *Rescuing History from the Nation: Questioning Narratives of Modern China*. London: University of Chicago Press.

(1998) 'The Regime of Authenticity: Timelessness, Gender, and National History in Modern China', *History and Theory*, 37(3): 287–308.

(2009) *The Global and Regional in China's Nation-Formation*. Routledge: London.

Dwyer, Arienne M (2005) 'The Xinjiang Conflict: Uyghur Identity, Language, Policy, and Political Discourse', *East-West Center Policy Studies*, 15.

East Turkestan Information Center (ETIC) (Available at: www.uygur.org/) [Last accessed: 09/07/19].

Economist, The (2008) 'The Second Long March' (www.economist.com/node/12758848), 11 December [Last accessed: 01/12/18].

Elliot, Mark (2001) *The Manchu Way: The Eight Banners and Ethnic Identity in Late Imperial China*. Stanford: Stanford University Press.

(2011) '*Hushuo*: The Northern Other and Han Ethnogenesis' in Mullaney, Thomas S. et al. (eds) *Critical Han Studies: The History, Representation, and Identity of China's Majority*. Berkeley: University of California Press.

Engels, Friedrich (1884/2010) *The Origin of the Family, Private Property, and the State*. London: Penguin Books.

Enloe, Cynthia (1990) *Bananas, Beaches, and Bases: Making Feminist Sense of International Politics*. Berkeley: University of California Press.

(2000) *Maneuvers: The International Politics of Militarizing Women's Lives*. Berkeley: University of California Press.

Ethnic Unity Education Board (EUAB) (2009) *Minzu Lilun Changshi* ('Common Knowledge of Ethnic Theory'). Beijing: Central Television and Broadcasting Publishing House.

Fairbank, John (ed) (1968) *The Chinese World Order*. Cambridge, MA: Harvard University Press.

Fairbank, John and Goldman, Merle (2006) *China: A New History*. Cambridge, MA: Harvard University Press.

Fanon, Frantz (2001) *Wretched of the Earth*. London: Penguin Books.

Fan, Wenlan (1954) 'Shilun Zhongguo zi Qin-Han shi Chengwei Tongyi Guojia de Yuanyin' ('Analysis of the Reasons China Became a Unified Nation during the Qin-Han Period') in Peng, Wulin et al. (eds) (2013) *Zhongguo Jindai Minzushi Yanjiu Wenxian (Research Documents on Modern China's Ethnic History)*. Beijing: Shehui Kexue Wenxian Chubanshe ('Social Science Academic Press'), pp.3–14.

Fei, Xiaotong (1980) 'Guanyu Woguo Minzu Shibie Wenti' ('On China's Ethnic Classification Project'), in *Zhongguo Shehui Kexue (Social Sciences in China)*, 1.

(1988) 'Plurality and Unity in the Configuration of the Chinese People', *Tanner Lectures on Human Values*, 15 & 17 November (Available at: https://tannerlectures.utah.edu/_documents/a-to-z/f/fei90.pdf) [Last accessed: 19/09/19].

Feng, Jianyong and Aney, Adil (2009) 'Build a Bridge that Binds Workers of All Hues', *China Daily*, 3 September.

Fiskesjö, Magnus. 2017. 'The Legacy of the Chinese Empires: Beyond "the West and the Rest"'. *Education About Asia*, 22(1): 6–10.

Fletcher, Joseph (1978) 'Ch'ing Inner Asia c.1800' in Fairbank, John (ed) *The Cambridge History of China*, vol. 10, *Late Ch'ing, 1800–1911*, pt. 1, Cambridge: Cambridge University Press.

Forbes, Andrew (1986) *Warlords and Muslims in Chinese Central Asia*. Cambridge: Cambridge University Press.

Foreign Correspondent's Club of China (FCCC) (2009a) 'TV Crew Detained in Urumqi' (Available at: www.fccchina.org/2009/07/06/tv-crew-detained-in-urumqi/), 6 July [Last accessed: 22/06/19].

(2009b) 'Reporter in Urumqi Shoved into Van' (Available at: www.fccchina.org/2009/07/07/reporter-in-urumqi-shoved-into-van/), 7 July [Last accessed: 22/06/19].

(2009c) 'China Must Stop Harassing Reporters in Xinjiang' (Available at: www.fccchina.org/2009/07/07/china-must-stop-harassing-reporters-in-xinjiang/), 7 July [Last accessed: 22/06/19].

(2009d) 'China Should Allow Reporters Free Movement in Xinjiang' (Available at: www.fccchina.org/2009/07/11/china-should-allow-reporters-free-movement-in-xinjiang/), 11 July [Last accessed: 22/06/19].

(2009e) 'Open Letter on Reporting Conditions in Xinjiang' 20 July (Available at: www.fccchina.org/2009/07/20/open-letter-on-reporting-conditions-in-xinjiang/) [Last accessed: 22/06/19].

(2009f) 'Urumqi Police Seize Cameras during Protest' (Available at: www.fccchina.org/2009/09/04/urumqi-police-seize-cameras-during-protest/), 4 September [Last accessed: 22/06/19].

(2009g) 'Urumqi Armed Police Beat Journalists, Confiscate Tapes' (Available at: www.fccchina.org/2009/09/04/urumqi-armed-police-beat-journalists-confiscate-tapes/), 4 September [Last accessed: 22/06/19].

(2009h) 'Urumqi Paramilitary Beat Journalists, Damage Gear' (Available at: www.fccchina.org/2009/09/05/urumqi-paramilitary-beat-journalists-damage-gear/), 5 September [Last accessed: 22/06/19].

(2009i) 'FCCC Condemns Beating of Journalists in Urumqi' (Available at: www.fccchina.org/2009/09/05/fccc-condemns-beating-of-journalists-in-urumqi/), 5 September [Last accessed: 22/06/19].

Foucault, Michel (1991/1976) *The Will to Knowledge*. Volume 1 of *The History of Sexuality*. London: Penguin Books.

Franks, Mary Anne (2003) 'Obscene Undersides: Women and Evil between the Taliban and the United States', *Hypatia*, 18(1): 135–156.

Fravel, Taylor (2005) 'Regime Insecurity and International Cooperation: Explaining China's Compromises in Territorial Disputes', *International Security*, 30(2): 46–83.

(2007) 'Power Shifts and Escalation: Explaining China's Use of Force in Territorial Disputes', *International Security*, 32(3): 44–83.

Freeman, Charles W. and Wen Jin Yuan (2012) 'The Influence and Illusion of China's New Left', *The Washington Quarterly*, 35(1): 65–82.

Freemuse (2019) 'China: Sanubar Tursun, Voice of the Uyghurs, Missing Presumed Detained in Xinjiang's Internment Camps' (Available at: https://freemuse.org/news/china-sanubar-tursun-voice-of-the-uyghurs-missing-presumed-detained-in-xinjiangs-internment-camps/), 8 February [Last accessed: 23/07/19].

Friederich, Michael (2007) 'Uyghur Literary Representations of Xinjiang Realities' in Bellér-Hann, I. et al. (eds) *Situating the Uyghurs between China and Central Asia*. Aldershot: Ashgate, pp.89–108

Fukuyama, Francis (1989) 'The End of History', *National Interest*, 16: 3–18.

Fuller, Graham and Lipman, Jonathan (2004) 'Islam in Xinjiang', in Starr, S. F. (ed) *Xinjiang: China's Muslim Borderland*. New York: M. E. Sharpe, pp.320–352.

Gaubatz, Piper Rae (1996) *Beyond the Great Wall: Urban Form and Transformation on the Chinese Frontier*. Stanford: Stanford University Press.

Geertz, Clifford (1973) *The Interpretation of Cultures: Selected Essays by Clifford Geertz*. New York: Basic Books.

(1980) *Negara: The Theatre-State in Nineteenth-Century Bali*. Princeton, NJ: Princeton University Press.

Gellner, Ernest (1996) 'The Nation: Real or Imagined?', *Nations and Nationalism*, 2(3): 357–370.

(2006) *Nations and Nationalism*. Oxford: Wiley-Blackwell.

Gladney, Dru (1990) 'The Ethnogenesis of the Uighur', *Central Asian Survey*, 9(1): 1–28.

(1996) *Muslim Chinese: Ethnic Nationalism in the People's Republic*. Cambridge, MA: Harvard University Press.

(2004) *Dislocating China: Muslims, Minorities, and Other Subaltern Subjects*, London: Hirst & Co.

Global Times (2009) 'Xinjiang Migrant Labour-Plan Combats Poverty' (Available at: http://china.globaltimes.cn/chinanews/2009-07/448670.html), 20 July [Last accessed: 11/06/19].

Gold, Thomas B (1989) 'Guerilla Interviewing among the Getihu' in Link, Perry et al. (eds) *Unofficial China: Popular Culture and Thought in the People's Republic*. Boulder, CO: Westview Press, pp.175–192.

Goldstein, Avery (2001) 'The Diplomatic Face of China's Grand Strategy: A Rising Power's Emerging Choice', *The China Quarterly*, 168: 835–864.

Gong, Yufeng (2009) 'Xinjiang: A Fairyland Ever and Forever' (Available at: http://eg.china-embassy.org/eng/rdwt/gert2444/t575748.htm), 28 July [Last accessed: 14/01/19].

Goodman, David (2002) 'The Politics of the West: Equality, Nation-Building and Colonisation', *Provincial China*, 7(2): 127–150.

—— (2004) 'The Campaign to "Open Up the West": National, Provincial-Level, and Local Perspectives', *The China Quarterly*, 178: 317–334.

Gramsci, Antonio (1935) *Selections from Cultural Writings* in Forgacs, David (ed) (1999) *The Antonio Gramsci Reader: Selected Writings 1916–1935*. London: Lawrence and Wishart.

Gries, Peter Hays (2004) 'Popular Nationalism and State Legitimation in China' in Gries, Peter Hays and Rosen, Stanley (eds) *State and Society in Twenty-first Century China: Crisis, Contention, and Legitimation*. London: Routledge, pp.180–194.

Grovogui, Siba N (2001) 'Come to Africa: A Hermeneutics of Race in International Theory', *Alternatives*, 26(4): 425–448.

Guardian, The (2012) 'China Steps Up Campaign against Ramadan in Xinjiang' (Available at: www.guardian.co.uk/world/2012/aug/03/china-restriction-ramadan-xinjiang-uighurs), 3 August [Last accessed: 23/10/18].

—— (2014) 'Chinese Authorities Offer Cash for Inter-ethnic Marriages' (Available at: (www.theguardian.com/world/2014/sep/02/chinese-authorties-cash-inter-ethnic-marriages-uighur-minority), 2 September [Last accessed: 23/07/19].

—— (2018) 'My Soul, Where Are You? Families of Muslims Missing in China Meet Wall of Silence' (Available at: www.theguardian.com/world/2018/sep/13/uighur-xinjiang-family-missing-china-kazakhstan), 13 September [Last accessed: 23/07/19].

—— (2019) 'Fears for Uighur Comedian Missing Amid Crackdown on Cultural Figures' (Available at: www.theguardian.com/world/2019/feb/22/xinjiang-fears-for-uihgur-comedian-missing-amid-crackdown-on-cultural-figures), 22 February [Last accessed: 23/07/19].

Hao, Shiyuan (2012) 'Zhongguo Minzu Zhengce de Hexin Yuanze bu rong Gaibian' ('China's Ethnic Minority Policies are not Easy to Improve'). *Zhongguo Gongchandang Xinwen Wang* (*Chinese Communist Party News Online*) (Available at: http://theory.people.com.cn/GB/17106132.html). 14 February [Last accessed: 24/08/17].

Harrell, Stevan (1990) 'Ethnicity, Local Interests, and the State', *Comparative Studies in Society and History*, 32(3): 515–548.

—— (1995) 'Introduction: Civilizing Projects and the Reaction to Them', in Harrell, Stevan (ed) *Cultural Encounters on China's Frontiers*. Seattle: University of Washington Press.

Harris, Rachel (2001) 'Cassettes, Bazaars and Saving the Nation: The Uyghur Music Industry in Xinjiang, China' in Craig, Tim and King, Richard (eds) *Global Goes Local: Popular Culture in Asia*. Vancouver: University of British Columbia Press, pp.265–283.

(2005) 'Wang Luobin: Folk Song King of the Northwest or Song Thief? Copyright, Representation, and Folk Songs', *Modern China*, 31: 381–408.

(2008) *The Making of a Musical Canon on Chinese Central Asia: The Uygur Twelve Muqam*. Ashgate: Aldershot.

(2011) 'Invitation to a Mourning Ceremony: Perspectives on the Uyghur Internet', *Inner Asia*, 13(1): 27–49.

Harrison, Henrietta (2000) *The Making of the Republican Citizen: Political Ceremonies and Symbols in China, 1911–1929*, Oxford: Oxford University Press.

Hechter, Michael (1975) *Internal Colonialism: The Celtic Fringe in British National Development*. Berkeley: University of California Press.

Hershatter, Gail (1993) 'The Subaltern Talks Back: Reflections on Subaltern Theory and Chinese History', *Positions*, 1(1): 103–130.

Hess, Steve (2009) 'Dividing and Conquering the Shop Floor: Uyghur Labour Export and Labour Segmentation in China's Industrial East', *Central Asian Survey*, 28(4): 403–416.

Hobsbawm, Eric J. (1990) *Nations and Nationalism since 1780: Programme, Myth, Reality*. Cambridge: Cambridge University Press.

Hobson, John (2007) 'Is Critical Theory Always for the White West and Western Imperialism? Beyond Westphillian towards a Post-racist IR', *Review of International Studies*, 33: 91–116.

Hu, Angang (2012) *Zhongguo 2020: Yige Xinxing Chaoji Daguo* ('China in 2020: A New Type of Superpower'). Zhejiang: Zhejiang Renmin Chubanshe ('Zhejiang People's Press').

Hu, Angang and Hu, Lianhe (2012) 'Di Er Dai Minzu Zhengce: Cujin Minzu Jiaorong Yiti he Fanhua Yiti' ('The Second Generation of *Minzu* Policies: Promoting *Minzu* Fusion and Prosperity in an Organic Whole') (Available at: www.mzb.com.cn/html/Home/report/293093-1.htm), 10 April [Last accessed: 24/08/18].

Hu, Jintao (2006) 'Zuohao Xinshiqi Minzu Gongzuo he Zongjiao Gongzuo' ('Doing good Minzu work and religious work in the new period') in Zhonggong Zhongyang Wenxian Yanjiushi ('CCP Central Committee Document Research Office') (ed) (2010) *Xinjiang Gonzuo Wenxian Xuanbian (Xinjiang Work – Selected Documents)*. Beijing: Zhongyang Wenxian Chubanshe ('CCP Central Committee Party Literature Publishing House'), pp.632–637.

(2007) 'Hold High the Great Banner of Socialism with Chinese Characteristics and Strive for New Victories in Building a Moderately Prosperous Society in All Respects: Report to the Seventeenth National Congress of the Communist Party of China on October 15, 2007' in *Documents of the Seventeenth National Congress of the Communist Party of China*. Beijing: Foreign Languages Press, pp.1–73.

(2009) 'Hu Jintao Zhute Zhongyang Zhengzhiju Changwu Weiyuan Huiyi Yanjiu Buzhi Weihu Xinjiang Shehui Wending Gongzuo' in Xinjiang Uyghur Autonomous Region Party Commission Ministry of Information (eds) *Jiaqiang Minzu Tuanjie, Weihu Xinjiang Wending: Xuanchuan Jiaoyu Cailiao Yi (Strengthening Ethnic Unity, Protecting Xinjiang Stability: Information Education Materials No. 1)*. Wulumuqi: Xinjiang People's Publishing Press.

Hughes, Christopher (2006) *Chinese Nationalism in the Global Era*. Routledge: London.
Human Rights Watch (HRW) (2009a) '"We Are Afraid to Even Look for Them": Enforced Disappearances in the Wake of Xinjiang's Protests' (Available at: www.hrw.org/sites/default/files/reports/xinjiang1009webwcover.pdf), 1 October [Last accessed: 16/06/18].
(2009b) 'China: Forcibly Returned Uighur Asylum Seekers at Risk' (Available at: www.hrw.org/news/2009/12/22/china-forcibly-returned-uighur-asylum-seekers-risk), 22 December [Last accessed: 20/06/18].
Human Rights Watch (HRW) (2011) 'China: Account for Forcibly Returned Uighurs' (Available at: www.hrw.org/news/2011/09/02/china-account-forcibly-returned-uighurs), 2 September [Last accessed: 20/06/18].
(2018) 'Eradicating Ideological Viruses' (Available at: www.hrw.org/report/2018/09/09/eradicating-ideological-viruses/chinas-campaign-repression-against-xinjiangs), 9 September [Last accessed: 23/07/19].
(2019) 'How Mass Surveillance Works in Xinjiang, China' (Available at: www.hrw.org/video-photos/interactive/2019/05/02/china-how-mass-surveillance-works-xinjiang) 2 May [Last accessed: 23/07/19].
Hunan Dianshitai (HunanTelevision) (2009) *Baqian Xiang Nu Shang Tianshan* ('8,000 Flowers Go Up the Mountain'), DVD. Hunan: Hunan Dianshita('Hunan Television').
Huntington, Samuel P (1996) *The Clash of Civilizations and the Remaking of World Order*. Touchstone: New York.
Jacobs, Justin (2008) 'How Turkestan Became Chinese: Visualising Zhang Zhizong's Tian Shan Pictorial and Xinjiang Youth Song and Dance Troupe', *The Journal of Asian Studies*, 47(2): 545–591.
(2016) *Xinjiang and the Modern Chinese State*. Seattle: University of Washington Press.
Jianfei, Jia (2011) 'Whose Xinjiang? The Transition in Chinese Intellectuals' Imagination of the "New Dominion" During the Qing Dynasty', *Harvard-Yenching Institute Working Paper Series*.
Jian, Bozan (1960) 'Guanyu Chuli Zhongguoshi shang de Minzu Guanxi Wenti' ('On the Question of How to Deal with *Minzu* Relations throughout Chinese History') in Peng, Wulin et al. (eds) (2013) *Zhongguo Jindai Minzushi Yanjiu Wenxian (Research Documents on Modern China's Ethnic History)*. Beijing: Shehui Kexue Wenxian Chubanshe ('Social Science Academic Press'), pp.14–31.
Ikenberry, John (2014) 'The Rise of China and the Future of Liberal World Order' (Available at: https://www.chathamhouse.org/sites/default/files/field/field_document/20140507RiseofChina.pdf), Chatham House Lecture [Last accessed: 12/03/20].
Independent, The (2012) '12 Children Hurt as China Police Raid Religious School' (Available at: www.independent.co.uk/news/world/asia/12-children-hurt-as-china-police-raid-religious-school-7820183.html), 6 June [Last accessed: 23/10/18].
Jarvis, Lee and Lister, Michael (2013) 'Vernacular Securities and Their Study: A Qualitative Analysis and Research Agenda', *International Relations*, 27(2): 158–179.
Jiang, Zemin (1990a) 'Guanyu Jinyibu Wending Bianjiang Minzu Diqu de Jidian Qingkuang he Yijian' ('A Few Situations and Suggestions Regarding the Progress

Bibliography

of Stabilising Frontier Minority Regions') in Zhonggong Zhongyang Wenxian Yanjiushi ('CCP Central Committee Document Research Office') (ed) (2010) *Xinjiang Gonzuo Wenxian Xuanbian (Xinjiang Work – Selected Documents)*. Beijing: Zhongyang Wenxian Chubanshe ('CCP Central Committee Party Literature Publishing House'), pp.303–308.

(1990b) 'Ba Xinjiang Shehui zhuyi Jianshe he Gaige Shiye Buduan Tuixiang Qianjin' ('The Unceasing Progress of the Mission of Socialist Building and Reform in Xinjiang') in Zhonggong Zhongyang Wenxian Yanjiushi ('CCP Central Committee Document Research Office') (ed) (2010) *Xinjiang Gonzuo Wenxian Xuanbian (Xinjiang Work – Selected Documents)*. Beijing: Zhongyang Wenxian Chubanshe ('CCP Central Committee Party Literature Publishing House'), pp.315–338.

Johnston, Alastair Iain (1995) *Cultural Realism: Strategic Culture and Grand Strategy in Chinese History*. Princeton, NJ: Princeton University Press.

(2003) 'Is China a Status Quo Power?', *International Security*, 27(4): 5–56.

Kaldor, Mary (2006) *New and Old Wars*. Redwood City, CA: Stanford University Press.

Kamalov, A. (2007) 'The Uyghurs as Part of Central Asian Commonality: Soviet Historiography on the Uyghurs' in Bellér-Hann, I. et al. (eds) *Situating the Uyghurs between China and Central Asia*. Aldershot: Ashgate.

Kardos, Amy (2010) 'A Rock and a Hard Place: Chinese Soldiers in Xinjiang Caught between Centre and Periphery After 1949', in Cochran, S. and Pickowicz, P. G. (eds) *China on the Margins*. Honolulu: University of Hawai'i Press, pp.135–157.

Kerr, David (2011) 'Paradoxes of Tradition and Modernity at the New Frontier: China, Islam, and the Problem of "Different Heavens"' in Callahan, William A. and Barabantseva, Elena (eds) *China Orders the World: Normative Soft Power and Foreign Policy*. Washington, DC: Woodrow Wilson Center Press, pp.143–179.

Krishna, Sankaran (1999) *Postcolonial Insecurities: India, Sri Lanka, and the Question of Nationhood*. Minneapolis: University of Minnesota Press.

Lam, Willy (2009) 'The Xinjiang Crisis: A Test for Beijing's Carrot-and-Stick Strategy', *China Brief*, 9(15). (Available at: www.jamestown.org/programs/chinabrief/single/?tx_ttnews%5Btt_news%5D=35307&tx_ttnews%5BbackPid%5D=459&no_cache=1) [Last accessed: 06/12/18].

Laogai Research Foundation (2008) *Laogai Handbook*. Washington DC: Laogai Research Foundation.

Leibold, James (2007) *Reconfiguring Chinese Nationalism: How the Qing Frontier and Its Indigenes Became Chinese*. New York: Palgrave.

(2010) 'The Beijing Olympics and China's Conflicted National Form', *The China Journal*, 63: 1–24.

(2012a) 'Can China Have a Melting Pot?' (Available at: http://thediplomat.com/china-power/can-china-have-a-melting-pot/), *The Diplomat*, 23 May [Last accessed: 11/07/18].

(2013) 'Ethnic Policy in China: Is Reform Inevitable?' (Available at: www.eastwestcenter.org/sites/default/files/private/ps068.pdf), *East-West Center Policy Studies*, 68 [Last accessed: 20/09/19].

Lewis, Bernard (1990) 'The Roots of Muslim Rage' (Available at: www.theatlantic.com/magazine/archive/1990/09/the-roots-of-muslim-rage/304643/), *The Atlantic*, September [Last accessed: 15/01/18].

Li, Dezhu (2007) 'Guojia Minwei Zhuren Li Dezhu Zai Quanguo Minwei Zhuren Huiyishang de Jianghua' ('National Commission for Ethnic Affairs Chairman Li Dezhu's Speech at the 2007 National Commission for Ethnic Affairs Conference') (Available at: http://news.sohu.com/20071229/n254377534.shtml) [Last accessed: 03/06/19].

Li, Sheng (2006) *'Dong Tujuesitan' Fenliezhuyi de Youlai yu Fazhan (The Origins and Development of 'East Turkestan' Separatism)*. Wulumuqi: Xinjiang People's Press.

Liu, Shaoqi (1954) 'Guanyu Minzu Quyu Zizhi Wenti' ('Regarding the Problem of Ethnic Regional Autonomy'), in Zhonggong Zhongyang Wenxian Yanjiushi ('CCP Central Committee Party Document Research Office') (ed) (2010) *Xinjiang Gonzuo Wenxian Xuanbian (Xinjiang Work – Selected Documents)*. Beijing: Zhongyang Wenxian Chubanshe ('CCP Central Committee Party Literature Publishing House'), pp.118–122.

Ma, Dazheng (2004) 'Xinjiang Lishi Yanjiu zhong de jige Wenti' ('Several Problems in Researching Xinjiang History'), *Xiyu Yanjiu (Western Regions Research)*, 2: 1–14.

— (2006) *Xinjijang Shijian (Reflections on Xinjiang History)*. Wulumuqi: Xinjiang Renmin Chubanshe ('Xinjiang People's Press').

Ma, Rong (2007) 'A New Perspective in Guiding Ethnic Relations in the 21st Century: "Depoliticization" of Ethnicity in China', *Asian Ethnicity*, 8(3): 199–217.

— (2009) 'The Development of Minority Education and the Practice of Bilingual Education in Xinjiang Uyghur Autonomous Region', *Frontier Education China*, 4(2): 188–251.

— (2010) 'Hanhua hai shi Xiandaihua' ('Hanification Is Still Modernisation') (Available at: www.21ccom.net/articles/zgyj/ggzhc/article_2010121726544 .html), *Gongshi Wang* ('Consensus Net'), 17 December [Last accessed: 13/07/18].

— (2018) 'Xi Jinping TongzhiJinqi Jianghua Zhudao Woguo Minzu Gongzuo de Fangxiang' ('Comrade Xi Jinping Guides the Direction of Our Country's *Minzu* Policy'), *Journal of the Central Institute of Socialism*, 3(213): 121–126.

Mahmut, Rahima (2020) *Surveillance and Repression of Muslim Minorities: Xinjiang and Beyond*, Conference presentation, SOAS (Available at: https://www.youtube .com/watch?v=rRgUg2P-l3I), 7 March [Last accessed: 28/03/20].

Mao, Zedong (1923) 'The Cigarette Tax' (Available at: www.marxists.org/reference/ archive/mao/selected-works/volume-6/mswv6_08.htm) [Last accessed: 29/05/18].

— (1926) 'Analysis of the Classes in Chinese Society' (Available at: www.marxists.org/ reference/archive/mao/selected-works/volume-1/mswv1_1.htm) [Last accessed: 29/05/18].

— (1937) 'On Contradiction' (Available at: www.marxists.org/reference/archive/mao/ selected-works/volume-1/mswv1_17.htm) [Last accessed: 29/05/18].

— (1949) 'Zhonggong Zhongyang Guanyu Xinjiang Wenti gei Peng Dehui de Dianbao' ('A Telegram from the CCP Central Committee to Peng Dehui Regarding the Xinjiang Problem') in Zhonggong Zhongyang Wenxian Yanjiushi ('CCP Central Committee Document Research Office') (ed) (2010) *Xinjiang Gonzuo Wenxian Xuanbian (Xinjiang Work – Selected Documents)*. Beijing: Zhongyang Wenxian Chubanshe ('CCP Central Committee Party Literature Publishing House'), pp.21–22.

(1956) 'Hanzu he Shaoshu Minzu de Guanxi' ('Relations between Han and *Shaoshu Minzu*') in Zhonggong Zhongyang Wenxian Yanjiushi ('CCP Central Committee Document Research Office') (ed) (2010) *Xinjiang Gonzuo Wenxian Xuanbian (Xinjiang Work – Selected Documents)*. Beijing: Zhongyang Wenxian Chubanshe ('CCP Central Committee Party Literature Publishing House'), pp.142–143.

Marx, Karl (1869/1963) *The Eighteenth Brumaire of Louis Bonaparte*. New York: International Publishers.

Mattern, Janice Bially (2005) 'Why "Soft Power" Isn't So Soft: Representational Force and the Sociolinguistic Construction of Attraction in World Politics', *Millennium*, 33(3): 583–612.

Mauk, Ben (2019) 'Weather Reports: Voices from Xinjiang' (Available at: https://believermag.com/weather-reports-voices-from-xinjiang/) [Last accessed: 09/04/2020].

McMillen, Donald H. (1979) *Chinese Communist Power and Policy in Xinjiang, 1949–1977*. Boulder, CO: Westview Press.

Mearsheimer, John J. (2010) The Gathering Storm: China's Challenge to US Power in Asia, *Chinese Journal of International Politics*, 3(4): 381–396.

Millward, James A. (1994) 'A Uyghur Muslim in Qianlong's Court: The Meaning of the Fragrant Concubine', *The Journal of Asian Studies*, 53(2): 427–458.

(1996) 'New Perspectives on the Qing Frontier' in Hershatter, Gail et al. (eds) *Remapping China: Fissures in Historical Terrain*. Stanford: Stanford University Press, pp.113–129.

(2004) 'Violent Separatism in Xinjiang: A Critical Assessment', *Policy Studies* 6. Washington, DC: East-West Center.

Millward, James A. (2005) 'Uyghur Art Music and the Ambiguities of Chinese Silk Roadism in Xinjiang', *Silk Road*, 3(1) (Available at: www.silk-road.com/newsletter/vol3num1/3_uyghur.php) [Last accessed: 13/04/19].

(2007) *Eurasian Crossroads: A History of Xinjiang*. London: Hurst and Company.

(2009a) 'Positioning Xinjiang in Eurasian and Chinese History: Differing Visions of the "Silk Road"' in Mackerras, Colin and Clarke, Michael (eds) *China, Xinjiang, and Central Asia: History, Transition, and Crossborder Interaction into the Twenty-first Century*. London: Routledge, pp.55–74.

(2009b) 'Does the Urumchi Violence Mark a Turning Point?', *Central Asian Survey*, 28(4): 347–360.

Millward, James A. and Perdue, Peter (2004) '*Political and Cultural History of the Xinjiang Region through the Late 19th Century*' in Starr, S. F. (ed) *Xinjiang: China's Muslim Borderland*. New York: M. E. Sharpe, pp.27–62.

Ministry of Foreign Affairs (MFA) (2014) 'The Central Conference on Work Relating to Foreign Affairs Was Held in Beijing' (Available at: https://www.fmprc.gov.cn/mfa_eng/zxxx_662805/t1215680.shtml), 29 November [Last accessed: 12/03/20].

Ministry of Information (MOI) (2008) *Kexue Fazhanguan Xuexi Duben (Scientific Development Outlook Study Guide)*. Beijing: Xuexi Chubanshe ('Study Press').

Ministry of Information, Theoretical Department (MOI TD) (2009a) *Liuge Weishenme: Dui Jige Zhongda Wenti de Huida (The Six Whys: Answers to Some Huge Questions)*. Beijing: Xuexi Chubanshe ('Study Press').

(2009b) *Lilun Redian Mianduimian (Face-to-Face Hot Theory Topics)*. Beijing: Renmin Chubanshe ('People's Publishing Press').

Ministry of Information, Education Department (MOI ED) (2009) *Minzu Tuanjie Jiaoyu: Tongsu Duben* (*Ethnic Unity Education: Basic Study Guide*). Beijing: Xuexi Chubanshe ('Study Press').

Mitter, Rana (2004) *A Bitter Revolution: China's Struggle with the Modern World*. Oxford: Oxford University Press.

Moore, Malcolm (2009) 'Xinjiang Protests: Han Chinese Demand Better Security after Syringe Attacks in Urumqi' (Available at: www.telegraph.co.uk/news/worldnews/asia/china/6131874/Xinjiang-protests-Han-Chinese-demand-better-security-after-syringe-attacks-in-Urumqi.html), *The Daily Telegraph*, 3 September [Last accessed: 22/06/18].

Morgan, Lewis (1944/2005) *Ancient Society*. New York: Adamant Media Corporation.

Morgenthau, Hans J. (1948) *Politics among Nations: The Struggle for Power and Peace*. New York: McGraw-Hill.

Mullaney, Thomas S. (2011) *Coming to Terms with the Nation: Ethnic Classification in Modern China*. Berkeley: University of California Press.

National Development and Reform Commission (NDRC) (2015) *Vision and Actions on Jointly Developing Silk Road Economic Belt and Twenty-first-Century Maritime Silk Road* (Available at: http://english.www.gov.cn/archive/publications/2017/06/20/content_281475691873460.htm), 20 June [Last accessed: 12/03/20].

National People's Congress Changwu Weiyuanhui (NPC) (2001) *Zhonghua Renmin Gonghheguo GuojiaTongyong Yuyan Wenzifa* (*The People's Republic of China National Language and Script Law*) (Available at: http://news.xinhuanet.com/legal/2003-01/21/content_699566.htm) [Last accessed: 06/04/19].

New York Times (NYT) (2007) 'Chinese Leave Guantanamo for Albanian Limbo' (Available at: www.nytimes.com/2007/06/10/world/europe/10resettle.html?pagewanted=all), 10 June [Last accessed: 01/09/18].

Newby, Laura J. (1999) 'The Chinese Literary Conquest of Xinjiang', *Modern China*, 25: 451–474.

―― (2005) *The Empire and the Khanate*. Leiden: Brill.

―― (2007) '"Us and Them" in Eighteenth and Nineteenth Century Xinjiang' in Bellér-Hann, I. et al. (eds) *Situating the Uyghurs between China and Central Asia*. Aldershot: Ashgate.

Nordin, Astrid (2012) 'Space for the Future: Exhibiting China in the World at the Shanghai Expo', *China Information*, 26(2): 235–249.

Nyíri, Pál (2005) 'The Yellow Man's Burden: Chinese Migrants on a Civilizing Mission', *The China Journal*, 56: 83–106.

Pakulski, Jan (2016) 'State Violence and the Eliticide in Poland, 1935–49', in Killingsworth, Matt et al. (eds) *Violence and the State*. Manchester: University of Manchester Press, pp.40–62.

Pan, Jiao (ed) (2008a) *Zhongguo Shehui Wenhua Renleixue / Minzuxue Bainian Wenxuan* (*Selected Works of 100 Years of Chinese Social and Cultural Anthropology / Minzu Studies*). Beijing: Zhishi Chanquan Chubanshe ('Intellectual Property Publishing House').

Pan, Jiao (2008b) 'Zuqun Jiqi Xiangguan Gainian zai Xifang de Liubian' ('Ethnicity and Related Concepts in the Later Developments of the West') in Pan, Jiao (ed) *Zhongguo Shehui Wenhua Renleixue / Minzuxue Bainian Wenxuan* (*Selected Works of 100 Years of Chinese Social and Cultural Anthropology / Minzu Studies*).

Beijing: Zhishi Chanquan Chubanshe ('Intellectual Property Publishing House'), pp.83–92.
Pan, Zhiping (1996a) 'Wulumuqi Dutong' ('Urumqi Military Governor') in Yu, Taishan et al. (eds) *Xinjiang Gezu Lishi Wenhua Cidian (Dictionary of History and Culture of Every Xinjiang Minzu)*. Beijing: Zhonghua Shuju Chubanshe ('Zhonghua Book Publishers'), p.51.
 (1996b) 'Hancheng' ('Han City') in Yu, Taishan et al. (eds) *Xinjiang Gezu Lishi Wenhua Cidian (Dictionary of History and Culture of Every Xinjiang Minzu)*. Beijing: Zhonghua Shuju Chuban Chubanshe ('Zhonghua Book Publishers'), p.86.
 (2008) *'Dongtu' de Lishi yu Xianzhuang (The History and Present Situation of 'East Turkestan')*. Beijing: Minzu Chubanshe ('Publishing House of Minority Nationalities').
PBS (2009) 'Tensions Remain High in China Following Deadly Riots' (Available at: www.pbs.org/newshour/bb/asia/july-dec09/china2_07-07.html), 7 July [Last accessed: 24/01/19].
PEN (2013) 'Nurmuhemmet Yasin' (Available at: https://pen.org/advocacy-case/nurmuhemmet-yasin/) [Last accessed: 26/07/19].
People's Daily (2011) 'Xinjiang AIDS Attack Rumour Denied' (Available at: http://english.peopledaily.com.cn/90882/7648910.html), 18 November [Last accessed: 21/06/18].
Perdue, Peter (2005) *China Marches West: The Qing Conquest of Central Eurasia*. Cambridge, MA: Harvard University Press.
 (2015) 'The Tenacious Tributary System', *Journal of Contemporary China* 24(96): 1001–1014.
Prakash, Gyan (1992) 'Postcolonial Criticism and Indian Historiography', *Social Text*, 31/32: 8–19.
 (1995) 'Orientalism Now', *History and Theory*, 34(3): 199–212.
Pye, Lucian (1990) 'Erratic State, Frustrated Society', *Foreign Affairs*, 69(4): 56–74.
Radio Free Asia (RFA) (2009) 'Witnesses Describe Two-Way Violence' (Available at: www.rfa.org/english/news/uyghur/witnesses-07172009121028.html), 17 July [Last accessed: 15/06/18].
 (2010) 'Police Raid Quran Group' (Available at: www.rfa.org/english/news/uyghur/raid-06082010112725.html), 8 June [Last accessed: 24/05/18].
 (2011a) 'Laid-Off Profs Reject Deal' (Available at: www.rfa.org/english/news/uyghur/deal-09272011172719.html), 27/09/2011 [Last accessed: 02/04/18].
 (2011b) 'Deported Uyghurs Face Terrorism Charges' (Available at: www.rfa.org/english/news/uyghur/charges-06142011163646.html), 14 June [Last accessed: 07/08/18].
 (2012a) 'Search for a Missing Son' (Available at: www.rfa.org/english/news/uyghur/search-05112012123934.html), 11 May [Last accessed: 16/06/18].
 (2012b) 'Party Member among Missing' (Available at: www.rfa.org/english/news/uyghur/member-06142012174311.html), 14 June [Last accessed: 16/06/18].
 (2012c) 'Student Battles Travel Ban' (Available at: www.rfa.org/english/news/uyghur/travel-12202012143138.html), 20 December [Last accessed: 13/03/18].
 (2013) 'Two Uyghurs Believed Killed in Hotan Violence' (Available at: www.rfa.org/english/news/uyghur/raid-06082010112725.html), 28 June [Last accessed: 24/05/18].

(2014) 'China Offers Cash for Marriages to Promote Assimilation in Xinjiang' (Available at: https://www.rfa.org/english/news/uyghur/scheme-08292014122418.html), 29 August [Last accessed: 23/07/19].

(2016) 'China Recalls Passports across Xinjiang amid Ongoing Security Crackdown' (Available at: www.rfa.org/english/news/uyghur/xinjiang-passports-10202016144107.html), 20 October [Last accessed: 02/06/17].

(2017) 'Uyghur Village Cadre Dismissed for Holding Islamic Wedding Vows at Home' (Available at: www.rfa.org/english/news/uyghur/weddings-04182017171857.html), 18 April [Last accessed: 24/05/17].

Rapport, Nigel (2002) 'The Truth of Movement, the Truth as Movement: 'Post-cultural Anthropology' and Narrational Identity' in Amit, Vered and Rapport, Nigel (eds) *The Trouble with Community: Anthropological Reflections on Movement, Identity, and Collectivity*. London: Pluto Press.

Rayila, M. (2011) 'The Pain of a Nation: The Invisibility of Uyghurs in China Proper', *The Equal Rights Review*, 6.

Roberts, Sean R. (2004) 'A "Land of Borderlands": Implications of Xinjiang's Transborder Interaction', in Starr, S. F. (ed) *Xinjiang: China's Muslim Borderland*. New York: M. E. Sharpe, pp.216–240.

(2007) 'The Dawn of the East: A Portrait of a Uyghur Community Between China and Kazakhstan', in Bellér-Hann, I. et al. (eds) *Situating the Uyghurs between China and Central Asia*. Aldershot: Ashgate.

(2009) 'Imagining Uyghurstan: Re-Evaluating the Birth of the Modern Uyghur Nation', *Central Asian Survey*, 28(4): 361–381.

(2009b) 'Ethnic Clashes in Xinjiang: Uighurs vs. Han Chinese', *The Washington Post* (Available at: www.washingtonpost.com/wp-dyn/content/discussion/2009/07/07/DI2009070701491.html), 8 July [Last accessed: 11/06/18].

(2012) 'Imaginary Terrorism? The Global War on Terror and the Narrative of the Uyghur Terrorist Threat', *Ponars Eurasia Working Paper*.

Roberts, Sean R. (2018) 'The Biopolitics of China's "War on Terror" and the Exclusion of the Uyghurs', *Critical Asian Studies*, 50(2): 232–258.

Robinson, Cedric (2000) *Black Marxism: The Making of the Black Radical Tradition*. Chapel Hill: University of North Carolina Press.

Roe, Paul (1999) 'The Intrastate Security Dilemma: Ethnic Conflict as a *"Tragedy"*?', *Journal of Peace Research*, 36(2): 183–202.

Ruan, Xihu (2004) 'Minzu Haishi "Zuqun" – Yi "Ethnic Group" Yici de Hanyi' ('Minzu or "Zuqun" – The Implications of Translating "Ethnic Group"'), Guangxi Minzu Xueyuan Xuebao *(*Journal of Guangxi University for Minority Nationalities*)*, 5.

Rudelson, Justin (1997) *Oasis Identities*. New York: Columbia University Press.

Said, Edward W. (1993) *Culture and Imperialism*. New York: Alfred Knopf.

(1997) *Covering Islam*. London: Vintage.

(2003) *Orientalism*. London: Penguin Books.

Sankara, Krishna (2001) 'Race, Amnesia, and the Education of International Relations', *Alternatives*, 26: 401–424.

Sautman, Barry (1997) 'Myths of Descent, Racial Nationalism, and Ethnic Minorities in the People's Republic of China' in Dikotter, F. (ed) The Construction of Racial Identities in China and *Japan*. London: Hurst & Co, pp.75–95.

(1998) 'Preferential Policies for Ethnic Minorities in China: The Case of Xinjiang', *Nationalism and Ethnic Politics*, 4(1): 86–118.
Schein, Louisa (1997) 'Gender and Internal Orientalism in China', *Modern China*, 23(1): 69–98.
(2000) *Minority Rules*. Durham, NC: Duke University Press.
Schluessel, Eric (2007) '"Bilingual" Education and Discontent in Xinjiang, *Central Asian Survey*, 26(2): 251–277.
(2009) 'History, Identity, and Mother-Tongue Education in Xinjiang', *Central Asian Survey*, 29(4): 383–402.
Scholars at Risk Network (2019) 'Rahile Dawut, China' (Available at: https://www.scholarsatrisk.org/actions/rahile-dawut-china/) [Last accessed: 23/07/19].
Scott, James C. (1985) *Weapons of the Weak: Everyday Forms of Peasant Resistance*. New Haven, CT: Yale University Press.
Seth, Sanjay (2011) 'Postcolonial Theory and the Critique of International Relations', *Millennium*, 40(1): 167–183.
Shambaugh, David (1996) 'Containment or Engagement of China? Calculating Beijing's Responses', *International Security*, 21(2): 180–209.
(2013) *China Goes Global: The Partial Power*. Oxford: Oxford University Press.
Shapiro, Michael J. (1988) *The Politics of Representation: Writing Practices in Biography, Photography, and Policy Analysis*. Madison: University of Wisconsin Press.
(1989) 'Textualizing Global Politics' in Shapiro, Michael J. and Der Derian, James (eds) *International/Intertextual Relations: Postmodern Readings of World Politics*. New York: Lexington Books, pp.11–22.
(2004) *Methods and Nations: Cultural Governance and the Indigenous Subject*. New York: Routledge.
Sheehan, Jackie (2009) 'China's Dangerous Dilemma in Xinjiang' (Available at: www.nottingham.ac.uk/cpi/publications/commentaries-reports/2009/sheehan-xinjiang-07-09-2009.aspx), *China Policy Institute*, 9 July [Last accessed: 11/07/18].
Shen, Jianhua (2009) 'Gaoxiao Wending Xingshi Fenxi Ji Duice Sikao' ('Analysis of Measures for an Effective and Stable Situation'), *Xinjiang Shifan Daxue Xuebao (Xinjiang Normal University Journal)*, 30(4): 12–14.
Shijian Bianji Bu (1965) 'Bixu Bawo Minzu Wenti de Jieji Shizhi' ('We Must Grasp the Class Essence of the Minzu Problem') in Pan, Jiao (ed) (2008) *Zhongguo Shehui Wenhua Renleixue / Minzuxue Bainian Wenxuan (Selected Works of 100 Years of Chinese Social and Cultural Anthropology / Minzu Studies)*. Beijing: Zhishi Chanquan Chubanshe ('Intellectual Property Publishing House'), pp.213–221.
Shue, Vivienne (1988) *The Reach of the State: Sketches of the Chinese Body Politic*. Redwood City, CA: Stanford University Press.
(2004) 'Legitimacy Crisis in China?' in Gries, Peter Hays and Rosen, Stanley (eds) *State and Society in Twenty-first-Century China*. New York: Routledge Curzon, pp.24–49.
Shule County Government (2009) 'Zhulao Fangxian Xiandi Shentou, Changzhi jiuan gujiben Shulexian Wucuo bing Jucuo Quebao Yishi Xingtai Lingyu Fanfenlie Douzheng Qude Shixiao' ('A Firm Line of Defence to Resist Infiltration, Ensure Long-Term Peace and Order, and Secure a Foundation. Five Measures of Shule County to Be Carried Out in Order to Ensure Success in the Ideological Fight

against Anti-separatism') (Available at: www.360doc.com/content/11/0512/16/ 6133644_116221536.shtml) [Last Accessed: 29/08/18].
Smith, Anthony D. (1991) *The Ethnic Origins of Nations*. Oxford: Blackwell.
—— (1995) 'Gastronomy or Geology? The Role of Nationalism in the Reconstruction of Nations', *Nations and Nationalism*, 1: 3–23.
Smith, Joanne, N. (1999) 'Changing Uyghur Identities in Xinjiang in the 1990s'. Unpublished PhD diss., University of Leeds.
Smith, Joanne N. (2000) 'Four Generations of Uyghurs: The Shift towards Ethno-Political Ideologies among Xinjiang's Youth', *Inner Asia*, 2: 195–224.
—— (2002) 'Making Culture Matter: Symbolic, Spatial, and Social Boundaries between Uyghurs and Han Chinese', *Asian Ethnicity*, 3(2): 153–174.
—— (2006) 'Maintaining Margins: The Politics of Ethnographic Fieldwork in Chinese Central Asia', *The China Journal*, 56: 131–147.
Smith Finley, Joanne N. (2007) 'Ethnic Anomaly or Modern Uyghur Survivor? A Case Study of the *Minkaohan* Hybrid Identity in Xinjiang' in Bellér-Hann, I. et al. (eds) *Situating the Uyghurs between China and Central Asia*. Aldershot: Ashgate.
—— (2011) 'No Rights without Duties: *Minzu Pingdeng* in Xinjiang since the 1997 Ghulja Disturbances', *Inner Asia*, 13(1): 73–96.
—— (2013) *The Art of Symbolic Resistance: Uyghur Identities and Uyghur-Han Relations in Contemporary Xinjiang*. Leiden: Brill.
Smith, Kristie N. (2006) 'Dance for Development', *East-West Center Working Papers*, No. 25.
Smith, Neil (1996) *The New Urban Frontier: Gentrification and the Revanchist City*. London: Routledge.
South China Morning Post (SCMP) (2014) 'President Xi Jinping Vows Peace, as PLA Top Brass Talks Tough and with Vietnam Ablaze' (Available at: https://www.scmp.com/news/china/article/1514570/president-xi-jinping-vows-peace-pla-top-brass-talks-tough-and-vietnam) 18 May [Last accessed: 23/07/19].
—— (2019) 'China Releases Video of "Dead" Uyghur Poet Abdurehim Heyit but Fails to Silence Critics' (Available at: https://www.scmp.com/news/china/politics/article/2185695/china-releases-video-dead-uygur-poet-abdurehim-heyit-fails) 11 February [Last accessed: 23/07/19].
Spegele, Brian (2011) 'No Foreign Tie Seen in China Attacks' (Available at: http://online.wsj.com/article/SB10001424053111904491704576574412601080364.html) [Last accessed: 30/05/18].
Spence, Jonathan D. (1990) *The Search for Modern China*. New York: W. W. Norton.
Spivak, Gayatri Chakravorty (1988) 'Can the Subaltern Speak?' in Nelson, C. and Grossberg, L. (eds) *Marxism and the Interpretation of Culture*. Basingstoke: Macmillan Education, pp.271–313.
Stalin, Josef (1913/1945) *Marxism and the National Question*. Moscow: Foreign Languages Publishing House.
Starr, Frederick (2004) 'Introduction' in Starr, F. (ed) *Xinjiang: China's Muslim Borderland*. New York: M. E. Sharpe, pp.3–24.
State Council (1950) 'Xinjiangsheng Renmin Zhengfu Weiyuanhui Muqian Shishi Fangzhen' ('Measures for Immediate Implementation by the Party Committee of the Xinjiang Provincial Government') in Zhonggong Zhongyang Wenxian Yanjiushi ('CCP Central Committee Document Research Office') (ed) (2010)

Xinjiang Gonzuo Wenxian Xuanbian (*Xinjiang Work – Selected Documents*). Beijing: Zhongyang Wenxian Chubanshe ('CCP Central Committee Party Literature Publishing House'), pp.45–48.

(2002) 'East Turkestan Forces Cannot Get Away with Impunity' (Available at: http://english.people.com.cn/200201/21/eng20020121_89078.shtml), 21/1/2002 [Last accessed: 29/05/19].

(2003) *Xinjiang de Lishi yu Fazhan* (*The History and Development of Xinjiang*) (Available at: http://english.gov.cn/official/2005-07/28/content_17948.htm). Beijing: Renmin Chubanshe ('People's Publishing Press').

(2006) *Xibu Da Kaifa 'Shiyiwu' Guihua* (*Western Development Project: 11th 5 Year Plan*) (www.chinawesthr.org/html/xiangmuyanjiuyurencaikaifa/zhengcefagui/20081017/40.html) [Last accessed: 10/04/19].

(2009a) *Zhongguo de Minzu Zhengce yu ge Minzu Gongtong Fanrong Fazhan* (*China's Ethnic Minority Policy and the Common Prosperity of all Ethnic Groups*). Beijing: Renmin Chubanshe ('People's Publishing Press').

(2009b) *Xinjiang de Fazhan yu Jinbu* (*The Progress and Development of Xinjiang*). Beijing: Renmin Chubanshe ('People's Publishing Press').

(2019) 'The Fight Against Terrorism and Extremism and Human Rights Protection in Xinjiang' (Available at: www.xinhuanet.com/english/2019-03/18/c_137904166.htm), March [Last accessed: 23/07/19].

State Ethnic Affairs Commission, *Minzu* Problem Research Centre (SEAC) (2009) *Xinjiang Wenhua Zhishi Duben* (*Xinjiang Cultural Knowledge Study Guide*). Beijing: Renmin Chubanshe ('People's Publishing Press').

Steele, Brent J. (2007) *Ontological Security in International Relations: Self-Identity and the IR State*. London: Routledge.

Stevens, Daniel and Vaughan-Williams, Nick (2014) 'Citizens and Security Threats: Issues, Perceptions, and Consequences beyond the National Frame', *British Journal of Political Science*, 46: 149–175.

(2016) 'Vernacular Theories of Everyday (In)Security: The Disruptive Potential of Non-Elite Knowledge', *Security Dialogue*, 47(1): 1–19.

Stewart, Phil (2019) 'China Putting Muslims in "Concentration Camps", US says' (Available at: https://www.reuters.com/article/us-usa-china-concentrationcamps/china-putting-minority-muslims-in-concentration-camps-us-says-idUSKCN1S925K), Reuters, 3 May [Last accessed: 23/07/19].

Szadziewski, Henry (2011) 'Commanding the Economy: The Recurring Patterns of Chinese Central Government Development Planning among Uyghurs in Xinjiang', *Inner Asia*, 13(1): 97–116.

Sylvester, Christine (2013) 'Experiencing the End and Afterlives of International Relations/Theory', *European Journal of International Relations*, 19(3): 609–626.

Taynen, Jennifer (2006) 'Interpreters, Arbiters, or Outsiders: The Role of the Minkaohan in Xinjiang Society', *Journal of Muslim Minority Affairs*, 26(1): 45–62.

Telegraph, The (2019) 'One Minute Felt Like a Year: A Day in the Life of Inmates in the Xinjiang Internment Camps' (Available at: https://www.telegraph.co.uk/news/2019/03/26/dispatch-day-life-inmate-xinjiang-internment-camps/), 26 March [Last accessed: 23/07/19].

Thornton, Patricia (2007) *Disciplining the State: Virtue, Violence, and State-Making in Modern China*. Cambridge, MA: Harvard University Press.

Tickner, J. Ann (2011a) 'Retelling IR's Foundational Stories: Some Feminist and Postcolonial Perspectives', *Global Change, Peace, and Security*, 23(1): 5–13.

(2011b) 'Dealing with Difference: Problems and Possibilities for Dialogue in International Relations', *Millennium*, 39(3): 607–618.

Tilly, Charles (1992) *Coercion, Capital, and European States, AD 990–1992*. Cambridge, MA: Wiley Blackwell.

Tobin, David (2014) 'Worrying about Ethnicity: A New Generation of China Dreams?' in Kerr, David (ed) *China's Many Dreams: Comparative Perspectives on China's Search for National Rejuvenation*. Basingstoke: Palgrave Macmillan.

Tohti, Ilham (2006) 'Xinjiang Jingji Fazhan Yu Minzu Guanxi' ('Xinjiang's Economic Development and *Minzu* Relations') (Available at: www.uighurbiz.net/archives/3639), *Uighurbiz*, 1 January 2006 [Last accessed: 10/03/18].

(2009) 'Zhongguo de Minzu Zhengce Bu xuyao Fansi Ma?' ('China's *Minzu* Policies Don't Need to Be Re-Considered?') (Available at: www.uighurbiz.net/archives/189), *Uighurbiz*, 12 November [Last accessed: 10/03/18].

(2012a) 'Duoshu Weiwuer Ren Renwei Zhengfu Shi Hanren Liyi de Biaoda' ('A Majority of Uyghurs Believe That the Government Represents Han Interests') (Available at: www.uighurbiz.net/archives/6493), *Uighurbiz*, 3 December [Last accessed: 10/03/18].

(2012b) 'Yilihamu Pinglun Weiwuer Daxuesheng Atike Huzhao Shenling Zaoju Shijian' ('Ilham Considers the Incident of Uyghur University Student Atika's Passport Application') (Available at: www.uighurbiz.net/archives/6714), 23 December [Last accessed: 13/03/18].

Toops, Stanley (1999) 'Tourism and Turpan: The Power of Place in Inner Asia/Outer China', *Central Asian Survey*, 18(3): 303–318.

Tu, Wei-ming (ed) (1995) *The Living Tree: The Changing Meaning of Being Chinese Today*. Palo Alto, CA: Stanford University Press.

Tu, Wei-ming (2005) 'Cultural China: The Periphery as Center', *Daedalus*, 134(4): 145–167.

Tu, Wei-ming and Vattiimo, Gianni (2007) 'Toward a Dialogical Civilization', in Dunhua, Zhao (ed) *Dialogue of Philosophies, Religions, and Civilizations in the Era of Globalization*, Cultural Heritage and Contemporary Change Series, 3/25. Washington DC: The Council for Research in Values and Philosophy, pp.11–21.

Turner, Frederick Jackson (1986) 'The Significance of the Frontier in American History' in Ridge, Martin (ed) *Frederick Jackson Turner: Wisconsin's Historian of the Frontier*. Madison: State Historical Society of Wisconsin, pp.1–19.

Tursun, Mihrigul (2018) 'Congressional-Executive Commission on China: Testimony of Tursun Mihrigul' (Available at: https://www.cecc.gov/events/hearings/the-communist-party%E2%80%99s-crackdown-on-religion-in-china), 28 November [Last accessed: 28/03/20].

Uighur (2008) 'Wulumuqi Laixin: Zhongqiu shi Shei de Jieri' ('A Letter from Ürümchi: Mid-Autumn Festival Is Whose Festival?') (Available at: www.uighurbiz.cn/socity/2008/1003/article_7240.htm), *Uighurbiz*, 3 October [Access no longer available].

US Department of State (2012) 'Country Reports for Human Rights Practices for 2011: China' (Available at: www.state.gov/j/drl/rls/hrrpt/humanrightsreport/index.htm#wrapper) [Last accessed: 23/08/18].

Uyghur American Association (UAA) (2012) 'Reports: Uyghur Asylum Seekers Deported from Cambodia Sentenced to Life, 17 Years in Prison' (Available at: http://uyghuramerican.org/old/articles/6721/1/Reports-Uyghur-asylum-seekers-deported-from-Cambodia-sentenced-to-life-17-years-in-prison/index.html), 26 January [Last accessed: 25/06/18].

Uyghur Human Rights Project (UHRP) (2011) 'A City Ruled by Fear and Silence, Urumchi Two Years On' (Available at: www.uhrp.org/uaa-and-uhrp-reports-press-releases/new-uhrp-report-city-ruled-fear-and-silence-urumchi-two-years) [Last accessed: 16/06/18].

(2012a) 'New Rules Issued by Hotan Company Discriminate against Uyghur Women' (Available at: http://uhrp.org/press-release/new-rules-issued-hotan-company-discriminate-against-uyghur-women.html), June 6 [Last accessed: 23/10/18].

(2012b) 'Notice Informs Locals of Mandatory Residence Searches in Hotan Community' (Available at: http://uhrp.org/press-release/notice-informs-locals-mandatory-residence-searches-hotan-community-police-reserve), 18 June [Last accessed: 23/10/18].

(2012c) 'China Launches Campaign to Search Houses of Uighur Muslims' (Available at: http://uhrp.org/news/china-launches-campaign-search-houses-uighur-muslims), June 21 [Last accessed: 23/10/18].

Wæver, Ole (1995) 'Securitization and Desecuritization' in Lipschutz, Ronnie D. (ed) *On Security*, New York: Columbia University Press, pp.46–87.

Walker, R. B. J. (1990) 'Security, Sovereignty, and the Challenge of World Politics', *Alternatives*, 15(1): 3–27.

(1997) 'The Subject of Security' in Krause, K. and Williams, M. (eds) *Critical Security Studies*. Minneapolis: University of Minnesota Press, pp.61–82

Walsh, Eileen Rose (2005) 'From *Nu Guo* to *Nu Er Guo*: Negotiating Desire in the Land of the Mosuo', *Modern China*, 31: 448–486.

Waltz, Kenneth (1979) *Theory of International Politics*. Reading, MA: Addison-Wesley.

Wang, Lequan (2009a) 'Jianjue Daji ge zhong Didui Shili de Shentou Fenlie Pohuai Huodong' ('Resolutely Strike Hard against the Infiltration of All Enemies' Separatist, Harmful Activities') (Available at: http://leaders.people.com.cn/GB/9087179.html) [Last accessed: 31/05/18].

(2009b) 'Wang Lequan Guanyu Muqian Shehui Zhian Xingshi de Dianshi Jianghua' ('Wang Lequan's Televised Speech Regarding the Present Public Order Situation') in Xinjiang Uyghur Autonomous Region Party Commission Ministry of Information (eds) *Jiaqiang Minzu Tuanjie, Weihu Xinjiang Wending: Xuanchuan Jiaoyu Cailiao (Yi) (Strengthening Ethnic Unity, Protecting Xinjiang Stability: Information Education Materials No. 1)*. Wulumuqi: Xinjiang Renmin Chubanshe ('Xinjiang People's Publishing Press').

(2009c) 'Wang Lequan zai Quanqu Wending Gongzuo Dianshi Dianhua Huiyi shang de Jianghua' ('Wang Lequan's Televised Speech at the Regional Stability Work Telephone Conference') in Xinjiang Uyghur Autonomous Region Party Commission Ministry of Information (eds) *Jiaqiang Minzu Tuanjie, Weihu Xinjiang Wending: Xuanchuan Jiaoyu Cailiao (Yi) (Strengthening Ethnic Unity, Protecting Xinjiang Stability: Information Education Materials No. 1)*. Wulumuqi: Xinjiang Renmin Chubanshe ('Xinjiang People's Publishing Press').

Bibliography

Wang, Yiwei (2014) 'Great Power Security Concept in the Age of Globalisation', *Frontiers*, 6: 6–13.

Watts, Jonathan (2009) 'Old Suspicions Magnified Mistrust into Ethnic Riots in Urumqi' (Available at: www.guardian.co.uk/world/2009/jul/10/china-riots-uighurs-han-urumqi), *The Guardian*, 10 July [Last accessed: 14/09/18].

Weber, Cynthia (1998) 'Performative States', *Millennium*, 27(1): 77–95.

Weber, Cynthia and Lacy, Mark (2011) 'Securing by Design', *Review of International Studies*, 37(3): 1021–1044.

Wiemer, Calla (2004) 'The Economy of Xinjiang' in Starr, S. F. (ed) *Xinjiang: China's Muslim Borderland*. New York: M. E. Sharpe, pp.163–189.

Winichakul, Thongchai (1994) *Siam Mapped*. Honolulu: University of Hawaii Press.

Wong, Edward (2009) 'New Protests Reported in Restive Chinese Region' (Available at: www.nytimes.com/2009/09/04/world/asia/04china.html?_r=1), *New York Times*, 3 September [Last accessed: 22/06/18].

World Bank (2012) *China 2030: Building a Modern, Harmonious, and Creative High-Income Society* (Available at: www.worldbank.org/en/news/2012/02/27/china-2030-executive-summary) [Last accessed: 24/08/18].

World Uyghur Congress (www.uyghurcongress.org/En/home.asp) [Last accessed: 09/03/19].

Wulumuqi Wanshibao (Ürümchi Evening Times) (2009) 'Benbao jiang Paisong 50,000 tao Guozhu Jinian tie' ('This Paper Will Distribute 50,000 National Day Commemoration Stickers'), 25 September, p.B17.

Xi, Jinping (2012) 'Jinyibu ba Xinjiang Jingji Shehui Fazhan Gaoshangqu, ba Changzhi jiuan Gongzuo gao Zhashi' ('Progressing Xinjiang's economic and social development, doing solid long-term peace and stability work') in Zhonggong Zhongyang Wenxian Yanjiushi ('CCP Central Committee Document Research Office') (ed) *Xinjiang Shengchan Jianshe Bingtuan Gongzuo Wenxian Xuanbian (Xinjiang Bingtuan Work – Selected Documents)*. Beijing: Zhongyang Wenxian Chubanshe ('CCP Central Committee Party Literature Publishing House'), pp.314–319.

(2013) 'Xi Jinping Calls for the Building of New Type of International Relations'. 23 March. Available at: http://www.fmprc.gov.cn/mfa_eng/topics_665678/xjpcf1_665694/t1024781.shtml [accessed: 28/03/20].

(2015) 'Speech on China–US Relations in Seattle'. 23 September (Available at: http://news.xinhuanet.com/english/2015-09/24/c_134653326.htm) [Last accessed: 28/03/20].

(2017) 'Juesheng Quanmian Jiancheng Xiaokang Shehui, Duoqu Xinshidai Zhongguo Tese Shehui zhuyi Weida Shengli – Zai Zhongguo Gongchandang Di Shi Jiu ci Quanguo Daibiao Dahuishang de Baogao' ('Secure a Decisive Victory in Building a Moderately Prosperous Society in All Respects and Strive for the Great Success of Socialism with Chinese Characteristics for a New Era') (Available at: www.xinhuanet.com//politics/19cpcnc/2017-10/27/c_1121867529.htm), 27 October [Last accessed: 27/07/19].

Xinhua (2009a) 'Xinjiang Riot Hits Regional Anti-Terror Nerve' (Available at: http://news.xinhuanet.com/english/2009-07/18/content_11727782.htm), 18 July [Last accessed: 11/06/18].

Bibliography 273

(2009b) 'Rumourmonger Held over South China Toy Factory Brawl' (Available at: http://news.xinhuanet.com/english/2009-06/29/content_11616274.htm), 29 June [Last accessed: 14/09/18].
(2009c) 'Innocent Civilians Make Up 156 in Urumqi Riot Death Toll' (Available at: http://news.xinhuanet.com/english/2009-08/05/content_11831350.htm), 5 August [Last accessed: 11/06/18].
(2009d) 'Many Countries Say Xinjiang Riot China's Internal Affair' (Available at: http://news.xinhuanet.com/english/2009-07/17/content_11726662.htm), 17 July [Last accessed: 11/06/18].
(2009e) 'Fresh Chaos Erupts in Urumqi' (Available at: http://news.xinhuanet.com/english/2009-07/07/content_11666941.htm), 7 July [Last accessed: 11/06/18].
(2009f) 'Chinese President Back Home after Italy Visit' (Available at: http://news.xinhuanet.com/english/2009-07/08/content_11674664.htm), 8 July [Last accessed: 19/06/18].
(2009g) 'Urumqi Quiets Down after Protest against Syringe Attacks', (Available at: http://news.xinhuanet.com/english/2009-09/04/content_11992622.htm), 4 September [Last accessed: 21/06/18].
(2009h) 'Chinese Medical Experts Examine Urumqi Syringe Attacks Victims' (Available at: http://news.xinhuanet.com/english/2009-09/05/content_12001983.htm), 5 September [Last accessed: 21/06/18].
(2009i) 'Four Prosecuted for Endangering Public Security in Urumqi Syringe Attacks' (Available at: http://news.xinhuanet.com/english/2009-09/05/content_12001771.htm), 5 September [Last accessed: 21/06/18].
(2011) 'Factbox: Mid-Autumn Festival and Its Traditions' (Available at: http://news.xinhuanet.com/english2010/culture/2011-09/12/c_131134150.htm), 12 September [Last accessed: 13/07/18].
(2012a) 'No Mercy for Terrorists: Xinjiang Party Chief' (Available at: http://news.xinhuanet.com/english/china/2012-03/07/c_131452573.htm), 7 March [Last accessed: 28/06/18].
(2012b) 'Xinhua Insight: China Never to Copy a Western System' (Available at: http://news.xinhuanet.com/english/special/18cpcnc/2012-11/12/c_131968691.htm), 12 November [Last accessed: 14/01/18].
(2012c) 'Xinhua Insight: Xinjiang to Get Tougher on Terrorists' (Available at: http://news.xinhuanet.com/english/china/2012-04/18/c_131535858.htm), 18 April [Last accessed: 24/05/18].
(2014) 'Yilihamu Tuheti Fenlie Guojia Anting Shenjishi' ('Court Trial Documentary: Ilham Tohti Splitting the Nation') (Available at: http://news.xinhuanet.com/legal/2014-09/24/c_1112614703.htm), 24 September [Last accessed: 13/06/18].
(2017) 'Xi Calls for Building "Great Wall of Iron" for Xinjiang's Stability' (Available at: http://news.xinhuanet.com/english/2017-03/10/c_136119256.htm), 10 March [Last accessed: 24/05/18].
Xinjiang Dushibao ('Xinjiang Reader') (2010) 'Yi Jia Ren Zhu Xin Chun' ('"One Family" Celebrates a New Spring') (Available at: http://epaper.xjts.cn/ftp/site1/xjdsb/html/2012-07/12/node_2.htm), 3 February [Last accessed: 12/07/18], p.C03.
Xinjiang Education Press (XEP) (2009) *50ge 'Weishenme': Weihu Guojia Tongyi, Fandui Minzu Fenlie, Jiaqiang Minzu Tuanjie Duben (The 50 Whys: Protecting*

274 Bibliography

National Unification, Opposing Ethnic Separatism, Strengthening Ethnic Unity Study Book). Wulumuqi: Xinjiang Jiaoyu Chubanshe ('Xinjiang Education Press').

Xinjiang Uyghur Autonomous Region Government (XUAR Government) (1996) *Xinjiang Weiwuer Zizhiqu Saochu Wenmang Tiaolie (Xinjiang Uyghur Autonomous Region Government: Regulations Regarding the Eradication of Illiteracy)* (Available at: http://gtt.xinjiang.gov.cn/10120/10190/2009/15754.htm) [Last accessed: 15/01/18].

Xinjiang Uyghur Autonomous Region Government (XUAR) (2007) *Xinjiang Weiwuer Zizhiqu Jiben Puji Jiunian Yiwu Pinggu Yanshou Banfa (Compulsory Nine-Year Education Mission: Evaluation and Acceptance Measures)* (Available at: http://gtt.xinjiang.gov.cn/10120/10185/2009/15679.htm) [Last accessed: 13/05/19].

(2010) *Xinjiang Weiwuer Zizhiqu Shehui Zhian Zonghe Zhili Tiaolie (Xinjiang Uyghur Autonomous Regional Government Public Order Comprehensive Administration Regulations)* (Available at: www.law-star.com/cacnew/201001/315051147.htm) [Last accessed: 08/06/18].

(2018) *2018 Nian Xinjiang Weiwuer Zizhiqu Zhengfu Gongzuo Baogao (Xinjiang Uyghur Autonomous Region Government's 2018 Work Report)*, http://cn.chinagate.cn/reports/2018-03/02/content_50636629.htm, March 2 [Last accessed: 23/07/19].

Xinjiang Uyghur Autonomous Region Government Department of Information (XUAR Dept of Information) (2009) *Xinjiang Fazhan Wending: Liuti (Xinjiang's Development and Stability: Six Questions)*. Wulumuqi: Xinjiang Renmin Chubanshe ('Xinjiang People's Press').

Xinjiang Uyghur Autonomous Region (XUAR) Party Commission Information Department (eds) (2009a) *Jiaqiang Minzu Tuanjie, Weihu Xinjiang Wending: Xuanchuan Jiaoyu Cailiao Yi (Strengthening Ethnic Unity, Protecting Xinjiang Stability: Information Education Materials No. 1)*. Wulumuqi: Xinjiang Renmin Chubanshe ('Xinjiang People's Publishing Press').

Xinjiang Uyghur Autonomous Regional (XUAR) Party Commission Information Department (2009b), *Yi Jiaren (One Family)*, DVD. Wulumuqi: Xinjiang Dianzi Yinxiang Chubanshe ('Xinjiang Electronic Audiovisual Press').

Xinjiang Uyghur Autonomous Region Party Committee (XUAR Party Committee) (1982) 'Xinjiang Weiwuer Zizhiqu Dangwei Guanyu zai Quanqu Jinxing Guanche Dang de Minzu Zhengce Zengqiang Minzu Tuanjie Jiaoyu de Tongzhi' ('XUAR Party Committee on the Implementation of *Minzu* Policy to Strengthen Ethnic Unity Education') in Zhonggong Zhongyang Wenxian Yanjiushi ('CCP Central Committee Document Research Office') (ed) (2010) *Xinjiang Gonzuo Wenxian Xuanbian (Xinjiang Work – Selected Documents)*, Beijing: Zhongyang Wenxian Chubanshe, ('CCP Central Committee Party Literature Publishing House') pp.256–262).

Xinjiang Uyghur Autonomous Regional Government Public Security Department (XUAR Gonganting) (2009) 'Xinjiang Weiwuer Zizhiqu Gonganting Gonggao' ('Xinjiang Uyghur Autonomous Regional Government Public Security Department Announcement'), *Chen Bao*, 7 September, A1.

Xinjiang Uyghur Autonomous Region (XUAR) Statistics Bureau (2007) *Xinjiang Tongji Nianjian (Xinjiang Statistical Yearbook)*. Beijing: China Statistics Bureau.

(2018) *Xinjiang Weiwuer Zizhiqu 2017 Guomin Jingji he Shehui Tongji Gongbao* (*Statistical Communique of Xinjiang on 2017 National Economic and Social Development*) (Available at: www.tjcn.org/tjgb/31xj/35514.html), April 25 [Last accessed: 11/04/19].

Xinjiang Victims Database (XVD) (2018) Available at: https://shahit.biz/eng/ [Last accessed: 23/07/19].

Xin, Kuan (2009) *Yi Jia Ren* (*One Family*) (Available at: http://hi.baidu.com/ouzhouzhannz/item/0cc93380621956ebe596e041), *Baidu* Kongjian, 19 August [Last accessed: 12/07/18].

Xu, Vikki Xiuzhong et al. (2020) *Uyghurs for Sale: 'Re-Education', Forced Labour, and Surveillance beyond Xinjiang*. Australian Strategic Policy Institute, International Cyber Policy Centre, Policy Brief 26.

Ya, Hanzhang (1962) 'Guanyu Minzu Yici de Yiming Tongyi Wenti' ('On the Problem of Unifying Translations of Minzu') in Pan, Jiao (ed) (2008) *Zhongguo Shehui Wenhua Renleixue / Minzuxue Bainian Wenxuan* (*Selected Works of 100 Years of Chinese Social and Cultural Anthropology / Minzu Studies*). Beijing: Zhishi Chanquan Chubanshe ('Intellectual Property Publishing House'), pp.115–126.

(1965) 'Minzu Wenti de Shizhi shi Jieji Wenti' ('The Essence of the Minzu Problem Is a Class Problem') in Pan, Jiao (ed) (2008) *Zhongguo Shehui Wenhua Renleixue / Minzuxue Bainian Wenxuan* (*Selected Works of 100 Years of Chinese Social and Cultural Anthropology / Minzu Studies*). Beijing: Zhishi Chanquan Chubanshe ('Intellectual Property Publishing House'), pp.222–229.

Yan, Xuetong (2013) *Ancient Chinese Thought, Modern Chinese Power*. Princeton, NJ: Princeton University Press.

Yang, Faren (2005) *Xibu Da Kaifa yu Minzu Wenti* ('The Western Development Project and the Ethnic Question'). Beijing: Renmin Chubanshe ('People's Press').

Yasin, Nurmehemmet (2005) 'Wild Pigeon' ('Yawa Kepter') (Available at: www.rfa.org/english/uyghur/wild_pigeon-20050627.html; www.rfa.org/english/uyghur/wild_pigeon2-20050627.html) [Last accessed: 09/03/19].

Yee, Herbert (2003) 'Ethnic Relations in Xinjiang: A Survey of Han-Uyghur Relations in Urumqi', *Journal of Contemporary China*, 12(36): 431–452.

Yeung, Yue Man and Fa, Jian (2004) *Developing China's West*. Hong Kong: Chinese University Press.

Yi, Xiaocuo (2019) 'A Road to Forgetting: Friendship and Memory in China's Belt and Road Initiative' (Available at: https://madeinchinajournal.com/2019/04/18/a-road-to-forgetting-china-belt-and-road-initiative/), *Made in China Journal*, 18 April [Last accessed: 08/07/19].

Young Nam, Cho and Jong Ho, Jeong (2008) 'China's Soft Power: Discussion, Resources, and Prospects', *Asian Survey*, 48(3): 453–472.

YouTube (2009) 'Race Riot in China' (Available at: www.youtube.com/watch?v=GUPHVf5yDM4), 29 June [Last accessed: 14/09/18].

(2011) 'Arbitrary Detentions of Uyghurs in Urumchi after July 5, 2009' (Available at: www.youtube.com/watch?v=pRcOZOygmZc), 1 July [Last accessed: 16/06/18].

Yuval-Davis, Nira (2008) *Gender and Nation*. Sage: London.

Zehfuss, Maja (2002) *Constructivism in International Relations: The Politics of Reality*. Cambridge: Cambridge University Press.

Zenn, Jacob (2011) 'Violence Escalates in China's Xinjiang Province' (Available at: www.ctc.usma.edu/posts/violence-escalates-in-china%E2%80%99s-xinjiang-province) [Last accessed: 30/05/18].

Zenz, Adrian (2018) 'Thoroughly Reforming Them towards a Healthy Heart Attitude,' *Central Asian Survey*, 38(1): 102–128.

——— (2019) 'Break Their Roots: Evidence for China's Parent-Child Separation Campaign in Xinjiang', *Journal of Political Risk*, 7(7) (Available at: www.jpolrisk.com/break-their-roots-evidence-for-chinas-parent-child-separation-campaign-in-xinjiang/).

Zhang, Haiyang (2006) 'Jianlun Zhongguohua yu Hexie Shehui' ('On Sinicisation and a Harmonious Society'), *Sixiang Zhanxian (Ideological Front)*, 2.

——— (2012) '"Xinren tuanjie hezuo" haishi "bilan bihei bizuo"? Jinian Zhonghua Renmin Gongheguo 62nian he Xinhai Geming Gonghe bainian" ("Trust, Unity, Solidarity' is better than 'Blue pen, Black pen'? Commemorating the PRC's 62nd Anniversary of the PRC and the Xinhai Revolution's Centenary') (Available at: www.mzb.com.cn/html/node/293068-1.htm) [Last accessed: 09/01/18].

Zhang, Weiwei (2011) 'An Apt Example of a Civilizational-State' (Available at: www.chinadaily.com.cn/opinion/2011-04/27/content_12401986.htm), *The China Daily*, 27 April [Last accessed: 24/01/18].

——— (2012) *Zhongguo Chudong (China Shock)*. Shanghai: Shanghai Renmin Chubanshe ('Shanghai People's Press').

Zhang, Yupo et al. (2014) *Zongjiao Jiduan Haisiren (Religious Extremes Kill People)*. Wulumuqi: Xinjiang Renmin Chubanshe ('Xinjiang People's Press').

Zhao, Suisheng (2004) *A Nation-State by Construction: Dynamics of Modern Chinese Nationalism*. Stanford: Stanford University Press.

——— (1998) 'A State-Led Nationalism: The Patriotic Education Campaign in Post-Tiananmen China', *Communist and Post-Communist Studies*, 31(3): 287–302.

Zheng, Yongnian (2007) *De Facto Federalism in China: Reforms and Dynamics of Central-Local Relations*. Singapore: World Scientific Publishing.

Zhongguo Minzu Zongjiao Wang (2012) 'Di er Dai Minzu Zhengce Tantao' ('Exploring The Second Generation of *Minzu* Policies') (Available at: www.mzb.com.cn/html/folder/292573-1.htm?utm_source=China+Policy&utm_campaign=0025fe4449-RSS_EMAIL_CAMPAIGN&utm_medium=email) [Last accessed: 24/08/18].

Zhonghua Renmingongheguo Minzu Diquyu Zizhifa ('National Law on Regional Autonomy') (2001) (Available at: http://hyconference.edu.cn/chinese/2001/Mar/22466.htm) [Last accessed: 09/11/18].

Zhou, Enlai (1949) 'Women Zhuzhang Minzu Quyu Zizhi, ba ge Minzu Tuanjie Cheng Yige Da Jiating' ('We Stand for *Minzu* Regional Autonomy, Every *minzu* Forms One Big Family') in Zhonggong Zhongyang Wenxian Yanjiushi ('CCP Central Committee Document Research Office') (ed) (2010) *Xinjiang Gonzuo Wenxian Xuanbian (Xinjiang Work – Selected Documents)*. Beijing: Zhongyang Wenxian Chubanshe ('CCP Central Committee Party Literature Publishing House'), pp.3–5.

——— (1950a) 'Dui Xibei Diqu Minzu Gongzuo de Jidian Yijian' ('A Few Suggestions Regarding *Minzu* Work in the Northwest Region') in Zhonggong Zhongyang Wenxian Yanjiushi ('CCP Central Committee Document Research Office') (ed) (2010) *Xinjiang Gonzuo Wenxian Xuanbian (Xinjiang Work – Selected*

Documents). Beijing: Zhongyang Wenxian Chubanshe ('CCP Central Committee Party Literature Publishing House'), pp.53–56.

(1950b) 'Renzhen Shixing Dang de Minzu Zhengce' ('Earnestly Implement the Party's *Minzu* Policy') in Zhonggong Zhongyang Wenxian Yanjiushi ('CCP Central Committee Document Research Office') (ed) (2010) *Xinjiang Gonzuo Wenxian Xuanbian (Xinjiang Work – Selected Documents)*. Beijing: Zhongyang Wenxian Chubanshe ('CCP Central Committee Party Literature Publishing House'), p.63.

(1951) 'Zhengwuyuan Guanyu Chuli Daiyou Qishi huo Wuru Shaoshu Minzu Xingzhi de Chengwei, Diming, Beijie, Bianlian de Zhishi' ('State Council Directives on Dealing with Names, Place Names, Stone Tablets, and Placards Which Discriminate Against or Humiliate Minorities') in Zhonggong Zhongyang Wenxian Yanjiushi ('CCP Central Committee Document Research Office') (ed) (2010) *Xinjiang Gonzuo Wenxian Xuanbian (Xinjiang Work – Selected Documents)*. Beijing: Zhongyang Wenxian Chubanshe ('CCP Central Committee Party Literature Publishing House'), pp.66–67.

Zhu, Weiqun (2012) 'Dui Dangqian Minzu Lingyu Wenti de Jidian Sikao' ('A Few Thoughts on Current Problems in the Field of Ethnicity') (Available at: www.studytimes.com.cn/2012/02/13/01/01_51.htm), *Xuexi Shibao* ('Study Times'), 13 February [Last accessed: 11/07/18].

Index

Abdurehim, Heyit, 146, 176, 184, 186, 188, 190, 237
Ai, Weiwei, 108
Aksu, 103
Albania, 102
Alim, Seytoff, 15, 128
Anderson, Benedict, 28–29, 163
assimilation, 1, 37, 44, 69, 75, 140, 148, 158, 174, 187, 194, 220, 229–230, 234, 236, 238, 242
  'ethnic extinction' (*minzu xiaowang*), 60, 62, 74–75, 77–78, 83–84, 141, 143, 146, 226, 231–232, 234
  'fusion' (*jiaorong*), 2, 44, 63–64, 72, 75–77, 79, 191, 205–206, 223, 234–238
  'teaching without discrimination' (*jiaohua*), 4, 78, 188, 194, 220, 234–235, 238
  Sinicisation, 185–186, 210–211, 214, 216–217, 220, 229
autonomy, 41, 106
  federalism, 45, 143
  independence, 41, 44, 92, 99, 107, 180–181, 204, 226
  regional, 8, 44–45, 54, 61, 79, 94, 105, 226, 234
  sub-autonomies, 44–45

Barth, Frederick, 29, 182
Beijing, 40, 66, 96, 108, 123, 147
  attitudes towards Uyghurs, 200
  in Uyghur identity narratives, 182–183, 197
  military parade, 209
  Olympics, 1, 114, 160
  time, 55
Bekri, Nur, 67, 74, 82, 99–101, 103–104, 120, 124, 205
Belarus, 128
Bermuda, 102
Bhabha, Homi, 11, 18, 29, 107, 163, 167–168, 172
Bo, Xilai, 59

Brubaker, Rogers, 28, 86, 140, 163, 182
Butler, Judith, 11, 13, 61, 68, 105, 121

Callahan, William A., 4, 10, 12, 28, 32, 46, 51, 84, 98, 114–115, 153, 161, 212, 239
Cambodia, 102, 128
Campbell, David, 12–13, 28, 88, 115–116, 193
Central Asia, 6, 17, 27, 39, 67, 91, 96, 110, 112
  Central Asian Studies, 48, 193
  Soviet, 53
  terrorism, 102
  Uyghurs as Central Asian, 4, 14, 28, 41, 46–47, 54, 63, 94, 104, 106–107, 182, 185, 223
Chan, Kuanchong, 108
Chen, Quanguo, 2, 235–237
China
  enemies of, 6, 14, 47, 88, 96–97, 104, 109, 113, 122, 129, 131, 137, 142, 152, 166, 192, 196, 232, 236
  guojia (nation), 3, 6, 126, 129
  new China, 4, 37, 44, 70, 73, 91, 156, 192
  PRC, 2, 6–7, 17, 24, 28, 32–33, 46, 85, 91, 106, 130, 140, 156, 161, 235, 239
  constitution, 50–51, 78, 232
  Yellow Emperor, 36, 161, 164, 224
  Zhongguo (China), 3, 114, 156, 170, 205
  Zhonghua Minzu, 2, 4–5, 26–27, 31–32, 36–37, 44, 47–50, 58–59, 61, 66–67, 69, 71–72, 75, 77–78, 80, 92–96, 98, 100, 107, 110–111, 122, 139–143, 145, 152, 158, 160–163, 173, 177, 179, 185–188, 197, 199, 201–202, 208, 214, 230–234, 237–238, 241
  zuguo (motherland), 59, 61, 130, 143, 156, 159
China's rise, 3, 6, 9–10, 75, 78, 87, 224, 235
China Dream, 1, 4, 114, 166
China threat, 9
development model, 242
Great Revival, 1–2, 114–115, 139, 166, 232, 235–236, 239, 242

Index

in Chinese debates, 79, 114, 140
in IR theory, 10, 243
in official narratives, 2, 6, 8, 93, 104, 114–115, 136, 141, 240
Chinese Communist Party (CCP)
  18th National Congress, 84, 240
  19th National Congress, 240
  Central Committee of the Chinese Communist Party (CCPCC), 1, 43, 60, 94
Chinese Studies, 3, 7, 16, 32, 45, 48, 107, 224, 231
  Eurocentrism in, 241
  nationalism literature, 240
  Sinocentrism in, 32, 223, 231
  Sinology, 6–7, 193
  Xinjiang's absence in, 7, 48
Civilisation, 88, 92, *See also* Confucianism
  5,000 years of, 4, 27–29, 44, 61, 68–69, 74, 87, 98, 106, 143, 166, 187, 241
  barbarians, 5, 23, 31–34, 36–38, 46, 51, 57, 63–64, 67, 69, 72, 78–79, 85, 112, 182, 191, 193–194, 224, 230, 238–241
  barbarism, 48, 51, 63, 66, 70–71, 143, 152, 177, 233
  civilisation-state, 4, 9, 223, 241
  exceptionalism, 3, 6, 37, 78, 84–85, 142, 178
  hua, 8, 106, 141, 168, 188
  hua / yi binary, 65–66, 78–79, 144, *156*, 177–178, 230–231
  timeless, 47, 51, 61–63, 69, 86, 96, 111, 141, 143, 146–148, 184–186, 200, 225, 230, 243
  Turkic, 40, 46, 106–107, 111, 113, 186, 188, 211
  unbroken, 6, 28, 35, 38, 69, 72–73, 76, 83, 86, 96, 144, 166, 239, 241
Colonialism, 7–8, 15, 35–36, 49–50, 70–71, 78, 93–94, 211, 225, 234, 238–240, 242, *See also* Imperialism, Orientalism
communications technology, 116
  internet closure, 18, 117
  official SMS texts, 17, 121, 131–132, 153, 159
  Uyghur blogs, 121, 161–164
  video-hosting sites, 123, 146
Communist era, 7, 66–67, 73, 129, 233, 241
community, 32, 35–36, 141, 146, 156, 177, 191, 198
  Han, 170, 172, 190
  imagined, 33, 55, 140, 208, 215–216, 224
  international, 128
  of destiny, 239
  Uyghur, 52, 55, 91, 110, 146, 174, 185, 187, 208, 216, 218

visceral, 55, 167–168, 182, 186–188, 198, 208, 210, 215–216
Confucianism, 85, 140, 161, 224, 230, *See also* Civilisation
  culturalism, 35, 37, 77, 140, 166, 168, 171, 178, 180, 189, 196, 218, 222–223, 230, 232, 239–240
  scholars, 7, 223, 230
Confucius, 148, 233, 247
  in Uyghur identity narratives, 214
contradictions
  ethnic, 173, 199–200, 232
  national, 67
  policy, 206, 234–235
Cultural Revolution, 170
  in Xinjiang, 43, 77, 98
  influence on current policy, 60, 77, 143, 235
  post-Cultural Revolution 'liberalisation', 99, 152

daily practices, 11, 15, 17, 48, 55, 96, 154, 173, 175, 185, 193, 195, 198–199, 208, 217–218, 220
danger, *See also* Security
  discourses of, 12, 26, 88, 97, 100, 104, 136–137, 194, 196, 200, 207–208, 210, 219, 240, 242
  existential threats, 2, 5, 9, 11–12, 14, 29, 31, 40, 42, 48, 56, 77, 83, 87, 93–94, 100, 108–109, 115, 117, 120–121, 125, 136, 139, 161, 193, 196, 198, 207, 212, 214, 218, 220, 222, 233, 242
  reactionaries, 4, 87, 92, 96, 125, 192
  Uyghur identity, 8, 25, 61–62, 68, 82–83, 89–90, 94, 103, 113, 121, 127, 131, 160, 180, 197–198, 206
  Xinjiang, 47, 68, 82, 104, 119
Daoguang Emperor, 39
Deng, Xiaoping, 4, 28, 37, 42–43, 45, 60, 68, 87, 96, 99, 105–106
development, *See also* modernisation
  agricultural, 63, 69, 178
  capitalism, 51, 65, 93, 96, 233
  cultural, 37, 60, 63, 67, 72, 75, 144
  economic, 2, 5, 7, 18, 27, 43, 63, 68, 77, 79, 84–86, 111, 120, 141, 149, 230, 240
  employment discrimination, 199
  ethnic, 77
  labour
    camps, 109
    employment discrimination, 19, 43, 232
    forced, 233
    migration, 22, 45, 99, 119, 190, 233
    transfers, 119–120, 122

development (cont.)
  model, 233
  natural resources, 232

East Turkestan, 91, *See also* Turks
  East Turkestan Islamic Movement (ETIM),
    93, 101–102
  in Chinese narratives, 90–105, 112, 120,
    125, 132, 211, 229, 238
  in Han identity narratives, 128, 197, 202
  in Uyghur identity narratives, 105–108
  Republics of, 41, 65,
    91, 105
East, the, 223
  in Chinese narratives, 11, 84, 114,
    239
  in IR theory, 223
empathy, 224–225, 242
Engels, Friedrich, 51, 65–66, 71, 85
ethnic boundaries, 3, 8, 23, 26, 29, 48, 50,
    54–55, 58, 83, 88–89, 103, 112, 121,
    140, 156, 163, 169, 173, 175, 181–182,
    189–190, 193–194, 199–200, 208, 212,
    220, 225, 230–231, 242
ethnic relations, 2–3, 16, 21, 25, 30, 32, 36, 42,
    46, 55, 75, 78, 80, 123, 138, 143, 155,
    170, 181, 201, 215, 225
ethnic unity (*minzu tuanjie*), 126, 139–165
  education, 19–20, 24, 59, 75, 77, 80, 103,
    123, 143, 149, 159, 209, 240
  'fragrant concubine', 47
  Han and Uyghur attitudes to, 166–191, 200,
    242
  'three cannot leaves' (*sange libukai*),
    143–144
ethnicity, 30, 34, 50–52, 58, 115, 142, 225,
    228, 239, *See also Minzu* (ethnicity)
  in Han identity narratives, 170, 179,
    195–196, 205
  in official narratives, 65, 74, 77–79, 87, 108,
    118, 124, 139–140, 146, 153, 160, 162,
    164, 234
  in Uyghur identity narratives, 188, 208, 214
ethnocentrism, 34, 37, 44, 51, 60, 63, 71, 86,
    140, 149, 169, 172–174, 188–189, 206,
    219, 232
  objectivisation of Han-ness, 8, 76, 142,
    152–154, 156, 159–160, 162, 164, 170,
    174, 189, 192, 198, 201, 228, 232
Eurocentrism, 10–11, 32, 34, 71, 85, 115,
    223–225, 241
Europe, 4, 9–10, 34
  colonialism, 8, 35, 49, 70, 78, 91, 94, 234,
    238, 240
  genocide, 237

imperialism, 35–36, 38, 40, 57, 68, 161, 239
nationalism, 86
'one-nation, one-state' model, 6
settlers, 86, 242
state-making, 33–34

Fairbank, John King, 4, 33
Fan, Wenlan, 51, 63, 65
Fei, Xiaotong, 3, 31, 37, 49–51, 63, 65, 68–69,
    140, 142–143, 178, 230
festivals, 25, 142, 164, 228
  Han chauvinism, 163–165
  in official narratives, 142, 152–154, 160
  in Uyghur identity narratives, 157, 160–161,
    165
  Mid-Autumn, 154, 162
  National Day, 126, 152, 155, 157
  Qurban, 157
  Roza, 157–158
  Spring, 147, 158
Foucault, Michel, 13, 17, 29, 88, 141
Frontier, 33, 64, 72, 129, 169, 179, 189
  exotic, 31, 41, 47, 49, 57, 92, 129

Gellner, Ernest, 28–29
gender
  in Han identity narratives, 204
  in official narratives, 71, 118–119, 145–147,
    212
  in Uyghur identity narratives, 110, 146, 194,
    207, 211, 215, 220, 230
  of interviewees, 21
Group of 8 (G8), 123
Guomindang (GMD), 41, 43, 60, 65, 75, 87,
    105
nationalists, 44

Hami rebellion, 39
Han, *See also* China
  attitudes
    class, 171–172, 180
    pork, 198–201, 232
    religion, 196–202, 206, 208, 231
    Uyghur food, 199
    Uyghurs as foreign, 201–203
  getihu entrepreneurs, 22, 25–26, 133–134,
    138, 169–175, 178–181, 196, 202–206,
    219, 229, 232
  identity
    hometown (*laojia*), 172, 178–179,
      190
    land (*tudi*), 178–179, 198
    lineage, 35–36, 50, 61, 65, 129, 190, 200,
      229
    local (*bendi ren*), 172–173, 179–180, 199

Index

insecurities, 127, 132, 136, 195–206, 218
intellectuals, 26, 168–173, 178–179, 190, 194, 201–202, 219, 229, 232
migration, 27, 76, 96, 119, 233
protestors, 129–136, 228
working-class, 17, 135, 173, 179, 202–203, 219, 232
Han dynasty, 32, 67, 106
  in official historiography, 64–66, 69, 72, 76, 94
  in Uyghur identity narratives, 106, 111
harmony, 145–146, 148
  ethnic relations, 80, 148, 159
  harmonious society, 160
  in Han identity narratives, 200, 204
  in Uyghur identity narratives, 162
Henan, 180
  Han from, 179
history, *See also* modernisation
  'distortions', 66, 227
  'mission', 74, 80, 84, 92, 103, 125, 239
  'overall direction', 63, 65, 74, 76, 84, 92, 98, 141, 164
  historiography, 46, 62–65, 72, 92, 226, 241
  national, 6, 24, 32, 34, 61, 63, 68
  'separatist', 44, 70, 94
Hu, Angang, 78–79, 84, 140, 235, 239
Hu, Jintao, 4, 44, 67, 84, 87, 98, 123, 127, 139, 143, 149, 166, 235, 240–241
Hubei
  Han from, 202, 204
Hui, 41, 198–199
  in Han identity narratives, 199
  in official narratives, 145
  Muslim category, 182
humiliation
  century of, 114, 143, 161, 166, 223, 225
  of minorities, 42, 161, 211, 220, 225

identity, *See also* Han, Uyghurs
  ambivalence, 5, 29, 32, 34, 36, 42, 46, 48–50, 62, 70, 112–113, 129, 149, 152, 159, 183, 226, 231, 238, 241
  ethnic, 16, 58, 68–69, 75, 85, 128, 139, 174, 218–219
  ethno-linguistic, 174, 187, 214
  national, 2, 7, 13, 28, 30, 34–37, 52–53, 57–58, 60, 62, 68, 75, 114, 137, 146, 162, 166–188, 230
  religion, 22, 95–96, 101, 108, 159, 167, 201, 243
  self-identification (*rentong*), 64, 79

status (*shenfen*), 95
trans-ethnic, 76, 78, 82, 142, 153, 159, 164, 177, 225, 228
Ilham, Tohti, 231–234
Imperialism, 5, 27, 34–40, 42–43, 53, 57, 62, 68, 87–93, 105, 161, 192, 239, *See also* Colonialism, Orientalism
  'hegemonism', 42, 87, 93
  empire, 6, 28, 33, 35–36, 42, 46–48, 53, 92, 182
India, 4, 6, 33, 201
intercultural translation, 34, 57
  semantic hybridity, 35, 53, 141, 182, 238
international relations, 10, 12
  ethnic relations and, 36, 139, 202, 225, 236
  China's foreign policy, 4, 98, 102, 112, 139
IR theory, 3, 9, 21, 243
  Chinese, 1, 79
  critical, 10
  eurocentric, 115, 223
  feminist, 10
  global, 223
  liberal, 10
  postcolonial, 10
  post-structuralism, 10
  realist, 10
Iraq, 114

Japan, 5, 11, 34, 42
  imperialism, 5, 34, 36, 40
  in 'patriotic education', 5, 60, 240
Jiang, Zemin, 4, 99–101, 108, 143, 152, 166
journalists, 108, 122, 133

Karamay, 171, 199
Kashgar, 41, 47, 53, 91–92, 138, 157
  in official narratives, 102–103
  in Uyghur identity narratives, 183–185, 188
  Literature Journal, 109
  officials, 102
  Uyghurs from, 107, 210
Kazakhs, 43, 182
  in official narratives, 77
Kazakhstan, 102, 209
Khotan, 41, 102–103, 134, 138, 158
  in official narratives, 103
Korla, 23, 231
Kucha
  in official narratives, 103
Kyrgyz, 147, 182
  in official narratives, 77
Kyrgyzstan, 91

Laos, 128
Li, Hongzhang, 39–40

Liang, Qichao, 36, 79
Liberalisation, 7, 99, 152
Liu, Shaoqi, 37, 42–43, 60

Ma, Dazheng, 73, 96
Ma, Rong, 5, 78–79, 82, 140, 156, 194, 230, 234–235
Malaysia, 102
Manchu, *See also* Qing Dynasty
  in Uyghur identity narratives, 188
Mao, Zedong, 4, 27, 37, 41–42, 44, 55, 60, 72, 87, 97, 105, 143, 161, 166, 198, 226
Marx, Karl, 66, 77, 85, 233
Marxism, 51, 67
  dialectics, 43, 51
  feudalism, 62, 68, 97
  historical materialism, 43, 54, 67, 71, 77, 84–85, 171, 188, 230
  mode of production, 71
  socialism, 4, 38, 44, 53, 63, 77, 79, 93, 97, 143, 190
Meng, Jianzhu, 135
methodology, 15–23
  discourse analysis, 15
  exhibitions, 17
  interviews, 8, 23
  newspapers, 17, 117
  participant-observation, 8, 15, 20, 24–25
  political slogans (*kouhao*), 17
  textbooks, 17, 19–20
  texts, 16–20
Minzu (ethnicity), *See also* Assimilation, Race
  'ethnic minority work' (*minzu gongzuo*), 67, 77
  56 *minzu*, 3, 8–9, 29, 31–32, 34, 50, 77–78, 115, 142, 160, 177
  alienation, 72, 148
  backwardness, 8, 36, 45, 50, 56, 63, 66–67, 69–70, 79, 92, 103–104, 115, 119, 170, 176, 180, 198, 217, 232, 239
  category, 52, 61, 78–79
  'core *minzu*' (*zhuti minzu*), 42, 55
  equality, 84, 227, 232
  ethnic minorities (*shaoshu minzu*), 3, 65–66, 76, 85, 140, 234–235
    'simple', 71, 76, 112, 145
    backwardness, 72–74
  ethno-taxonomy (*minzu shibie*), 50–52, 65, 182
  Han category (*Hanzu*), 24, 34, 68–69, 74, 76, 140, 143, 177, 179, 201, 219
    'socialist *minzu*', 65
    centripetal force, 3, 104, 144
    frontier-building culture (*tunken wenhua*), 70–72, 130

    nucleus, 37, 69, 140, 142, 160, 230, 232
    superiority, 63, 144, 231
    trans-ethnic, 76, 159
    Xinjiang person, 171, 173, 177–180, 190, 203
    hatred, 119–120, 124, 127, 242
    love, 47, 129, 145, 148, 154–157
    problem, 43, 50, 66–68, 77, 96, 120, 124, 139, 173, 191, 197, 205, 220, 223, 242
  Uyghur category (*Weiwuerzu*), 4, 66–67, 71, 182, 185
  modernisation, 32, 72–74, 78, 80, 82, 103, 119, 122, 148, 159, 174, 185–186, 214, 233–234, 240, 243, *See also* Development
  'scientific development', 43, 59, 67, 103
  complementary economy, 69–70, 110
  cultural evolution, 71–72, 75, 77, 91–92, 103, 145, 180, 223, 231
  progress, 29, 64, 70, 74, 77, 81, 92, 144, 241
  prosperity, 63, 81, 123, 148–151, 200
  'tall buildings', 45, 73
  teleology, 10, 43, 61, 64–65, 67, 76–77, 79, 85, 188, 192, 241
Mongolians, 4, 6, 33, 80, 103, 159
  Daur, 50
  in Chinese narratives, 36–37, 44, 147, 154, 228
  in Han identity narratives, 179
  in relation to Uyghur category, 66
  in Uyghur identity narratives, 188
  interviewees, 62
  Qing expansion, 33, 39–40
multiculturalism, 65, 76, 78, 93, 98, 139, 190
  'plurality and unity' (*duoyuan yiti*), 3, 31, 37, 69

nationalism, *See also* Ethnicity
  banal, 141, 156–157, 163
  civic, 34, 82, 86, 140, 157
  ethnic, 34, 37, 75, 86, 139, 168, 177, 180, 189, 191, 195, 230, 232, 240
  Han chauvinism, 37, 41–43, 46, 54, 59–60, 72, 75, 84, 105, 135, 140, 143, 163, 166, 193, 198, 200–206, 231
  legitimacy, 5, 16, 60, 63, 182
  'local nationalism', 43, 60
nation-building, 3, 8–9, 11, 23, 26, 28–30, 38–56, 64, 66, 71, 78, 86, 88, 90, 94–95, 105–107, 110, 120, 140–141, 144, 169, 171, 174, 179, 182, 184, 186, 190, 194, 206, 214, 217, 220, 222, 225, 229, 231
  integration, 31–32, 35, 37–40, 47–48, 52–53, 56, 59, 106, 111, 175, 194, 233

Index

state-making, 33–35, 38–39, 41
tensions, 26, 28–29, 37, 44, 47, 50, 61, 63, 75, 79, 82, 86, 88, 162, 166, 169, 177, 189–190, 218, 223, 231, 238–242
nomads, 34, 176
  in Chinese narratives, 34, 71, 103, 198
  in relation to Uyghur category, 40–41, 106, 182
Nurmehemmet, Yasin, 89, 105, 109–111

Opening and Reform era, 7, 43, 45, 52, 54–55, 67, 84, 107–108, 140, 143, 153, 166, 192, 210, 223, 230, 233, 239, 241
Opium War, 39, 142
Orientalism, 32, 35, 49–50, 118, *See also* Colonialism, Imperialism

Pakistan, 102, 202
Palau, 102
Pan, Zhiping, 96, 101
Patriotic Education, 5, 96
  ethnic unity education, 59
  in Xinjiang, 43, 60
  literature on, 60, 240
  post-Cultural Revolution, 43
performance, 11–14, 29–32, 51, 111–113, 125, 141, 147–149, 154–156, 160, 168, 184, 186, 188, 191, 204, 207, 230
re-performance, 11, 106, 157, 166–221
Perride, Mamut, 184–185, 190
policy. *See also* Development, Modernisation, *Minzu* (ethnicity)
  'de-extremification' (*qu jiduanhua*), 2, 119, 158, 184, 201, 205, 232, 236
  'strike hard' (*yanda*), 15, 100–101, 108, 149, 151, 160–161
  abnormal behaviour law, 132
  ethnic
    'great wall of iron', 138
    'preferential policies' (*youhui zhengce*), 73, 199, 232, 240
    ethnic dispersion (*minzu fensan*), 119
    internment camps, 2, 138, 184, 192, 205–206, 223, 235–238, 241, 243
    stability work, 138
  foreign, 4, 98, 102, 113, 139, 236
  language, 80, 185, 187
    'bilingual education', 74, 79–84, 185–186, 188, 213–214, 234–235
    experimental bilingual classes, 80, 213
    national language and script law, 80
  martial law, 46, 126, 129, 133, 149, 152
  surveillance, 125–127, 137–138, 152, 162, 228
  Western Development Project, 73
political stability, 2, 18, 28, 43, 73, 97

awards, 96
critical stability period, 236
development and, 103–104, 232, 234
ethnic relations and, 143, 147, 155, 192, 225
Han as source of, 73, 96
identity transformation and, 28, 44–45, 76
in Uyghur identity narratives, 174
nationalism, 60
stability work, 138, 218, 223
Uyghurs as threat to, 138
power
  global, 8, 113, 115, 142, 235–237
  'national strength', 139, 181
  omnipresence, 13, 17, 46, 141, 143
  relations, 11–12, 18, 32, 71, 142, 172, 196
  soft, 139
  to identify, 18, 167, 193
propaganda slogans (*kouhao*), 1, 17, 45, 60, 77, 108, 114, 124, 126, 129–130, 143, 146, 149, 151, 154, 162, 166, 170, 173, 175, 177–178, 200, 235
protest, 97
  1980s & 90s, 98–100
  2009, 121–123, 128, 132–137, 204–205, 228
  conflation with violence, 89, 97, 123–126
Public Health
  biopolitics, 130–131, 236
  China's Academy of Military Medical Sciences', 130
  HIV / AIDS, 131
  Ministry of Health, 131
public intellectuals, 1, 16, 84, 93, 239
Pye, Lucian, 4, 231, 241

Qianlong Emperor, 39–40
Qing Dynasty, 32, 35, 41, 133, 182, *See also* Manchu
  anti-Manchu sentiment, 34–36, 87, 238
  expansion, 6, 27, 33, 37, 47
  frontier, 32–33, 38, 44
  in official historiography, 46, 65, 73, 76, 94, 97
  policy, 35–36, 39–41
  rule by custom, 39

race, 36, 79, 129, 177, 240–241, *See also Minzu* (ethnicity)
  Chinese, 79, 235
  'five races', 36, 79
  race-state (*guozu*), 6, 36, 79, 140, 234, 236
  racial capitalism, 233
  racism, 36, 42, 75, 93, 206, 212, 240
Rahile, Dawut, 237
Rebiya, Qadir, 134, 202

religion
  fasting, 158
  freedom of, 42, 94–96
  local leaders (*begs*), 39
  mosques, 22, 96, 99, 126, 158, 162, 183
  pork taboo, 54, 183, 198–201
  prayers, 95, 158, 199, 238
  Ramadan, 157–158
Republican era, 36, 41, 65, 79, 182, 200
resistance, 7, 13, 16–18, 23, 29, 88, 237
  conflation of armed and vernacular, 8–9, 240
  everyday, 54, 111, 167, 195
  Han, 134–135, 204
  in China, 108, 184
  in official narratives, 74, 84, 104, 211
  in Xinjiang, 39, 56, 212, 242
  nationalism, 5
  Uyghur, 6, 40, 90, 99, 107, 109, 111, 122, 158, 160, 163, 185, 242
Russia, 6, 91, 96
  imperialism, 27, 48, 53, 92
  Turkestan, 53, 91, 181

Said, Edward, 17, 49, 88, 90, 101
Sanubar, Tursun, 184, 237
security. *See also* Danger
  de-securitisation, 120, 227
  dilemma, 56, 111–113, 191, 220
  identity, 12–13, 18, 26, 31, 46, 54, 56, 62, 74, 82, 89, 93, 97–98, 102, 105, 110, 113, 116, 119, 124, 127–129, 132–135, 137, 157, 160, 175, 193, 196–197, 201, 206, 208, 210, 213, 220
  insecurity, 3, 8–9, 13, 54, 127–129, 132, 137–138, 192–223, 225, 243
  national, 1, 13–14, 46, 67, 73, 75, 92, 96, 108, 117, 121, 131, 137, 203
  ontological, 9, 11–12
  physical, 12, 196, 200, 209–210, 212, 220
  re-securitisation, 194–212
  securitisation, 11–15, 29, 38, 44, 48, 55, 84, 93, 97–113, 116, 118, 129, 133, 135–138, 148, 158, 192–221, 223, 225, 229–231, 233–234, 236, 241
  vernacular, 8, 116, 240
security services
  cadre patrols, 138, 218
  military patrols, 126–127, 147, 149, 154, 228
  military roadblocks, 133, 151
  neighbourhood patrols, 126–127
  paramilitary patrols, 162
  People's Liberation Army (PLA), 70, 72, 126, 132–133, 143, 149, 196

People's Armed Police (PAP), 126, 128, 133–134, 138, 148–149, 196
Public Security Bureau (PSB), 18, 121, 131–132, 135, 210
SWAT police, 159
volunteers, 127, 208
Shandong, 180
  attitudes towards Uyghurs, 200
  Han from, 179–180
Shanghai
  Han from, 170, 178
  in Uyghur identity narratives, 183
Shanghai Co-operation Organisation (SCO), 102
Sheng, Shicai, 65, 200
Sichuan, 180
  Han from, 172, 180, 199
Sinocentrism, 36, 66, 223
SINOPEC, 199, 232
social anthropology, 11, 48, 55
  in China, 71
sovereignty, 4, 28, 30, 35–36, 80, 88, 99, 239, 241
  cultural integrity, 130–131, 146
  territorial integrity, 28, 46, 48, 56, 58, 76, 143
Soviet Union, 7
  as a threat to the West, 13, 101
  federalism, 143
  'hegemonism', 42
  influence in Xinjiang, 42, 53, 181
Stalin, Josef, 66
  four principles of nationhood, 51, 65
State Council, 8, 45
  Foreign Ministry, 101–102
  Ministry of Information, 18–19, 43, 65, 67, 69, 73
  State Ethnic Affairs Commission (SEAC), 18, 40, 61, 65–66, 69, 71–73, 76, 78
  white papers, 51, 63, 69–70, 80, 85, 92, 101–102, 159, 236
struggle, 129, 151, 164
  against separatism, 99–100, 183
  against terrorism, 101–103, 119, 124
  against bourgeois liberalism, 143
  anti-imperialist, 4, 27, 36, 42
  century of, 143, 166, 225
  class, 43
  for ethnic unity, 130–131, 142, 145, 148
  'life or death', 2, 14, 47, 104, 115, 138, 149, 175, 236
  'persistence', 73
Sun, Yat-Sen, 5, 36–37, 58, 87

Index

Tajikistan, 91
Tajiks, 147
Tang dynasty, 46, 64
　in official historiography, 64, 69, 72, 76
Tarim Basin, 33, 72, 102
tensions, nation-building
　tensions, 35, 37
terrorism. *See also* Three Evils
　9/11, 14–15, 89, 93, 100–101, 224
　Al-Qaeda, 102
　Bin Laden, 101
　frontline, 103, 132, 183, 211
　Guantanamo Bay, 101
　war on terror, 15, 101–102, 104, 113
Thailand, 102, 128, 209
Three Evils (separatism, terrorism, and extremism), 14, 24, 47, 75, 77, 87–101, 103–104, 115, 120–121, 123–125, 127, 133, 136, 147, 149–152, 161, 164, 227–228
　in Han identity narratives, 197–198, 202, 220
　in Uyghur identity narratives, 175
Tibet, 6, 32–33, 37, 44, 179
　2008 violence, 1, 114
　in official narratives, 98
　in Uyghur identity narratives, 188
　religious leaders, 39
Tibetans, 4, 33, 36, 201
Tohti, Tunyaz, 108
Tu, Wei-ming, 7, 224, 239
Turghun, Almas, 106
Turkey, 67, 96, 201
Turks, 53, 91, 107, 202
　Chagatai, 184
　in official narratives, 66–67, 77, 88, 92–96, 149
　Khanate, 67
　Pan-Turkism, 7, 91
Turpan, 66
　Qocho Kingdom, 52
　Uyghurs from, 107, 183

United Nations (UN), 102, 128
Universalism, 34, 50, 84–86, 139, 223
Ürümchi
　beimen (north-gate), 132, 154
　erdaoqiao / döngköwrük, 41, 123, 126, 128, 134, 159, 197, 200, 210
　hongshan, 154
　nanhu, 132, 154
　nanmen (south-gate), 121, 128, 133, 196
　People's Square, 121, 123, 132, 149, 154, 162, 205
　saimachang, 123, 134
　Xinjiang University, 99, 123, 126, 154–155

USA, 86, 101–102, 114, 140
　colonialism, 71
　frontier, 72
　identity, 13, 121
Uyghurs. *See also* religion, Turks
　attitudes
　　alcohol, 100, 217
　　dress, 54, 217
　　food, 183, 198
　　hospitality, 159, 171, 176, 185, 213
　　mother-figure, 146
　　mother-tongue, 110, 146, 186–187, 216
　desettlement, 177
　ethnonym, 51–54, 66–67, 105, 181–182
　getihu entrepreneurs, 107
　identity
　　chthonic, 106, 110–111, 176–177, 207
　　ethno-national, 52, 117, 174, 208
　　homeland, 41, 111, 176, 183, 213
　　in-between-ness, 6, 33, 58, 88, 97, 175, 209, 223–225, 239, 242
　　linguistic, 91, 110, 185, 187, 213–216, 230
　　local / oasis, 40, 53, 177, 181, 214
　insecurities, 117, 120–121, 124, 128, 153, 158, 172, 207–218, 227, 232, 235, 243
　intellectuals, 53, 107, 157, 181
　Minkaohan / minkaomin categories, 26, 110, 195, 212–218, 230
　music
　　dance, 159–160
　　folk, 146, 184
　　muqam (classical), 95, 187, 215
　nationalism, 53, 57, 181
　neighbourhoods (*mähällä*), 157, 216
　passports, 209–210, 237
　protestors, 100

violence
　1990s, 2, 54–55, 89, 98–101, 122–123, 138
　Bachu, 138
　Baren, 1990, 98–100, 122, 143
　casualty figures, 119, 124, 128, 132, 208
　epistemic, 17, 105, 175, 220, 242
　Ghulja, 1997, 100–101, 122
　July 2009, 1, 14–16, 18, 46, 93, 96, 102, 114–139, 146, 149, 160, 196, 199–200, 202, 205, 207, 209, 228, 234–235, 242–243
　Pishan, 138
　Shanshan, 138
　Shaoguan incident, 117, 119–121, 127, 205, 227
　syringe attacks, 129–136
　Yecheng, 2012, 119, 138

Wang, Lequan, 103, 120, 124, 134–135
Wang, Yang, 1, 234
West, the, 5, 9–11, 49, 223–224, 240
   in Chinese narratives, 6, 14, 16, 27, 58, 60, 97, 141, 212, 220, 236, 238, 241
   in Chinese Studies, 32
   in ethnic policy, 42, 75, 79, 139, 238
   in Han identity narratives, 197
   in Uyghur identity narratives, 175
   in Xinjiang policy, 14, 40, 47, 93, 96–97, 104, 126, 227
World Order, 1, 11, 223
   Chinese, 33
   in Chinese debates, 6, 84, 239
   in IR theory, 10, 223
World Uyghur Congress (WUC), 15, 91, 106, 128

Xi, Jinping, 1, 44, 87, 103, 105, 138, 146, 166, 222, 234–235, 237–238, 240–241
Xi, Zhongxun, 105–106
Xi'an
   Han from, 170
   syringe assaults, 131
Xibe
   in Uyghur identity narratives, 188
Xinhua
   books, 19, 96
   news, 81, 130, 132

Xinjiang
   'peaceful liberation' of, 37–38, 45, 69–70, 73, 94, 200, 219
   ambivalent position of, 7, 23, 27, 45, 57, 179, 182, 190, 225
   'barren wasteland', 40, 71
   demographic transformation of, 26–27, 54, 63, 73, 76, 171, 182, 194, 229
   establishment of province, 6, 27, 40–41
   geopolitical buffer, 27, 38, 40, 42
   'new frontier', 6, 27, 40, 105, 185, 206, 241
   'problem', 99
   Western Regions, 6, 27, 38, 41, 72, 94
Xinjiang Production and Construction Corps (*Bingtuan*), 22, 43, 54, 76

Yuan dynasty, 64
   in official historiography, 65
Yunnan
   in official narratives, 71
   Yi people, 52

Zhang, Binglin, 36
Zhang, Chunxian, 119, 138
Zhang, Weiwei, 4, 84, 93, 239, 241
Zhang, Zhizhong, 41, 65
Zuo, Zongtang, 40

CPSIA information can be obtained
at www.ICGtesting.com
Printed in the USA
LVHW082144080421
683963LV00002B/106